Treasures

A Reading/Language Arts Program

Mc Graw Hill **Macmillan McGraw-Hill**

Acknowledgments

The publisher gratefully acknowledges permission to reprint the following copyrighted material:

"Black Cowboy Wild Horses" by Julius Lester, illustrations by Jerry Pinkney. Text copyright © 1998 by Julius Lester. Illustrations copyright © 1998 by Jerry Pinkney. Reprinted by permission of Dial Books, a member of Penguin Putnam Inc.

"The Bottom of the World" is from ANTARCTIC JOURNAL: FOUR MONTHS AT THE BOTTOM OF THE WORLD by Jennifer Owings Dewey. Copyright © 2001 by Jennifer Owings Dewey. Reprinted by permission of HarperCollins Publishers.

"Carlos and the Skunk" by Jan Romero Stevens, illustrations by Jeanne Arnold. Text copyright © 1997 by Jan Romero Stevens. Illustrations copyright © 1997 by Jeanne Arnold. Reprinted by permission of Rising Moon, Books for Young Readers from Northland Publishing.

"Davy Crockett Saves the World" by Rosalyn Schanzer. Copyright © 2001 by Rosalyn Schanzer. Reprinted by permission of HarperCollins Publishers.

"Goin' Someplace Special" by Patricia C. McKissack, illustrations by Jerry Pinkney. Text copyright © 2001 by Patricia C. McKissack. Illustrations copyright © 2001 by Jerry Pinkney. Reprinted by permission of Atheneum Books for Young Readers, an imprint of Simon & Schuster Children's Publishing Division.

"The Golden Mare, the Firebird, and the Magic Ring" by Ruth Sanderson. Copyright © 2001 by Ruth Sanderson. Reprinted by permission of Little, Brown and Company.

"The Gri Gri Tree" is from THE COLOR OF MY WORDS by Lynn Joseph. Copyright © 2000 by Lynn Joseph. Reprinted by permission of HarperCollins Children's Books, a division of HarperCollins Publishers.

"Hidden Worlds: Looking Through a Scientist's Microscope" is from HIDDEN WORLDS: LOOKING THROUGH A SCIENTIST'S MICROSCOPE by Stephen Kramer. Copyright © 2001 by Stephen Kramer. Reprinted by permission of Houghton Mifflin Company.

"Home on the Range" is from I HEAR AMERICA SINGING, FOLK SONGS FOR AMERICAN FAMILIES collected and arranged by Kathleen Krull. Copyright © 1992 by Kathleen Krull. Reprinted by permission of Alfred A. Knopf, an imprint of Random House Children Books.

"Hurricanes" is from HURRICANES by Seymour Simon. Copyright © 2003 by Seymour Simon. Reprinted by permission of HarperCollins Publishers.

"I'm Building a Rocket" by Kenn Nesbitt. Copyright © 2003 by Kenn Nesbitt.

(Acknowledgments continued on page 783.)

Contributors

Time Magazine, Accelerated Reader

Students with print disabilities may be eligible to obtain an accessible, audio version of the pupil edition of this textbook. Please call Recording for the Blind & Dyslexic at 1-800-221-4792 for complete information.

A

Treasures

A Reading/Language Arts Program

Program Authors

Donald R. Bear
Janice A. Dole
Jana Echevarria
Jan E. Hasbrouck
Scott G. Paris
Timothy Shanahan
Josefina V. Tinajero

Macmillan
McGraw-Hill

Challenges

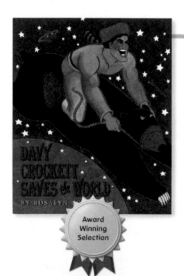

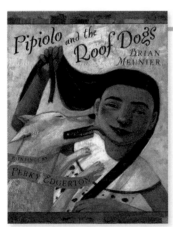

Turning Points

Award Winning Selection

Award Winning Selection

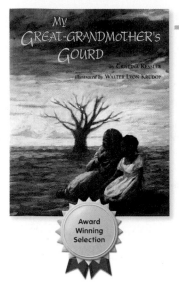

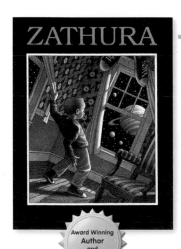

Test Strategy: Author and Me

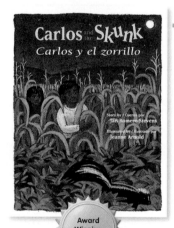

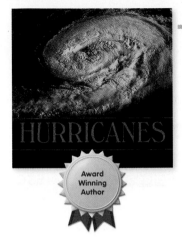

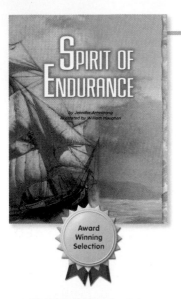

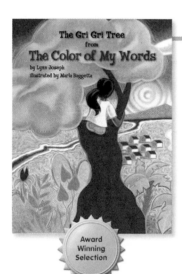

Unit 6

Great Ideas

The Golden Mare, the Firebird, and the Magic Ring

Award Winning Selection

SKUNK SCOUT
by Laurence Yep
illustrated by Winson Trang

Award Winning Author

Improving Lives

TIME FOR KIDS

School
Contests

Talk About It

What challenges and responsibilities come with entering a contest? What emotions can affect the contestants?

LOG ON Find out more about school contests at **www.macmillanmh.com**

Vocabulary

slumped	strands
soggy	gigantic
capable	credit
categories	luminous

Context Clues

Synonyms are words that mean the same or almost the same thing as other words. For example, *huge* is a synonym for *gigantic*. When you read an unfamiliar word, check to see if there is a synonym nearby to use as a context clue.

The Talent Contest

by Howard Gabe

As Danny put his lunch tray onto the cafeteria table, milk spilled all over his sandwich. He sat down, hung his head forward, and **slumped** over the food in front of him. Frowning, he began peeling the **soggy** milk-soaked bread from his sandwich. "This is the most ridiculous thing I've ever done!" he said.

"It's not that bad," said his friend Elena, who was sitting across from him. "Just get another sandwich."

"Sandwich? What sandwich? I am talking about the talent contest. It's only two weeks away and I don't know what I'm doing! Everybody will laugh at me. It's inevitable. There's no way to avoid it!"

"Don't be so negative, Danny," said Elena as she rolled her eyes. "You're going to be great. You're very **capable**. You have the skills to do just about anything."

Danny moved his lunch tray to the side and rested his head on the table.

"Sit up Danny," ordered Elena. "I have an idea. Let's brainstorm a list of things you could do. We'll divide the list into **categories** or groups. Let's start with music. You play the piano, right?"

"I stopped taking lessons in third grade," said Danny.

"What about singing a song?" suggested Elena.

Danny shook his head no. "Let's move on to another category."

"What about juggling?" asked Elena, as she twisted thin **strands** of hair around her finger.

"I don't know how to juggle!" Danny almost shouted. "Elena, how did I get myself into this huge, **gigantic** mess?"

"Stop being so…" Elena paused. "That's it, DRAMATIC!" Elena shouted excitedly. "You could do a dramatic

reading. You definitely have the talent for it. Mrs. Pace always calls on you to read aloud in class. You could read a play aloud. Maybe you could even get extra **credit** from Mrs. Pace. She rewards students with points for doing extra reading work."

Danny thought for a minute. Then he smiled. "Elena," Danny said, "you are a great friend!"

Elena smiled back. "I just want to make sure you are a bright, shiny, **luminous** star when you step out onstage."

Reread for **Comprehension**

Story Structure
Character and Plot

A Character and Plot Chart helps you figure out a character's personality and events of the plot. These traits and events are part of story structure. Use your Character and Plot Chart as you reread "The Talent Contest" to figure out Elena's traits and how her actions affect the plot of the story.

Character	Plot

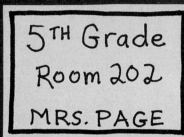

Comprehension

Genre

Realistic Fiction uses settings, characters, and events that could actually exist.

Story Structure

Character and Plot

As you read, use your Character and Plot Chart.

Character	Plot

Read to Find Out

How does the kind of person Sage is affect the plot?

Miss Alaineus

A VOCABULARY DISASTER

**written and illustrated by
Debra Frasier**

None of this would have happened if it wasn't for Forest.
Forest is not a *thicket of trees*. Forest is a boy. A sick boy. A
boy sneezing and coughing all over my desk and pencils.

I caught Forest's cold and had to stay home from school
on Tuesday. Tuesday is Vocabulary Day at Webster School.
Follow my advice: Never get sick on Vocabulary Day.

On Tuesday afternoon I called my best friend, Starr, who is
not *a luminous celestial object seen as a point of light in the
sky*, but a very smart girl who listens perfectly on Vocabulary
Day. She was late for baseball practice, so she spelled the first
fourteen vocabulary words as fast as she could.

I had to scribble them quickly because her mom was calling
her to the car. "This last one's 'Miss Alaineus'!" Starr yelled.
"I gotta go. I hope you feel better tomorrow, Sage." And she
hung up the phone with a crash.

I didn't feel much better on Wednesday, so my mom called Mrs. Page, who is not *a single side of a printed sheet of paper usually found bound in a book.* She's my teacher, and actually Mrs. Page is a good name for her because she reads to us every day. My mom told her yes, I had my math problems and vocabulary words, and yes, I would get better soon.

Plot

How do you think Starr's rush to give Sage the vocabulary words will affect what happens next?

VOCABULARY WORDS

1. dinosaur
2. snake
3. museum
4. reptile
5. constrictor
6. herpetologist
7. fossil
8. carnivore
9. herbivore
10. nest
11. species
12. theory
13. hypothesis
14. category
15. Miss Alaineus

Every week Mrs. Page gives us a list of words with a theme, like Story Writing or Musical Performance or Electricity. We're supposed to look up each word in the dictionary, but sometimes I already know the words, so I try to make the definitions sound like I looked them up.

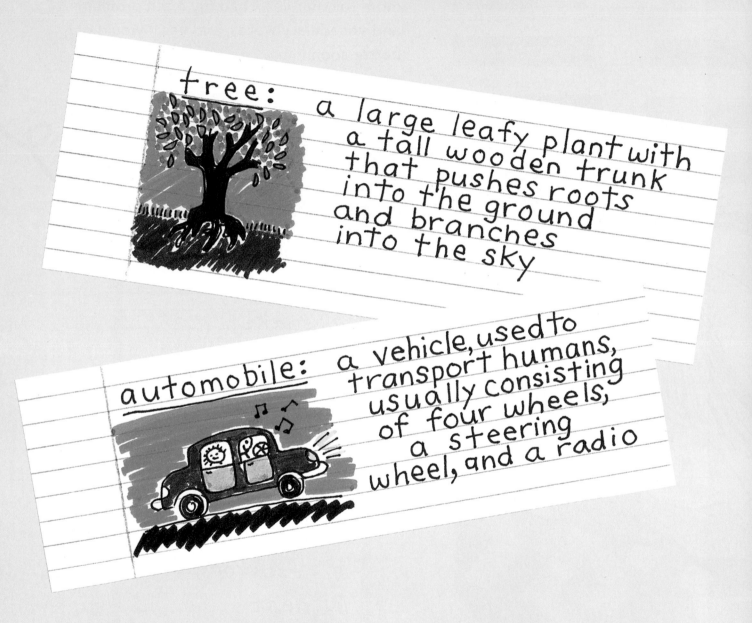

tree: a large leafy plant with a tall wooden trunk that pushes roots into the ground and branches into the sky

automobile: a vehicle, used to transport humans, usually consisting of four wheels, a steering wheel, and a radio

I thought I was pretty good at definitions until this week.

My mom says, "Pride goeth before a fall."

Pride: *an unduly high opinion of oneself.*

Goeth: *Old English for "to go."*

Fall: *what happened on Monday, Vocabulary Test Day.*

By Thursday afternoon my head felt like it was stuffed with cotton and my throat felt swollen shut. I finished defining my vocabulary words while propped up in bed with a box of tissues on one side and a **gigantic** red dictionary on the other. It's hard to look up words in a huge book while you're in bed blowing your nose, so I made my own dictionary language for as many of them as I could.

13. hypothesis: what you guess will happen in your science experiment

14. category: a bunch of things that are alike

15. Miss Alaineus:

The last word seemed a little odd to me because I couldn't figure out what she had to do with snakes or **categories** or theories. Mrs. Page rarely gives us people's names on our vocabulary lists, but we have had a few that turned into words, like Louis Pasteur for **pasteurization** and George Washington for **Washington, D.C.**, so I decided she must have been included for a reason.

You should know that for years I had wondered who Miss Alaineus was. When I was little I figured out that she had something to do with the kitchen, because the Miss Alaineus drawer held the spoons too big to fit anywhere else, the sharp corn holders shaped like tiny cobs, and the spaghetti spork, that weird cross between a spoon and a fork that perfectly lifts slippery spaghetti out of the bowl. I thought maybe she was an **ancestor:** *an ancient relative long dead*, who left us all these odd things in the drawer.

Then just last year my mom and I were at the grocery store and it all fell into place. We were in one of those Very Big Hurries when she said, "You go get some of that long Italian bread and two sticks of butter. I'll get Miss Alaineus' things and meet you here at the cash register."

I found the bread and butter, and my mom came back with spaghetti sauce, a can of Parmesan cheese, a can of corn, and a big green box of spaghetti with a beautiful woman on the front. She was drawn so that her hair tumbled perfectly across the box and ended in a little plastic window, making the spaghetti look just like the ends of the **strands** of her hair.

There she was—Miss Alaineus.

So, propped up on pillows in my bed, with a tissue in one hand and a pencil in the other, I wrote:

15. Miss Alaineus: the woman on green spaghetti boxes whose hair is the color of uncooked pasta

and turns into spaghetti at the ends

And then I fell asleep.

I finally got better over the weekend and felt great on Monday. I turned in my homework to Mrs. Page and sat down at my desk, glad to be back at school with my friends. I was even glad to see Forest at our morning circle meeting.

"First, I want to remind you of the Tenth Annual Vocabulary Parade on Friday," said Mrs. Page. "I hope you are all working on your word costumes. Second, please remember to bring your bus money and permission slips for our science museum field trip tomorrow. And third, instead of our usual Monday test, we are going to have a Vocabulary Bee today.

"Everyone line up here by the chalkboard, and I'll choose a word from our list. After I pronounce the word, please spell and define it. If you are correct, go to the end of the line. If you miss the word, please sit down at your desk and look it up in the dictionary. Write the word five times and define it once."

Starr was first with **museum**: "M-U-S-E-U-M: *a building for exhibiting objects about art or history or science,*" she said, and went to the back of the line.

Cliff, not *a high, steep face of rock,* but one very tall boy, answered to the word **dinosaur**: "D-I-N-O-S-A-U-R: *a prehistoric, extinct reptile, often huge,*" and he went to the back of the line.

I was tenth, and when Mrs. Page called out my word, I spelled: "Capital **M-I-S-S**, capital **A-L-A-I-N-E-U-S**," and added, *"the woman on green spaghetti boxes whose hair is the color of uncooked pasta and turns into spaghetti at the ends."*

There was a moment of silence in the room. I smiled at Mrs. Page. She waited to see if I would add anything else, and when I didn't, she grinned. Not smiled—**grinned:** *to draw back the lips and bare the teeth, as in a very wide smile*—and the entire class burst into one huge giggling, laughing, falling-down mass of kids. Forest was doubled over. Starr, my best friend, was laughing so hard tears came to her eyes. By now, even Mrs. Page was laughing.

Pride goeth before a fall. I was **Sage:** *one who shows wisdom, experience, judgment.* Why were they laughing? "Wise-girl-with-words" my dad always called me. What had I said? I was beginning to turn red. **Red:** *the color of embarrassment.*

Finally the room quieted. Mrs. Page opened her dictionary and wrote on the chalkboard:

Miscellaneous: *adj. 1. consisting of various kinds or qualities 2. a collection of unrelated objects*

My jaw dropped as I looked at the spelling. My eyes bulged as I read the definition. I didn't bother to tell anyone about my mom and the spaghetti spork and the grocery store. **Humbled:** *aware of my shortcomings, modest, meek,* I dragged back to my seat and wrote **miscellaneous** five times and defined it once. And that's when I remembered I had even drawn a picture of the spaghetti box for extra **credit.** I was **devastated:** *wasted, ravaged.* **Ruined:** *destroyed.* **Finished:** *brought to an end.*

Character
What does Sage's reaction to her mistake tell you about her character?

They called me Miss Alaineus for the rest of the day. Sometimes a person couldn't even get the words out before bending over with laughter. The day took a week to end. When I got off the bus I **slumped** home—devastated, ruined, finished.

I told my mom the whole story, from the kitchen drawer to the grocery store to the Vocabulary Bee. Even my own mother laughed a little at the part about the drawing for extra credit, but at least she stopped fast and said, "You know what I always say . . . There's gold in every mistake."

Gold? *A bright yellow precious metal of great value?*

Mistake? *Something done, said, or thought in the wrong way?*

"Impossible," I told her. **Impossible:** *not capable of happening.*

I couldn't believe I *ever* had to go back to school. But the next day we went to the science museum, and everyone forgot all about Miss Alaineus at the snake exhibit and the dinosaur bone lab. Then the guide said, "The field of bone archaeology has been influenced by a wide and unusual array of miscellaneous discoveries around the world." The class burst out laughing, and the guide was pleased with herself for entertaining us so easily. And I **knew:** *to apprehend with certainty*, that my mistake was still alive and well, and nothing like gold.

After school I lay on my bed and stared at the wall. How could I have been so stupid?

My mom came in and said it was time to work on my costume for the Vocabulary Parade. We had finished the cape for **Capable**, but I still needed to make the lettering down the back.

"Mom," I said, "I could only be a mistake this year. **Miss Stake.**"

Suddenly I sat up.

I looked at my mom. She looked at me.

I smiled.

She smiled.

"Sweetheart," she said, "let's take another look at that cape."

It took the most courage I've ever had to walk out on that stage as **Miss Alaineus,** *Queen of All Miscellaneous Things.* But when Mr. Bell read my word and definition, everyone applauded and laughed **wildly:** *in a manner lacking all restraint,* and I grinned at my mom across the auditorium.

Forest came right after me. When he bowed, his **Precipitation** watering-can hat rained on Mr. Bell's new suit, and the entire audience gasped, then cheered when Mr. Bell smiled at his **soggy** clothes.

To my **astonishment**: *great shock and amazement*, I won a gold trophy for The Most Original Use of a Word in the Tenth Annual Vocabulary Parade.

So this time Mom was right. There was gold in this mistake.

And next year I think I'm going to be . . .

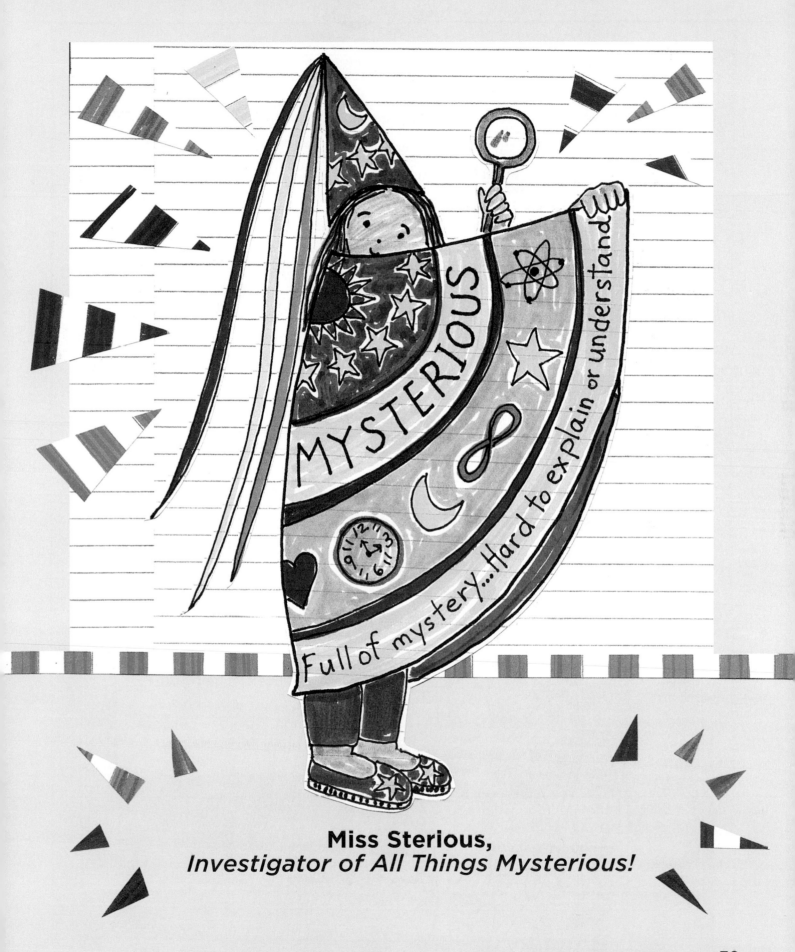

Miss Sterious,
Investigator of All Things Mysterious!

A Few Words About Debra Frasier

Debra Frasier's fifth-grade daughter said to her one day, "Mom, today I figured out that *miscellaneous* is not a person." Her daughter's new wisdom gave Debra two gifts: a good laugh and the idea to write *Miss Alaineus*. Debra says her books take a long time because she loves the creative process. Being creative is nothing new for Debra. As a child in Florida, she used to make collages with old wood she found on the beach and miles of tape.

For the illustrations, Debra again turned to her daughter for inspiration. Papers, glue, scissors, and pencils that were crammed in her daughter's desk gave her the idea for the story's school setting. At last Debra had completed a fun adventure about the usually tame world of vocabulary.

Another book by Debra Frasier:
Out of the Ocean

Author's Purpose

Authors of fiction usually write to entertain, but they may have another purpose. What clues can help you figure out if Debra Frasier had more than one purpose for writing *Miss Alaineus*?

 For more information about Debra Frasier visit **www.macmillanmh.com**

Comprehension Check

Summarize

Use your Character and Plot Chart to help you summarize *Miss Alaineus*. Include only the most important events that lead to Sage's creative solution to her problem.

Character	Plot

Think and Compare

1. *Miss Alaineus* is written from Sage's point of view. How does this help you know what she is like? What words or phrases would you use to describe her? Use story details in your answer. **Story Structure: Character and Plot**

2. Reread page 38. What does Sage mean when she says, "there was gold in this mistake"? Use details from the story to support your answer. **Analyze**

3. Even the most **capable** people make mistakes. How do you feel when you make a mistake? Compare your feelings to Sage's feelings. **Analyze**

4. Why might it be helpful to have a sense of humor when you are trying to solve a problem? **Evaluate**

5. Look back at "The Talent Contest" on pages 18–19. How is Danny's experience similar to Sage's? Use details from each selection. **Reading/Writing Across Texts**

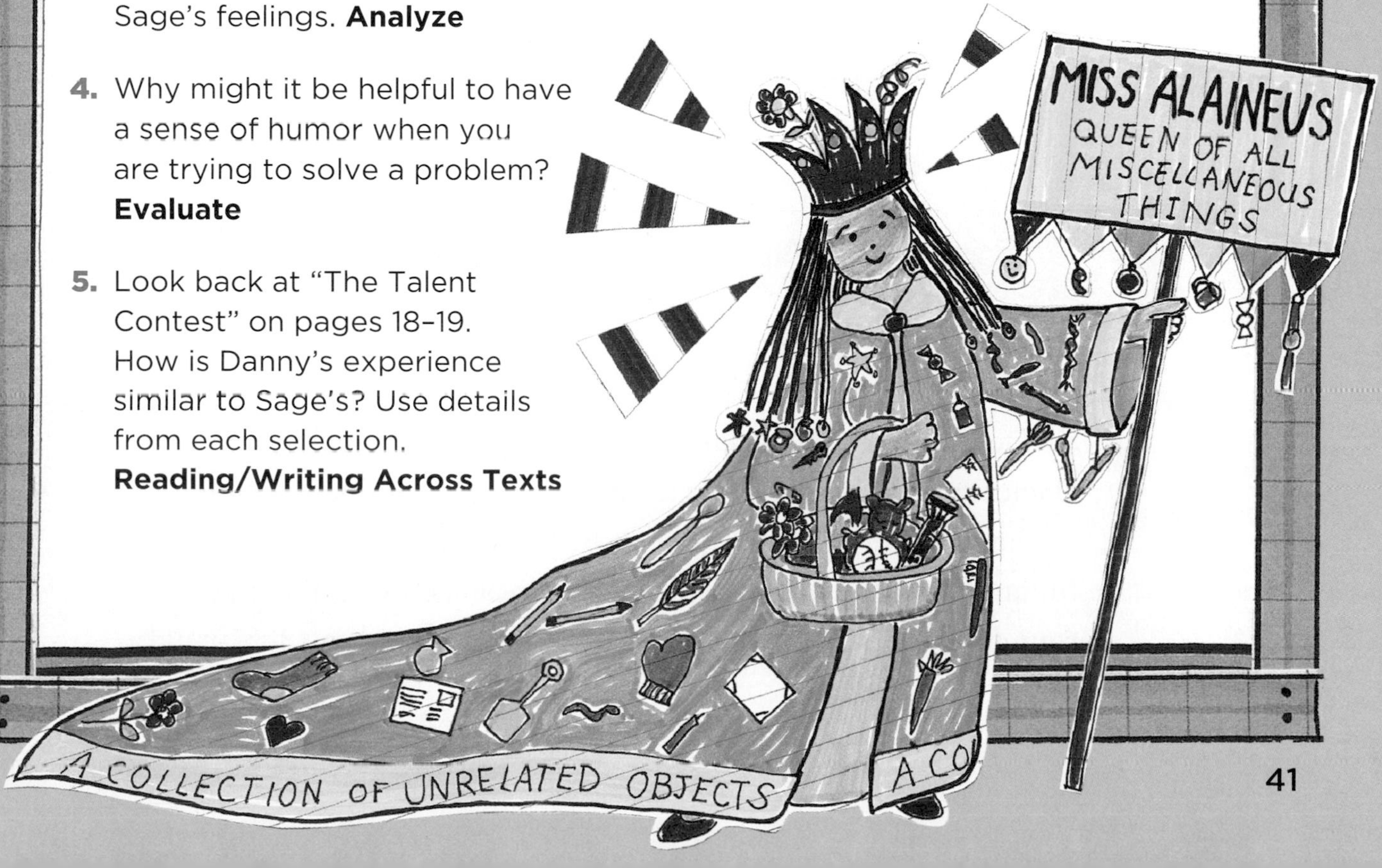
MISS ALAINEUS
QUEEN OF ALL MISCELLANEOUS THINGS
A COLLECTION OF UNRELATED OBJECTS
A CO

The National

SPELLING BEE

by Nicole Lee

Does the word *autochthonous* sound familiar? Luckily, to David Tidmarsh, it did. David correctly spelled *autochthonous* to win the 77th National Spelling Bee. David, from South Bend, Indiana, won the spelling championship at age 14. In the final round of **competition**, David beat Akshay Buddiga, a 13-year-old boy from Colorado.

Welcome to the exciting and intense world of spelling bees. The National Spelling Bee takes place each June in Washington, D.C. The competition has been around for a long time. It began in 1925 with only nine contestants. In 2004 there were 265 contestants ranging in age from 8 to 15. Contestants for the National Spelling Bee come from English-speaking countries all over the world. Students from Jamaica, Puerto Rico, and even Saudi Arabia have competed in the National Spelling Bee.

It takes a lot of hard work and dedication to advance to the National Spelling Bee finals. Students spend a lot of time preparing for competition. The words chosen for the competition are chosen from the dictionary by a panel of word experts. There are more than 470,000 words in the dictionary, and any one of these words could be chosen for the competition. David spent several months preparing for the finals. He spent many hours studying a dictionary, and a list of 10,000 words that he created. Fortunately for David, *autochthonous* was one of the words on his list. After David won he said, "I was just hoping I got a word I studied."

Spelling contestants spend months poring over the dictionary.

arete

Intense moments on David's road to V-I-C-T-O-R-Y!

The purpose of the National Spelling Bee is to encourage students to improve their spelling, broaden their vocabularies, and develop correct English usage. During round one of the championships, the spellers have to take a 25-word written test. In round two, each student spells a word **orally**. Next, the judges score the students. The top 90 students move on to round three. Any mistake during round three or the later rounds **eliminates** the speller. Some of the words that David had to spell before the 15th and final round were *gaminerie*, *arete*, *balancelle*, and *sumpsimus*.

Akshay (left) and David anxiously await their turns.

44

Spellers qualify for the finals by winning locally sponsored spelling bees in their home communities. Qualifying for the national competition is a significant accomplishment. Every student who advances to the national competition is awarded a prize. The champion gets $17,000, a set of encyclopedias, an engraved trophy, and several other prizes. When asked what he would do with the prize money, David said, "I might put it in a savings account," and "I'll probably take a little and spend it at the mall."

autochthonous

gaminerie

Connect and Compare

1. Look at the photo of the spellers sitting on the stage. What feelings do you think the contestants experienced during the competition? **Photographs and Captions**

2. What advice do you think David would give to someone who wanted to enter a spelling bee? **Evaluate**

3. Think about this article and *Miss Alaineus*. Compare how Sage prepared for the vocabulary bee and David prepared for the spelling bee. **Reading and Writing Across Texts**

Language Arts Activity

Does your state have spelling bees? Research spelling bees in your state and write a paragraph about what you need to do to enter a local spelling bee.

 Find out more about the National Spelling Bee at **www.macmillanmh.com**

SCHOOL CONTEST

Writer's Craft

A Good Paragraph

A **good paragraph** has a topic sentence that lets a reader know what the subject of the paragraph will be. Supporting details add information about the subject.

My topic sentence is a clue that practicing spelling words is the main idea of the paragraph.

I use supporting details to add information about my topic sentence.

Always One Hundred Percent

by Christina M.

Every Friday morning my friends and I sit on the rug in class and practice our spelling words before the weekly test. We have a contest to see who can spell the words the fastest. One of us sits in our teacher's chair and reads the spelling words. Whoever slaps the floor first gets a two-second head start spelling the word.

A few weeks ago, Miguel had been reading the words, and Kevin and I were spelling them. For one of the words, I lifted my hand in such a hurry that it flew back and hit my nose. We all laughed hysterically. Miguel laughed so hard he fell out of the teacher's chair, and that started us laughing all over again.

Our weekly contest works out well even when nothing funny happens. We get one hundred percent on our spelling tests! You should try it. It's a fun way to study spelling words.

Your Turn

Write two or three paragraphs about a school contest that you have entered or that you would like to enter. Tell about what happened to you and how you felt. Be sure to use a topic sentence and supporting details in each paragraph. Use the writer's checklist to check your writing.

Writer's Checklist

✓ **Ideas and Content:** Are my ideas clear?

☑ **Organization:** Did I use a topic sentence to create a strong beginning for my **paragraph**?

✓ **Voice:** Do the details tell how I feel? Do they make my writing sound like something I would have written?

✓ **Word Choice:** Did I choose strong words to tell what is happening?

✓ **Sentence Fluency:** Did I join related sentences to make compound sentences?

✓ **Conventions:** Did I capitalize proper nouns? Did I check my spelling?

PAUL BUNYAN
WELCOMES YOU TO THE
TREES MYSTERY

Talk About It

Who are some of the legendary figures of American history? What qualities must a person have to become a legend?

LOG ON Find out more about American legends at **www.macmillanmh.com**

American Legends

Grandma's Tales

by Daniel Fritz

My grandma lives in a town in Tennessee near the place Davy Crockett was born. She is a distant relative of his and thinks people should get all the **original** facts about this American legend straight. She is determined to **wring** the truth from all those wild stories about him. She feels those stories are like the words in an **advertisement**: they exaggerate and try to convince readers that Davy Crockett could accomplish impossible feats! My grandma agrees he was a man full of energy and enthusiasm. But she wants people to remember he was a talented human being—not a superhero.

It was a cold, snowy night the last time Grandma told me Davy Crockett's life story. We were sitting on the couch, sipping hot chocolate when she **commenced** telling me facts about Davy's early life. "Davy Crockett was born in 1786," she began. "The woods around here were beautiful then, but life wasn't easy. His family moved around a lot."

50

"Was Davy a boy when he caught a flaming **fireball** with his bare hands?" I asked. "Is that when he picked up a rattlesnake and used it for a lasso?" I continued, trying to **impress** Grandma with my knowledge. She didn't smile or laugh.

"Davy got married and had children. He farmed, hunted, and joined the army. He got interested in politics and was **elected** to Congress. He lived by the rule: 'Be sure you are right. Then go ahead,'" Grandma said.

"When he left politics, Davy decided to explore Texas," she continued. "That was where he had his last great adventure."

"Yes!" I said. "That's where he died a hero in the famous battle at the Alamo."

That statement of fact brought a huge smile to Grandma's face. "You got THAT right," she said, happily. Then she **sauntered** slowly over to the coonskin cap sitting on her mantel and plopped it on my head.

Reread for **Comprehension**

Story Structure
Plot and Setting

A Plot and Setting Chart helps you identify why the setting is important to the plot of the story. Use your Plot and Setting Chart as you reread "Grandma's Tales" to find out how the setting is an important part of the story's structure.

Plot	Setting

Comprehension

Genre

A **Tall Tale** is a story about a larger-than-life character that is so exaggerated you know it is not believable.

Story Structure

Plot and Setting

As you read, use your Plot and Setting Chart.

Plot	Setting

Read to Find Out

What problem does Davy Crockett try to solve?

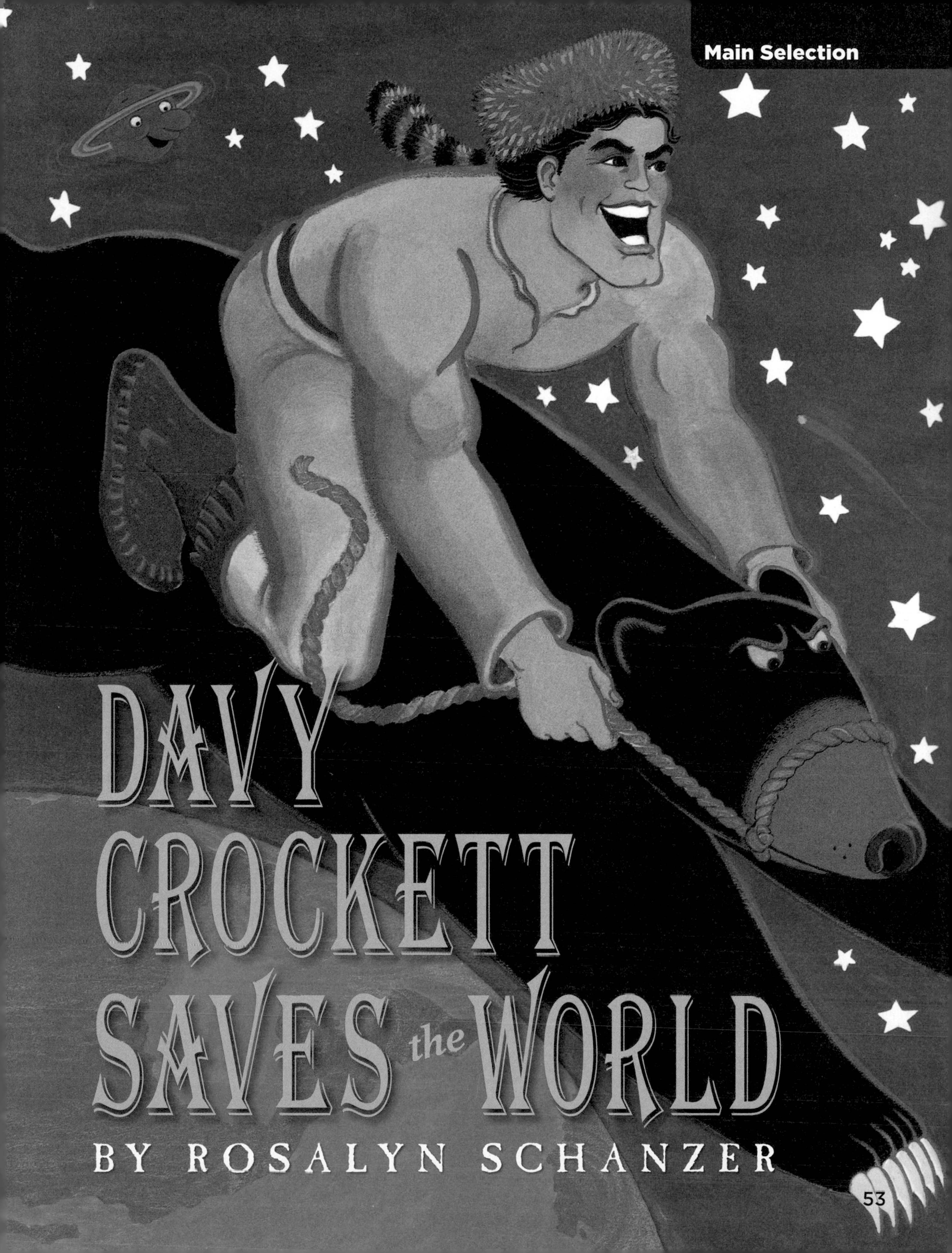

DAVY CROCKETT SAVES the WORLD

BY ROSALYN SCHANZER

I reckon by now you've heard of Davy Crockett, the greatest woodsman who ever lived. Why, Davy could whip ten times his weight in wildcats and drink the Mississippi River dry. He combed his hair with a rake, shaved his beard with an ax, and could run so fast that, whenever he went out, the trees had to step aside to keep from getting knocked down.

Folks always crow about the deeds of Davy Crockett, but the biggest thing he ever did was to save the world. This here story tells exactly how he did it, and every single word is true, unless it is false.

Setting
Where and when does the story take place? What clues help you to identify the setting?

About the time our tale begins, the world was in a heap of trouble. A way past the clouds and far beyond all the stars and planets in outer space, scientists with telescopes had discovered the biggest, baddest ball of fire and ice and brimstone ever to light up the heavens.

Its name was Halley's Comet, and it was hurling itself
lickety-split straight toward America. Why, its tail alone was
two million miles long. If it were to hit the earth, everyone would
be blown to smithereens!

The President of the United States started getting big piles of letters telling him to stop Halley's Comet before it was too late. He made a law telling the comet it couldn't crash into the earth, but the comet paid no attention. It just kept speeding toward America and growing bigger every day.

Finally the President had an idea. He had heard of a brave man named Davy Crockett, who lived somewhere in the mountains far away. He put an **advertisement** in all the newspapers in America that said:

> ## WANTED
> ### BY THE PRESIDENT
> ### OF THE UNITED STATES
> ## DAVY CROCKETT
> ### TO PULL THE TAIL OFF OF
> ### *HALLEY'S COMET*

Meanwhile, Davy Crockett didn't know a thing about any comet. He had no idea that the earth was even in danger. Davy was off in the forest with his pet bear, Death Hug. He was teaching himself to dance so that he could **impress** a real purty gal named Sally Sugartree, who could dance a hole through a double oak floor. He was not reading any newspapers.

It took two whole weeks, but once Davy had learned all the latest dances, he combed his hair nice and slow with his rake, shaved his face real careful-like with his ax, and **sauntered** off toward Sally Sugartree's cabin just as easy as you please.

All this time, of course, Halley's Comet was getting closer and closer to the earth and moving faster by the minute.

Now, Sally Sugartree was not just purty, but she was right smart too. Sally read the newspaper front to back every day, and she knew all about Halley's Comet. She had also seen the advertisement from the President.

Sally climbed up a fifty-foot hickory tree and commenced to look for Davy Crockett. Before long, she spotted him a way far off in the forest. Sally grabbed up her newspaper and waved it around just as hard as she could. When Davy saw her, he grinned and started to walk a mite faster.

As soon as Davy got close enough, Sally jumped right out of that tree. Davy caught her in his arms and gave her such a hug that her tongue stuck out half a foot and her eyes popped out like a lobster's. Then she showed Davy the want ad from the President.

Davy still didn't know what Halley's Comet was, but if the President of the United States wanted to see him, he would waste no time getting to Washington. He bridled up Death Hug and set out like a high-powered hurrycane. He could dance with Sally later.

Death Hug was so fast that rocks and trees and cows and snakes and other varmints all flew out behind him.

Plot

Why is Davy's decision to go to Washington an important event in the plot?

By the time they reached the White House, Halley's Comet was getting so close that there wasn't a minute to lose.

The President told Davy to climb the highest mountain he could find right away, and to **wring** that comet's tail off before it could destroy the earth. Then the President posed with Davy for pictures and pretended to look calm.

Davy combed his hair with his rake, rolled up his sleeves, and ate a big plateful of pickled rattlesnake brains fried by lightning to give him energy. Then he **commenced** to climb all the way to the top of Eagle Eye Peak in the Great Smoky Mountains.

Eagle Eye Peak was so high you could see every state and river and mountain in a whole geography book.

You could also look a way far off into outer space. By the time Davy reached the top, it was night.

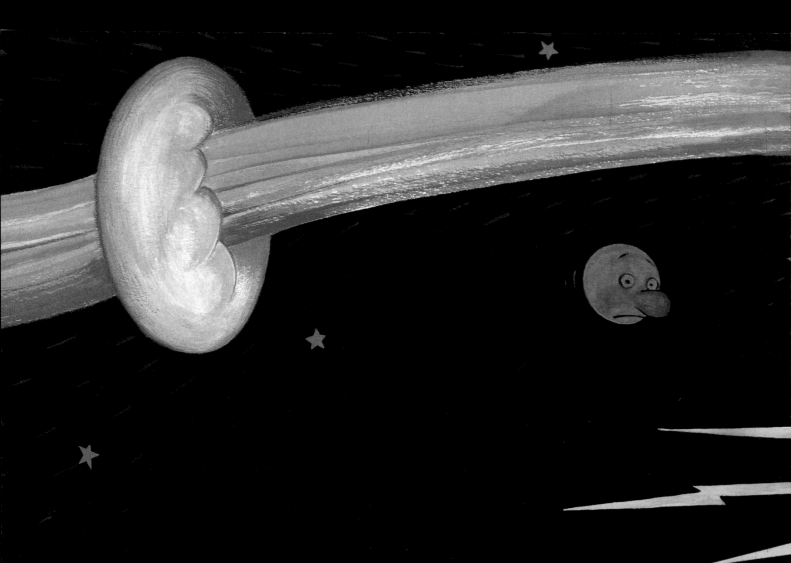

Halley's Comet spotted Davy Crockett right away. It took a flying leap and zoomed past all the stars and planets. Then it laughed and headed straight toward Davy like a red-hot cannonball!

Lightning and thunder shot out of its eyes! So many sparks flew out of its tail that, even though it was night, the entire countryside lit up and all the roosters set to crowin'!

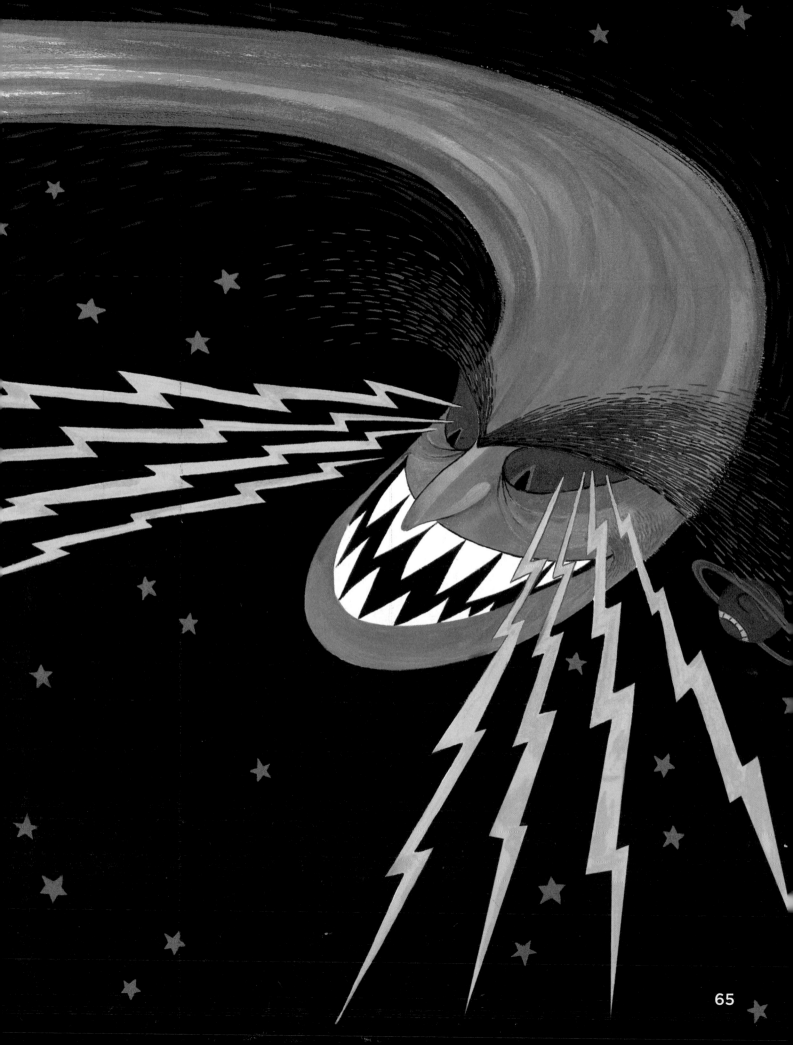

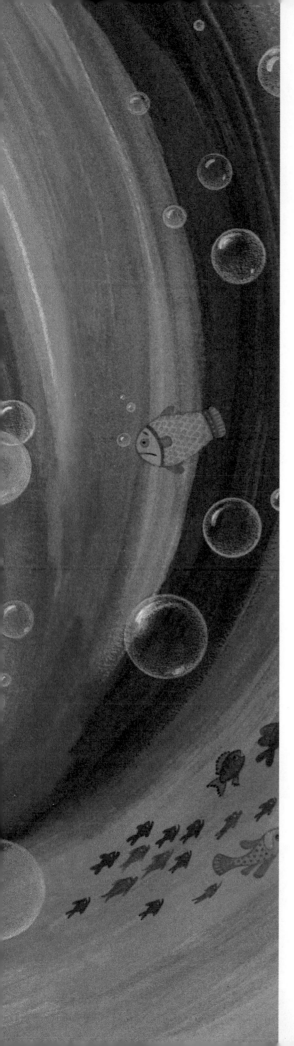

That comet must have thought Davy looked mighty tender, for it licked its chops, howled louder than a hundred tornadoes, and roared toward him with its mouth wide open!

This made Davy so mad that he jumped right over its shoulders and onto its back. Then he planted his teeth around the comet's neck and hung on. Halley's Comet spun around and around like a whirlwind trying to throw Davy off, but it couldn't.

Next off, that comet tried to drown Davy by diving into the Atlantic Ocean. The water got so all-fired hot that it boiled! The whole world was covered with steam, and the sun didn't shine as bright as usual for a month.

Just in time, the ocean put out that comet's fire and melted all its ice. It washed up on an island, and before it could grow back to its **original** size, Davy grabbed what was left of Halley's tail, spun around seventeen times, and hurled the comet back into outer space. It was so discombobulated that the next time it ever came in this direction, it missed the earth by 39 million miles.

That's how Davy Crockett saved the world. In fact, he did such a good job that there was a huge parade in his honor, he got to marry Sally Sugartree, and he was even **elected** to Congress.

Of course, that infernal **fireball** singed the hair right off Davy's head.
A whole new crop grew back in tufts like grass and kept in such a snarl
that he couldn't even comb it without breaking his rake.

That's why these days Davy Crockett always wears a coonskin cap.

Go Exploring with
Rosalyn Schanzer

Rosalyn Schanzer loves adventure just as much as Davy Crockett. She swam with sharks in Belize; kayaked with whales in Alaska; fished for piranhas in South America; and even sailed a boat through the Bermuda Triangle. When Rosalyn wants to create a new story, she treks to a different part of the globe to seek an unusual adventure.

Before words ever hit the page, Rosalyn illustrates her books. While traveling she asks questions, snaps pictures, and researches facts that can be used for artistic inspiration. After Rosalyn illustrates her new ideas and adventures, she brings the story to life with words. It seems only fitting that Rosalyn, who has gone on such unique adventures, takes such an unusual and adventurous approach to creating books.

Other books by Rosalyn Schanzer:
Gold Fever: Tales of the California Gold Rush and *How Ben Franklin Stole the Lightning*

Author's Purpose
Tall tale heroes and heroines do amazing things. Why might Rosalyn Schanzer have written this story besides wanting to explain Halley's Comet to readers?

LOG ON Find out more about Rosalyn Schanzer at **www.macmillanmh.com**

Comprehension Check

Summarize

Use your Plot and Setting Chart to help you summarize *Davy Crockett Saves the World.* When preparing your summary, be sure to include only important events and characters.

Plot	Setting

Think and Compare

1. How does the setting of the Atlantic Ocean add to the excitement of the story? **Story Structure: Plot and Setting**

2. Reread page 54. Should you believe everything that is said about Davy Crockett? Why or why not? **Analyze**

3. If you were President, whom would you ask to save the world? Explain your answer. **Evaluate**

4. How would the President's **advertisement** to Davy Crockett be different if the story took place now? Explain. **Analyze**

5. Reread "Grandma's Tales" on pages 50–51. Describe how Grandma would react to *Davy Crockett Saves the World.* Use details from both stories to explain your answer. **Reading/Writing Across Texts**

Social Studies

Genre

Online Articles present facts about real people, living things, places, or events.

Text Features

A **Toolbar** is a strip of icons, or symbols, on a computer that allows you to visit different features on the Web page.

A **Link** is an electronic connection on a Web page that provides direct access to other documents or information.

Content Vocabulary

exaggerating   **features**
superhuman

Links related to this topic

Related Articles

▶ Paul Bunyan
▶ John Henry
▶ Davy Crockett
▶ Pecos Bill

THE TALES ARE GETTING TALLER

by Kyle Seulen

Have you ever visited or seen pictures of Puget Sound in Washington State or the Black Hills of South Dakota? If so, you have seen some of Paul Bunyan's greatest work. One time, when Paul was headed out West, he dragged his giant pickax behind him, and the ditch he made with it was the Grand Canyon. This statement may be **exaggerating** the facts just a little. Paul Bunyan really did not make these beautiful places, but the stories we like to tell about him make him one of the heroes of American tall tales.

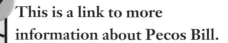

This is a link to more information about Pecos Bill.

72

Home **Browse** **Search** Tall Tales

SKILL ✓ This strip of icons is called a toolbar.

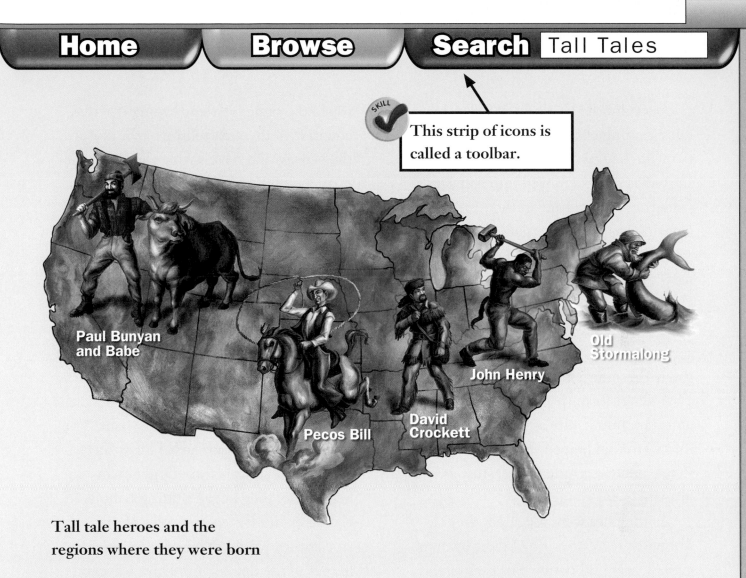

Paul Bunyan and Babe

Pecos Bill

David Crockett

John Henry

Old Stormalong

Tall tale heroes and the regions where they were born

What is a tall tale? Four **features** make a story a tall tale. First, the hero must seem larger than life and have **superhuman** skills. Second, the hero usually has a certain job that he does better than anyone else. The hero might be a lumberjack or a cowhand, for example. Third, the hero must solve a problem in a way that surprises the reader or makes the audience laugh. Fourth, the details of the tale are exaggerated to be made greater than they really are. Often, the hero is bursting with courage and ready to conquer any difficulty. As a rule, the heroes would be a little rough on the outside. Still, they had tender hearts and souls and possessed the most admirable qualities. They were helpful, always available to solve problems and determined to create a better world for their neighbors and friends.

How did the tradition of inventing tales starring characters that were larger-than-life begin? Tall tales probably started as settlers moved into America's wilderness areas. Life on the American frontier was difficult, exhausting, dangerous and uncertain. For the most part, the future was unknown and scary. When the day was done, pioneers gathered around the fire in search of relaxation and entertainment. Telling stories became a favorite pastime. It was a handy art form that could not only entertain but inspire as well. The tales that were told helped the people feel they could overcome danger, just as their favorite heroes had.

As the tales were repeated, they somehow took on a life of their own and grew bigger and better. For example, if someone roped a fierce bear and swung it across town, then in the retelling he

roped the same bear and swung it across country. In the next telling of the story the hero would have swung the bear so far it landed on the moon. Even though no one believed a bear landed on the moon, people certainly enjoyed listening to the story as much as the storyteller enjoyed telling it.

A brand-new tall tale often had the fellow who told it or somebody from the "neighborhood" as its hero. But as the tale became more famous, people began to feel it wasn't "right" that such a wonderful story be told about an ordinary man. The pioneers decided that larger-than-life stories needed to feature larger-than-life heroes. So, they began putting famous characters in the leading roles of the stories they would tell. Some were real heroes of the day such as Davy Crockett or Jim Bridger. Others, like Paul Bunyan and Pecos Bill, were products of the imaginations of good storytellers.

A particular tall tale might also be influenced by events in the region where it was born. People who made their living from the sea liked to hear stories about the adventures of Old Stormalong and his ship. Railroad workers liked to hear stories about John Henry, who could hammer railroad spikes faster than anyone else. Ranchers and cowboys enjoyed hearing about Pecos Bill who roped a mountain

lion and rode it a hundred feet at a step. They also enjoyed hearing about Slue-foot Sue who rode a catfish down the Rio Grande.

Speaking of roping, if you feel up to it, you might try to catch a ride to the lumber camp on Paul Bunyan's blue ox, Babe. It shouldn't be too hard to catch him. The distance between Babe's horns is just a little over seven ax handles. Once you rope him and he takes you to the camp, relax by the campfire. The lumberjacks there will probably have another tale or two to share with you!

Connect and Compare

1. If you were on this Web page what feature would you select to help you find out more information about Babe, Paul Bunyan's ox? **Using Toolbars and Links**

2. If you were to write a tall tale, who would be the hero? Explain your answer. **Synthesize**

3. Think about "The Tales Are Getting Taller" and *Davy Crockett Saves the World.* How do you know that *Davy Crockett Saves the World* is a tall tale? **Reading/Writing Across Texts**

Social Studies Activity

Use an online encyclopedia to learn more about one hero on the map on page 73. Write a tall tale about the person you choose. Remember to exaggerate the tale.

 Find out more about tall tales at **www.macmillanmh.com**

Writer's Craft

Topic Sentence
The first sentence in a paragraph is usually the **topic sentence**. It tells what the paragraph will be about.

Write About a Hero

My topic sentence tells about my own hero.

I wasn't afraid to tell how I really feel about Aliyah.

Aliyah, My Hero

by Carla M.

My hero, my neighbor Aliyah, is only seven years old, but she is the bravest person I know. Aliyah has cerebral palsy. Her muscles don't work properly, so she uses a wheelchair. I'd probably be mad at the world if I were Aliyah, but you never even know when Aliyah is having a tough day. She is always smiling.

Doing many everyday tasks is a challenge for Aliyah. Picking up a dropped pencil or getting into a car are complicated tasks. Aliyah gets everything done, but she needs to move slowly and carefully. It's amazing how much patience she has. She almost never gets frustrated.

Aliyah loves jokes, riddles, and games like "Twenty Questions" and "I Spy." Aliyah is so smart that she usually wins.

I know I am lucky to be friends with Aliyah. She has taught me what it really means to be special.

Your Turn

Write a few paragraphs about your own personal hero. Why is he or she your hero? Tell how you feel about this person. Use the writer's checklist to check your writing.

Writer's Checklist

✓ **Ideas and Content:** Does my writing say what I mean?

☑ **Organization:** Does my topic sentence let the reader know what I am writing about?

✓ **Voice:** Did I express my feelings about my hero?

✓ **Word Choice:** Did I use words that are fresh and new?

✓ **Sentence Fluency:** Did I use different sentence types?

✓ **Conventions:** Did I use commas in a series correctly? Did I check my spelling?

Talk About It

What would happen if trees disappeared from the world?

LOG ON Find out more about trees at **www.macmillanmh.com**

TREES for LIFE

TREE-RIFIC!

Vocabulary

- quest
- settings
- reduce
- buffet
- major

The hollow trunk of this Australian boab tree was once used as a prison.

Thomas Pakenham stands at the foot of a Montezuma cypress in Mexico.

Thomas Pakenham set out on a **quest**. Armed with 30 pounds of camera equipment, the British historian went searching for fascinating trees. As Pakenham says, he was in search of trees with "noble brows and strong personalities." He wrote a book about his experiences, with photographs of the many different "personalities" he found. His portraits show the wide range in tree sizes and shapes. Some of the tiny bonsai trees of Japan are less than a foot tall, even though they are full-grown and many years old. On the other hand, in California, Pakenham found "General Sherman"—the name given to a giant sequoia tree that is considered to be the largest single living thing on Earth.

Pakenham's search brought him face to leaf with many remarkable trees in beautiful **settings** all around the world. A tree in Mexico, the Montezuma cypress, has a trunk that is 190 feet around. Similarly, a tree called a "dancing lime" in Germany once held an orchestra on its bottom branches! Pakenham hopes these and other trees will help his message grow: "We shouldn't take them for granted."

TREES at WORK

From steamy rain forests to snowy mountainsides, trees are among nature's hardest workers in any climate!

KEEP IT DOWN!

In noisy areas such as near airports and freeways, trees can absorb sound. They **reduce**, or cut down, the noise almost as effectively as stone walls.

EARTH FRIENDLY

Trees reduce the effects of carbon dioxide, a cause of global warming. Trees absorb and "lock up" carbon dioxide, keeping it from harming the environment.

TAKE A BREATHER

In just one season, a mature tree can produce as much oxygen as ten people inhale in one year.

STAY COOL

Trees can reduce heating costs by breaking the force of winter winds that **buffet** and batter homes. In summer, trees can keep areas of cities as much as 12 degrees Fahrenheit cooler than areas without trees.

STRONG ROOTS

Top layers of soil can be carried away by wind and water. This can cause **major** environmental problems, such as floods and clogged waterways. Trees hold soil in place.

TOP 5 MOST COMMON TREES IN THE U.S.

In the United States, the last Friday in April is Arbor Day. More than 1 million trees were planted on the first Arbor Day in 1872. In 2002, 130 years later, Americans celebrated by planting 18 million trees during the year. Here are the most common trees in this country. Are any of them in your neighborhood?

 1. Silver Maple

 2. Black Cherry

 3. Box Elder

 4. Eastern Cottonwood

 5. Black Willow

LOG ON Find out more about identifying trees at **www.macmillanmh.com**

Forests of the WORLD

How are geography and climate related to the kinds of trees, plants, and animals that inhabit different forests around the world?

Monteverde Cloud Forest Preserve, Costa Rica

Giant redwoods in California. Redwoods are cone-bearing trees.

Have you visited any biomes lately? A biome is a large community of plants and animals that is supported by a certain type of climate. Biomes like the Arctic tundra—where cold winds **buffet** anything that appears on the barren landscape—are treeless. Many other areas in the world are covered with different kinds of trees. Here are three types of forest biomes.

82

Deciduous forest in autumn

Coniferous Forest

If you are on a **quest** to find a coniferous forest biome, you will want to head south of the Arctic tundra. This type of forest stretches from Alaska southward across North America as well as across Europe and Asia.

Coniferous forests consist mainly of cone-bearing trees such as spruce, hemlock, and fir. The soil is not very rich, because there are no leaves to decompose and make the ground suitable for growth. This will **reduce** the growth of other kinds of plant life.

Some animals that thrive in this biome are ermine, moose, red fox, snowshoe rabbits, and great horned owls.

Deciduous Forest

Do you want to visit a deciduous forest in person? This biome is in the mild-temperate zone of the Northern Hemisphere. **Major** deciduous forests are found in eastern North America, Europe, and eastern Asia.

Deciduous trees lose their leaves in the fall. The natural decaying of the fallen leaves enriches the soil and allows all kinds of plant life to grow.

83

This Costa Rican rain forest has many layers of plant life.

Oak, beech, ash, and maple trees are typical of deciduous forests, and many types of insect and animal life abound. In the U.S., these forests are home to many animals, including deer, American gray squirrels, rabbits, raccoons, and woodpeckers.

Rain Forest

Tropical rain forests are found in Asia, Africa, South America, Central America, and on many of the Pacific islands. Almost half the total area of the world's rain forests is in Brazil.

Tropical rain forests receive at least 70 inches of rain each year and have more species of plants and animals than any other biome. The thick vegetation absorbs moisture, which then evaporates and falls as rain.

A rain forest grows in three layers, like the levels in a stadium. The canopy, or tallest level, has trees between 100 and 200 feet tall. The second level, or understory, contains a mix of small trees,

Biomes of the World

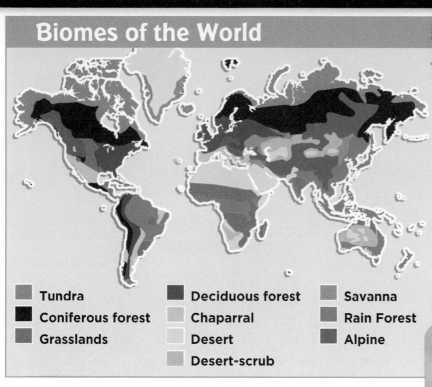

- ■ Tundra
- ■ Coniferous forest
- ■ Grasslands
- ■ Deciduous forest
- ■ Chaparral
- ■ Desert
- ■ Desert-scrub
- ■ Savanna
- ■ Rain Forest
- ■ Alpine

Orangutan

vines, and palms, as well as shrubs and ferns. The third and lowest level is the forest floor, where herbs, mosses, and fungi grow.

The combination of heat and moisture makes tropical rain forests the perfect **settings** for more than 15 million types of plants and animals. Some of the animals of the tropical rain forest are the anteater, jaguar, lemur, orangutan, macaw, sloth, and toucan. Among the many plant species are bamboo, banana trees, and rubber trees.

The floor of this rain forest is covered with ferns and mosses.

Think and Compare

STRATEGY
SKILL

1. What three types of forest biomes does this article describe?

2. How is the soil in a coniferous forest different from the soil in a deciduous forest?

3. Think of a forest you have visited or that grows near where you live. Describe the plants and animals that live there.

4. The trees listed in the "Top 5 Most Common Trees in the U.S." on page 81 can be classified into a single category. Based on "Forests of the World," what category do you think that is?

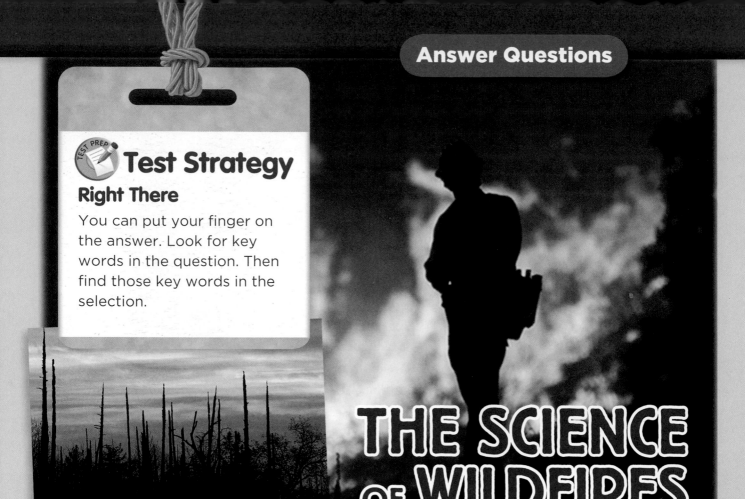

The aftermath of a wildfire

THE SCIENCE OF WILDFIRES

Wildfires result from a combination of fuel, dryness, and a trigger. Each factor determines how strong the blaze will be. Fuel means flammable solids that, with oxygen, feed the fire. Dryness can be caused by short-term periods with little rain or by lengthy drought. Triggers can be as natural as a lightning strike, as innocent as a campfire, or as careless as a stray match.

Weather is the primary force that creates or ends wildfires. Once wildfires start burning, they create their own weather. First, smoke and heat from fires can rise thousands of feet in the air, creating an empty space below them. Cooler air rushes in to fill the space, but the fresh air brings oxygen that fuels the flames. This convection system creates powerful, hot winds that dry out and preheat fuel ahead of the fire. This helps the fire move forward and even jump natural barriers, such as rivers.

A fire dies when it cannot get fuel, heat, or oxygen. The main strategy for fighting wildfires is containment: surround the fire and starve it. Helicopters and tanker airplanes can drop water or chemicals to slow the spread of flames. Firefighters can also set up fire lines—areas cleared of any fuel that would allow the fire to spread. Controlled fires are sometimes set to deny fuel to an approaching blaze.

Directions: Answer the questions.

1. **Which term means a strategy to fight a wildfire by depriving it of fuel?**

   A triggering
   B flame retardant
   C containment
   D convection system

Tip
Look for key words.

2. **What triggers wildfires?**

   A Matches, campfires, or lightning can trigger a wildfire.
   B Controlled fires provide fuel for the blaze.
   C Hot, dry winds preheat fuel to create a convection system.
   D Tanker airplanes spread the flames.

3. **Why do firefighters set up fire lines?**

   A to create a fuel-free area
   B to create a fire-resistant forest
   C to restore grassland
   D to create safe zones for forest homes

4. **How might dropping chemicals and creating fire lines be more effective together than if used separately?**

5. **Describe the role weather can play in both creating and ending wildfires. Use details from the article to support your answer.**

Write to a Prompt

In the selection "The Science of Wildfires," you read about forest fires. Explain what strategies you would use to fight a wildfire that was moving rapidly toward your community. Use examples from the selection to support your answer. Include specific details to support your main idea.

Let's Fight Fires!

 The fire in our community is spreading too quickly for firefighters to put out. Our tanker planes have not improved the situation at all.

 If we want to save our homes, we must fight fire with fire. We need to cut all the trees and brush on the edge of our community. This will steal the fire's fuel and, we hope, stop the fire before it reaches our town.

 There are no guarantees. The wind can carry embers half a mile. We will have to do more. We will need to set a backfire. This means setting fire to the forest between the wildfire and the fire line we create. The prevailing wind will spread the fire toward us. I know it sounds crazy, but we really won't be helping the wildfire. By setting this smaller, more controllable fire, we hope to stop the wildfire more easily at the fire line. The backfire will burn away all the fuel between us and the wildfire. When the wildfire reaches the burned out area, it will go out.

I used details to make my point and support my ideas.

Writing Prompt

In the selection "The Science of Wildfires," you read different ideas about the best way to deal with forest fires. Explain which two of the approaches described in the article you think will work the best. Write your response in two paragraphs, and include specific details that support your main ideas.

Writer's Checklist

☑ Ask yourself, who is my audience?

☑ Think about your purpose for writing.

☑ Use details to support your main idea.

☑ Plan your writing before beginning.

☑ Be sure your ideas are clear and organized.

☑ Use your best spelling, grammar, and punctuation.

EXPLORING SPACE

Talk About It

What draws people to want to explore space? Why should we continue to explore space?

LOG ON Find out more about exploring space at **www.macmillanmh.com**

Vocabulary

mission	gravity
disasters	maze
environment	adjusted
zone	function

Context Clues

Descriptions or explanations can be **Context Clues** that will help you figure out the meaning of unfamiliar words. Sometimes you can find these clues if you keep reading until the end of a sentence or paragraph.

by Latasha Pearson

In the early years of space travel, an astronaut's job was to pilot a spacecraft. Astronauts of today do many other types of jobs. These jobs change depending on the goal of the **mission** that needs to be accomplished.

Astronaut Pilots control and direct the space shuttle. One astronaut pilot is the captain. Captains must make sure the mission is a success. Their job is to keep the crew safe. Captains know that working as a team can prevent **disasters** in space.

Mission Specialists run tests and take care of the equipment on board. The equipment may need to be **adjusted** to fit the task. Sometimes they walk in space or handle the shuttle's robot arm. Astronaut pilots and mission specialists work for the National Aeronautics and Space Administration (NASA). They learn to live and work in an unusual **environment**. They learn to move in a special **zone** where there is zero **gravity**, the force that pulls things back to Earth. They also figure out how to operate the confusing **maze** of equipment that fills the space shuttle.

Payload Specialists do not work for NASA. These crew members have specific skills and are usually in charge of special projects. They train with the astronauts. Like everyone else getting settled on the shuttle, these specialists have to get used to life in space.

Educator Astronauts are teachers who travel into space. Their job is to encourage students to study science and math. This will help the next generation of astronauts **function** well in space and carry out their jobs successfully.

Reread for **Comprehension**

Generate Questions
Summarize

A Summary Chart helps you ask questions about the main ideas in a selection. Use your Summary Chart as you reread "Jobs in Space" to summarize the main ideas.

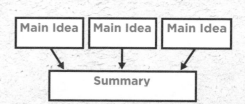

Comprehension

Genre

Nonfiction gives facts about real people, living things, places, or events.

Generate Questions

Summarize

As you read, use your Summary Chart.

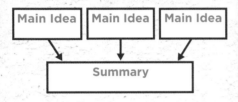

Read to Find Out

How do astronauts prepare for space travel?

94

ULTIMATE FIELD TRIP 5

BLASTING OFF TO SPACE ACADEMY

BY
SUSAN E. GOODMAN

PHOTOGRAPHS BY
MICHAEL J. DOOLITTLE

95

Countdown to Adventure

What's the best part of being an astronaut? Is it the thrill of rocketing out of Earth's atmosphere at 25,000 miles per hour? Is it the chance to make new scientific discoveries? Or is it the adventure of leaving the familiar behind and going, as someone once put it, "where no man has gone before?"

Few people actually get to answer these questions by traveling into space. But some kids took the first step by going to U.S. Space Academy at the United States Space and Rocket Center in Huntsville, Alabama.

AMAZING SPACE FACTS

At least half the astronauts experience space sickness at the beginning of their voyage. That's why John Young didn't do Gus Grissom any favor when he smuggled him a corned beef sandwich on the Gemini 3 mission. The story is Grissom threw up; in weightless conditions, that's a difficult cleanup job.

"I can't tell whether this fits or not," said Shane. "Do I look like an astronaut?" Another kid's comment: "If you have to go to the bathroom quick, these flight suits are a bummer."

For almost a week they used the same simulators that real astronauts use and learned how to walk on the Moon and work without **gravity**. They built their own rockets and visited the ones scientists used to launch the Apollo astronauts to the Moon. They tried tasting space food and wearing space suits. They learned how to eat in space, sleep in space, even how to go to the bathroom without any gravity.

During their training they became a team, Team Europa, named after one of Jupiter's seven moons. Then, Europa blasted off on a mission of its own . . . .

The Habitat, where kids sleep at Space Academy, was designed as an earthbound space station with stairs and handrails to get from floor to floor. In space, you'd float where you need to go.

On the Training Floor

"**E**uropa, the training center is a dirt-free **zone**," said Paul. "Gum and drinks can create **disasters** here."

Paul, one of Europa's team leaders, led the kids through a **maze** of strange-looking machines. As they walked, the kids peeked at other teams jumping high enough to dunk a basketball and spinning in what looked like a giant gyroscope. Paul explained that astronauts trained for years before going into space. It takes a lot of practice to learn how to **function** in such a different **environment**. On space walks, for example, they must make delicate repairs while floating upside down. In their ships they must learn how to drift rather than walk through the air.

How do they learn these things while anchored by Earth's gravity? To find out, Europa tried some of the simulators that astronauts have used.

The training center is equipped with many simulators.

The ⅙ Gravity Chair

"The Moon has only one-sixth of our gravity," explained Paul. "If you weigh one hundred twenty pounds here, you'd only weigh twenty pounds on the Moon. And you'd have to learn to walk differently because there isn't as much traction."

To practice this movement, the kids used a ⅙ Gravity Chair similar to the Apollo astronauts'. In fact, Europa learned from the astronauts' experiences. The best ways to get around were a slow jog and the bunny hop.

John waited impatiently while Paul **adjusted** the chair to offset five-sixths of his weight.

"Bunny hop for me," said Paul.

"You've got to be kidding," answered John. "I can barely reach the ground."

Soon, however, he was leaping across the training floor.

"This looks like good practice for the high jump," said Stephanie.

"It shouldn't be; you want to jump for distance, not height," said Paul. "Astronaut Charlie Duke of *Apollo 16* tried to set a height record. But his life-support pack changed his center of gravity. He landed on his back and couldn't get up, just like a beetle. If John Young hadn't been around to help him, he could have been stuck there until *Apollo 17!*"

"I felt like I was on a trampoline," said Lindsay, "but I didn't go down—just up!"

Summarize
What did the kids of Team Europa do to help them prepare for a possible trip into space?

99

The Multi-Axis Trainer (MAT)

"Remove everything from your pockets," said Bethany, Europa's other team leader. "Take off your necklaces, too, so you don't get whacked in the face."

To get ready for the MAT, some kids took off jewelry; others just took a few deep breaths. The MAT looks like an atom gone wild, with each of its three outer circles spinning separately and you as its whirling nucleus. The Mercury astronauts used it to learn how to regain control of a tumbling spacecraft.

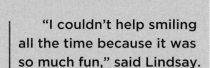

The MAT never turns more than twice in the same direction, which is supposed to keep you from feeling sick. That didn't keep a lot of kids from getting nervous. But once they tried it, the glint of silver braces flashed through their smiles.

"It was terrific," said Stacy, "but next time, I'll tie my hair back so it doesn't keep hitting my face."

"It's awesome," Stephanie agreed.

When asked how she'd feel doing it for a ten-minute stretch in a spaceship, Stephanie added, "Your head spins like crazy, but it doesn't feel bad."

"I couldn't help smiling all the time because it was so much fun," said Lindsay.

The Five Degrees of Freedom (5DF) Chair

On Earth, when you jump up, gravity pulls you back down. In space, you just keep going up. If you push away from a wall, you keep going backward. Bending quickly to grab something could make you do somersaults. To get used to the weightless tumble of space, the Gemini and Apollo astronauts—and the kids at Space Academy—used the 5DF Chair. This chair glided over the floor on a cushion of air like the puck in an air hockey game.

"This is what an EVA, an extravehicular activity, or space walk, feels like," Bethany said, tipping and rolling the chair in all direction to give the kids a taste of the different movements.

Bethany held on to the 5DF Chair to keep it safe. In space, astronauts are tethered to their ship. It's a good thing, too. When astronaut Pete Conrad went on his space walk, he lost hold of *Skylab*. That tether was the only thing that kept him from floating away.

In the 5DF Chair, kids practiced inching their way along a wall. Once Lindsay pushed herself away by accident, she had a hard time getting back.

"Swim, Lindsay, swim!" Courtney called out.

Lindsay tried to breaststroke her way back to the wall—it was hopeless.

"Oh, well," said Charles, "she's *Lost in Space!*"

Space Shot

"This is your last chance to change your mind," said the operator. "Once the generator has been charged, we cannot stop."

In just seconds, the kids were blasting off on the Space Shot. They would rocket skyward with a force of 4 Gs, one more than astronauts experience during their launches. All that force meant that, for a few seconds at the top, before gravity pulled them back, the kids could feel what it was like to be weightless.

Some people call the Space Shot "an elevator with an attitude."

AMAZING SPACE FACTS

The last time astronauts walked on the Moon was in 1972, but all of their footprints are still there. Since the Moon does not have an atmosphere, there is no wind to blow the prints away.

NASA doesn't use the Space Shot to simulate weightlessness; it trains astronauts aboard its KC-135 airplane. The plane climbs sharply and then free-falls straight toward the ground, up again, then down again, and again. For twenty-five seconds, at the top of each roller-coaster ride, the plane's passengers are weightless. But many astronauts have paid a price for this amazing experience. The KC-135 is nicknamed the "Vomit Comet" for good reason.

"I wish I hadn't eaten so much breakfast," said Erin as she waited for her turn on the Space Shot. "I'm going to scream. It helps you not throw up."

Before her second ride, Erin was too excited to feel sick. "I love that feeling of just shooting up there," she said.

"Then you rise up out of your chair and float there for a second," said Stacy. "Weightlessness, I wish it lasted a lot longer."

Summarize
How did each machine Team Europa used help them to experience what it's like to travel in space?

This is the way Frank and most kids feel going up on the Space Shot . . .

. . . and they feel this way coming down. Devin was amazed that one kid in line thought the experience would cure his fear of heights.

The Pool

Another way the earthbound astronauts simulate working in weightlessness is by going underwater. At Houston's Lyndon B. Johnson Space Center, astronauts practice in a huge water tank holding a full-scale model of the Shuttle's payload bay. At Space Academy, the kids went to a swimming pool.

"Your job is to build a cube underwater as fast as possible," said Bethany. "It takes teamwork, an ability to work in weightlessness, and—something astronauts don't need, I hope—an ability to hold your breath."

Each strut, or tube, belonged in a specific place.

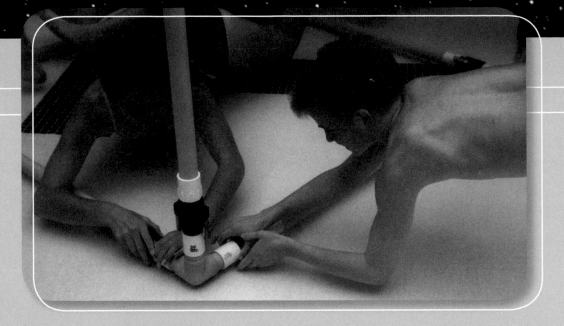

The water started boiling as kids grabbed struts and dove underwater. It kept boiling as they came up for air again and again, slowly realizing they needed a better plan. . . .

"Ten minutes and fifty-six seconds," Bethany said when they finally finished. "Well, every astronaut has to start somewhere. How could you have gone faster?"

"Talk more to each other?" said Isabelle.

"That's right," Bethany agreed. "Communication, letting your leaders lead, and teamwork. It's true in the pool, and it will be even more important when you work to make your own space mission a real success."

Once the kids started working together, the cube was built quickly.

AMAZING SPACE FACTS

Flawed when it went into orbit in 1990, the Hubble Space Telescope was repaired in 1993 during a spectacular mission that required five space walks. Located above our hazy atmosphere, the Hubble sees deep into the universe to reveal black holes, new galaxies, the birth of some stars and the death of others. Its "eagle-eyed vision" is so acute that if the Hubble were on Earth, it could spot a firefly ten thousand miles away!

BLAST OFF WITH SUSAN E. GOODMAN

Susan E. Goodman writes her stories by trying them out first. For this story she actually went to Space Camp at the U.S. Space Academy. There she learned how to do everyday things at zero gravity, like brushing her teeth and "walking." Experiencing different ways of living helps Susan find the right words when it comes to writing about them. For other stories Susan has stayed in an underwater hotel and even balanced on a girder fifty stories above the ground.

Another book by Susan E. Goodman:
On This Spot: An Expedition Back Through Time

 Find out more about Susan E. Goodman at **www.macmillanmh.com**

Author's Purpose

Authors of nonfiction often write to inform readers about something. Do you think that is why Susan E. Goodman wrote *Ultimate Field Trip 5*? Explain what clues in the text and captions make you think so.

106

Summarize

Use your Summary Chart to summarize *Ultimate Field Trip 5: Blasting Off to Space Academy*. Your summary should include the main ideas from the selection. These will usually appear at the beginning of each paragraph.

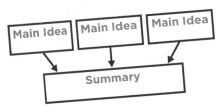

Think and Compare

1. Summarize one section of *Ultimate Field Trip 5: Blasting Off to Space Academy*. Be sure to only include important events and information. **Generate Questions: Summarize**

2. Reread page 99. Why do Team Europa and actual astronauts use a gravity chair? Give reasons for your answer. **Analyze**

3. Which activity from space camp would you enjoy most? Explain your answer. **Evaluate**

4. Do you think a future **mission** into space will improve our lives on Earth? **Analyze**

5. Reread "Jobs in Space" on pages 92–93. What aspects of the jobs described aboard a space shuttle would Team Europa be prepared to do? Use details from both stories to explain your answer. **Reading/Writing Across Texts**

I'm Building a Rocket

by Kenn Nesbit

I'm building a rocket.
As soon as I'm done
I'm taking my friends
On a trip to the sun.

The rhyme scheme for this stanza would be *a, b, c, b.*

But what do you mean
That the sun is too hot?
Oh, well, I suppose
I'll just pick a new spot.

I'm building a rocket.
I'm finishing soon
And taking my friends
On a trip to the moon!

But what do you mean

That the moon has no air?

Well, dang, then I guess

That we can't go up there.

I'm building a rocket.

It's going to fly.

I'm taking my friends

Way up high in the sky.

But what do you mean

When you ask how we'll land?

This rocket is harder

To build than I planned.

To heck with the rocket.

It's out in the shed.

I'm taking my friends

Out for pizza instead.

> There are six syllables in lines 1 and 4 and five syllables in lines 2 and 3. This is an example of *rhythm.*

Connect and Compare

1. What are some other examples of rhyme schemes and rhythm that make this a simple poem? **Rhyme Schemes and Rhythm**

2. Read the poem aloud. How does the rhythm help you read the poem with expression? **Evaluate**

3. Compare this poem with *Ultimate Field Trip 5: Blasting Off to Space Academy.* What is the difference between the children in the book and the speaker in this poem? **Reading/Writing Across Texts**

 Find out more about poetry at **www.macmillanmh.com**

Writer's Craft

Important Details

Important details that describe or explain make writing interesting. Readers need detailed descriptions, explanations, and examples to better understand your experience.

I included important details to tell my teacher about a great experience.

I used descriptive details to describe the costumes.

September 19

Dear Mrs. Hansen,

I miss my old school and friends. I know you said I would have some great experiences in my new town. Now I know you were right! I'm writing to tell you about last weekend.

We went to an international parade called Folkmoot. People in costumes from all over the world came to sing, dance, and perform their music.

The colorful costumes were decorated with red, blue and green beads and some even had feathers. The beads were so sparkly they nearly blinded me. Who would have thought I'd have this incredible experience in a small North Carolina town?

Sincerely,
Marcella W.

Your Turn

Write a letter about an exciting experience you have had. Choose descriptive details that help the person you are writing to share the experience with you. Use the writer's checklist to check your letter.

Writer's Checklist

☑ **Ideas and Content:** Does my letter include important details?

✓ **Organization:** Did I separate my letter into paragraphs so it is easy to read?

✓ **Voice:** Will the person who reads my letter know I wrote it before he or she sees my signature?

✓ **Word Choice:** Did I use precise words related to sight, sound, smell, taste, and touch?

✓ **Sentence Fluency:** Did I sometimes use long sentences instead of short, choppy sentences?

✓ **Conventions:** Did I use the correct punctuation? Did I check my spelling?

RESCUE DOGS

Talk About It

In what situations do you hear about dogs coming to the rescue? What abilities do dogs have that make them useful for rescue work?

LOG ON Find out more about dogs at **www.macmillanmh.com**

IT'S A DOG'S LIFE

by Shawna Telman

Vocabulary

variety	fragrance
transformed	cooperation
celebration	canceled
moistened	theory

Thesaurus

A **Thesaurus** is a tool that can help you find synonyms for a particular word. For example, the word *fragrance* may have the following synonyms listed: *aroma*, *perfume*, or *scent*.

My name is Sparky and I work for Ms. Toni Graham. I am her in-home companion. My trainer calls what I do "work" but I think my job is fun! I especially enjoy the **variety** in my job: I do many different things for Ms. Toni every day. She says I have **transformed** her life. I have changed things so her daily routine is easier.

Ms. Toni suffers from an illness that makes her hands shake and causes her muscles to stiffen up. She has a hard time bending over. On a bad day, Ms. Toni can lose her balance and fall. Whenever she drops something, I pick it up for her. It's part of my job.

Another part of my job is to help Ms. Toni with her work. She has an office in her home. Last week she was preparing to mail invitations for some major **celebration** that will raise money for a charity. How did I help? I learned how to lick the flaps of envelopes. They needed to be **moistened**, so that they could seal shut. For once my slimy doggy tongue came in handy!

Every afternoon I accompany Ms. Toni on a walk around town. Exercise is important for her health so we never miss a day. We often see a new sight or smell a new **fragrance** along our route. Ms. Toni rests when we get back. She needs my **cooperation** during this time. I help her by being very quiet. I stay by the front door and keep my eye on things. If Ms. Toni needs me, she rings a bell.

Every so often Ms. Toni can't sleep, so naptime is **canceled**. At these times she likes me to hang out and relax with her. The **theory** behind this is that petting me makes her feel calm. The idea makes sense. She talks to me and brushes me. This is one of the best parts of my job.

I am very lucky to be a part of Ms. Toni's life. People who have a hard time with day-to-day chores can become sad and lonely. Dogs like me help them feel happy.

Reread for **Comprehension**

Generate Questions
Cause and Effect

A Cause and Effect Chart helps you ask questions to figure out what happens in a story (an effect) and why it happens (a cause). Use your Cause and Effect Chart as you reread "It's a Dog's Life" to find several effects and their causes.

Cause → Effect
→
→
→
→

Comprehension

Genre

Fantasy tells a story about characters and events that could not exist in real life.

Generate Questions

Cause and Effect

As you read, use your Cause and Effect Chart.

Cause ➔ Effect
➔
➔
➔
➔

Read to Find Out

How does Pipiolo change the lives of the roof dogs?

Pipiolo and the Roof Dogs

written by **Brian Meunier**   illustrated by **Perky Edgerton**

The village of San Pablo Etla is on the edge of a wide valley in southern Mexico. My father built our house on the mountainside overlooking the village. From there I can see the whole valley, the distant villages, and every house in San Pablo.

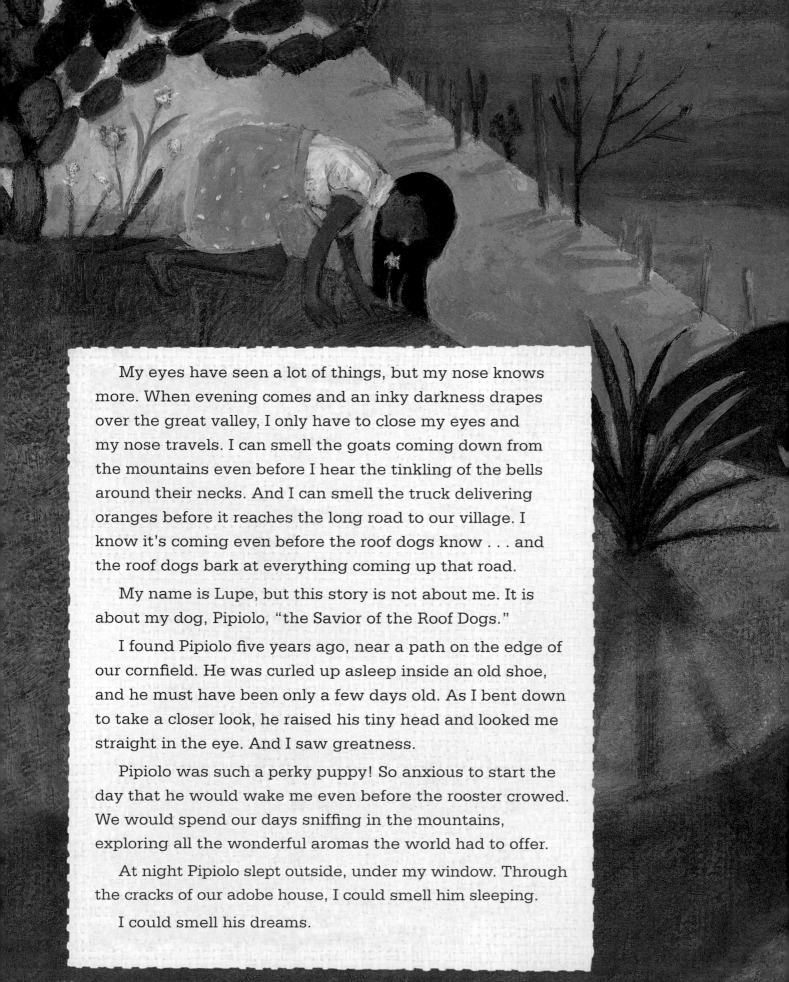

My eyes have seen a lot of things, but my nose knows more. When evening comes and an inky darkness drapes over the great valley, I only have to close my eyes and my nose travels. I can smell the goats coming down from the mountains even before I hear the tinkling of the bells around their necks. And I can smell the truck delivering oranges before it reaches the long road to our village. I know it's coming even before the roof dogs know . . . and the roof dogs bark at everything coming up that road.

My name is Lupe, but this story is not about me. It is about my dog, Pipiolo, "the Savior of the Roof Dogs."

I found Pipiolo five years ago, near a path on the edge of our cornfield. He was curled up asleep inside an old shoe, and he must have been only a few days old. As I bent down to take a closer look, he raised his tiny head and looked me straight in the eye. And I saw greatness.

Pipiolo was such a perky puppy! So anxious to start the day that he would wake me even before the rooster crowed. We would spend our days sniffing in the mountains, exploring all the wonderful aromas the world had to offer.

At night Pipiolo slept outside, under my window. Through the cracks of our adobe house, I could smell him sleeping.

I could smell his dreams.

Pipiolo walked with me to school each morning. As we passed through the village, the roof dogs would run to the edge of their roofs and furiously bark down at us. They never scared me much, because I knew they were the ones who were frightened. Pipiolo would race around barking, flaunting his own freedom. Much too proud, I thought. "Poor roof dogs!" I said to Pipiolo. "To be put up on roofs as puppies to serve as guard dogs, imprisoned on a small patch of hot concrete their whole lives. Never to smell the wet earth and feel the delicious squish of mud between their toes."

"You're lucky, Pipiolo, that we don't have a flat roof, or Papa would have put you up there a long time ago. Besides," I added, "I know you're just showing off for the cute one, Chulita."

He looked at me with his clear brown eyes, and I knew he understood.

One day, as we were traipsing through a field, Pipiolo gave out a sudden yelp. He then buried his nose in a tuft of grass. I got down and took a sniff. It had a kind of musty goat smell, with a hint of mint. Suddenly, I understood what Pipiolo was trying to tell me!

Using my school ruler as a shovel, I dug up a clump and stuffed it into my backpack. We ran to the village, where I broke the clump into many pieces. I tossed a piece to each angry roof dog, saving the piece with the flower in it for Chulita.

You should have heard the dogs as they experienced their first whiff of real earth—their barks turned from anger to delight. A unified howl of surprise and discovery! And Pipiolo and I howled right along with them in their symphony of **celebration**.

We had made a difference!

Cause and Effect
Why doesn't Pipiolo share the same fate as the other dogs in San Pablo Etla?

Every day, Pipiolo and I would dig up another **fragrance** and share it with the roof dogs. We worked hard to find a good **variety**, sometimes overlooking the very pungent for the rare and unusual.

Life went on like this for some time, until it dawned on me that, on many days, Pipiolo would not even get up with me in the morning to walk to school. He was spending more and more time sleeping in the shade during the day, while I was doing all the work myself in the hot sun!

One night, as I stepped out into our yard to smell the evening air, I saw Pipiolo's shadow slip into the cornfield. I crouched down so he wouldn't see me and followed him on all fours as he sauntered down the mountainside. Wherever he sniffed, I sniffed. I followed him through several cornfields, through a drainage pipe, and under fences. Straight to the only store in town that was still open, Tienda Soliz.

Now I understood why he was so tired during the day.

He had a night life!

Even before I saw the flickering of blue light, I could smell the heated plastic of a television waft through the cool dark night. Tienda Soliz had the only television set in our village. We are so high up in these mountains that this television can only get one channel. And that one channel only shows old American westerns.

Pipiolo walked right up to the front of the television and plopped down. The mayor of our village, El Presidente, greeted him nonchalantly.

It was obvious Pipiolo was a regular.

My dog has been watching TV every night! I thought as I hid behind a corner to watch Pipiolo—and the movie, too.

The actor, Juan Wayne, was trapped on the roof of a burning building. Just when it looked as though all was lost, four horses pulling a hay wagon galloped through the town, and as it passed by, Juan Wayne jumped down into the hay to safety. At that moment, Pipiolo jumped up and let out an earthshaking howl. The men in the *tienda* sprang to their feet, visibly shaken. "Get that dog out of here!" shouted El Presidente.

Pipiolo raced out into the street, and I ran after him.

He ran down the main street of San Pablo. I looked up at the roof dogs and saw that they were all quietly watching Pipiolo.

They had been waiting for him!

I had never heard Pipiolo bark so long and so eloquently. He spoke of freedom, courage, **cooperation**, and action—and of all the smells yet to be experienced. The roof dogs and I were transfixed. And when he was through barking, they were **transformed**.

At his command, they all sat down to wait.

I must have fallen asleep, because suddenly I awoke to the tang of ripe oranges, followed by the familiar sound of a truck grinding its gears as it climbed along the long, steep road to our village.

Pipiolo barked, and the roof dogs stood up and began to leap from house to house toward the last two roofs at the end of the village. All, that is, except for Chulita, who shivered, frozen with terror.

The truck stopped at Tienda Soliz to make the delivery of oranges, then drove on to the end of the village to turn around. Pipiolo barked again, and the dogs all jumped down onto the pile of oranges in the back of the truck.

Chulita was now the only dog left. She barked forlornly as the truck started to make its way back through the village—and to leave Chulita behind.

The only roof dog in San Pablo Etla.

Just as the truck began to pass the house of Chulita, Pipiolo ran out in front of it. "Pipiolo!" I screamed as the driver blasted his horn and slammed on his brakes. But Pipiolo stood his ground. With the loudest bark I ever heard him make, he commanded Chulita to "Jump!" Chulita closed her eyes and took a great leap of faith, landing safely on top of the oranges. Only then did Pipiolo move out of the way, and the truck drove off out of town.

Cause and Effect
Why does Pipiolo run out in front of the truck?

126

Just before the truck disappeared down the road, I saw all the dogs, one by one, leap off the back of it and follow Pipiolo into the cornfield and out of sight.

As they did, I whispered, "*Tierra y Libertad*—Land and Freedom."

I slowly walked home and crawled into bed. Closing my eyes, I could smell the roof dogs racing through the fields, exhilarated by the first touch of soft earth beneath their paws, their fur **moistened** by the tall grass. They were headed for the mountains.

As I listened, I heard the joyous barking of the newly free. And in that sound, the voice of one dog stood out among them all. My Pipiolo!

In my small village, things remain the same from day to day. The mysterious disappearance of the roof dogs was the biggest event ever to happen in San Pablo Etla. El Presidente called an emergency meeting and even **canceled** school. Everyone had a **theory**, but most agreed that it had to have been some kind of supernatural event. My little cousin, Inocencia, stood up and pronounced it *"El Milagro de San Pablo!"*—the Miracle of San Pablo!

The next morning, I got up especially early to take the long route to school, through the neighboring village of Viquera.

When I stepped out into my yard, I saw Pipiolo curled up in his usual spot under my window! I ran over to give him a big hug, but he was so deeply asleep, I decided not to wake him. Instead, I softly whispered in his ear, "Sleep, my dear Pipiolo. You've been busy, but you have much more to do."

On my long walk to the next village, I explored several different aromas, finally settling on the very best. And this I shared with the roof dogs of Viquera.

As I did, I whispered to each dog in turn:

"Be patient. Pipiolo will be here soon."

Come Along With
Brian Meunier and Perky Edgerton

Brian Meunier wrote this story, but he is an artist, too. His large wood and metal bird sculptures are in museums and galleries all around the country. Brian is also a professor of fine arts. When he started writing, he didn't stop with this story. It is the first in a trilogy, which means there are two more books on a similar theme coming out soon.

Perky Edgerton worked on this story with her husband, Brian. She illustrated this story with paintings that are warm, complex, and dreamlike, which makes them a great fit for Brian's story. The original paintings for this book were in an exhibition. Perky and Brian live in Pennsylvania with their two daughters and a dog named Chulita.

 LOG ON Find out more about Brian Meunier and Perky Edgerton at **www.macmillanmh.com**

Author's Purpose
Pipiolo and the Roof Dogs is a fantasy because not all of the events could take place in real life. Do you think Brian Meunier wrote just to entertain, or could he have had another purpose? Explain.

Comprehension Check

Summarize

Use your Cause and Effect Chart to help you summarize *Pipiolo and the Roof Dogs*. In your own words, tell how Pipiolo changed the lives of the roof dogs.

Cause → Effect
→
→
→
→

Think and Compare

1. What caused Pipiolo to want to free the roof dogs from their lives as guard animals? Use what you know about Pipiolo's character from the story. **Generate Questions: Cause and Effect**

2. Reread page 131. Predict what will happen when Pipiolo gets to the town of Viquera. **Synthesize**

3. What **fragrances** would you share with the roof dogs? Explain your choices. **Evaluate**

4. Pipiolo used creative thinking to free the roof dogs. Explain how thinking creatively can help solve a problem. **Analyze**

5. Reread "It's a Dog's Life" on pages 114–115. Both Sparky and Pipiolo help others. Describe the similarities and differences between the jobs that both dogs do. Use details from both stories to support your answer. **Reading/Writing Across Texts**

DOGGONE WORK

by Lori Marquez

In January 1925 many of the children in Nome, Alaska, were very ill with a serious disease called diphtheria. Their only hope was a serum used to cure the disease.

The serum was nearly a thousand miles away in Anchorage, Alaska. It was the middle of winter and blizzards had brought heavy snows, making it impossible for planes to land. Dogsleds were the only way to get the medicine from Anchorage to Nome.

Balto at the lead of a dog team

Dog teams and their drivers began a series of dangerous journeys. The teams worked in **relays**, one team handing the serum off to the next team. Balto was the lead dog of the twentieth team. Strong and smart, Balto led the team safely across icy paths. His team reached Nome with the serum and the children were saved.

Why could Balto and the other dog teams make this journey? Different dogs have changed or adapted over centuries for different functions. Sled dogs like Balto have **characteristics** that help them pull sleds. They move their feet quickly and have remarkable strength for their size. Their double coat of fur protects them from cold, snow, and ice. These dogs have great **stamina** and keep going no matter what the conditions are. Also, they know how to find the safest way to travel. These qualities make them well adapted to pulling a sled in the worst winter weather.

Sledder Gunnar Kasson hugs his famous dog Balto

✔ Reading a Chart

This chart helps you organize information about dog breeds, their adaptations, and the work that each breed does.

DOG ADAPTATIONS

Breed	Adaptation	Job
Husky	Strong; fast; thick fur	Pulling sleds
Collie	Instinct for herding other animals; good eyesight	Tending sheep and cattle
Bloodhound	Excellent sense of smell	Searching and rescuing

SAR DOGS

Sled dogs are not the only dogs who work for a living. For example, Bronte is a search-and-rescue dog, or a SAR dog. Bronte is a rottweiler who helps find missing people. In 1995, after an explosion in a building in Oklahoma City, Oklahoma, Bronte was brought in to search through the rubble. When she began to scratch and sniff in one place, her handler knew that she had found someone. Rescuers dug quickly and found a 15-year-old girl who was alive under the debris.

What makes a good SAR dog? First, SAR dogs need an especially good sense of smell. Dogs use their whiskers to help them smell. Whiskers help dogs know the direction of the wind so they can tell where a scent is coming from. SAR dogs use scents in the air to find a person in a certain area. They can also sniff an item of human clothing and then track the scent of the person who wore it.

It takes about a year to train a SAR dog. These dogs are likely to be friendly, eager to please, and happy to **retrieve** things. Trainers use different forms of the game hide-and-seek to teach SAR dogs. The trainer hides an object. When the dog finds the hidden item, it drags the object back to the trainer. This training along with the dog's natural characteristics make it perfectly suited for search-and-rescue missions.

A rescue dog named Tracer picks up the scent of a diver in ten feet of water.

SERVICE DOGS

Other dogs have other jobs. Service dogs provide people with different types of services, depending on their needs. If you visit a sheep farm, you might see dogs herding sheep. Sheep dogs help move sheep from field to field or into holding pens. Some dogs help people. These dogs are trained to cross streets, open doors, and even make beds! You might even see an agriculture dog working at an airport. These dogs smell suitcases and packages, looking for harmful insects that might be hiding in food.

This service dog helps a blind woman cross the street.

Connect and Compare

1. Look at the dog adaptations chart on page 135. What characteristics do dogs that tend sheep have? **Reading a Chart**

2. If your family decided to adopt a dog, what characteristics would you look for? **Evaluate**

3. Think about "Doggone Work" and *Pipiolo and the Roof Dogs*. What characteristics do Pipiolo and a SAR dog have in common? **Reading/Writing Across Texts**

 Science Activity

Research three other dog breeds. Make a chart listing the work the dogs do and the characteristics that help each dog do that work.

 Find out more about dogs at **www.macmillanmh.com**

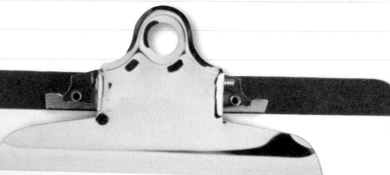

Writer's Craft

Unimportant Details
Delete **unimportant details** that do not tell about your topic. Also delete details that may tell something about your topic but are not really important.

My teacher encourages us to keep a journal. Here are details about last night.

I decided I should give descriptive details about African gray parrots.

Monday, October 3

I've had my African gray parrot for about three years. His name is Frank. He's about a foot tall, with gray feathers all over, except for his brilliant red tail. His eyes are yellow.

I've been talking to Frank for three years, but in all this time he's only squawked back at me.

Last night all of that changed. I was reading in bed. All of a sudden I heard, "Hi, Bao!" I glanced over, and Frank was staring at me. Then he said it again, "Hi, Bao!" I couldn't believe it! Not only was Frank talking to me, but he was using my name! I answered him: "Hi, Frank!" He was quiet. I reached over to turn off my bedside lamp. Just then I heard Frank's voice again. "Goodnight!" he said. "Goodnight, Frank!" I replied.

Your Turn

Write a journal entry about an encounter you have had with an animal. The animal could be a pet, one you saw at the zoo, or a wild animal. Use lots of details so that the reader can understand your experience. Use the writer's checklist to check your writing.

Writer's Checklist

☑ **Ideas and Content:** Did I delete unimportant details that do not help the reader to understand my ideas?

✓ **Organization:** Do my ideas flow together in a logical way?

✓ **Voice:** Does my journal entry sound like something I would say?

✓ **Word Choice:** Did I use strong and colorful words?

✓ **Sentence Fluency:** When I read my journal entry aloud, does it sound pleasing?

✓ **Conventions:** Are all of my sentences complete? Did I check my spelling?

Test Strategy

Think and Search

The answer is in more than one place. Keep reading to find the answer.

Job	Workers	Date Done
Sharpen Axes	Elmer	Postponed due to Snow
Cut Trees	Elmer	Postponed due to Snow
Hire Workers	Paul Bunyan	Postponed due to Snow
Shoe Babe	Olé	Postponed due to Snow
Make Griddle	Olé	Postponed due to Snow

The Year of the Two Winters

retold by Tricia Gentle

Characters

PAUL BUNYAN, superhuman lumberjack
SIX LUMBERJACKS, each named Elmer
LUCY, the purple cow
SOURDOUGH SAM, the cook
OLÉ, the blacksmith

[*Setting: A lumber camp in Michigan. It is May, but snow covers the trees. Paul Bunyan is digging through the snow and finds three of the Elmers, Lucy, and Sourdough Sam frozen underneath.*]

PAUL BUNYAN: If I wait for the spring thaw, we won't get any work done this year. (*Shouts back over his shoulder.*) Olé, I found Sam and some others, but they're frozen stiff! Let's get a fire going over here!

Go On ▶

Olé: (*Calls from offstage.*) Okay, Paul, I'm on my way!

(*Olé arrives and builds a fire near the frozen characters. When the fire begins to roar, the characters caught in the frozen scene come to life.*)

Sourdough Sam: (*Rubs warmth back into his body.*) Thank you, Olé. I was starting to think it would be summer before I'd lay eyes on you again. I know everyone must be hungry, like me. Snow doesn't make much of a meal, you know.

Paul: I sent my ox for a load of pork and beans. Babe should be back any time now.

Sourdough Sam: Great! Paul, will you lend me some Elmers to get a meal going?

Paul: Be glad to, Sam. (*Turns and shouts over his shoulder.*) Elmer!

(*The three Elmers from the frozen scene appear along with three others who come from offstage.*)

Paul: (*Chuckling.*) Best idea I ever had, hiring all of these Elmers. It saves me a lot of time.

Sourdough Sam: Elmers, go build fires on the shore all around that icy lake over there. (*They leave.*) We'll boil the water in that lake and make a pot of pork and beans. We'll have hot food for the rest of the year.

Paul: But what will we wash it all down with?

Sourdough Sam: I'd suggest milk, but judging by the looks of Lucy over there, I guess we're out of luck. She produces only when the grass is green, and last time I saw that color on the ground was last month!

PAUL: (*Taking green glasses from his pocket.*) If green is what she needs, then green is what we'll give her. If she wears these glasses, the snow will look like grass. (*Paul goes to Lucy and puts glasses on her. Lucy starts grazing. An Elmer arrives with a pail and begins milking her.*)

(*It starts to snow.*)

SOURDOUGH SAM: (*Disgusted.*) Snow, again! How many winters are we going to have this year?

PAUL: It's hard to say, Sam. Sure looks like we're not having much of a spring. I'm going to tell the Elmers to let their beards grow. They can wrap themselves in their beards until summer.

SOURDOUGH SAM: That's a good idea, Paul. 'Cause from the looks of things, this is going to be a Paul Bunyan–sized winter or winters. (*Laughs and claps Paul on the back.*)

Go On ▶

Directions: Answer the questions.

Tip

Keep reading. The answer may be in more than one place.

1. How do the Elmers help Paul save time?

   A They like to cook pork and beans.
   B They help with many jobs.
   C They shoe Babe.
   D They give Lucy glasses.

2. What foods does Sourdough Sam suggest they prepare?

   A pork and beans and snow
   B green grass and milk
   C pork and beans and milk
   D They cannot cook because of the snow.

3. Look at the chart and the play. What jobs could the Elmers do?

   A sharpen axes, cut trees, milk the cow
   B start the fire, shoe Babe, cook pork and beans
   C cook pork and beans, shovel snow, light a fire
   D make a griddle, cook pork and beans, milk the cow

4. Summarize the play. Briefly tell what happens in the beginning, middle, and end.

5. Using what you know and what you have read, explain why tall tales are fun to read. Include examples from the selection in your answer.

Writing Prompt

Have you ever had a problem due to weather? What happened? Write a letter to a friend about a time weather caused a problem for you. Write three to five paragraphs and include details to tell what happened.

STOP

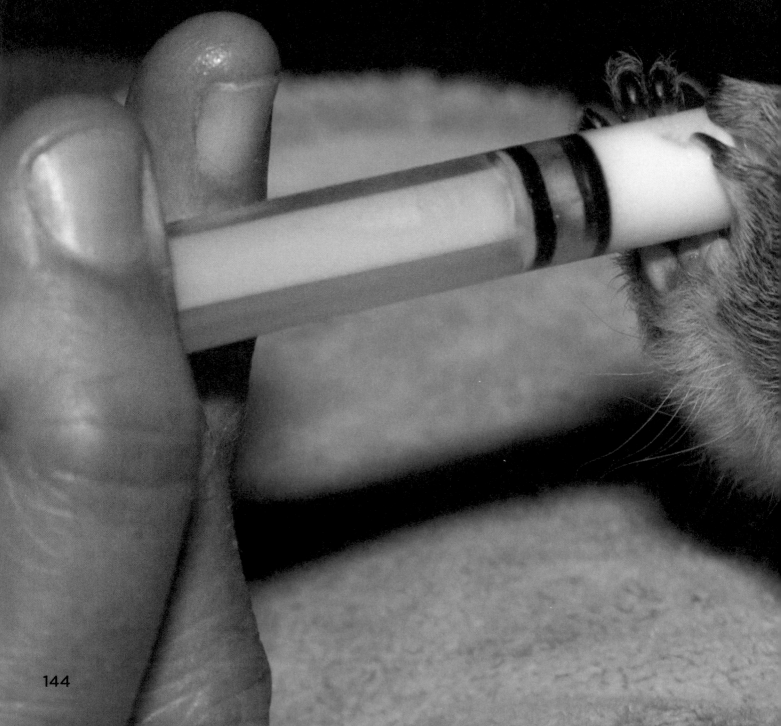

People Helping Animals

Talk About It

How do people help animals? What are the differences between helping wild animals and helping pets?

LOG ON Find out more about helping animals at **www.macmillanmh.com**

Vocabulary

injury	slurp
mournful	shrieks
sympathy	decency
delivering	bulletin board

Idioms

An **Idiom** is a phrase that cannot be understood from the meanings of the separate words in it. To *pull a person's leg* is an idiom that means to trick or tease. You can often find idioms in a dictionary.

A REAL SURVIVOR

by Todd Sampson

"**W**hat was that?" Mom gasped as she suddenly stepped on the brakes of the van. "I think a big bird just hit our windshield," she said. "We've got to go look for it! I bet it has an **injury** that might be causing it some pain."

At first, I thought she was pulling my leg. Then Mom pulled off to the side of the road and I found the bird within minutes. It was a **mournful** sight, lying there with its sad eyes and broken wings.

"Do you think it's going to make it?" I whispered to Mom.

Mom's face was full of caring and **sympathy**. She checked that the bird was breathing and then said we should get help. "There's a place about an hour away from here called the Raptor Trust. The people there know how to care for injured birds," she said.

"Let's go!" I said excitedly. Both of us were intent on **delivering** the bird to the people at the Raptor Trust.

The hawk didn't make a sound during our drive. Mom and I didn't say much either. All we did was **slurp** the icy smoothies we bought with lunch as we hoped for the best.

When we finally found the place, I was amazed. So many beautiful birds lived there—hawks, owls, falcons, and eagles. Their loud **shrieks** filled the air. The knowledgeable workers told us the bird we had rescued was a female red-tailed hawk. They explained that sometimes injured birds can be set free. I hoped that would be the case with our hawk.

A veterinarian checked our bird and assured us that she would recover. When it was time to leave, I thanked all the workers for their kindness and **decency** in helping the birds. I took a picture of my hawk that I planned to pin on the **bulletin board** in my room and I promised her we'd be back to visit. That's when I knew I had chosen the perfect name for her: Survivor.

Reread for Comprehension

Monitor Comprehension
Make Inferences

To make inferences you take clues from the story and combine them with information you already know. This will help you monitor your comprehension, or understanding, of the story. Use your Inferences Chart as you reread "A Real Survivor" to make inferences about the characters and events in the story.

Text Clues	What You Know	Inferences

Comprehension

Genre

Realistic Fiction tells an invented story that could have happened in real life.

Monitor Comprehension

Make Inferences

As you read, use your Inferences Chart.

Text Clues	What You Know	Inferences

Read to Find Out

How does Marty's family feel about Shiloh?

Shiloh

written by Phyllis Reynolds Naylor

illustrated by Joel Spector

Marty Preston is faced with a dilemma when a young beagle turns up at his home near Friendly, West Virginia. Marty feels sure the dog is being abused by his owner but Marty's parents say he must take him back. It hurts Marty to return the runaway dog to his cruel master. That's when Marty secretly decides he'll do anything to save the dog he names Shiloh.

Sure seems strange having Shiloh in the house that night, after trying so hard to keep him secret. Strange, too, the way Ma takes to him. Seems like she can't hardly pass his box next to the stove without reaching down to pet him, making low **sympathy** noises in her throat, way she does when Dara Lynn or Becky or me gets sick.

Dad don't say much. He come home to find Shiloh there, he just stands off to one side, listening to what Doc Murphy said about him; he don't get close enough for Shiloh to take a lick.

But when supper's over and I go off to the bathroom to brush my teeth, I peek back through the doorway, and Dad's over by Shiloh's box, letting him lick his plate clean. Dad crouches there a minute or two, scratching all down Shiloh's back and up again.

What I'm figuring, see, is by the time Shiloh's better, everybody will love him so much they just can't let him go—even Dad. I'm hoping Dad will go over to see Judd Travers, make him an offer for Shiloh, and then he'll be ours. The trouble with this kind of thinking, though, is we don't have the money.

I'll probably be through junior high school, almost, before I earn enough to pay Doc Murphy's bill. To buy Shiloh from Judd, even if Judd's willing to sell, I'd have to collect aluminum cans all through high school, too. Can't make very much with cans. I try to think about what other kind of work I can do that would pay me more, but except for **delivering** the county paper on Friday afternoons, nothing else comes to mind. And somebody's got that job already.

Make Inferences
How does Marty's Dad feel about Shiloh? What clues tell you how he feels?

It's sort of like Shiloh's there and he's not. In the next couple of days, everybody's pettin' him every chance they get. Becky feeds him the crusts off her toast—breaks off little bits, and **shrieks** every time she feels Shiloh's mouth **slurp** them out of her fingers.

Ma's putting up beans in jars, and all the while she hums to Shiloh like he's a baby in a cradle, not a dog in a box. Dara Lynn's got an old hairbrush, and she just can't seem to brush that dog enough. Even Dad sits down one evening and gets out every tick Shiloh's got on him. Takes a little dab of turpentine and rubs it on the tick's rear end, and the tick backs out of Shiloh's skin mighty quick.

The thing that makes it seem like Shiloh's *not* there is that nobody except me and Dara Lynn and Becky talks about him. Ma and Dad don't even once mention his name out loud, as though saying it makes him ours, which he ain't. As though if you don't talk about him, maybe he'll disappear as quietly as he come that day in the rain.

What everyone's waiting for, I guess, is something to happen. Every day Shiloh's getting a little stronger. Two days after Doc Murphy brought him here, Shiloh's up limping around on his bad leg. Ma puts some papers beside his box for him to do his business on, but he won't, so for the first couple days I pick him up, carry him out to the yard, and after he's done his business there, I bring him in again. But now he's pushing open the back screen himself and going down into the yard, then comin' back and tapping on the screen with one paw, so we'll let him in. Somebody, sometime, is bound to see him. Becky, sometime, bound to say something. Even David Howard, when his ma came to pick him up the other day, opens his mouth right off and says something about Shiloh.

"Who's Shiloh?" she asks, and David realizes he's let it slip.

"Old stray cat," he says, and now I've got David lying.

Worse part about having Shiloh here in the house where I can play with him anytime I like is that it's hard to leave him when I go out collecting cans. But I've got to earn money now more than ever, so each day, when Shiloh takes his long nap, I set out with my plastic garbage bag hanging out one jeans' pocket.

One day I walk all the way to Friendly and ask at the grocery, where the county paper is dropped, if they'll put in my name as a carrier. Mr. Wallace says he'll turn my name in, but he's already got six names ahead of me, and one of 'em is a grown man with a car. Don't see how I can match that.

I study the **bulletin board** at the back of the store where people put up notices. Stand on one foot and then the other reading the whole danged board, and seems like everybody got something to sell, or want to be hired, nobody wants to buy. Only two jobs listed, one for an appliance salesman and some woman who wants her house painted.

Mr. Wallace sees me looking at the board, and he comes over and takes down the notice about a woman wanting her house painted.

"That's already taken," he tells me.

That night, while we finish supper, Shiloh's going around the table, putting his nose in everyone's lap, looking **mournful**, waiting for somebody to slip him something to eat. I can tell Ma and Dad's trying their best not to laugh. Ma won't let us feed him at the table.

What I'm dying to ask Dad is did he tell Judd Travers about his dog being here. Dad won't mention it so I don't ask. Maybe I don't want to know, I tell myself.

And then, just as Ma's dishing up a peach cobbler that we're going to eat with hot milk, I hear a sound outside that makes my bones feel like icicles inside me.

154

Shiloh hears it, too, and I know right away it's what I think it is, because Shiloh sticks his tail between his legs, puts his belly low to the floor, and climbs back into his box.

Ma and Dad look at Shiloh. They look at each other. Then there's the slam of a truck door outside, footsteps on the ground, footsteps on the porch, and a *rap, rap, rap* at the back door. Everybody stops eating, like we was all froze to death in our chairs.

Dad gets up and turns on the porch light, and there he is, Judd Travers, looking as mean and nasty as I ever seen him look. He don't even ask can he come in; just opens the screen and steps inside.

"Ray Preston," he says, "somebody told me you got my dog."

Dad's looking serious. He nods and points toward the box by the stove. "Over there, Judd, but he's hurt, and we've been taking care of him for you."

Judd stares at Shiloh and then at Dad. "Well, I'll be danged," he says, almost softly. "Somebody knows my dog is missing, takes him in, and don't even have the **decency** to tell me?"

"We *were* going to tell you," Dad says, and he's looking straight at Judd. "Nobody wants to hear his dog's been hurt, though, and we wanted to make sure he was going to pull through." Then he turns to me. "Marty," he says, "you want to tell Mr. Travers how his dog come to be here?"

He knows I don't. He knows I'd rather swim a river full of crocodiles than face Judd Travers. But it's my story to tell, not Dad's, and he always did make us face up to what we'd done.

"Your dog come over here twice because you been mistreatin' it," I say, and my voice don't sound near as strong as Dad's. Sort of quavery. I clear my throat and go on: "So second time it come over, I built it a pen up in the woods and Dad didn't know it, and that German shepherd of Baker's got in and fought Shiloh."

Make Inferences
What are some of the ways Marty shows his concern for Shiloh?

"Fought who?"

"The beagle. Shiloh, that's what I've been callin' him. And Shiloh got hurt bad. It was my fault for not making the fence higher. We took him to Doc Murphy and he patched him up."

Judd Travers is still staring around the room like he never saw the likes of us before. Finally he lets out his breath through his teeth and slowly shakes his head: "And I got to find out all this from Doc Murphy?"

I couldn't believe Doc would go tell him.

"Somebody goes to the doc the other day and sees a beagle lying out on his back porch. Tells me about it later. Says he thinks maybe the dog's mine. So I ride over to Doc's this evening, and he tells me it was you who brought him in."

Judd walks across the kitchen, and at the thud of each footstep, Shiloh huddles down farther and farther in the box, like maybe he can make himself disappear. His whole body is shaking. Ma sees it, I know, because she watches for a minute, then turns her face away quick.

Judd stares down at Shiloh—at his bandage and the shaved place where he's all stitched up—the rip on his ear. "Look what you done to my *dog*!" he yells at me, eyes big and angry. I swallow. Nothin' I can say to that.

Travers squats down by the box. He puts out his hand, and Shiloh leans away, like he's going to be hit. If that don't prove the way he treats 'em, I don't know what would, but Judd's saying, "I never mistreated my dogs. This one was shy when I got him, that's all. I sure never caused him an **injury** like this one. Wouldn't never have happened if you'd brought him back like I told you." I close my eyes.

When I open 'em again, Judd's putting his hand on Shiloh's head, roughlike, sort of patting him, and you can tell he ain't got much practice being kind. Still, hard to prove Shiloh was mistreated *before* he got to Judd's. How do you go about proving something like that?

"It was wrong of Marty to pen up your dog, Judd, and we've already talked about that," Dad says. "He's the one who's going to pay Doc Murphy for patching him up, and soon as the dog is strong, we'll drive him over to your place. Why don't you let us keep him until then, in case he needs more care?"

Judd stands up again and looks at me. I stare back, but I don't say nothing.

And then Ma can't take it anymore. She says, "Judd, Marty's got awful attached to that dog, and we'd like to know how much you want for it. Maybe we can scrape up the money to buy him."

Judd looks at her like she's talking some kind of nonsense, like we are all getting crazier by the minute.

"That dog's not for sale," he says. "Paid good money to get me a hunting dog, and he could be one of the best I've had. You want to keep and feed him till he's better, okay with me. It's you that got him all tore up, and you paying the bill. But I want him back by Sunday."

Screen door slams again, truck starts up, and then he's gone.

Walk Along with Phyllis Reynolds Naylor

Phyllis Reynolds Naylor may look as if she is walking, swimming, or playing the piano, but often she is really thinking about her next book. "I'm always listening," she says. "I look at what kids are doing, and listen to what they are talking about. I am thinking back to when I was that age, and I discover that feelings don't change over the years."

Phyllis kept up with the story of the real Shiloh as years passed. Thankfully, his life has changed for the best. The once-abused dog has even become a celebrity in the town of Shiloh, West Virginia. Fans from as far away as Canada come to visit and see the dog, people, and places that inspired Phyllis to write this story.

Other books by Phyllis Reynolds Naylor:
Saving Shiloh and *Shiloh Season*

LOG ON Find out more about Phyllis Reynolds Naylor at www.macmillanmh.com

Author's Purpose

Authors of fiction often write to entertain, but sometimes they have more than one purpose in mind. Why do you think Phyllis Reynolds Naylor wrote *Shiloh*? Explain.

Comprehension Check

Summarize

Use your Inferences Chart to help you summarize *Shiloh*. Include only important information from the excerpt you read.

Text Clues	What You Know	Inferences

Think and Compare

1. Do you think Marty will return Shiloh to Judd on Sunday? Explain your answer. Use what you know about Marty and knowledge from your own experience. **Monitor Comprehension: Make Inferences**

2. Reread page 156. Why does Marty's father make Marty explain to Judd what caused Shiloh's **injury**? **Critical**

3. What would you do to earn money for something that you really wanted? **Analyze**

4. Marty rescues Shiloh by hiding him. In what other ways do people try to save animals from harm? **Evaluate**

5. Reread "A Real Survivor" on pages 146–147. Compare and contrast the experiences the injured hawk and Shiloh have with people who offered them help. Use details from both stories to explain your answer. **Reading/Writing Across Texts**

Love at First Sight

by Amy Yin

At age 14 Rexanne Struve fell in love during a visit to a dairy farm. No, Rexanne did not fall in love with a boy on the trip but with a cow. Right then she knew she wanted to work with animals and become a **veterinarian**. To achieve her goal, she had to finish high school, college, and veterinary school. Struve eventually became the first woman veterinarian in Carroll County, Iowa.

As a teenager Struve started preparing for her future. Science was not her favorite subject in high school, but she took as many courses as she could. During the summers she worked as a horseback-riding instructor.

When Struve finished high school, she attended a university in Kansas. Struve says that her high school courses and summer job helped prepare her for her college studies. Struve took more science courses in college. These courses helped her better understand animals and how their bodies work. After college Struve went to veterinary school for four more years. Finally, she graduated and was ready to begin her career as an animal doctor.

In the beginning it was not easy being a female veterinarian. In fact, Struve's grandfather told her that being a vet was not a job for a woman. Even some of her clients felt uneasy around her as she took care of their large animals.

Today, however, Struve has a busy practice where she treats both small and large animals. The farmers with whom she works no longer question her or wonder whether she can do the work. She has proven herself to be the right person for the job.

When animals cannot come to her office, Dr. Struve brings the office to them.

When animals are sick or hurt, Dr. Struve works to make them better. Each year she sees about 800 small animals, such as birds and cats, in her office. She also has about 300 farm clients, including many who own large animals. It is difficult for farmers to bring large animals to Dr. Struve's office, so she brings her office to them. Dr. Struve drives a special truck that holds medicines, equipment, and supplies for surgery. Sometimes Dr. Struve has to operate on animals. She also treats **fractures**, or broken bones, and gives medicine to sick animals.

Dr. Struve sees many different breeds of animals. Once she saw 16 different kinds in one day! Many days start with Dr. Struve traveling in her truck to farms where she treats sheep, hogs, horses, and cattle. Sometimes she even cares for llamas and ostriches. Then she comes back to her office to deal with people's pets.

This variety poses a challenge because Dr. Struve must know the **anatomy** of every animal in order to care for their injuries. She feels rewarded when she can **diagnose** and then treat an illness that is hard to recognize.

Like all veterinarians Dr. Struve does not just take care of sick animals. She also works to keep healthy animals well. She helps bring baby animals into the world. Another big part of her job is to give vaccinations, or shots of medicine, to animals to prevent disease.

This cattle chute holds the cattle still and in the right position. It allows a veterinarian to work safely.

Dr. Struve must be very careful not to spread disease. She does not want germs from one farm to spread to another farm and cause **contamination**. To prevent the spread of disease, Dr. Struve wears coveralls. After she treats a sick animal she takes off her coveralls and washes her boots, too.

Dr. Struve has a tough job. She is on call around the clock, so people often call her late at night. She often works 80 to 90 hours in one week. Dr. Struve also faces danger from some of the animals she works with. They can weigh as much as 1,000 pounds. She has been kicked and bitten by some of her patients. She has even had bones broken. Even so, it was love that led Rexanne Struve to choose her job, and it is love that keeps her there.

Connect and Compare

1. Look at the photograph of the cattle chute on page 166. How does the chute help the vet work safely?
   Photographs and Captions

2. Why is Dr. Struve's job important to farmers? **Evaluate**

3. Think about "Love at First Sight" and *Shiloh.* How could someone like Dr. Struve have helped Marty?
   Reading/Writing Across Texts

Social Studies Activity

Through research, find a photograph of someone doing a job that you might like to do someday. Find out facts about what the job requires. Write a caption, explaining what training the person needed to get this job.

 Find out more about careers at **www.macmillanmh.com**

Writer's Craft

A Strong Opening

When writers want to persuade audiences, they start with a **strong opening.** Good writers may lead with an interesting question or quotation.

We included this question at the opening of our radio ad.

We told people how we will raise money for the shelter.

Radio Advertisement

ANNOUNCER: Hi! We're Scout Troop Number 92. We're having a fundraiser to help friends in our community. Did you know the folks who run the Marion Animal Shelter are having trouble making ends meet? We're raising money to help them buy pet food.

Show your support by coming with your dirty dog to the school parking lot at Fifth and Main this Saturday. We'll lovingly wash, dry, and brush your pet for only five dollars.

Your happy, sweet-smelling pet will thank you for the treat. Speaking of treats, we've got tasty biscuits for all our dog friends.

Remember, it's this Saturday at Fifth and Main. We'll be there from 9:00 A.M. until 5:00 P.M. Together we can raise money to save our animals.

Your Turn

Write an advertisement for radio or television that will convince listeners to support an event sponsored by kids. Create a strong opening that will make listeners consider your cause. Use the writer's checklist to check your writing.

Writer's Checklist

☑ **Ideas and Content:** Are the listeners interested in the advertisement because of the **strong opening**?

✓ **Organization:** Do the supporting details of the advertisement keep the audience's attention?

✓ **Voice:** Can the listeners tell from the ad that I really care about the event?

✓ **Word Choice:** Does the advertisement include lots of words with positive connotations?

✓ **Sentence Fluency:** When I read the advertisement aloud, does it flow well?

✓ **Conventions:** Did I capitalize proper nouns? Did I check my spelling?

Slithery Snakes!

Talk About It

When you hear the word "snake" what do you think of? What are some facts that you know about snakes?

LOG ON Find out more about snakes at **www.macmillanmh.com**

Poisonous SNAKES

by Thomas Kane

There are about 130 different **species** of snakes found in the United States and Canada. Many people are afraid of snakes because they think they are poisonous. However, only four kinds of poisonous snakes live in the United States. One, the coral snake, is in the cobra family. The other three snakes belong to the pit viper family. A bite from a poisonous snake can kill a person. However, most people bitten by snakes **survive** if they are treated quickly.

All snakes have some characteristics in common. For example, none of them hear well. Instead, they are constantly aware and **alert** for times when the ground **vibrates**, or shakes slightly. They feel, rather than hear, something coming.

copperhead snake

Snakes also have a keen sense of smell. They use their tongues to pick up smells from the air. They sort out these smells to find out whether an animal in their nearby **surroundings** is **prey**. Snakes are **predators** that hunt other animals for food. Snakes usually eat small animals, sometimes swallowing them whole.

coral snake

Coral Snakes

Coral snakes live in the southern part of the United States. Their shiny red, yellow, and black bands make them easy to spot. A coral snake has a small head. You can see its fangs at the front of its mouth. When a coral snake bites, it shoots poison into its prey. The animal soon stops breathing and dies.

Pit Vipers

A pit viper is named for the two large pits or dents on each side of its head. When both pits feel the same temperature, the pit viper knows it is facing its prey

and it springs forward. **Lunging**, the viper digs its fangs into the animal. The poisonous bite causes bleeding and swelling that leads to death.

The three types of pit vipers in the United States are rattlesnakes, copperheads, and cottonmouths. Copperheads and cottonmouths are sometimes called moccasins.

Pit vipers live in the southeastern United States, the West, and the Midwest.

Reread for Comprehension

Summarize
Main Idea and Details

A Main Idea Web helps you decide which information is important to include in a summary. Use your Main Idea Web as you reread "Poisonous Snakes" to summarize the main idea and the important details of the selection.

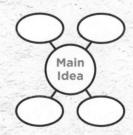

Comprehension

Genre

A **Nonfiction Article** gives information and facts about a topic.

Summarize

Main Idea and Details

As you read, use your Main Idea Web.

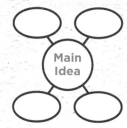

Read to Find Out

How do rattlesnakes catch their prey?

174

RATTLERS!

by Ellen Lambeth

Are you rattled by rattlesnakes? Well, don't be. Just sink your teeth into the real truth about these amazing reptiles.

Rattlesnakes have a bad reputation. No wonder! They look mean. They sound spooky. And you *know* about their nasty bite. But mostly they're misunderstood. So here is all you ever wanted to know about rattlesnakes.

What are rattlesnakes?

They're a group of snakes that have what no other snakes have: rattle-tipped tails. They also have thick bodies, wide heads, cat-like eyes, and long, hollow fangs that fold away when they're not needed. Their dull colors and patchy patterns help them blend in with their **surroundings**.

Where do rattlers live?

There are about 30 different **species** (kinds), and you can find at least one kind or another in almost every state. Rattlers also live in southern Canada, Mexico, and Central and South America.

Different rattlers hang out in different habitats. For example, sidewinders are in deserts, and many timber rattlers live in rocky woodlands. Canebrake rattlers can be found in swamps, while prairie rattlers live in grasslands.

Main Idea
Name two details that support the main idea in the paragraph "Where do rattlers live?"

Are rattlesnakes dangerous?

To their **prey**, they're deadly! To people, their bite is painful . . . and *sometimes* deadly. But it's very unusual for a person to be bitten: People and rattlers aren't often in the same place at the same time.

Even when they are, most rattlers would rather stay hidden or slither away than attack. The prairie rattler in the photo **(see right)** has been surprised by a hiker. Its vibrating rattle is giving the hiker a clear warning: *Don't take another step forward!*

177

What's the rattle made of, and how does it work?

The rattle is a stack of hard sections of skin **(see drawing)**. In other snakes, all of the skin comes off during shedding. In rattlesnakes, some stays attached at the end of the tail.

The beginning of the rattle is called the button. It stays stuck to the end of the tail the very first time a young rattlesnake sheds its skin. The next time the snake sheds, a new section is added underneath the button, and so on.

Each section fits loosely over the one under it. When the snake **vibrates** its tail, the sections rattle against each other and make a buzzing sound.

Can you tell a rattlesnake's age by counting the sections in the rattle?

No. A section is added each time a rattlesnake sheds. But some snakes shed several times a year. Others shed not as often. Also, one or more of the rattle's sections may have broken off.

button

What happens when a rattlesnake bites?

First it strikes by **lunging** toward the prey or enemy. The mouth opens wide, and the fangs swing out **(see above)**. When the snake hits its target, the fangs sink in deep. The rattler may—but doesn't always—pump venom (poison) through each fang. All this happens in about a second.

Can a rattlesnake bite be cured?

Yes, especially if a doctor treats it right away. If the kind of snake is known, the person may be treated with medicine made from the venom of the snake. And how do people get venom to make medicine? By "milking" the snake! **(see right)**

nostril

heat-sensing pit

What do rattlers eat?

Most kinds go for small mammals—such as mice, squirrels, and rabbits—and sometimes birds. Some kinds eat mostly lizards, and others eat mostly frogs.

How does a rattlesnake find its prey?

It picks a good spot and waits. When prey comes along, all the snake's senses are on **alert**. First it may feel vibrations in the ground. Next it looks about and gathers scent molecules on its tongue. It sticks the tip of the tongue into a special smelling organ on the roof of its mouth. Then it uses deep pits on its face to sense body heat coming from the prey. Finally the snake knows exactly where the prey is—and STRIKES!

How does a rattlesnake eat its prey?

It sinks in its fangs and pumps in venom. Then it lets go and waits. If the dying prey crawls away, no problem. The snake can follow the scent trail with its tongue. Then the snake grabs the prey headfirst and swallows it whole.

(see above)

Do rattlesnakes drink?

Rattlers, like all snakes, get water from the food they eat. But sometimes they suck some in from a puddle or pond, as the western diamondback rattler **(see below)** is doing.

How big are rattlers?

All sizes. The eastern diamondback probably is the biggest. It can get to be 6 feet (1.8m) long or more. But usually it grows no more than 4 feet (1.2m) or so. Most of the smallest species, such as the pygmy rattlesnake, are less than 20 inches (50 cm).

Do rattlesnakes have any natural enemies?

Sure. Big animals, such as bison, sometimes crush them underfoot—by mistake or on purpose. And some animals eat rattlesnakes. Red-tailed hawks nab lots of them. And so do other snakes—especially king-snakes **(see black-and-white snake above)**. Other animals, such as coyotes, may gobble up a rattler once in a while.

How can **predators** eat a rattler without getting hurt? Some are quick enough to keep from being bitten. Others don't seem to be bothered by the venom.

STRATEGY SKILL

Main Idea
Name two details that support the main idea on this page.

182

Are any rattlesnakes endangered?

Two kinds—the New Mexican ridge-nosed and the Aruba Island rattlesnakes—are on the U.S. endangered species list as "threatened." That means they could easily become endangered. So they must be protected by law. Many other kinds also are a lot rarer than they once were. Here's why:

Humans have changed many of the places rattlesnakes live—by plowing under grasslands or draining wetlands, for example. That can make it hard for the rattlesnakes to find food or hiding places.

Humans have also killed way too many rattlers—sometimes for the skin or meat, but more often just for "fun" or out of fear.

Do rattlers lay eggs?

No. They give birth to live young— usually at summer's end. A mother rattlesnake may have only one baby . . . or more than twenty! But the average number is eight.

Each young rattler is inside a thin sac when it comes out of the mother. Soon it wriggles itself free.

Like the newborn timber rattler **(see left)**, the young snakes may stay near their mother for several days or longer. But then they all go their separate ways.

Rare Rattler Rescue!

- John Cancalosi

Most people want to know how to protect themselves from rattlesnakes. But one scientist and his family want to help protect rattlesnakes from people.

Hugh McCrystal is a herpetologist (her-pih-TOL-uh-jist). And his two best helpers are his kids, Rachel and James.

The McCrystals are studying the ridge-nosed and rock rattlesnakes. These shy, rare snakes live in the mountains of southeastern Arizona. The more the McCrystals learn about them, the easier it will be to protect them.

But how do you study a dangerous creature up close? Carefully! First Dad catches a rattler and sticks it headfirst into a plastic tube so it can't bite. Then James scans it with a special machine **(below)**. If the McCrystals have caught the snake before, it will have an ID tag that they had put under its skin. The machine works like a store scanner to "read" the tag.

Rachel writes down which snake it is and then records the animal's weight, length, and temperature. (If it's a new snake, they give it a tag and number.) She also jots down other information, such as where the snake was found and what it was doing. After they let the snake go, they hunt for another one.

The family compares the information with other information they've already collected. That way, they can keep track of each rattler and find out more about what it needs to survive.

Rattle Around with
ELLen Lambeth

Ellen Lambeth writes for magazines, mostly about animals. Besides meeting monkeys and avoiding snake bites, she talks with scientists, watches videos, and visits zoos. It's a lot of hard work, but the more Ellen learns, the more she wants to know. She has a pet dog and a horse at home. Ellen has taught each of them tricks, but sometimes feels they are the ones teaching her.

LOG ON Find out more about Ellen Lambeth at **www.macmillanmh.com**

Author's Purpose

Ellen Lambeth used a question-and-answer text structure. How does this information help you to determine her purpose for writing?

Comprehension Check

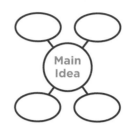

Summarize

Use your Main Idea Web to help you summarize "Rattlers!" Be sure to include only the most important information in your summary.

Think and Compare

1. What is the main idea of the three passages on page 180? Make a list of details to help you find the main idea. **Summarize: Main Idea and Details**

2. Reread the first page of "Rattlers!" How do you think the author feels about rattlesnakes? Include specific examples from the text to support your answer. **Apply**

3. Explain whether you think rattlers and other snakes are misunderstood. Discuss any personal encounters that you may have had with snakes. **Evaluate**

4. Rattlers are on the endangered **species** list. What can be done to help keep these snakes from becoming extinct? **Analyze**

5. Reread "Poisonous Snakes" on pages 172–173. How are coral snakes and rattlesnakes similar? How are they different? Use evidence from both selections to support your answer. **Reading/Writing Across Texts**

Language Arts

Legends are stories that come down from the past, based on the traditions of a people or region.

Literary Elements

The **Hero** is the main character in a legend who usually does something brave to help others.

Personification is the assignment of human characteristics to an animal, thing, or idea.

How Poison Came Into the World

retold by Paul Sirls

Long ago, when Earth was young, the Choctaw people loved to swim in the cool waters of the bayou. But the Choctaw had to be very careful when swimming because a poisonous plant grew in the heart of the bayou. This plant lived below the surface, so swimmers could not see it until it was too late.

> The plant is the *hero* in this legend.

The plant, however, did not want to hurt his friends the Choctaw. As more people fell ill, the poor plant became sadder and sadder. Finally, he decided to give away his poison. The plant called the chiefs of the wasps and snakes to meet with him. He asked them to take his poison.

Wasp shouted out his answer first. "I will put a little poison in my tail. It will help me keep my nest safe." Wasp also promised to make a buzzing sound before he stung anyone.

A water moccasin that speaks is an example of *personification*.

Water Moccasin spoke next. "I will put some poison in my mouth to use only if people stomp on me." Water Moccasin promised to open his mouth wide so people could see the white poison and run before he struck anyone.

Finally, Rattlesnake slithered up slowly, shaking his rattle as he spoke. "I will take a lot of your poison. I will rattle my tail loudly before I strike anyone."

And so the plant's poisonous leaves fell off. In their place, beautiful water lilies grew. The waters of the bayou became safe. And that is how poison came into the world.

Connect and Compare

SKILL ✓

1. What are some ways that the author personifies the plant and the animals? **Personification**

2. What is the purpose of this legend? What does it provide an explanation for? **Analyze**

3. Think about "How Poison Came Into the World" and *Rattlers*! Compare how each author gives information about nature. **Reading/Writing Across Texts**

Writer's Craft

A Strong Conclusion
A persuasive letter flows smoothly from beginning to end. Base a **strong conclusion** on the details you have written. Be sure to sum up your thoughts about your topic.

Write About Your Opinion

I wanted to explain my opinion about reptiles. I included these details.

I summed up my thoughts with a strong conclusion.

Springfield Herald
22 Main St.
Springfield, TX
July 1

Dear Editor:

My favorite exhibit at the zoo is the Reptile House. Every time I visit I am more convinced that reptiles are not as dangerous as people think.

These creatures are no threat to people passing through the Reptile House. They are kept in locked cages and a security guard patrols every aisle.

Outside in the woods people are also too afraid of reptiles. Very few humans are attacked by reptiles each year. They usually need to be provoked before they will bite. If people knew all the facts about reptiles, they would appreciate them much more.

Sincerely,
Isabel S.
Fifth-Grade Student

190

Your Turn

Write a letter to the editor about how you would improve your school or community. State your opinion clearly and include a strong conclusion. Remember that people will be more likely to read your letter if you give good reasons for your opinion. Use the writer's checklist to check your writing.

Writer's Checklist

☑ **Ideas and Content:** Does the letter have a strong conclusion?

✓ **Organization:** Do the ideas in the letter follow in a logical order?

✓ **Voice:** Did I make it clear that I care about my topic? Do I sound as though I am talking to the reader?

✓ **Word Choice:** Did I choose words that express my feelings?

✓ **Sentence Fluency:** Did I use a variety of sentence types?

✓ **Conventions:** Did I use proper punctuation for a formal letter? Did I check my spelling?

Talk About It

Is it important to remember what happened in the past? Why or why not?

LOG ON Find out more about national monuments at **www.macmillanmh.com**

REMEMBERING THE PAST

Vocabulary

dedicated

equality

artifacts

exhibits

site

A stop on the Underground Railroad

Toward FREEDOM

The National Underground Railroad Freedom Center was **dedicated** in August 2004. The museum is located in Cincinnati, Ohio, and sits just across the river from Kentucky, a former slave state.

Journey to a Better Life

In the mid-1800s, there were more than 4 million slaves in the United States. They were denied **equality** with other people. Under the law, slaves had no civil rights, including such basic rights as owning property.

The Underground Railroad was the name for a series of places where slaves could stay during their journey north to escape slavery in the South. Code words were used to protect slaves on their trip. The places they stopped were called "stations," the people being guided toward freedom were called "packages," and the guides were called "conductors."

Preserving the Past

Artifacts—human-made objects from the past—and lectures at the museum teach about slavery and the trail to freedom. One of the **exhibits** is a slave pen where a slave dealer once locked up slaves. Visitors can enter the small building and imagine what it was like to be locked up in a cramped space with dozens of other people.

In the Hall of Everyday Heroes, museum visitors learn about people who stood up for what they believed. These heroes helped bring the basic right of freedom to many people. Visitors might learn that they, too, can stand up and make a difference.

The slave pen at the National Underground Railroad Freedom Center

ON SACRED GROUND

Senator Ben Nighthorse Campbell

In September 2004 the Smithsonian Institution's National Museum of the American Indian in Washington, D.C., opened. What is the museum's goal? "To show and tell the world who and what we really are, and to use our own voices in the telling," says museum director Rick West. West is a member of the Southern Cheyenne tribe.

Senator Ben Nighthorse Campbell of Colorado, a Northern Cheyenne, helped get the project started. Exhibits represent more than 1,000 tribes. The sad chapters of the Native American story, in which millions died at the hands of settlers, are part of the museum's message. Native Americans insisted that Indian art and modern culture be key features of the museum.

Before the building was constructed, Chief Billy Redwing Tayac blessed the **site**. His tribe, the Piscataway, lived in the Washington, D.C., area. "The water is still here. The Earth is still here. And we are still here," he said. "We're very proud that Indian people today have a place to remember our ancestors."

TOP 5 MOST VISITED NATIONAL MONUMENTS

In 1906 President Theodore Roosevelt established Devils Tower in Wyoming as the first national monument in the United States. Today there are more than 60. Here are the 5 most popular ones.

		VISITORS A YEAR
1	**Statue of Liberty (New York)**	5,200,633
2	**Castle Clinton (New York)**	4,390,268
3	**Cabrillo National Monument (California)**	1,095,638
4	**Muir Woods National Monument (California)**	860,378
5	**Montezuma Castle (Arizona)**	853,821

LOG ON Find out more about national monuments at **www.macmillanmh.com**

(Source: National Park Service)

MAYA LIN
ARCHITECT OF MEMORY

How did one architect create two of the most powerful memorials in the United States?

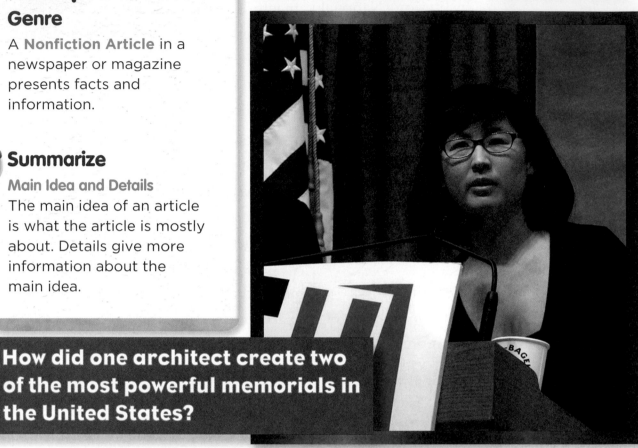

Maya Lin

As is her habit, architect Maya Lin stayed away from the crowds—and the limelight. She stood behind the tinted windows of the Southern Poverty Law Center in Montgomery, Alabama. Outside, hundreds of visitors arrived at the **site** for the opening of the Civil Rights Memorial, which Lin designed. "I like standing back quietly," Lin said. "You create your message, and then it is out there on its own."

Lin's message can be found in the memorial's **exhibits**. This memorial honors those who died fighting for **equality** during the Civil Rights Movement. Some visitors reached out to touch the names of loved ones carved into a black granite disk. Their faces were wet with tears. "I'm so thankful," said Sarah Salter, whose husband, Willie Edwards, Jr., was killed in Montgomery in 1957. "At last he's being recognized."

Remembering Vietnam Veterans

Nine years before the opening of the Civil Rights Memorial, Lin had been a senior at Yale University. She sent in the winning design for the Vietnam Veterans Memorial in Washington, D.C. After it was **dedicated**, angry veterans at first called the stark, V-shaped granite wall a "black gash of shame." Yet the memorial soon became the most visited monument in the capital. Millions of Americans touched—and were touched by—the more than 58,000 names carved into the stone. They are the names of Americans who died in Vietnam.

The Vietnam Veterans Memorial, with the Washington Monument in the distance

Lin's Vietnam Memorial does not present any **artifacts** of the Vietnam era. It is just a wall. This simple wall, however, helped the United States begin the long process of healing after years of bad feelings over the war. The memorial made it possible for the country to come together and honor those who had served.

A Different Way of Looking

"I'm an architect, I'm an artist, I make things," Lin said. "I just love the fact that I can make a work and put it out there and walk away from it and then look at it like everyone else."

As Lin grew up in her hometown of Athens, Ohio, one of the subjects she did well in was mathematics. That skill first led her toward architecture and now shapes her outlook on work. "If you present me with a problem, and if I like it and think I can work with it, I'll do it." In fact, Lin finds herself driven to solve a problem immediately.

Paying respects on a rainy day

Throughout Lin's career, she has shown her range as an architect. Her other projects include the design of a stage set in Philadelphia; an open-air gathering place at Juniata College in Pennsylvania; a "playful park" outside the Charlotte Coliseum in North Carolina (with trees shaped like spheres); and a 38-foot clock for a New York City train station that has moving rays of light instead of hands.

Lin's work shows a thoughtful approach to building design. "It's the kind of thing," Lin said, "that requires patience, awareness, and added sensitivity."

Inspiration from a Great Leader

Too young to remember the Civil Rights Movement firsthand, Lin researched it for months while working on the design for the Civil Rights Memorial. She was struck by a line from Martin Luther King, Jr.'s "I Have a Dream" speech. That line said, "We will not be satisfied until justice rolls down like waters and righteousness like a mighty stream." Lin thought the calm, soothing quality of water

The words of Martin Luther King, Jr., carved on the wall in the background, inspired Lin's design.

At the Civil Rights Memorial, Sarah Salter touches the name of her husband, who was killed during the Civil Rights Movement.

and its quiet, constant sound would be perfect for the area in front of the center. This is a place "to appreciate how far the country has come in its quest for equality and to consider how far it has to go."

Using King's quote as her theme, Lin designed a granite disk that is 12 feet in diameter. Inscribed on it are the names of 40 freedom fighters and landmark events of the Civil Rights Movement. Behind it she designed a black granite wall nearly 9 feet high and 39 feet long, also covered by water. King's words were carved into the rock of this wall. "I'm trying to make people become involved with the piece on all levels," Lin said, "with the touch and sound of the water, with the words, with the memories."

Memories of the past are very important to Lin. After all, she asked, "If you don't remember history accurately, how can you learn?"

Think and Compare

1. What does Maya Lin love about her work?

2. What is the main idea of this article?

3. What people and events are honored with statues and monuments in your city or town?

4. What are some things the National Underground Railroad Freedom Center, the National Museum of the American Indian, the Civil Rights Memorial, and the Vietnam Veterans Memorial all have in common?

★ ☆ ★ A SALUTE to ★ ☆ ★ SERVICEWOMEN

Throughout our nation's history, nearly 2 million women have served in the armed forces. Their brave work is remembered at the Women in Military Service for America Memorial. The memorial opened in Arlington National Cemetery in Virginia in 1997. The Vice President at the time, Al Gore, helped dedicate the memorial. He thanked servicewomen for "their countless acts of bravery and sacrifice."

The memorial covers more than four acres and is surrounded by a semicircular stone wall 30 feet tall. In front of the memorial are a fountain and reflecting pool. The use of light and water symbolizes life. Two hundred jets of water create a sound that represents the voices of women blended together in one purpose. The reflecting pool is a symbol that these women's lives and stories are unified, or brought together, into one history.

The 33,000 square foot education center includes a theater and a computer register. Visitors can use the computer database to read about all the women who served in the armed forces. The memorial roof is an arc of curved glass, 250 feet in diameter. Quotations by and about servicewomen are etched on it. Like diary entries, they give a voice to women who have served their country honorably.

Directions: Answer the questions.

1. This selection is MAINLY about

    A   how a memorial honors American servicewomen.
    B   Arlington National Cemetery.
    C   a speech given to dedicate a memorial.
    D   the progress women have made in gaining rights.

2. What is the purpose of the quotations etched on the memorial?

    A   to explain the monument more clearly
    B   to express thanks for the contributions of women
    C   to provide first-hand descriptions of the experiences of servicewomen
    D   to describe the effects of war on women

> **Tip**
> You have to think about the entire passage to choose the best answer.

3. Which statement BEST expresses the feelings of gratitude shown by the government toward servicewomen?

    A   A four-acre memorial was built in Arlington National Cemetery to honor servicewomen.
    B   Vice President Gore thanked all servicewomen for their bravery.
    C   The fountain and reflecting pool symbolize life.
    D   Two million women have served in the armed forces.

4. The selection talks about the voices of servicewomen. Why do you think this is important? What do you think you can learn from listening to their stories?

5. What are the features of the memorial? Describe them and tell why they are appropriate to honor women in the military. Use information in the selection and the photographs to write your answer.

Write to a Prompt

In "A Salute to Servicewomen" you read how America honored the women who have served in the American armed forces. Think of a time you or someone you know has been honored or thanked for doing something. Write a one-page story about this event and how you (or the person honored) felt about it. Be sure to include a beginning, a middle, and an ending.

Giving and Receiving

Last Friday we had an assembly for all the classes in school. This one was outside. That is very unusual.

Ms. Jones, the principal, stood beside a big oval plot filled with flowers planted in three circles of red, blue, and gold. She said, "This is a special occasion." We were dedicating our new school flower garden.

Our fifth-grade class was especially proud. We had worked on the garden after school every day for weeks. This was our project to give something to our school. In just a week, we would leave Tyler School behind forever.

My story has a clear sequence of events. →

Then Ms. Jones surprised us. She called our class up to stand with her. "We will not forget what you did for us," she said.

Then she gave each of us a paper. It read, "Certificate of Caring." I was so proud! Making the garden was fun, but knowing how much our school appreciated it was the best.

Writing Prompt

People who have helped their country, their community, or their family deserve recognition. Think of a time when you thanked someone for doing something special for you, your class, or your family. Write a one-page story giving details about what you said and did. Tell how the person responded and how you felt afterwards.

Writer's Checklist

☑ Ask yourself, who will read my story?

☑ Think about your purpose for writing.

☑ Plan your writing before beginning.

☑ Use details to support your story.

☑ Be sure your story has a beginning, a middle, and an ending.

☑ Use your best spelling, grammar, and punctuation.

Talk About It

What would it be like to live in the Caribbean? What makes island culture different from mainland culture?

LOG ON Find out more about the Caribbean Islands at **www.macmillanmh.com**

THE CARIBBEAN ISLANDS

Johanna in Jamaica

by Katy Morales

e-mail

TO: Ron@example.com

Subject: The Jamaican Festival

Hi Ron:

Mama and Papa have not yet decided that I can go to the Mermaid Festival in Jamaica when I'm there this summer visiting my grandparents. My parents have always refused to let me go. They said it was **forbidden** for me to go until I could swim well.

Last month when I started asking Papa if I could go, he was **reluctant** to answer me. He was unwilling to make a decision. Mama said that I should show him that I was a strong swimmer. She also said I should prove to him that I was responsible enough to go.

Here's what I did. Last Sunday at the pool, I showed my father that I could swim ten laps in a row. Then when he was relaxing on the deck, I didn't interrupt him once.

What a long afternoon that was! Everyone in my family **gossiped** about who was going to be the Queen Mermaid at the festival. I heard so many rumors!

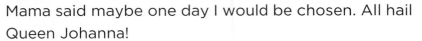

e-mail

Mama said maybe one day I would be chosen. All hail Queen Johanna!

I wanted to join in the noisy conversation. Chatting with my sisters about being queen one day was very tempting, almost **irresistible**. I wanted to describe how **elegant** I would look, dressed in a shimmering costume and glittering crown. I stayed quiet because I knew I'd get too excited and the noise might wake my father, who had fallen asleep.

Do you remember how the music **blared** from speakers on the beach during the festival last year? We could hear it all the way in town. With my eyes closed I pretended that I was on the beach celebrating with everyone. I'm excited that this year I might actually take part in the festivities.

Today Mama warned me to stay on my best behavior. If I'm **mischievous** or naughty Papa will not let me go. I will follow her advice without **hesitation** because I am so anxious to go. Wish me luck!

Hope to see you at the festival,

Johanna

Reread for **Comprehension**

Summarize
Problem and Solution

A Story Map helps you summarize information about the problems and solutions that characters encounter. Use your Story Map as you reread "Johanna in Jamaica" to identify the problems and solutions in the story.

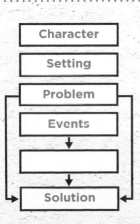

Character
Setting
Problem
Events
Solution

Comprehension

Genre

Fiction tells a story about characters and events that are not real.

Summarize

Problem and Solution
As you read, use your Story Map.

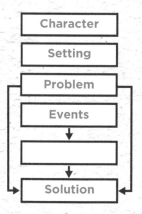

```
┌─────────────┐
│  Character  │
├─────────────┤
│   Setting   │
├─────────────┤
│   Problem   │
├─────────────┤
│   Events    │
├─────────────┤
│             │
├─────────────┤
│  Solution   │
└─────────────┘
```

Read to Find Out

How do the sisters help their friend José Manuel?

The Night of San Juan

written by **Lulu Delacre**
illustrated by **Edel Rodriguez**

Back in the 1940s, in Puerto Rico's walled city of Old San Juan, everybody knew everybody else. We neighborhood children played freely together on the narrow streets, while from windows and balconies adults kept a watchful eye on us. It was only my lonely friend José Manuel who was **forbidden** from joining us.

"Look, Evelyn," whispered Amalia. "He's up there again, watching us play."

Aitza and I looked up. There he was, sitting on his balcony floor. He peered sadly down at us through the wrought iron railing, while his grandma's soap opera **blared** from the radio inside. No matter how hard José Manuel tried, he could not convince his grandma to let him play out on the street.

"Too many crazy drivers! Too hard, the cobblestones! *¡Muy peligroso!*" His grandma would shake her head and say, "Too dangerous!"

209

Besides her fear of danger on the street, José Manuel's grandma kept to herself and never smiled, so most of us were afraid of her. That is, until my sisters and I changed all that.

"One day," Amalia suddenly announced, "I'm going to ask his grandma to let him come down and play." If anyone would have the courage to do that, it was my little sister Amalia. Even though she was only seven, she was also the most daring of the three of us.

We never knew what she would do next. In fact, at that very moment I could see a **mischievous** grin spreading across her freckled face as two **elegant** women turned the corner of Calle Sol. Once they strolled down the street in front of us, Amalia swiftly snuck up behind them and flipped their skirts up to expose their lace-trimmed slips.

"*¡Sinvergüenza!*" the women cried out. "Little rascal!"

We could hardly hold our laughter in. We all looked up to make sure none of the neighbors had seen her. If anyone had, we would surely have been scolded as soon as we got home. News traveled fast in our neighborhood.

Luckily, only José Manuel was watching us with amusement in his wistful eyes. Grateful for an audience, Amalia smiled at him, curtsied, and ran down the street toward the old cathedral with us chasing after her. I couldn't help but feel sorry for my friend as we left him behind.

Problem and Solution
How do you think Aitza, Amalia, and Evelyn will try and solve José Manuel's problem?

There was hardly any sea breeze that day, and running in the humidity made us quite hot.

"Let's get some coconut sherbet," said Amalia, peeling her damp red curls away from her sweaty neck.

"*Sí, sí!*" we agreed, and we chattered excitedly about our plans for that night all the way to the ice-cream vendor's wooden cart by the harbor.

It was June twenty-third, and that night was the Night of San Juan. For this holiday, the tradition was to go to the beach, and at exactly midnight, everyone would walk backward into the sea. People say that doing this three times on the Night of San Juan brings good luck. I thought of my friend José Manuel. Perhaps if he did this with us, his luck would change, and his grandma would allow him to play with us outside on the street.

I thought about this as we bought our coconut sherbet and then ate it perched on the knobby roots of the ancient tree above the port. Excitement stirred in me while the distant ships disappeared over the horizon.

"How can we get José Manuel to go to the beach tonight?" I asked my sisters.

"Evelyn, you know very well his grandma will never let him go," Aitza said. "You know what she will say—"

"*¡Muy peligroso!*" Aitza and Amalia teased at once. "Too dangerous!"

It was getting close to dinnertime, and we knew we had to be home soon if we wanted our parents to take us to the beach that night. So we took the shortcut back across the main square. In the plaza, groups of men played dominoes while the women sat by the fountain and **gossiped**. Back on the street we heard the vegetable vendor chanting:

"*¡Vendo yuca, plátanos, tomates!*"

He came around every evening to sell his fresh cassava, plantains, tomatoes, and other fruits and vegetables.

Leaning from her balcony, a big woman lowered a basket that was tied by a cord to the rail. In it was the money that the vendor replaced with two green plantains. As we approached our street I saw José Manuel and his grandma on the second floor. She gave José Manuel money and went back inside. He was about to lower his basket when I had an idea. Maybe there was a way we could ask him to join us.

"What if we send José Manuel a note in his grandma's basket inviting him to go to the beach with us tonight?" I offered.

"It will never work," Aitza said. "His grandma will not like it. We could get into trouble."

"Then we could ask her personally," I said.

"But what excuse could we use to go up there?" said Aitza. "Nobody ever shows up uninvited at José Manuel's house."

"Wait! I know what we can do," Amalia said, jumping up and down. "We'll tell him to drop something. Then we'll go up to return it."

Even though Aitza was very **reluctant**, we convinced her to try our plan. We wrote the note and asked the vegetable vendor to please place it in José Manuel's basket next to the vegetables. We impatiently waited on the corner as we watched. When he opened the note, he looked puzzled. He took the tomatoes he had purchased in to his grandmother. Soon he returned with his little red ball. He had just sat down to play when suddenly the ball fell from the balcony. It bounced several times, rolled down the hill, and bumped into a wall. Amalia flew after it. "I got it!" she called triumphantly, offering me her find.

With José Manuel's ball in my hand we climbed up the worn stairs of his pink apartment house. And while Aitza and I stood nervously outside his apartment trying to catch our breath, Amalia knocked loudly on the wooden door. With a squeaking sound it slowly opened, and there stood José Manuel's grandma wearing a frown as grim as her black widow's dress.

"¿Sí?" she said. "How can I help you?"

Aitza and I looked at each other. She looked as afraid as I felt. But without **hesitation**, Amalia took the little ball from my hand and proudly showed it to José Manuel's grandma. I wanted to run, but a glimpse of José Manuel's hopeful expression made me stay.

"This belongs to José Manuel," Amalia declared. "We came to return it." Amalia took a deep breath, then took a step forward. "We also wanted to know if he could come to the beach tonight with our family."

Aitza and I meekly stood behind Amalia.

"The beach?" José Manuel's grandma asked, surprised, as she took the little ball from Amalia's palm.

"Y-y-yes," I stuttered. "Tonight is the Night of San Juan, and our parents take us to the beach every year."

José Manuel's grandma scowled at us. How silly to think she would ever let him go. I suddenly felt embarrassed and turned to leave, pulling both sisters with me by their arms.

"Wait," we heard her raspy voice behind us. "Come inside for a *surullito de maíz*."

It was then that I smelled the aroma of the corn fritters that was escaping from the kitchen. José Manuel's grandma was making *surullitos* for dinner.

"Oh, yes!" Amalia followed her in without a thought. And before we knew it, we were all seated in the living room rocking chairs next to José Manuel, eating the most delicious corn fritters that we dipped in garlicky sauce. Somehow, sitting there with José Manuel, his grandma seemed less scary. After we finished, José Manuel's grandma thanked us for our invitation and said she would let us know.

José Manuel smiled.

When we got home we found Mami waiting with her hands on her hips. She had just hung up the phone with José Manuel's grandma. She had reason to be upset. Not only were we late for supper, but in our excitement we had forgotten to ask for permission before inviting José Manuel to the beach. We all looked down, not knowing what to do or say.

"It wasn't my fault. It was Evelyn and Amalia's idea," volunteered Aitza, the coward.

"*Bendito*, Mami," I said. "Don't punish us, we forgot."

"Forgot?" Mami asked.

"*Sí*, Mami," we all said at once. "We are sorry."

"Actually it was very nice of you girls to invite him," said Mami. "But please remember to ask me first next time."

Problem and Solution
What is the problem the girls face when they return home? How is it solved?

Late that night the whole family went to the beach as was our tradition on the Night of San Juan. But this time was special, for we had José Manuel with us.

The full moon shone against the velvet sky. The tide was high, and the beach swarmed with young revelers who, like us, had waited all year for this night's **irresistible** dip in the dark ocean. The moment we reached the water we all turned around, held hands, and jumped backward into the rushing waves. Amalia stumbled forward, Aitza joyfully splashed back, and so did I as I let go of my sister's hand. But my other hand remained tightly clasped to José Manuel's. When my friend and I took our third plunge into the sea, I wished good luck would come to him, and that from then on, his grandma would allow him to play with us out on the street. And as a wave lifted us high in the water, I suddenly knew this wish would come true.

Travel with Lulu Delacre

Lulu Delacre was born in Puerto Rico. While her parents were at work, she stayed with her grandmother in an old pink house. She drew pictures on sheets of white paper, and saved them in the corner of her closet. When Lulu was ten, she had her first real art lesson, and she has been writing and drawing ever since. Lulu is happiest when she is telling stories about growing up on an island of blazing sunshine, and of warm summer nights surrounded by friends, family, and traditions.

Other books by Lulu Delacre:
The Bossy Gallito and *Golden Tales: Myths, Legends, and Folktales from Latin America*

LOG ON Find out more about Lulu Delacre at **www.macmillanmh.com**

Author's Purpose

What was the author's main purpose for writing this story? Did Lulu Delacre want to entertain readers or inform them about the Night of San Juan and its traditions? Explain.

Comprehension Check

Summarize

Use your Story Map to create a summary of *The Night of San Juan*. Explain Evelyn's problem and the steps she and her sisters took to solve it.

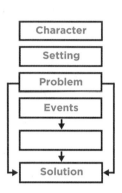

| Character |
| Setting |
| Problem |
| Events |
| |
| Solution |

Think and Compare

1. What was the biggest problem Evelyn had to overcome to get José Manuel to join her and her sisters? Explain your answer. **Summarize: Problem and Solution**

2. Reread page 219. Why does Evelyn hold onto José Manuel's hand during their **irresistible** dip in the ocean? Include details from the story to support your answer. **Analyze**

3. Would you choose a person like Evelyn to be your friend? Why or why not? Explain your answer. **Evaluate**

4. Amalia and the other children fear José Manuel's grandmother, yet Amalia finds the courage to ask her an important question. Describe why sometimes it is important to speak up in a difficult situation. **Analyze**

5. Reread "Johanna in Jamaica" on pages 206–207. Both Evelyn and Johanna want to change an adult's mind about something. Compare the strategies each of them uses. Use details from both selections. **Reading/Writing Across Texts**

Islands of the Caribbean

by Kaneesha Smith

On his first voyage to the New World in 1492, Christopher Columbus found sparkling blue water, warm sunshine, and a green tropical heaven. He had landed on the large Caribbean island he named Hispaniola. He described the island as "a land to be desired, and, once seen, never to be left."

Columbus was the first of many explorers who came to the Caribbean islands looking for gold. Spanish, English, Dutch, and French adventurers came to make their fortunes. After the search for gold ended, settlers who followed the explorers began to farm the rich soil. Many of the islands became rich and important colonies of European countries. Later the people of many of these islands would rule themselves.

Puerto Rico

During his second trip to the Americas, Columbus landed on the island of Puerto Rico, the fourth largest island in the Caribbean Sea. He claimed the land for Spain.

The name *Puerto Rico* means "rich port" in Spanish. Puerto Rico was once the name for San Juan, now Puerto Rico's largest city and capital. Gradually, the name came to be used for the entire island.

Spain gave Puerto Rico to the United States in 1898 after losing the Spanish-American War. In 1917 people in the **commonwealth** of Puerto Rico became U.S. citizens. However, their Spanish **heritage** remains in their language and customs. Puerto Rico's pleasant climate, interesting sights, and beautiful mountains and beaches make it a popular vacation spot. Tourism has become an important business.

You can find more facts about the Caribbean Islands in an almanac. The chart below comes from an almanac entry about Puerto Rico.

Reading a Chart

SKILL

This chart provides information about Puerto Rico. The facts and statistics are organized in a way that makes them easy to read and remember.

Commonwealth of Puerto Rico

Population (2003):	3,885,877
Official Languages:	Spanish and English
Total land area:	3,425 square miles
Capital:	San Juan
National Flower:	Maga
National Bird:	Reinita
National Tree:	Ceiba
Climate:	mild

Dominican Republic

Hispaniola is now two countries, Dominican Republic and Haiti. Dominican Republic covers two-thirds of the island. Santo Domingo, a busy port city, is the capital and largest city.

Dominican Republic was a colony of Spain. As a result its people speak Spanish and follow many of the customs of Spain.

Today most Dominicans live in cities and work in factories or for the government. However, some people farm, often on large sugar plantations.

African customs also have an important place in Dominican Republic. Dominicans particularly love music and dancing that mix the sounds of African instruments with those of Spain.

Haiti

Haiti covers the western third of Hispaniola. The island was formed by the peaks of two undersea mountain chains. The name *Haiti* comes from an Indian word for "high ground." Port-au-Prince is Haiti's capital and largest city.

Haiti is the second oldest self-ruling nation in the Western **Hemisphere**, after the United States. It was a French colony until 1804, when it won its independence. Since then Haiti has been a republic, but at times it has been led by a series of **dictators**.

Haiti is one of the most densely populated countries in the Western Hemisphere. Most of its people are descended from the Africans that were brought to Haiti as slaves, so there is a varied culture. Today its people speak French and Creole, a mix of French and African languages. Most of the people are sugarcane farmers.

Cuba

Cuba is another large, mountainous island country. Cuba gained its independence in 1902. In 1959 Cuba became the only communist country in the Americas. The island lies at the **intersection** of major sea routes. This central location is one reason that Cuba was an important Spanish colony. Its people still speak Spanish and share many of the same customs you would find in Spain.

About three-quarters of Cuba's people live in cities. Havana is Cuba's capital and largest city. Many city people work in small factories or for the government. Cubans who live in the country tend to be farmers. Sugarcane is Cuba's most important crop.

With its beauty, interesting people, and mix of farm and city life, the Caribbean Islands are truly "a land . . . never to be left."

Connect and Compare

1. Look at the chart on page 223. What are the two official languages of Puerto Rico? **Reading a Chart**

2. Compare the countries you read about in this article. How are they alike? How are they different? **Analyze**

3. After reading *The Night of San Juan* and page 223 of "Islands of the Caribbean" what images of Puerto Rico do the two selections make you think of? **Reading/Writing Across Texts**

Social Studies Activity

Choose another Caribbean country from the map on page 222. Look it up in an almanac. Using the information you find, create a brochure for tourists who might visit the country.

 Find out more about the Caribbean islands at **www.macmillanmh.com**

Writer's Craft

Multiple Paragraphs

A **paragraph** starts with a topic sentence. The detail sentences work together to support the main idea. Transition words can help connect ideas between paragraphs. A strong conclusion sums up all the paragraphs.

My paragraphs start with topic sentences. Details support the main ideas.

I used transition words to connect ideas between paragraphs.

Rochester: A City for Families

by Maria L.

Let me tell you about beautiful Rochester, New York. The city's attractions are so much fun, and there are so many cool places to visit.

You can spend hours at the Toy Hall of Fame in the Strong Museum. Its collection is huge and displays the best children's toys!

In addition, you can enjoy the outdoors in Rochester too. Our family loves to hike around Mendon Ponds Park and bike along the Erie Canal Heritage Trail. Of course, I shouldn't forget to mention lovely Ontario Beach Park!

No matter what you and your family enjoy, Rochester has it all. My friends and I know that you'll love New York's third largest city.

Your Turn

Write an essay about your hometown. Tell why people should move there. Think about your audience. Choose ideas that will appeal to them. Include topic sentences and transition words. Use the writer's checklist to check your writing.

Writer's Checklist

 Ideas and Content: Did I choose the best details to present to my audience?

 Organization: Does each paragraph start with a topic sentence and include supporting details?

 Voice: Do I sound sincere and believe what I say?

Word Choice: Did I choose words that are persuasive?

 Sentence Fluency: Can the reader move smoothly from sentence to sentence?

Conventions: Did I check to be sure all of the plural nouns are spelled correctly? Did I make sure possessive nouns have apostrophes?

227

Talk About It

What do you know about cowboys and cowgirls? What kinds of skills do you need to be a cowboy or cowgirl?

 Find out more about cowboys and cowgirls at **www.macmillanmh.com**

COWBOYS & COWGIRLS

The LIFE of a COWBOY

by Nancy Vilelli

The cowboy lifestyle became popular in America in the middle 1800s. One group that affected the rise of the professional American cowboy was the *vaqueros* (vah KAYR ohs). Vaqueros were cattle workers from Mexico. They knew how to keep animals together in the **vastness** of wide, open countryside. The American cowboys were eager to learn this ability. They accepted the vaqueros' ways with **enthusiasm** and excitement.

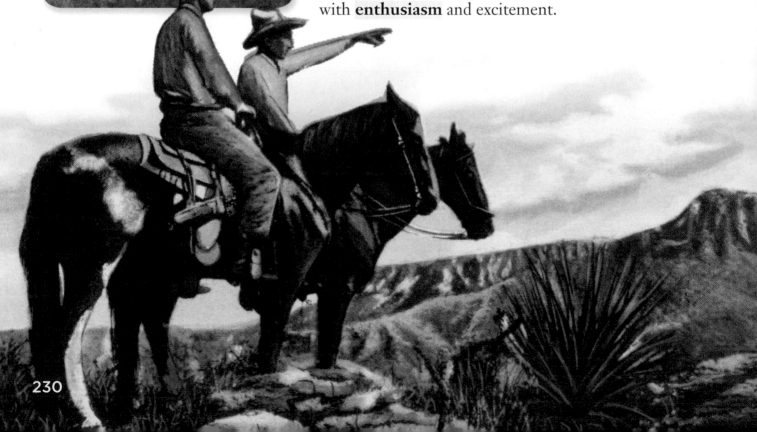

Soon cattle ranches sprang up from Texas to the Dakotas. It was hard work to keep track of hundreds of cows. Cows spread out as far as the **horizon**, where land meets the sky. No fences held them in. The cowboys rode their horses for miles every day to watch over the cattle.

There were many dangers in the open fields. A cow could fall into a **ravine** and hurt itself in the deep, narrow valley. Or a cow could be frightened by the **presence** of another animal that is nearby. One frightened cow can cause a stampede.

When spring came the cattle were rounded up to be counted. Afterwards the cowboys would move the cattle across the plains during the summer. Cowboys would ride inside the herd. They **swerved** as they rode, turning in and out, to move the cattle in the right direction.

A cowboy's job was tiring, so he would need a good place to set up camp, eat, and rest. After the cook fixed dinner, cowboys

would sit around a campfire that **flickered** unsteadily whenever a gust of wind blew by. Like the vaqueros, they would tell stories or sing songs. Eventually, all but one would fall asleep as the moon hung **suspended** in the huge, dark sky. As with vaqueros' tradition, one cowboy always remained awake because the safety of the herd came first.

Reread for **Comprehension**

Monitor Comprehension
Make Inferences

To make inferences, you take clues from the story and combine them with information you already know. This will help you monitor your comprehension, or understanding, of the story. Use your Inferences Chart as you reread "The Life of a Cowboy" to make inferences about the personality traits a successful cowboy would need.

Text Clues	What You Know	Inferences

Comprehension

Genre

Biography is an account of an actual person's life told by another person.

Monitor Comprehension

Make Inferences
As you read, use your Inferences Chart.

Text Clues	What You Know	Inferences

Read to Find Out

What does it take to be a real cowboy?

BLACK COWBOY WILD HORSES

A TRUE STORY

BY
JULIUS LESTER

ILLUSTRATED BY
JERRY PINKNEY

Award Winning
Author
and
Illustrator

F IRST LIGHT. Bob Lemmons rode his horse slowly up the rise.
When he reached the top, he stopped at the edge of the bluff.
He looked down at the corral where the other cowboys were beginning
the morning chores, then turned away and stared at the land stretching
as wide as love in every direction. The sky was curved as if it were a lap
on which the earth lay napping like a curled cat. High above, a hawk
was **suspended** on cold threads of unseen winds. Far, far away, at what
looked to be the edge of the world, land and sky kissed.

He guided Warrior, his black stallion, slowly down the bluff.
When they reached the bottom, the horse reared, eager to run across
the **vastness** of the plains until he reached forever. Bob smiled and
patted him gently on the neck. "Easy. Easy," he whispered. "We'll have
time for that. But not yet."

He let the horse trot for a while, then slowed him and began peering intently at the ground as if looking for the answer to a question he scarcely understood.

It was late afternoon when he saw them—hoofprints of mustangs, the wild horses that lived on the plains. He stopped, dismounted and walked around carefully until he had seen all the prints. Then he got down on his hands and knees to examine them more closely.

Some people learned from books. Bob had been a slave and never learned to read words. But he could look at the ground and read what animals had walked on it, their size and weight, when they had passed by, and where they were going. No one he knew could bring in mustangs by themselves, but Bob could make horses think he was one of them— because he was.

He stood, reached into his saddlebag, took out an apple, and gave it to Warrior, who chewed with noisy **enthusiasm**. It was a herd of eight mares, a colt, and a stallion. They had passed there two days ago. He would see them soon. But he needed to smell of sun, moon, stars, and wind before the mustangs would accept him.

Make Inferences
What clues in the story help you know when it takes place?

237

The sun went down and the chilly night air came quickly. Bob took the saddle, saddlebag, and blanket off Warrior. He was cold, but could not make a fire. The mustangs would smell the smoke in his clothes from miles away. He draped a thick blanket around himself, then took the cotton sack of dried fruit, beef jerky, and nuts from his saddlebag and ate. When he was done, he lay his head on his saddle and was quickly asleep. Warrior grazed in the tall, sweet grasses.

As soon as the sun's round shoulders came over the **horizon**, Bob awoke. He ate, filled his canteen, and saddling Warrior, rode away. All day he followed the tracks without hurrying.

Near dusk, clouds appeared, piled atop each other like mountains made of fear. Lightning **flickered** from within them like candle flames shivering in a breeze. Bob heard the faint but distinct rumbling of thunder. Suddenly lightning vaulted from cloud to cloud across the curved heavens.

Warrior reared, his front hooves pawing as if trying to knock the white streaks of fire from the night sky. Bob raced Warrior to a nearby **ravine** as the sky exploded sheets of light. And there, in the distance, beneath the ghostly light, Bob saw the herd of mustangs. As if sensing their **presence**, Warrior rose into the air once again, this time not challenging the heavens but almost in greeting. Bob thought he saw the mustang stallion rise in response as the earth shuddered from the sound of thunder.

Then the rain came as hard and stinging as remorse. Quickly Bob put on his poncho, and turning Warrior away from the wind and the rain, waited. The storm would pass soon. Or it wouldn't. There was nothing to do but wait.

Finally the rain slowed and then stopped. The clouds thinned, and there, high in the sky, the moon appeared as white as grief. Bob slept in the saddle while Warrior grazed on the wet grasses.

The sun rose into a clear sky and Bob was awake immediately. The storm would have washed away the tracks, but they had been going toward the big river. He would go there and wait.

By mid-afternoon he could see the ribbon of river shining in the distance. He stopped, needing only to be close enough to see the horses when they came to drink. Toward evening he saw a trail of rolling, dusty clouds.

In front was the mustang herd. As it reached water, the stallion slowed and stopped. He looked around, his head raised, nostrils flared, smelling the air. He turned in Bob's direction and sniffed the air again.

Bob tensed. Had he come too close too soon? If the stallion smelled anything new, he and the herd would be gone and Bob would never find them again. The stallion seemed to be looking directly at him. Bob was too far away to be seen, but he did not even blink his eyes, afraid the stallion would hear the sound. Finally the stallion began drinking and the other horses followed. Bob let his breath out slowly. He had been accepted.

The next morning he crossed the river and picked up the herd's trail. He moved Warrior slowly, without sound, without dust. Soon he saw them grazing. He stopped. The horses did not notice him. After a while he moved forward, slowly, quietly. The stallion raised his head. Bob stopped.

When the stallion went back to grazing, Bob moved forward again. All day Bob watched the herd, moving only when it moved but always coming closer. The mustangs sensed his presence. They thought he was a horse.

So did he.

The following morning Bob and Warrior walked into the herd. The stallion eyed them for a moment. Then, as if to test this newcomer, he led the herd off in a gallop. Bob lay flat across Warrior's back and moved with the herd. If anyone had been watching, they would not have noticed a man among the horses.

When the herd set out early the next day, it was moving slowly. If the horses had been going faster, it would not have happened.

The colt fell to the ground as if she had stepped into a hole and broken her leg. Bob and the horses heard the chilling sound of the rattles. Rattlesnakes didn't always give a warning before they struck. Sometimes, when someone or something came too close, they bit with the fury of fear.

The horses whinnied and pranced nervously, smelling the snake and death among them. Bob saw the rattler, as beautiful as a necklace, sliding silently through the tall grasses. He made no move to kill it. Everything in nature had the right to protect itself, especially when it was afraid.

The stallion galloped to the colt. He pushed at her. The colt struggled to get up, but fell to her side, shivering and kicking feebly with her thin legs. Quickly she was dead.

Make Inferences
What clues in the story point to the fact that Bob respects nature?

Already vultures circled high in the sky. The mustangs milled aimlessly. The colt's mother whinnied, refusing to leave the side of her colt. The stallion wanted to move the herd from there, and pushed the mare with his head. She refused to budge, and he nipped her on the rump. She skittered away. Before she could return to the colt, the stallion bit her again, this time harder. She ran toward the herd. He bit her a third time, and the herd was off. As they galloped away, Bob looked back. The vultures were descending from the sky as gracefully as dusk.

It was time to take over the herd. The stallion would not have the heart to fight fiercely so soon after the death of the colt. Bob galloped Warrior to the front and wheeled around, forcing the stallion to stop quickly. The herd, confused, slowed and stopped also.

Bob raised Warrior to stand high on his back legs, fetlocks pawing and kicking the air. The stallion's eyes widened. He snorted and pawed the ground, surprised and uncertain. Bob charged at the stallion.

Both horses rose on hind legs, teeth bared as they kicked at each other. When they came down, Bob charged Warrior at the stallion again, pushing him backward. Bob rushed yet again.

The stallion neighed loudly, and nipped Warrior on the neck. Warrior snorted angrily, reared, and kicked out with his forelegs, striking the stallion on the nose. Still maintaining his balance, Warrior struck again and again. The mustang stallion cried out in pain. Warrior pushed hard against the stallion. The stallion lost his footing and fell to the earth. Warrior rose, neighing triumphantly, his front legs pawing as if seeking for the rungs on which he could climb a ladder into the sky.

The mustang scrambled to his feet, beaten. He snorted weakly. When Warrior made as if to attack again, the stallion turned, whinnied weakly and trotted away.

Bob was now the herd's leader, but would they follow him? He rode slowly at first, then faster and faster. The mustangs followed as if being led on ropes.

Throughout that day and the next he rode with the horses. For Bob there was only the bulging of the horses' dark eyes, the quivering of their flesh, the rippling of muscles and bending of bones in their bodies. He was now sky and plains and grass and river and horse.

When his food was almost gone, Bob led
the horses on one last ride, a dark surge of flesh
flashing across the plains like black lightning.
Toward evening he led the herd up the steep
hillside, onto the bluff, and down the slope toward
the big corral. The cowboys heard him coming
and opened the corral gate. Bob led the herd, but
at the last moment he **swerved** Warrior aside, and
the mustangs flowed into the fenced enclosure.
The cowboys leaped and shouted as they quickly
closed the gate.

Bob rode away from them and back up to
the bluff. He stopped and stared out onto the
plains. Warrior reared and whinnied loudly.

"I know," Bob whispered. "I know.
Maybe someday."

Maybe someday they would ride with the
mustangs, ride to that forever place where
land and sky kissed, and then ride on.
Maybe someday.

RIDE ALONG WITH
JULIUS LESTER AND JERRY PINKNEY

Julius Lester was a musician before he wrote books. He even recorded two albums and hosted a radio show. When an editor asked him to write a children's book, he found he loved doing it. Julius believes it is important to be the voice for people who can't tell their own stories, people like Bob Lemmons. His advice to young writers is read, read, read. He should know—he has about 15,000 books!

Jerry Pinkney started drawing by copying from comic books and magazines, just like his two older brothers. In junior high school, he sketched people he saw on the street. He's been drawing and painting ever since. Jerry has even drawn eleven postage stamps for the U.S. Postal Service. "I'd rather draw than do anything else!" he says.

 Find out more about Julius Lester and Jerry Pinkney at **www.macmillanmh.com**

Another book
by Julius Lester
and Jerry Pinkney:
John Henry

Author's Purpose

This biography is full of adventure. Could Julius have written it for more than one purpose? Explain.

Comprehension Check

Summarize

Summarize the story of Bob Lemmons and the mustangs in *Black Cowboy, Wild Horses.* Use your Inferences Chart to help you include important information about the story.

Text Clues	What You Know	Inferences

Think and Compare

1. Warrior rears once at the beginning of the story and once at the end. What do you think Warrior is telling Bob? **Monitor Comprehension: Make Inferences**

2. Reread page 235 of *Black Cowboy, Wild Horses.* Make a list of descriptive words and phrases that the author uses to describe the **vastness** of the plains. Why do you think the author begins the story by using imagery? **Analyze**

3. Would you want to ride with the wild mustangs? Explain why or why not. **Evaluate**

4. Bob says that everything in nature has a right to protect itself. Do you agree or disagree with this opinion? Explain your answer. **Evaluate**

5. Reread "The Life of A Cowboy" on pages 230–231. How was Bob Lemmons's life similar to the life described in the article? How was it different? Give specific examples using both selections. **Reading/Writing Across Texts**

Poetry

Song Lyrics are the written words of a song. Long ago poems were not just recited but were often sung.

✓ Literary Elements

Repetition occurs when a line or sequence of lines appears more than once in a selection. In a song these repeating lines are often called the *chorus*.

Assonance is the repetition of the same or similar vowel sounds in a series of words, usually with different consonant sounds. The long "o" sound in *buffalo* and *roam* is an example of assonance.

Home on the Range

words by John A. Lomax
music by Daniel Kelley

Oh, give me a home where the buffalo roam,
Where the deer and the antelope play,
Where seldom is heard a discouraging word
And the skies are not cloudy all day.

Home, home on the range,
Where the deer and the antelope play
Where seldom is heard a discouraging word
And the skies are not cloudy all day.

This line is an example of *repetition*.

Oh, give me a land where the bright diamond sand

Flows leisurely down the stream,

Where a graceful white swan goes gliding along

Like a maid in a heavenly dream.

The short "a" sound in *land* and *sand* is an example of *assonance*.

Home, home on the range,

Where the deer and the antelope play

Where seldom is heard a discouraging word

And the skies are not cloudy all day.

Where the air is so pure, the zephyrs so free,

The breezes so balmy and light,

That I would not exchange my home on the range

For all the cities so bright.

Home, home on the range,

Where the deer and the antelope play

Where seldom is heard a discouraging word

And the skies are not cloudy all day.

Connect and Compare

1. What are some other examples of repeating lines or words in this song? **Repetition**

2. Read the poem aloud. How does assonance help you read the poem more smoothly? **Apply**

3. Compare "Home on the Range" to *Black Cowboy, Wild Horses*. What are some differences between the range described in the song and the land described in the story? **Reading/Writing Across Texts**

LOG ON Find out more about song lyrics at **www.macmillanmh.com**

Writer's Craft

Vary Sentences

Good writers use sentences that begin in a **variety** of ways. For example, they may start a sentence with an introductory clause or phrase.

Our teacher asked us to write a review of a TV show, movie, or book.

I made my review interesting by starting my sentences in different ways.

A Review of Wrango

by Maria D.

<u>Wrango</u> by Brian Burks is one of the best books I've ever read.

Based on facts, <u>Wrango</u> tells the story of an African-American cowboy named George McJunkin. After the Civil War ended, he and his family gained their freedom from slavery. George decided to ride the Chisholm Trail with a friend, and the two men's adventures began.

George survived a rattlesnake bite. He saved someone from drowning. Using lots of details, the author describes terrible storms, attacks from enemies, and other exciting events.

Besides telling a great story, <u>Wrango</u> also includes a glossary of words used by cowboys.

I urge you to read this book now!

Your Turn

Write a review of a TV show or movie you have seen, or tell about a book you have read. State your opinion, and give examples to support it. Use variety in your sentences and word choices. Use the writer's checklist to check your writing.

Writer's Checklist

✓ **Ideas and Content:** Did I choose to review a show, movie, or book that I feel strongly about?

✓ **Organization:** Does the review begin in an interesting way and hold the reader's attention throughout?

✓ **Voice:** Can my readers tell that I feel strongly about what I am reviewing?

✓ **Word Choice:** Did I choose words that bring the show, movie, or book to life for the reader?

☑ **Sentence Fluency:** Did I start my sentences in a **variety** of ways?

✓ **Conventions:** Did I use correct capitalization and punctuation? Did I check my spelling?

Test Strategy

Author and Me
The answer is not directly stated. Connect the clues to figure it out.

THE STORY OF RADIO

by Jill Seidman

It's one of those discoveries that you take for granted. You probably listen to it in the car or early in the morning at home. You push a button or turn the dial, then sound fills the air. Right away you can hear the latest song or a message about a snow day at your school. That little radio is an amazing device.

How It Works

Every radio has two parts: a transmitter and a receiver. First, sound is changed into radio waves. Then, those waves are transmitted. The signals can go through solid objects like walls or trees and are turned back into sounds once they are received.

The idea behind the radio is mathematical, not musical. About 150 years ago, J.C. Maxwell discovered that radio waves were possible. People used this idea to figure out how to send radio signals. The Italian scientist Guglielmo Marconi was the first to send a radio signal across the ocean. In 1901 he sent messages between England and Canada. The first radio was more like a wireless telegraph than the radio you have today. These first messages were sounds that stood for letters, not music or talking.

Go On ▶

Marconi's wireless radio began to signal ships at sea. The first time people heard voices and music over the radio was on December 24, 1906. A man in Massachusetts sent out a three-part broadcast. Ships picked up the signal. They heard a man speaking, then a woman singing. Finally, they heard a person playing a violin.

By the early 1920s, the first radio station, KDKA, started broadcasting in Pittsburgh. It was the first station to send out voice broadcasts. Within a few years, people eagerly bought radio sets to hear news and music. In 1930 the first broadcast was heard "around the world." Radio signals traveled from tower to tower across the globe. The golden age of radio had begun.

Vital Link During World War II

In those days radio was as important to people as television is today. In the days leading up to World War II, the President's important speeches were broadcast on the radio. The whole world tuned in to listen to the news of the war overseas. Radios became even more important once the United States joined World War II. Soldiers and sailors were able to use two-way radios to communicate with one another and get news about events happening around the world.

Radio was also a great source of entertainment then, much as television is today. Families and friends gathered around the radio to listen to music, comedy programs, quiz shows, and serious dramas. Companies that made laundry and cleaning products sponsored some of these dramas, which were called "soap operas." That's right; the first soap operas were on the radio and actually had something to do with soap.

During the golden age of radio, families frequently gathered around the radio. People would stop what they were doing to listen to a favorite program.

Go On 257

Radio Today

By the beginning of the 1950s, television took over as the leading form of home entertainment. However, that didn't mean that people turned off their radios. Most radio stations changed their programs and focused on playing the latest news and the newest music. In the 1950s, as rock and roll became all the rage, many stations began playing only popular music. Today most stations choose a particular type of program or music. Stations specialize in rock music, country tunes, classical music, sports, or news and weather.

Your parents might have a favorite radio station that plays music from their teen years. You, on the other hand, might enjoy a different station that plays the latest hits. Push a button or turn a dial. It's easy to find something you like!

Today's households enjoy home entertainment systems.
Families can listen to the news or enjoy their favorite programs.

Go On ▶

Directions: Answer the questions.

Tip

Connect the clues or ideas from the selection to figure out the best answer.

1. Why was radio first invented?

A to send sound waves
B for communication
C to teach others to play the violin
D to give families time together

2. Why are radios still important today?

A to listen to news and music
B to help soldiers communicate
C to listen to soap operas
D to signal ships at sea

3. Why do many families today have more than one radio?

A to listen to radio ads
B because they want to honor Guglielmo Marconi
C because they like different music or radio programs
D to use electricity

4. What problem did radio stations face when television appeared? How did radio stations try to solve the problem?

5. What do you think the future of radio and television will be? Write two paragraphs and include details from the selection in your response.

Writing Prompt

Your favorite radio station is going off the air. Write an essay to persuade people to listen to the station. Use reasons to support your opinion.

THE AMERICAN REVOLUTION

Talk About It

Why is the American Revolution important? Why did the colonists decide to fight the British?

LOG ON Find out more about the American Revolution at **www.macmillanmh.com**

Vocabulary

navigation	tyrant
instruct	stark
swagger	governor
patriots	spunk

 Word Families

Knowing about **Word Families** can increase your vocabulary. A prefix or suffix added to a base word can change its meaning. For example, *unpatriotic* and *patriotism* have *patriot* as a base word but each word means something different.

Letters from the Revolution

by Aryeh Gross

London, England
July 1, 1772

Dear Richard,

We were shocked to hear about the British ship, the *Gaspee* that sank off the coast of Rhode Island. Is it close to where you live? Do you know anyone who was aboard? It is hard to believe that the *Gaspee* was sunk by the tricky **navigation** of a colonist's boat. This smaller boat was able to steer the *Gaspee* into some hidden rocks. Then it quickly turned to attack the sinking ship.

Who would be bold enough to **instruct** the colonists to act like this? It could only be their rebel leader. I have heard that he walks with a **swagger** and is too proud for his own good. They are hiding him and calling him one of the best **patriots** because he loves Rhode Island more than England. It is not good that so many colonists have turned against King George. We should all be his loyal subjects. Please come home to England.

Sincerely,

Thomas

Rhode Island
September 10, 1772

Dear Thomas,

Thank you for your letter, but you are wrong about the *Gaspee*. The British commander in the colonies was a cruel **tyrant** who ruled as he pleased. People who once had plenty of food stored in their homes now have cupboards that are **stark** and bare. When our leader, the **governor** of Rhode Island complained, the British commander paid no attention. The colonists took matters into their own hands. I think it shows **spunk** and courage for our small colonies to fight the mighty England.

I disagree with the comments you made in your letter. We do take pride in our act of revolt on the open seas and against England. This is patriotism. I am in Rhode Island to stay.

My best wishes to you, my aunt and uncle.

Yours truly,

Richard

Reread for Comprehension

Make Inferences and Analyze
Draw Conclusions

To draw conclusions, you make inferences about two or more pieces of information from a story and arrive at a new understanding of a character or event. A Conclusions Chart can help you use information in the story to draw a conclusion. Use your Conclusions Chart as you reread the selection.

Text Clues	Conclusion

Comprehension

Genre

Historical Fiction tells a story in which fictional characters take part in actual historical events with real people from the past.

Make Inferences and Analyze

Draw Conclusions
As you read, use your Conclusion Chart.

Text Clues	Conclusion

Read to Find Out

What was it like to be a child in Boston at the time of the Revolutionary War?

SLEDS on BOSTON COMMON

A Story from the American Revolution

written by LOUISE BORDEN

illustrated by ROBERT ANDREW PARKER

Award Winning Selection

In December of 1774, times were hard for all of us in Boston. Few good folk had coins to spare when they walked past the window of my father's shop on King Street . . . the best place to buy English and Dutch toys, spectacles, flutes, or the maps that my father drew with his own hand.

Sometimes he let me color the maps with his paints and his pens. "In a few years, Henry, your steady hand will be better than mine." That's what my father, William Price, said.

Months ago, on the first day of June, the British closed our harbor

By order of the King of England, George III.

King George wanted to punish those in Boston who spoke against his laws that were made across the sea: **patriots** like Sam Adams and John Hancock and other town leaders . . . and patriots like my father and my friends' fathers . . . All over Boston, south and north, people were not happy with King George III.

Or with our new royal **governor**, General Thomas Gage. General Gage was King George's top general, the commander of every British soldier in North America. Since May, he had lived in one of the biggest, tallest houses in all of Boston. Whenever my brothers and I walked to school, we passed by the redbrick front of Province House. I always looked up at the weather vane high on the cupola: a gold Indian archer that shone in the sun. Thomas Gage was a powerful man indeed.

Draw Conclusions
Why would the closing of Boston Harbor lead to hard times for the people of Boston?

On the day he closed our harbor, church bells rang in every colony in America. Other patriots in other towns said: "We will stand beside Boston in these hard times. We are all Americans together."

Now only the king's ships could enter or leave our harbor. And so there was no trade. There was little work for the men on Long Wharf, once the busiest dock in New England, filled with the tall masts of ships that had sailed to China and to Spain, to the West Indies and back. Now there was only the salt smell of the sea and the cry of gulls in an empty port.

Every day, there were more and more of the king's soldiers marching on Boston Common. Or walking with a **swagger** in their bright red coats along the streets of our town. Or cutting down our fences and our trees for their firewood. King George wanted General Gage to make sure that we kept his new laws and that we paid our taxes to England. Every penny. My father said that by now there was one British soldier for every five of us in Boston. People called them "lobster backs" because of their coats. Most of us didn't like General Gage's troops in our town. Most of them didn't like us either.

But King George's laws hadn't closed the South Writing School on West Street. No one had told our schoolmaster, Mr. Andrews, to stay home and not teach. So my brothers, Colin and Ben, and I still had to study our lessons each day: first reading, then writing, then arithmetic and **navigation**.

One thing His Majesty King George couldn't stop was the winter snow in the colony of Massachusetts.

After days of hard frost and ice, the snow fell for three nights in a row, fine and thick.

Then, on my ninth birthday, the gray clouds blew out to sea, and the sun shone above the steeples of our town.

It was the best kind of New England day: a day for coasting on Boston Common for any boy or girl who had a sled. And now I had my very own. It was small but it was mine, made by my father's strong, steady hands, with slick beef bones for runners and a wood plank seat . . . a present to me at breakfast in a year of hard times.

That morning at school, we practiced our handwriting in our copybooks. I had written the day's date five times for Mr. Andrews:

22 December, 1774

Then, just before noon, I tucked my copybook, pen, and ink pot under the back bench of our schoolroom. I grabbed my wool coat from a high hook. Other students at the South Writing School tramped home through the snow for hot bean porridge. But not Colin or Ben or I. We had brought our sleds to school. Our sister, Kate, was waiting for us outside the school door with three slabs of corn bread and apple jam. Some girls were afraid to go to the Common because of General Gage's troops. But my sister loved to sled ride.

We had to hurry. Mr. Andrews would expect all boys back for lessons at two o'clock sharp.

We pulled our sleds along the icy ruts of West Street. The December wind was cold, and I was glad to be wearing Kate's old mittens and Ben's patched leather boots.

We crossed to the Common, a wide, hilly field with fine new snow and a frame of blue sky. We hurried on past the **stark** row of lime trees that John Hancock had given as a gift to the town . . . and past the town's Wishing Stone, but we had no time to stop and wish that King George would change his harsh laws.

For over a hundred years the Common had belonged to *everyone* in Boston. Now it was covered by the barracks of General Gage's troops. And they were everywhere, these troops, officers and soldiers, drummers and cooks. Three thousand of them, here on Boston Common, setting up their tents, carrying letters and orders, polishing boots and bayonets, drilling, marching.

Everywhere across the Common, my brothers and Kate and I heard the shouted orders of officers and the constant *tramp-tramp* of British boots.

Our father had told us to listen with our eyes and with our ears every time we went to the Common. "Look sharp but don't look like you're looking." Every patriot who thought King George was wrong helped out the Sons of Liberty* in his own small way.

Suddenly, I stopped and pulled on Colin's sleeve. Some of General Gage's soldiers had placed their tents and their cooking fires right in the middle of our sled runs. They had broken the ice on the Common's ponds so no one could skate. And they had knocked down the snow forts the town boys had worked yesterday to build.

We were steaming mad, all four of us. This was *our* Common. These were *our* ponds to skate on. And there were no better hills to sled on anywhere in Boston. It seemed as if the British troops had made it *their* Common.

Now there was no open run to sled on. So instead, we walked among the barracks, and listened with our eyes and with our ears. Ben began to count new sheds and tents and horses. Kate and I counted kegs of powder and barrels of fish. Colin counted officers.

---

* A group of local Boston patriots who opposed the actions of the British. They often met in secret to discuss plans for independence.

Kate and I saw General Gage. He was right there in front of us, almost close enough to touch. He looked like a general, and he stood like a general.

But he didn't look mean. Not like a **tyrant** who would close our harbor. Not like a bully for King George. And not like an old woman, as some Boston newspapers called him. He had slate-blue eyes and was speaking kindly to his soldiers who were setting up a tent. General Gage looked like a man who would listen, a good man, a man like my father.

If I could just speak to General Gage for a few minutes, maybe he would help us. Maybe he would let us sled on our Common. But I was just a town boy. General Gage was the royal governor. I'd have to be as brave as the Boston patriots who told the king of England that his taxes were not fair.

I held on to my sled tightly and took a deep breath. "Hurry," I whispered to Kate. "Go find Colin and Ben. We're going to talk to General Gage."

And so we did, right there in the middle of the Common, with British soldiers all about us.

I walked up to General Gage, tugged hard on his scarlet sleeve, and asked if he would hear a town boy's complaint. Some of his officers glared at me sternly and began to order us away. But the tall general turned and held up his hand to still them. Then he said, "Let this boy have his words."

And so I talked. And General Gage listened.

I told him that the Boston Common belonged to all of us, not just his soldiers. I told him his troops had knocked down our snow forts, and ruined our ponds for skating, and that they had built their cook fires in the middle of the best sled runs.

Then, with Colin and Ben and Kate right beside me, I said: "And it's my birthday, sir, and I wish to use my new sled on the steepest hill in our town. But I can't, you see, because of your men. And we have to be back at our school by two o'clock for our lessons."

General Gage crossed his arms and looked out across the snowy Common. His officers stood nearby with stony faces. No one spoke a word.

Then the general put his hand on my shoulder. He told me I had a fine sled and asked who had made it. "My father," I said proudly.

He leaned down to inspect the other sleds. Then he stood up and said in a general's voice: "I'm a father as well as a soldier for my king . . . I have sons, and daughters, too," he added, nodding at Kate. "And I know my own children would like to sled this hill if they were here. But they're back in England in school."

Then General Gage asked me my name. "Henry, sir," I said, standing as tall as I could. "Henry Price."

"Henry." The general nodded. "That's a good name, indeed." He shook my hand, man to man. "My oldest son is named Henry."

"I'm the youngest in our house," I said.

"You may be the youngest," said General Gage, "but you have the courage of a good soldier as well as the **spunk** of your local rebels." He turned swiftly on his heel to one of his officers.

Draw Conclusions
General Gage has children of his own. How might this influence his decision to let the children sled?

"**Instruct** all troops that they are to allow the town children to sled where they wish. And keep the ice unbroken in one of those ponds. Tell the men they are to clear a good run. And be quick about it. It's my young friend's birthday, and he needs to try out a new sled before two o'clock this day."

I'll never forget the first time I came down that hill on a sled I could call my own: down, down, down the snowy path beneath my runners, the tents and barrels blurring past, the red coats of soldiers rushing past, the wind on my face and in my eyes, faster, faster, over bumps and more bumps, straight through the sprawling camp of British troops till I reached the bottom of the Common, then slower, slower, slow, till I slid to a stop, never wanting that ride to end.

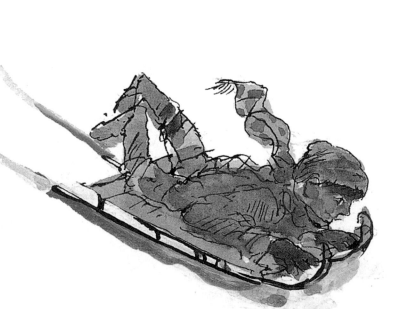

Again and again, my brothers and my sister and I sledded down the best hill in Boston and then dragged our sleds to the top, until it was time to hurry back to the South Writing School for Mr. Andrews's afternoon lessons.

And from December 22 on, Colin and Ben and Kate and I had other days of good sledding on the Common. And skating, too. Because General Thomas Gage was a man of his word.

Spring came, and in April of 1775, the War for Independence began after General Gage ordered his troops to Lexington and Concord. Our new country was at war, and the lobster backs in our town would soon be under siege. The next October, the good folk of Boston were glad when King George sent orders for his top general to return to England. Thomas Gage was the last royal governor of a colony that wanted to choose its own.

On the night that his ship left Boston Harbor and set sail for England, I stood on Long Wharf with my brothers and Kate. We were Americans now, my family and I. We were Boston patriots hoping to win a war against a king. But we'd never forget the tall British general that we'd met on my birthday. General Gage had given us back a pond and our sled runs on Boston Common because he had children of his own. Indeed, he was a good man.

Go Back in Time with
Louise Borden & Robert Andrew Parker

Louise Borden's stories often start with a compelling image. She found the idea for this story while reading a magazine article about children wanting to sled on Boston Common during the Revolutionary War. Louise followed that lead and tracked down the story. She even corresponded with people in England about General Gage.

Robert Andrew Parker lives in an old house in a valley surrounded by wooded hills. Inside the house he keeps his collection of miniature soldiers, which inspired him to create the images for Louise's book. His studio is out back, next to a garden. It holds his paintings, and a six-foot model airplane he built. When he is not working on a painting or illustration, he can be found tubing down the river that runs in front of his house.

Another book by Louise Borden:
A. Lincoln and Me

Author's Purpose
Do you think the author wrote this selection only to inform readers about the events that took place in Boston in the winter of 1774? Explain.

LOG ON Find out more about Louise Borden and Robert Andrew Parker at **www.macmillanmh.com**

Comprehension Check

Summarize

Use your Conclusions Chart to help you summarize *Sleds on Boston Common* in your own words.

Text Clues	Conclusion

Think and Compare

1. Draw a conclusion about General Thomas Gage's abilities as a leader. Explain why your conclusion is logical. **Make Inferences and Analyze: Draw Conclusions**

2. Reread the first paragraph on page 266. How did the closing of Boston Harbor affect Henry and his family? Use details from the story in your answer. **Analyze**

3. Pretend you were one of many **patriots** who had been listening carefully as you walked through the soldiers' camp on Boston Common. What might you have seen and heard? **Evaluate**

4. As Henry finds out, first impressions about others can be misleading or inaccurate. Do you agree with this statement? Why or why not? Explain your answer. **Analyze**

5. Reread "Letters from the Revolution" on pages 262–263. Which letter would Henry and his family agree with? Why? Use evidence from both selections to support your answer. **Reading/Writing Across Texts**

Poetry

Narrative Poetry is poetry that tells a story or gives an account of events.

Literary Elements

Meter is the regular arrangement of accented and unaccented syllables in a line of poetry.

Alliteration is the repetition of the same first letter or sound in a series of words.

"Paul Revere's Ride"

an excerpt from the poem by
Henry Wadsworth Longfellow

Paul Revere was a hero of the American Revolution. With two other patriots, he rode across the countryside to warn the colonists of a British attack.

Listen, my children, and you shall hear
Of the midnight ride of Paul Revere,
On the eighteenth of April, in seventy-five;
Hardly a man is now alive
Who remembers that famous day and year.
He said to his friend, "If the British march
By land or sea from the town tonight,
Hang a lantern aloft in the belfry arch
Of the North Church tower as a signal light—
One, if by land, and two, if by sea:
And I on the opposite shore will be,
Ready to ride and spread the alarm
Through every Middlesex village and farm,
For the country folk to be up and to arm."
Then he said, "Good night!" and with muffled oar
Silently rowed to the Charlestown shore,
Just as the moon rose over the bay,
Where swinging wide at her moorings lay
The *Somerset*, British man-of-war;
A phantom ship, with each mast and spar
Across the moon like a prison bar,
And a huge black hulk, that was magnified
By its own reflection in the tide.
Meanwhile, his friend, through alley and street,
Wanders and watches, with eager ears,
Till in the silence around him he hears
The muster of men at the barrack door,
And the measured tread of the grenadiers,
Marching down to their boats on the shore.

The repetition of the initial "w" and "e" sounds in this line are examples of *alliteration*.

Then he climbed to the tower of
Old North Church
By the wooden stairs, with stealthy tread,
To the belfry-chamber overhead,
And startled the pigeons from their perch
On the somber rafters, that round him made
Masses and moving shapes of shade—
By the trembling ladder, steep and tall,
To the highest window in the wall,
Where he paused to listen and look down
A moment on the roofs of the town,
And the moonlight flowing over all. . . .
You know the rest in the books you have read
How the British Regulars fired and fled,—
How the farmers gave them ball for ball,
From behind each fence and farmyard wall,
Chasing the red-coats down the lane,
Then crossing the fields to emerge again
Under the trees at the turn of the road,
And only pausing to fire and load.
So through the night rode Paul Revere;
And so through the night went his cry of alarm
To every Middlesex village and farm,
A cry of defiance and not of fear,
A voice in the darkness, a knock at the door,
And a word that shall echo forevermore!
For, borne on the night-wind of the Past,
Through all our history, to the last,
In the hour of darkness and peril and need,
The people will waken and listen to hear
The hurrying hoof-beats of that steed,
And the midnight message of Paul Revere.

There are four accented syllables in this line. The arrangement of these syllables with unaccented syllables is an example of *meter*.

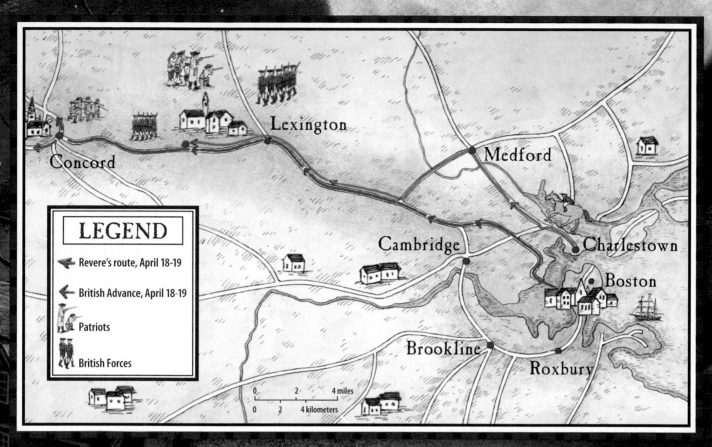

The first battle between the patriots and the British
took place at Lexington. They fought again at Concord.

Connect and Compare

1. What is another example of alliteration in this poem? **Alliteration**

2. Read the poem aloud. How might the meter help you memorize the poem? **Analyze**

3. Compare this poem with *Sleds on Boston Common*. In both the poem and the story, the authors describe the British. How are the descriptions similar? How are they different?
Reading/Writing Across Texts

LOG ON Find out more about narrative poetry at **www.macmillanmh.com**

Writer's Craft

A Good Topic

To choose a **good topic**, first think about what interests you. Then narrow the focus so you can cover the topic completely.

I narrowed the focus to be about my character's own thoughts about one incident.

I tried to show how General Gage felt about Henry's request.

Sledding Can Bring People Together
by Louisa P.

Today the most remarkable thing happened. I was doing my job supervising Boston Common when a brave young boy approached me. He asked my permission to sled on the nearby hills. All my troops were stationed there. I had a big decision to make. Should I allow the boy to sled or not?

Memories of my own children flashed before my eyes. How much they too would enjoy sledding on the Common if they had a chance. My heart felt tender towards the young lad. He saw his favorite sledding spot occupied by troops on his birthday. If I said yes, I would make his special day even more extraordinary.

My officer was standing by to see how I would react to this strange request. He probably could not understand why I was being so gracious. I figured it was a small kindness. Even during a time of war it is easy enough to do an act of peace.

Your Turn

Write a brief character sketch from a first-person point of view. You may base your character on somebody you know, or choose a character from a book, movie, or TV show. Choose words that express the character's personality and feelings. Use the writer's checklist to check your writing.

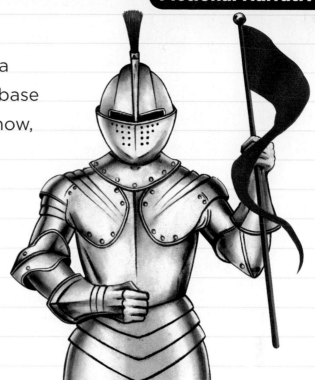

Writer's Checklist

☑ **Ideas and Content:** Did I choose a good topic and narrow the focus to include the most interesting details about my character?

✓ **Organization:** Does the sequence of ideas make sense?

✓ **Voice:** Does the first-person point of view express my character's feelings and thoughts?

✓ **Word Choice:** Do the words reveal my character's personality?

✓ **Sentence Fluency:** Do the sentences match the way the character would speak?

✓ **Conventions:** Do my subjects and verbs agree? Did I check my spelling?

THE RIGHT TO VOTE

Talk About It

Why should people vote? Why do you think it took women so long to win the vote in the United States?

LOG ON Find out more about women's suffrage at **www.macmillanmh.com**

MRS. PANKHURST LEADER of the ENGLISH SUFFRAGETTES

VOTES FOR WOMEN

Vocabulary

representative	postpone
colonel	submit
attorney	legislature
qualify	satisfactory

Dictionary

A **Dictionary** entry includes information about pronunciation in parentheses near the definition. The word is separated into syllables with symbols to show how to sound it out. For example, *colonel* is pronounced (kûr′nl). To figure out the symbols, look for the pronunciation key in the front of the dictionary.

U.S. Capitol Building in Washington, D.C.

YOUR VOTE YOUR VOICE

by Wyatt Thatcher

The word *democracy* comes from two Greek words which, when combined, mean "the people rule." The belief behind any democracy is that the people make the laws.

In the United States, everyone could not possibly gather and vote on every law. That's why the Founding Fathers set up a special type of democracy in which people elect a **representative** who will speak for them. This is the best kind of government to have.

Each person plays an important part in a representative democracy. One of their main responsibilities is to vote during an election. Everyone, from a teacher to an army **colonel**, has the right to vote as long as they are citizens.

Before the 1970s you had to be 21 years old to vote. Some people thought the age should be lowered to 18 years old, so an **attorney** challenged the law in court. Lawyers argued their case all the way to the Supreme Court. Finally, the debate was settled by Congress who created a new law that lowered the voting age to 18 years old for all elections.

Unfortunately, in recent years fewer and fewer Americans are voting. As the twenty-first century began, only one-third of those who **qualify** and are eligible to vote were registered to do so. Younger voters have the worst turnout of any age group.

People who are old enough to vote should not **postpone** signing up or they might find they will need to **submit** to laws they don't agree with. In Washington, D.C., and every state capital, the **legislature** decides about future laws. These laws might not be **satisfactory** for your needs. By voting, your voice can be heard in our governments. In this way, YOU can make a difference.

Reread for **Comprehension**

Evaluate
Fact and Opinion

A Fact and Opinion Chart helps you decide which statements can be proven to be true (facts) and which are somebody's personal feelings or beliefs (opinions). Use your Fact and Opinion Chart as you reread "Your Vote, Your Voice" to evaluate what is fact and what is opinion in the selection.

Fact	Opinion

293

Comprehension

Genre

A **Biography** tells the story of a person's life and is written by another person.

Evaluate

Fact and Opinion

As you read, use your Fact and Opinion Chart.

Fact	Opinion

Read to Find Out

What opinions does the author give about Esther Morris?

When Esther Morris Headed West

By Connie Nordhielm Wooldridge

Illustrated by Jacqueline Rogers

Award Winning Selection

er name was Esther Mae Hobart McQuigg Slack
Morris, and in 1869 she headed out to South Pass
City in the Wyoming Territory. She was fifty-five
years old.

South Pass City was a place that sprouted out of nearly
nothing at the mention of the word "gold." The space
around it was large and wide open. That was a good
thing because Mrs. Morris was a large woman with wide-
open ideas that needed more room than could be had in
New York or Illinois, where she'd come from. You see, she
thought a woman should be able to vote and hold office,
the same as a man.

Fact and Opinion
Find one example of fact and
one of opinion on this page.

After she got herself settled in South Pass City, she paid a call on a man who had already argued hard for the same new and crazy-sounding idea she was bringing in from the East. That man was **Colonel** William Bright, and he thought women's being able to vote and hold office made all kinds of sense. Since he was an elected member of the Wyoming Territory Council, he proposed An Act to Grant to the Women of the Wyoming Territory the Right of Suffrage and to Hold Office.

Colonel Bright was opposed by a feisty young lawyer named Benjamin Sheeks, another **representative** from South Pass City, who thought the idea was hogwash. His plan was to keep the thing from ever being voted on at all. He made a motion to **postpone** discussion until July Fourth, which any fool knew was a holiday.

But Mr. Ben Sheeks lost the day, and the heretofore unheard-of up and happened. In the closing months of 1869, a **legislature** full of men voted to give the women of Wyoming rights no other women in the world had: They could vote and hold office the same as men.

"The Deed Is Done," read one newspaper. "Ladies, Prepare Your Ballots!" read another. "Reckless Copperheads!" read a third, referring to the legislators who'd voted in such a fool thing. Back in South Pass City, the justice of the peace resigned.

Fact and Opinion

One newspaper had the headline "Reckless Copperheads!" Is this a fact or an opinion? How do you know?

Now that women had the right to vote, it was time to prove they could hold office just as well. Mrs. Morris had no hankering for power or highfalutin titles. But she knew an idea—even one voted into law—wasn't worth a hill of beans as long as it stayed words on a page. Her boys were grown and it was time to step away from her cooking and gardening for a spell and do a thing that might help women coming along later on. So Mrs. Morris applied for the position of South Pass City Justice of the Peace. The whole Wyoming Territory let out a gasp. But the only fellow who opposed her for the position failed to **qualify**. So there she was: a judge. And that made her the first female in the United States to hold a public office.

A test of her ability came early on from the very man she was replacing. He refused to hand over the court docket. He didn't think Mrs. Morris should have it. He didn't think any woman should have it.

"You can keep your dirty docket," Mrs. Morris told him, and got herself a nice clean one.

Then there was the time young Ben Sheeks, back to lawyering, argued a case in her court. The opposing **attorney** was having a heyday picking at every little thing and getting Mr. Sheeks's dander up real good. After he'd had about all he could take, Mr. Sheeks escorted his opponent out of the room when it didn't appear the fellow was of a mind to go.

When Mr. Sheeks came back into the courtroom, he knew he'd gone and done it. His views on the woman question were no secret and here he'd misbehaved in front of the first woman judge in the country. The situation called for humbleness and that was not a thing that came easy to Ben Sheeks.

"Your honor," he said, "I apologize for my behavior and I **submit** to any punishment you might inflict. I was in contempt."

Mrs. Morris was not educated in the fine points of the law. But she'd raised three sons in rough-and-tumble places, and she knew a thing or two about common-sense fairness. "Your behavior was justified, Mr. Sheeks," was all she said. And that was an end to it.

Along with seven other South Pass City women, the judge cast her vote for the very first time on September 6, 1870. She later claimed she had her personal physician by her side, and he determined the operation of voting had no ill effects on a woman's health.

Her term ended the following month. "My position as justice of the peace was a test to woman's ability to hold public office," she said, "and I feel that my work has been **satisfactory**, although I have often regretted I was not better qualified to fill the position. Like all pioneers, I have labored more in faith and hope." When she stepped down from the bench, Mrs. Morris handed the court docket over to the same judge who wouldn't turn his loose eight months before.

The gold fever that had brought three thousand people to South Pass City died down. Colonel Bright moved to Denver and then finished out his days in Washington, D.C.

Ben Sheeks headed for Salt Lake City and then west to Washington State. Somewhere along the way he took up the crazy notion that women should be able to vote and hold office the same as men.

Mrs. Morris moved to Laramie, Wyoming, and then on to Cheyenne. She was close to ninety when she died.

In the summer of 1920, a professor from the University of Wyoming made her way out to what was left of South Pass City. She got herself a wheelbarrow and took a stone from the broken-down home of William Bright, who once had the courage to propose a crazy new idea.

She took another stone from the home of Esther Morris, who had the courage to show how the idea looked in the living of it. She took a third from the home of Ben Sheeks, who hated the idea, saw how it looked in the living, and had the courage to change his way of thinking.

The professor piled the stones into a monument and invited the remaining inhabitants of South Pass City to a dedication ceremony. As the sun sank behind the mountains, nineteen human beings, two dogs, and a cow remembered for a moment that once in time a thing bigger and better than gold had happened here.

In Washington, D.C., later that same summer of 1920, the Secretary of State announced a change to the United States Constitution. He said women in all states were now allowed to vote, the same as men.

It wasn't a new idea for the state of Wyoming. The folks back East just took a little longer getting to it is all.

Heading West with Connie Nordhielm Wooldridge and Jacqueline Rogers

Connie Nordhielm Wooldridge tried a lot of things before she started writing. She studied Greek culture and archaeology in Greece, worked as a flight attendant, and taught school in Korea. But when Connie started writing, she knew she found the right job. She loves writing stories that tell children what life was like before they were born and how much life has changed.

Jacqueline Rogers grew up as the youngest child in a family of artists. While growing up she followed her mom to her sculpture class and her sisters to their drawing classes. When Jacqueline started drawing on her own, she focused on horses. Today she illustrates children's books because it allows her to be most creative. "It pushes me and scares me and that makes my work more exciting," she says.

Other books by Connie Nordhielm Wooldridge: *Wicked Jack* and *The Legend of Strap Buckner*

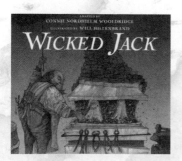

Author's Purpose

Does Connie Nordhielm Wooldridge admire Esther Morris? What details from the story indicate the author's opinion of her subject?

 Find out more about Connie Nordhielm Wooldridge and Jacqueline Rogers at **www.macmillanmh.com**

 Comprehension Check

Summarize

Use your Fact and Opinion Chart to help you write a summary of *When Esther Morris Headed West*. Opinions you have about events in the selection should not appear in your summary.

Fact	Opinion

Think and Compare

1. Identify two facts in the story about Esther Morris's term as a judge. Then identify two opinions that she had about herself. Do you agree or disagree with Morris's opinions? Explain your answer. **Evaluate: Fact and Opinion**

2. Reread page 305. What is the "thing bigger and better than gold" that happened? Explain why the author compares this event to gold. **Analyze**

3. What would you have done to help women get the right to vote? What would you have said to the Wyoming **legislature**? **Evaluate**

4. Explain why it takes courage to change people's way of thinking. **Synthesize**

5. Reread "Your Vote, Your Voice" on pages 292–293. Compare and contrast women's desire to vote in Wyoming in 1869 with the decrease in voting in recent years. Find evidence from both selections to support your answer. **Reading/Writing Across Texts**

Suffrage for Women

by Maria Chan

After more than 50 years of struggle and hard work, women finally won the right to vote in national elections in 1920.

The fight for **suffrage**, or the right to vote, began with the Seneca Falls Convention in New York state in 1848. As voting rights pioneer Susan B. Anthony argued, suffrage was "the pivotal right, the one that underlies all other rights." Suffragist leaders gained strength in 1870 when an **amendment** to the U.S. Constitution granted African American men the right to vote. Why not award the vote to all citizens?

In 1872 Anthony and a group of women marched into a **polling** place in Rochester, New York, and cast their votes in a presidential election. The women were arrested and fined. Finally, in 1878 after six more years of protests, a women's suffrage amendment was introduced in Congress.

Congress did not pass the women's suffrage amendment in 1878. Still, the amendment was reintroduced in every session of Congress for the next 40 years.

Suffragist leaders, such as Carric Chapman Catt, traveled across the country giving speeches and organizing workers. Catt led a "suffrage army" of 1 million volunteers. She used the **media** to spread her arguments. Newspapers and magazines were able to reach a large amount of people.

In 1920 these efforts paid off. Congress passed the Nineteenth Amendment, which guarantees every adult woman the right to vote. On August 26, 1920, the states approved this amendment. Here is what the Nineteenth Amendment to the Constitution says:

"The right of citizens of the United States to vote shall not be denied or abridged [limited] by the United States or by any state on account of sex." After a half-century of struggle, women finally won the right to have their voices heard in governing this country.

Biography

Carrie Chapman Catt was born Carrie Lane in Ripon, Wisconsin, in 1859. After college she became a teacher in Mason City, Iowa, and then the superintendent of schools in 1883. Around that time Catt became involved in fighting for the right to vote.

Over time Catt supervised thousands of volunteers and gave hundreds of speeches in favor of women's right to vote. She was elected president of the National American Woman Suffrage Association from 1900 to 1904, and again from 1915 to 1920.

Catt worked against great odds but held firm to her beliefs. "There will never be a true democracy until every responsible and law-abiding adult in it has his or her own voice in government." When American women won the right to vote in 1920, it was largely because of Catt's work.

That year Catt founded the League of Women Voters, which still exists today. She also founded the National Committee on the Cause and Cure of War in 1925. She died in 1947.

Reading a Time Line

One way to review major historical events is to look at them on a time line. Here are some of the major events of the women's suffrage movement:

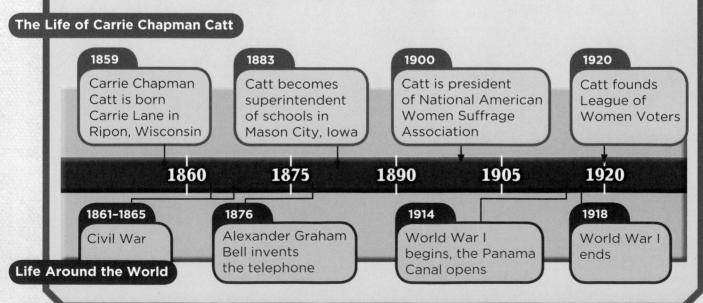

The Life of Carrie Chapman Catt

1859 Carrie Chapman Catt is born Carrie Lane in Ripon, Wisconsin

1883 Catt becomes superintendent of schools in Mason City, Iowa

1900 Catt is president of National American Women Suffrage Association

1920 Catt founds League of Women Voters

1860   1875   1890   1905   1920

1861–1865 Civil War

1876 Alexander Graham Bell invents the telephone

1914 World War I begins, the Panama Canal opens

1918 World War I ends

Life Around the World

Connect and Compare

1. Use the time line on page 310 to find out how old Carrie Chapman Catt was when she founded the League of Women Voters? **Reading a Time Line**

2. How did Carrie Chapman Catt help women win the vote? **Analyze**

3. Compare *When Esther Morris Headed West* with this article about women's suffrage. How are the two selections similar? How are they different? **Reading/Writing Across Texts**

 Social Studies Activity

Research another suffragist leader, such as Lucretia Mott, Elizabeth Cady Stanton, or Lucy Stone. Write a summary of her life. Include a time line that shows the main events in the life of the person you choose.

 Find out more about suffrage at **www.macmillanmh.com**

Word Choice
Word choice means choosing the right words to help readers understand what you mean. Strong adjectives and action verbs make the writing more specific.

Write a Poem

I used the verb "stride" because it packs a lot of meaning.

I chose the words "super cool" to show my enthusiasm about voting.

Vote Your Way

by Brian P.

At eighteen you're allowed to vote.
It keeps our country strong.
Stride to the polls with notes you wrote
On issues right and wrong.

You choose the candidates you like.
It's only up to you.
With your vote you make a strike
For right, and good, and true.

Don't waste the chance to vote your way.
This right is super cool.
Learn all you can; then have your say.
If you don't, you're just a fool!

Your Turn

People often write poems to celebrate ideas, people, or events. Choose a person, event, or topic from American history to honor with a poem that you write. Your poem does not have to rhyme. Use the writer's checklist to check your writing.

Harriet Tubman (1820-1913)

Writer's Checklist

✓ **Ideas and Content:** Is the main idea of my poem apparent to the reader?

✓ **Organization:** Does each line and stanza of my poem follow in a logical order?

✓ **Voice:** Can the reader tell how strongly I feel about this topic?

☑ **Word Choice:** Did I use action verbs whenever possible to strengthen my word choice?

✓ **Sentence Fluency:** Do the lines of poetry have a certain rhythm even if they don't rhyme?

✓ **Conventions:** Is every word in my poem spelled correctly?

Talk About It

Why should people care about the environment?

LOG ON Find out more about
the environment at
www.macmillanmh.com

Protecting the ENVIRONMENT

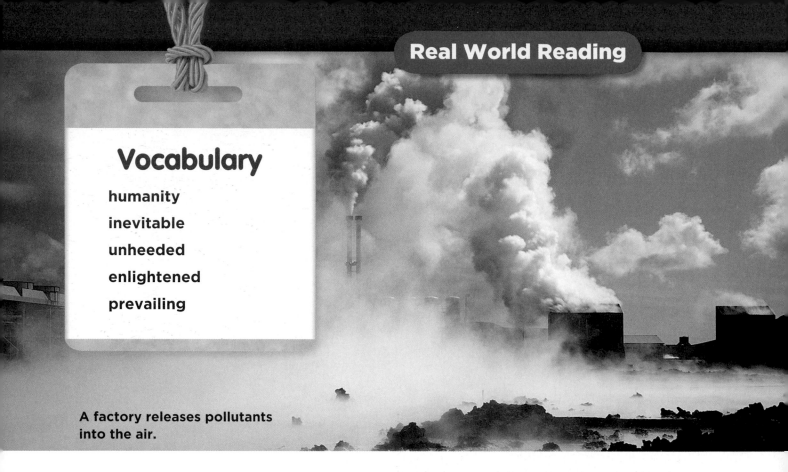

Vocabulary

humanity

inevitable

unheeded

enlightened

prevailing

A factory releases pollutants into the air.

ENVIRONMENTAL DANGERS

The following threats to the health of Earth's environment could affect all of **humanity**. They could also harm plant and animal life.

Damage to the Ozone Layer:

A thin layer of invisible ozone gas surrounds Earth. It protects us from the sun's harmful rays. In recent years, the amount of ozone has decreased. Scientists believe pollution is the cause. Less ozone means the sun's rays can reach us more directly and cause more harm.

Global Warming:

Some scientists think pollution is raising Earth's surface temperature. If global warming continues, some problems seem **inevitable**. Melting of ice at the North and South Poles would be one unavoidable problem. Then ocean levels would rise. Coastlines would be flooded. The weather would change. There could be more storms, more heat waves, and more droughts.

Acid Rain:

Acid rain occurs when rainwater mixes with certain pollutants. Burning fossil fuels—mainly coal—is the cause. Acid rain can harm trees and wildlife. It can even damage buildings.

AN EARTH DAY OF THEIR OWN

Trash tossing at Environmental Awareness Day

What's the biggest problem for the environment? "Ignorance!" say Lisa Wollett's fifth-graders in Parma, Michigan. These kids knew that many urgent warnings about the environment have gone unheeded. They wanted people in their town to start paying attention. So they created Environmental Awareness Day.

The students got information from environmental organizations. They made sure the local newspapers covered the event. They even started their own paper to get the word out. Some kids worked on plays, games, and skits. Everyone worked to become more enlightened. They did research on natural resources, conservation, pollution, and recycling. They learned that Americans throw away 40 million tons of paper a year and 65 million aluminum cans.

Hundreds of people from all over their county showed up for the event. The prevailing mood was upbeat. Everyone was excited and surprised. We weren't expecting so many people," said Benjamin Scott, 11. "My aunt from California even came."

Recycle These Facts!

Recycling one ton of paper saves 17 trees and 7,000 gallons of water.

Recycling one aluminum can saves enough electricity to run a TV for three hours.

Recycling one glass bottle or jar saves enough electricity to light a 100-watt bulb for four hours.

More than 30 million trees are cut down to produce a year's supply of newspapers.

Recycling one ton of plastic saves the equivalent of 1,000 to 2,000 gallons of gasoline.

LOG ON Find out more about recycling at **www.macmillanmh.com**

Comprehension

Genre

A **Nonfiction Article** in a newspaper or magazine presents facts and information.

Evaluate

Fact and Opinion

A fact is something that can be proven to be true. An opinion is a belief that may not be supported by facts.

BEYOND *the* HORIZON

Can people around the world improve their standard of living and still protect the environment?

Kofi Annan

Kofi Annan, as Secretary-General of the United Nations, made a speech to world leaders. The topic was the health of the environment. He described two visions of the future. If environmental warning signs go unheeded, he said, the future looks grim. But if people are willing to change their ways, the future can be bright. Here is a summary of what he said:

Imagine a future of constant storms and floods. Islands and coastal regions are flooded. Because of drought, nothing can grow in the hard soil. People are at war with each other over water and other natural resources.

Then imagine a future with cities and towns that are clean and pleasant. Homes, transportation, and industry are energy-efficient. The standard of living for all the world's people is improving.

The choice between these different visions is ours to make. Current trends may not be very encouraging. We know enough about ecological problems to fear the worst. But there is time to draw back from the edge of disaster. Most important, another path is possible. That path is better for **humanity** and less harmful to the environment.

The challenge of living in harmony with Earth is as old as human society itself. Things changed with the Industrial Revolution. The steam engine and the internal combustion engine were invented. People learned to take advantage of the energy locked in such fossil fuels as coal, oil, and gas. Improvements in farming methods and machinery pushed people from farms into factories and cities. The result was a revolution in living standards that the world had never seen or even imagined possible.

A dried-up lake bed in California

Today we need another revolution. We need to change our attitude toward the global environment. For too long, too many people have believed that we can overcome anything that limits us. And too many have believed that technology is the **inevitable** answer to any problem we might face.

Slowly, however, we have become **enlightened**. We have begun to see the dangers in the **prevailing** way of doing things. We can see the dangers in continuing to cut down forests and use up natural water supplies. We know that an atmosphere filled with poisons puts us at risk. We realize that we cannot continue to over-fish the oceans. The climate itself has begun to talk back in the form of storms and droughts.

People who believe all forms of development are bad do not help either side. For the poorest members of the human family, development offers hope. It means the chance to feed, school, and care for themselves and their children. But prosperity that destroys the natural

environment is no prosperity at all. We are faced with another kind of choice.

We know that development is possible without using up natural resources or ruining the environment. The people of the world must come together. We must show our strong sense of common destiny. We must take this challenge seriously. In the end we must exercise greater responsibility for one another. And we must take responsibility for the Earth on which we depend.

Think and Compare

1. What is the topic of this speech?

2. Do you agree with the main idea of this speech? Why or why not?

3. Would you describe this selection as mostly fact or mostly opinion? Explain your answer.

4. Which of the problems described in "Environmental Dangers" are also referred to in "Beyond the Horizon"?

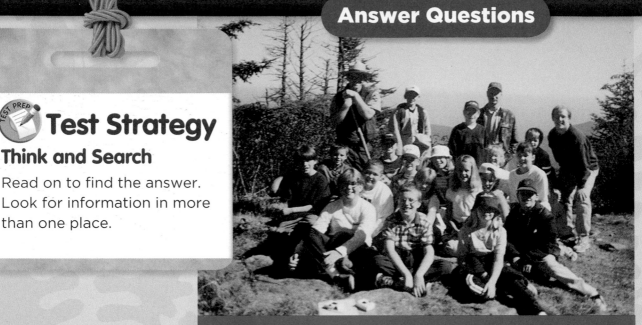

Jason McDougald's fourth-grade class poses for a picture during a visit to Graybeard Wilderness.

Test Strategy

Think and Search

Read on to find the answer. Look for information in more than one place.

KEEPING THE WILDERNESS WILD

Robin Tynes, age ten, often goes hiking with her family in leafy Graybeard Wilderness, a nature preserve in Montreat, North Carolina. "It's really nice and quiet," she says.

Robin's fourth-grade class at Black Mountain Elementary School is so fond of Graybeard that they chose it as their precious place. A lot of hikers, backpackers, and mountain bikers feel that way, too. The preserve's popularity has caused problems. Many visitors create their own paths, called "switchbacks." Robin's teacher, Jason McDougald, explains, "If there's a bend on the trail, a lot of people will go straight across it" to make their route shorter. They trample plants and cause erosion.

Other threats to Graybeard include campers who cut down trees for firewood and developers who build homes nearby. Development threatens the natural habitats of Graybeard's animals and can cause water and air pollution.

To protect their precious place, McDougald's class has presented programs on ways to enjoy the wilderness responsibly. They organized a group to spread the message. Among their tips: Stay on the trail and leave campsites just as you found them.

Go On ▶

Directions: Answer the questions.

1. **Which of the following statements is an opinion the fourth-grade class would agree with?**

   A Graybeard Wilderness is a nature preserve in North Carolina.

   B Graybeard Wilderness is a quiet place, loved by hikers.

   C It is okay to cut down trees inside the preserve.

   D Camping causes soil erosion and pollution.

2. **What are some threats to Graybeard Wilderness?**

   A the peace and quiet

   B wilderness programs

   C loud noises

   D switchbacks and development

3. **"Switchbacks" are made by**

   A park rangers creating hiking trails in the wilderness.

   B animals such as deer walking through the forest.

   C people who do not stay on the trail and who crush plants.

   D water rushing down the mountain and flooding campsites.

4. **How will the tips offered by Robin's class help save Graybeard Wilderness?**

5. **Do you think natural habitats and wilderness parks should be protected? Explain your answer.**

> **Tip**
>
> Look for information in more than one place.

Write to a Prompt

The rangers at Green Place State Park are thinking about allowing snowmobilers to use its trails in the winter. Do you think this is a good or a bad idea? Write an essay giving your opinion. Explain your reasons for feeling as you do.

I stated my opinion in my introduction.

Help Save Our Park

Imagine a beautiful, snowy forest. All is quiet. Suddenly, a loud, whining engine roars to life. A snowmobile whizzes past, leaving muddy ruts in the path and the smell of gasoline in the air. Snowmobilers should be barred from using Green Place State Park.

The park is a beautiful and peaceful place where people can go when they are stressed out. With snowmobiles around, being in the park is like being on the highway—it's noisy, smelly, and crowded.

Finally, the health of the environment is at stake. If we allow the park to go downhill, we may lose it altogether. Green Place State Park will become unfit as a habitat for wildlife. The ecosystem will be disturbed, and that will affect everyone in the community. All parts of an ecosystem depend on each other—and that includes people!

Writing Prompt

A company wants to buy a large meadow in your community and make it into a water park. There will be an entrance fee. The mayor of your city wants the parks department to buy it and turn it into a public park. Which do you think is the better use of the land? Write an essay giving your opinion and reasons why the land should be a water park or a public park.

Writer's Checklist

- ☑ Ask yourself, who is my audience?
- ☑ Think about your purpose for writing.
- ☑ Choose the correct form for your writing.
- ☑ Plan your writing before beginning.
- ☑ Use details to support your main idea.
- ☑ Be sure your ideas are clear and organized.
- ☑ Use your best spelling, grammar, and punctuation.

DeSeRT HaBiTaTs

Talk About It

What images come to mind when you think of deserts? How do animals and people survive in the desert?

LOG ON Find out more about desert habitats at **www.macmillanmh.com**

Vocabulary

brimming	parched
gushed	scrawny
landscape	gnarled
scorching	progress

Connotations

A thesaurus entry will include several different synonyms for a word. Each synonym will carry negative or positive feelings, called **Connotations**. For example, *scrawny* has a negative connotation. It would not be a positive word to describe a trim athlete.

The Best Place To Be

by Carmela Rameriz

My new friend Janine just moved here from North Carolina. She is always talking about how different Arizona is from her old home.

"I really miss the mountains," Janine said before soccer practice last week. "North Carolina is the best place to be."

"How can you say that?" I exclaimed as I closed the top of the team's ice chest. It was **brimming** with ice and so many drinks that I could hardly press it shut. "There are plenty of mountains here!"

"It's different in North Carolina," Janine explained. "Our mountains have tall, leafy trees," she said as we walked to the field. "The forests are filled with raccoons, deer, and bears. My dad and I used to hike along a stream near our house. The water there **gushed** over the rocks and would splash us. The **landscape** and scenery was rocky, but what a view!"

"Arizona's mountains are filled with wild flowers and animals," I said. "The bighorn sheep are my favorite!"

"Don't you mind the **scorching** sun burning your lawn?" Janine asked. "The grass around here always looks **parched** and thirsty from the lack of water.

"The ground is cracked and dry. The trees are **scrawny** and thin. Their **gnarled** and twisted branches grow so slowly."

"Still, you won't see mountains like these anywhere," I said. "People think Arizona's mountains glow from the sun," I continued, sounding like a travel book.

All my talking paid off, though. This week at soccer practice I found that I had made **progress** convincing Janine that Arizona was a great place to live. I felt there was a definite improvement in her attitude towards her new home.

"I saw the neatest thing," she said. "The tiniest bird flew into a hole in this huge cactus. There are so many beautiful things to see in the desert, don't you think?"

"It's the best place to be," I told her, as we both ran out onto the field.

Reread for **Comprehension**

Make Inferences and Analyze
Compare and Contrast

STRATEGY SKILL ✓

Making inferences and analyzing what happens in a story allows you to notice similarities and differences between characters, events, and settings. A Venn Diagram will help you to compare and contrast these similarities and differences. Use your Venn Diagram as you reread "The Best Place to Be" to compare and contrast the two states described in the story.

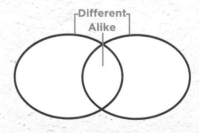

Different
Alike

Comprehension

Genre

Realistic Fiction tells an invented story that could have happened in real life.

Make Inferences and Analyze

Compare and Contrast
As you read, use your Venn Diagram.

Read to Find Out

How do Fatima's feelings about her grandmother change from the beginning of the story to the end?

My Great-Grandmother's Gourd

by Cristina Kessler
illustrated by Walter Lyon Krudop

Award Winning Selection

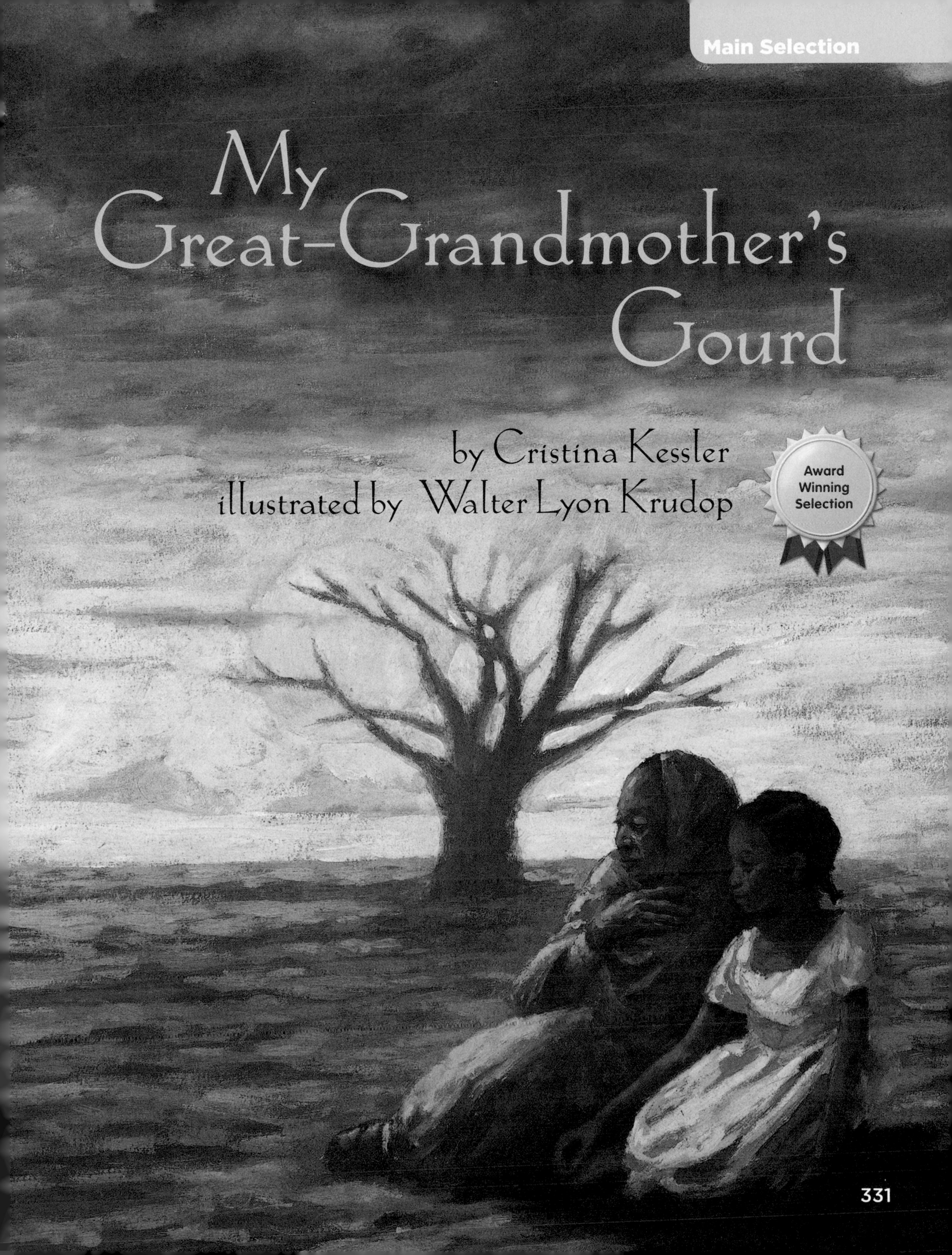

I'll always remember the first day the blue pump worked. The men in their turbans and the women in the *towbs* laughed and chattered as the bright, shining pump was fixed on top of the old well.

"Imagine," said Ibrahim, the village chief, "no more camels pulling water for drinking and washing and cooking. No more filling of the old trees to get us through the dry season. **Progress** has come to our village."

Compare and Contrast
Think about the new pump in the village. In what ways is getting water from the pump different from the old ways?

Ahmed, the barber, called out, "Who shall take the first pump of this fancy new machine?"

Silence filled the air until Hanan, the neighbor, said, "Let it be a child, to show just how easy it will be. Fatima, you pump and we will watch the water flow. *Inshallah*."

I stepped to the long handle, so hard and smooth in my hand, and pulled down. A soft creaking noise filled the silence. Everyone watched without speaking a word. But not a drop fell.

I pulled again, and a second soft *creeeeak* was surrounded by stillness—something rare in our village. Out **gushed** a stream of clear water. As if a spell had been broken, a sudden cheer filled the air and drums began beating.

Was it for me or the water? I wondered. I looked for my grandmother, who always says she is so proud of me, but I didn't see her face in the excited crowd. As people pushed forward to try the pump, I pushed outward to find my grandmother.

There she stood all alone beneath her best friend, an old baobab tree. I rushed to her, caught up in the drumbeats welcoming the pump.

"Grandmother, come see the new pump. The water is so easy to get now, our work will be less. Come dance."

I could see my friends and cousins dancing with arms flung wide. Turning circles, they kicked up small dust devils around their feet. I wanted to dance, too, for the drumbeat was powerful and the excitement was calling me.

Grandmother looked at me, then patted the **gnarled** trunk of the giant baobab tree with her work-worn hand and said, "Go dance, child. Drink the fresh, cold water. And soon I'll be there too."

I ran back and danced with my friends, celebrating the new pump. But my grandmother did not come.

Every morning I raced the girls of the village to the pump. The first one there got to pull down the long, shimmering handle for as long as she wanted, filling buckets and tins, head pans and gourds. I raced to the well each day, hoping to be the first.

My grandmother spent more and more time with her friend the baobab. Leaning against its great trunk. Resting beneath its wide-reaching shadow. Watching the girls and women walk to and from the well. Watching and waiting for what, I didn't know.

Compare and Contrast
How is Grandmother's reaction to the pump different from the rest of the people in her village?

Early one evening, after the food had been eaten and the sun's heat was only a whisper on my skin, I joined my grandmother beneath the tree.

Grandmother took my hand and placed it on the ancient bark of the giant trunk. She didn't say a word, but her sadness was loud.

"Tell me, Grandmother, what makes you so sad?" I asked as I looked deep into her eyes. "Is it the pump? Don't you like it?"

With tired eyes she looked at me and said, "The rains are nearly here, and still no one works to prepare the trees. All the years of my life, drumbeats would fill the village, and voices would sing and chant as we all worked together. But now there's only the *creeak*, *creeak* of metal. And no one works together, or works at all, to prepare the trees."

Gently patting the trunk, she said, "I always called this my great-grandmother's gourd. The name my grandmother called it. And her grandmother before her."

I smoothed the *towb* around her wrinkled face and said, "But, Grandmother, with the pump we don't need the trees. The days of storing water in trees are past."

She let go of my hand.

"Grandmother," I said, "that was then and this is now."

I couldn't sleep that night, for the air seemed heavy, so I sat outside. The moon cast great pools of darkness across the flat **landscape**. I was thinking about my stubborn grandmother, when, silent as a shadow, she sat down beside me.

I gazed upon our family's only baobab and let my eyes wander up the tree to the **scrawny** branches. Each branch looked small and separate in the light of the moon.

As if she read my mind, Grandmother said softly, "She gives us shade in the day. Shelter in the rain. And water in the dry season. She is the tree of life."

"No, Grandmother, the baobab will give us shade in the day and shelter in the rain. *Khalas*. And the pump will give us water in the dry season."

Shaking her head, she said, "Good-night, Granddaughter," and walked back to our hut.

I rose that next day with the first rays of the sun, when the air was still cool. Dressing quickly, I rushed to the well to pump away all the questions that my old-fashioned grandmother stirred in me.

I was first and I pumped till my shoulders ached. *Creeak, creeak* sang the pump. Nagla, the neighbor who always had something to say, called out, "Fatima is pumping like a woodpecker hammering a tree, and she fills your bucket before it is settled on the ground."

A long line of girls, with **brimming** buckets and tins, head pans and gourds balanced on their heads, streamed back and forth between the huts and the pump.

The hut was empty when I returned. I looked toward our field to find Grandmother. Instead, I saw her bent over her hoe at the base of her baobab tree.

I ran to her and shouted, "Grandmother, people will laugh at you, preparing your tree." I wanted to take the hoe from her hands, but she stood straight and said to me in a voice as hard as the dry earth, "Some may laugh. What do I care? I have work to do."

She worked in silence, for as the sun rose the heat was great. *Creak, creak* sang the pump. *Hack, hack* went my grandmother's hoe. Working alone, she looked as thin as one of the tree's skinny branches.

"Can I help?" I asked.

"No," she said. She wiped the sweat dripping from her brow with the end of her *towb* and bent back to her work.

One day Ahmed, the barber, passed our tree and shouted with a laugh, "For some people new ideas are like puddles on the clay: they never sink in."

Balgeese, the midwife, called out, "To fight progress is to fight the wind, old woman. Come, let's go to the pump."

But Grandmother kept right on working. Her back bent over her hoe, she was slowly digging out what looked like a large necklace around the base of the baobab's trunk.

Another day Nagla, the neighbor who never stops talking, passed. With a voice louder than the call to prayer, she said, "Who but a fool makes extra work? Myself, I use the well." Then she laughed. And I realized she was laughing at my grandmother. Old-fashioned or not, *my* grandmother.

I nearly knocked Nagla down as I grabbed my hoe and ran to the tree. Without a word, I started digging beside my grandmother. We worked side by side.

For days we dug, deepening the circle around the trunk. We didn't talk. In peaceful silence, we shared the work of my grandmother's great-grandmother.

People passed us, but now no one said a word. They still looked at us from the sides of their faces, balancing buckets and head pans, pots and gourds full of water on their heads. We worked on.

Creak, creak went the blue pump.

One day as the sun dipped below the earth's edge, Grandmother put away her hoe. "Now," she said, "we must wait for the rains."

The first rain comes as fiercely as the first winds of the *haboob*. Grandmother and I stood in it, feeling the water dripping down our faces. We watched our necklace around the giant old tree's trunk slowly fill with water. The **parched** earth turned a shiny red as the giant raindrops plopped upon it.

When the rain stopped, I climbed the tree and sat by a small hole at the top of the trunk. The hole that had been made by my grandmother's great-grandmother's great-grandmother.

I dropped the bucket tied to my waist down to Grandmother, who filled it to its brim from the baobab's necklace. Slowly I pulled the bucket up, then poured its contents into the tree. It took two breaths before we heard the splash of water hitting bottom, deep inside the tree. Grandmother's eyes sparkled at the old, familiar sound.

Ahmed, the barber, passed by, and, shaking his head in wonder, said, "I guess some people like extra work." But we took no notice of him as the sweet splash of water rose higher and higher inside the old tree.

Day after day now, I climbed the tree, and Grandmother filled the bucket. We worked together, filling our tree. Finally, when the rains ended, the tree was full.

The **scorching** dry season came early. Each day the horizon danced where the shimmering blue sky met the earth's baking red clay. Lines formed at the well, and the girls in their colorful *towbs* looked like a python stretched across the desert floor sunning itself. As the temperatures rose, people made many more trips to the well.

From the first rays of light till the sky glowed hot, red, and dusty as the sun slipped away, people pumped. The steady *creeak, creeak* turned to *screech! screech!* as people pumped water from sunup to sunset.

And then one day the pump stopped.

"We will fix it," said the chief, Ibrahim. Omar, the baker, and Musa, the butcher, brought out all the tools needed to take the pump off the well. People stood in silence, waiting for the news.

Musa pulled a large metal piece, sharp along one edge, from the pump's neck. "It has broken clean, from too much use. *Malesh*," he said to the quiet crowd. "I don't know what we shall do, for I have no spare part like this."

The men passed the broken metal rod from hand to hand in silence, each examining its sharp edge. "I will make another piece," said Boubacar, the cart builder. "But it will take some days."

"How can we wait days?" cried Nagla. "What shall we do without water?"

"We go back to the old ways," said Ahmed. "We shall use the camels to pull the water out of the well, just like in days past." Then he looked straight at my grandmother and told Nagla, "And two smart villagers can use their tree."

"This year we will share our tree," said Grandmother. "Maybe it's wise to mix old with new. We shall see."

Ahmed looked at her a moment, then nodded his head yes. He turned to the two men and said, "Get the camels and ropes."

His son, Abu Bakar, called to his friends Ali, Salah, and Osman, "Get the buckets. We'll go to the tree."

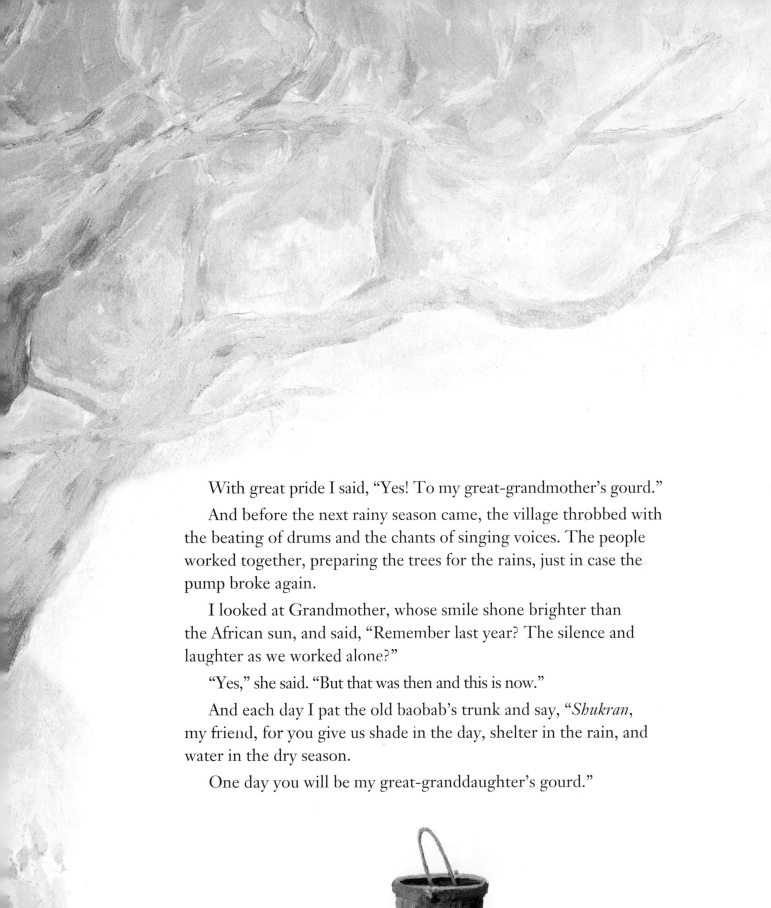

With great pride I said, "Yes! To my great-grandmother's gourd."

And before the next rainy season came, the village throbbed with the beating of drums and the chants of singing voices. The people worked together, preparing the trees for the rains, just in case the pump broke again.

I looked at Grandmother, whose smile shone brighter than the African sun, and said, "Remember last year? The silence and laughter as we worked alone?"

"Yes," she said. "But that was then and this is now."

And each day I pat the old baobab's trunk and say, "*Shukran*, my friend, for you give us shade in the day, shelter in the rain, and water in the dry season.

One day you will be my great-granddaughter's gourd."

Share Stories with Cristina Kessler and Walter Lyon Krudop

Cristina Kessler has visited more than 100 countries. She and her husband have been traveling the world ever since they were volunteers in the Peace Corps. She makes sure she gets to Africa, her favorite place, once or twice a year. When she is there, she looks for stories that will "get the good news out about Africa." Cristina especially likes to tell a story that combines the wisdom of both the old and the new ways, such as in this story. It is set in Sudan, and is based on a true event.

Walter Lyon Krudop uses pictures to tell stories. He started taking drawing lessons at age five, and after a decade as an artist, he has illustrated 17 books. He is also passionate about animation and is working on several animated stories. Walter lives in New York with his wife Sara.

Another book by Cristina Kessler: *Jubela*

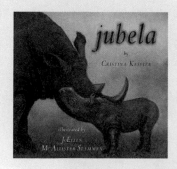

Author's Purpose

The author's main purpose here is to entertain. Realistic fiction also includes true-to-life details. Point to examples.

LOG ON Find out more about Cristina Kessler and Walter Lyon Krudop at **www.macmillanmh.com**

Comprehension Check

Summarize

Use your Venn Diagram to help you summarize *My Great-Grandmother's Gourd*. By comparing and contrasting different details, you will be able to understand how the story is organized.

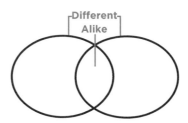

Think and Compare

1. Compare and contrast the grandmother's feelings about the traditional ways of collecting water with that of her village's. **Make Inferences and Analyze: Compare and Contrast**

2. Reread page 340. Why did the narrator suddenly decide to help her grandmother? **Analyze**

3. Give an example from your own life of mixing an old way of doing something with a new way. Explain the results. **Evaluate**

4. Explain how **progress** can be good and bad. **Analyze**

5. Reread "The Best Place to Be" on pages 328–329. Compare and contrast how Janine and Fatima adjust to a new situation. Give examples from each story to explain your answer. **Reading/Writing Across Texts**

MORE THAN SAND

by Haritha Gupta

Cold deserts? Deserts on mountains? Read on to find out some cool facts about deserts.

You probably know some basic facts about deserts. For example, most people know that deserts are dry places where more water **evaporates** each year than falls as **precipitation**, or rain. You might also know that **nomads** move frequently from place to place and often call deserts home. However, there are many facts about deserts that you may *not* know. Take the quiz below to help you find out more about these remarkable regions.

True or False?

No rain falls in the desert.

FALSE Most deserts have less than 10 inches of rain each year. However, in some South American deserts, it is true that rain almost never falls. In one desert in Chile, no rain has fallen for 45 years in a row! In other deserts, such as those in Madagascar, an island nation off the coast of southeastern Africa, about 24 inches of rain falls each year. All of this rain falls within a single month!

purple flowers in desert in Chile

True or False?

All deserts are hot.

FALSE Temperatures in deserts can reach above 100°F during the day, but can fall below freezing at night. Some scientists also consider any place that has almost no plants a desert. Regions that are too cold for anything to grow are called "frigid deserts." Examples are the ice deserts of Antarctica and Greenland. Other deserts are cold for long periods. The Gobi in Asia has freezing temperatures for as long as six months at a time.

Still other deserts are the hottest places on Earth. The hottest temperature ever recorded was 136.4°F in a desert in Libya, in northern Africa.

frozen desert region in Greenland

Water Cycle

Reading a Process Diagram

This diagram shows the stages of the water cycle.

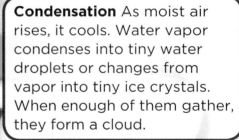

Condensation As moist air rises, it cools. Water vapor condenses into tiny water droplets or changes from vapor into tiny ice crystals. When enough of them gather, they form a cloud.

Precipitation Water droplets from clouds fall down to Earth in the form of rain, sleet, snow, or hail. In hot deserts, winds blow precipitation from dry lands to wetter regions.

Evaporation Heat from the Sun makes water evaporate and change into a gas state.

Collection Some of the water flows into streams, lakes, and rivers. Some of it soaks into the ground. Lots of the water slowly finds its way back into Earth's oceans.

True or False?

Deserts are flat and sandy.

FALSE Although deserts can be low and flat, some have rocky hills and even mountains. Some also have lakes and plains covered with gravel. Sand makes up only about 2 percent of North American deserts, 10 percent of the Sahara in northern Africa, and 30 percent of the Arabian Desert.

mountains in a South American desert

True or False?

There is no life in the desert.

FALSE To survive in a dry desert environment, plants and animals, including humans, must make some adaptations. Desert plants cannot grow too close together because each plant would not get enough water. In fact, many desert plants do not grow at all during dry periods. However, after a rainfall, they quickly sprout, flower, and die. Some desert plants get their water from deep underground. The mesquite tree has roots that can reach as deep as 263 feet. Other plants store water in their leaves, roots, or stems.

Like plants, most desert animals are inactive during dry periods. Other animals stay in burrows underground or rest in the shade during the heat of the day. They come out to eat at night after the temperature has dropped.

When rain does come, every living thing in the desert seems to celebrate. Colorful flowers cover the desert floor, and animals leave their hiding places to drink and eat.

Namib desert in Africa

True or False?

There are many deserts in the world.

TRUE Deserts cover about one fifth of Earth's land area. The largest desert in the world is the Sahara. The Sahara stretches from the Atlantic Ocean eastward to the Red Sea, spreading across parts of Morocco, Algeria, Tunisia, Libya, Sudan, Chad, Niger, Mali, and Mauritania. It covers an area about the size of the United States.

Sahara desert

Connect and Compare

1. Look at the water cycle diagram on page 351. What role does water vapor play in the water cycle? **Reading a Process Diagram**

2. Compare and contrast the different types of deserts discussed in this article. Put this information in a Venn diagram. **Apply**

3. Think about "More Than Sand" and *My Great-Grandmother's Gourd.* Describe ways that people adapt to living in desert regions. **Reading/Writing Across Texts**

Science Activity

Research the life cycle of a desert animal or plant. Using this information, create a process diagram like the one on page 351.

 Find out more about deserts at **www.macmillanmh.com**

Writer's Craft

Dialogue

Well-chosen **dialogue** makes characters sound natural and believable. It can also help further the plot. Quotation marks and punctuation in dialogue make the characters' words stand out from the rest of the text.

Write a Dialogue

The Great Debate
by Louis G.

"Of course cats are superior to dogs. We can climb trees," said the orange cat.

"Ridiculous! Dogs are stronger," growled the bulldog.

I wanted the dialogue between a cat and a dog to sound natural.

"Strength isn't everything, you know," said the cat. "We're so much more independent than you dogs. We don't need to be walked. We don't need to be bathed. As a matter of fact, most of us hardly need any attention at all from humans."

I used quotation marks correctly.

"Boring. Boring. Boring," said the dog. "You cats tip-toe around so quietly, your owners hardly even know you're there."

"Well all you dogs do all day is bark. We cats know how to catch mice. That's a useful talent," sniffed the orange cat.

The bulldog snorted. "Ha! We keep our humans safe from burglars. That's more important than catching a pathetic little mouse!"

"You can have your opinion. However, one of those pathetic little mice is stealing food from your bowl," said the orange cat, yawning.

The bulldog turned and barked, "Hey, come back here you thieving mouse!"

Your Turn

Write a dialogue between two characters. Include quotation marks, commas, and correct punctuation in the dialogue. Then read your dialogue aloud to see if the characters sound natural. Use the writer's checklist to check your writing.

Writer's Checklist

✓ **Ideas and Content:** Does my dialogue show what my characters think?

✓ **Organization:** Does the sequence of sentences make sense?

✓ **Voice:** Do my words express each character's feelings and thoughts?

☑ **Word Choice:** Did I choose words for the dialogue that reveal each character's personality?

✓ **Sentence Fluency:** Do the sentences match the way the characters would speak?

✓ **Conventions:** Did I use quotation marks correctly in dialogue? Did I check my spelling?

Talk About It

What kinds of new technology do you know about? What inventions would you like to see in the future?

LOG ON Find out more about life in the future at **www.macmillanmh.com**

Into the FUTURE

Who Says Robots Can't Think?

by Jane Schnelling

Dad and I are watching the Olympic Games in our media room. The giant screen drops down to cover one wall. I jiggle the lever and my seat turns around, to face the screen. We give our **robot**, Sylvia, our orders for popcorn and fresh lemonade. She is only a machine but she looks like a human and helps with the housework.

We are having popcorn for dinner tonight because our oven is **defective**. It is broken and keeps on repeating that it doesn't remember how to cook. Dad thinks the huge **meteor** passing by Earth is messing with its radio waves.

"I did see a shooting star yesterday," I said. "Maybe that's why I had trouble getting Sylvia started this morning. She **rotated** around and around, **staggered** when she tried to take a step, and almost fell backwards. She finally started moving towards me, but then suddenly **reversed**, and went backwards. I thought she was going to crash into a wall. Luckily, she grabbed hold of the wind chimes we have **dangling** down from the ceiling, and got her balance."

At last, Sylvia arrives with our popcorn and drinks. I look at the screen and see the Olympic torch burning brightly. Sylvia sees it too. Dad gives her **tokens** from an old board game as a tip. Sylvia thanks him for the pieces and starts to leave the room. Then she reverses direction and comes back to where we are sitting. I hear humming and then some clicking sounds. The sounds mean that she is searching her memory chips for information. "During the Olympics, I should get medals, not tokens," she says.

Dad and I just stare at each other. Sylvia doesn't seem to know that robots aren't supposed to think. Then we burst out laughing and award Sylvia a gold medal.

Reread for **Comprehension**

Make Inferences and Analyze
Draw Conclusions

Making inferences about what happens in a story will help you draw conclusions about characters and events and come to a new understanding of the story. Use your Conclusions Diagram as you reread the selection to help you to make inferences and draw conclusions.

Evidence   Conclusions

Comprehension

Genre

Science Fiction tells a story of imagined events usually set in the future and based on science or technology.

Make Inferences and Analyze

Draw Conclusions
As you read, use your Conclusions Diagram.

Evidence   Conclusions

Read to Find Out

What can you conclude about the relationship of the two brothers at the end of the story?

ZATHURA
A SPACE ADVENTURE

Award Winning
Author
and
Illustrator

written and Illustrated by Chris Van Allsburg

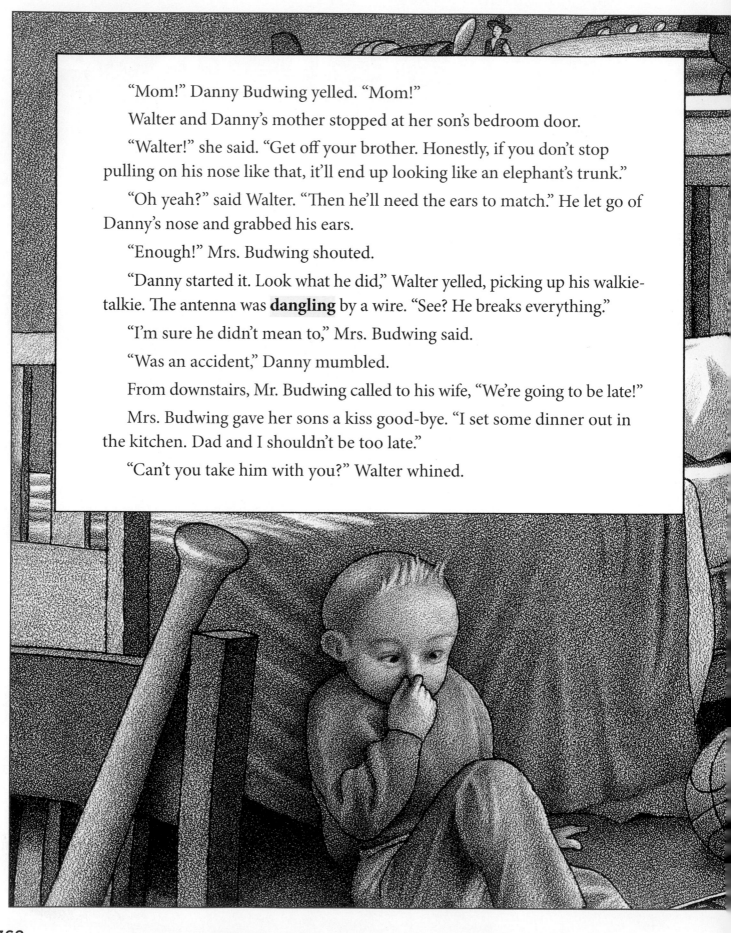

"Mom!" Danny Budwing yelled. "Mom!"

Walter and Danny's mother stopped at her son's bedroom door.

"Walter!" she said. "Get off your brother. Honestly, if you don't stop pulling on his nose like that, it'll end up looking like an elephant's trunk."

"Oh yeah?" said Walter. "Then he'll need the ears to match." He let go of Danny's nose and grabbed his ears.

"Enough!" Mrs. Budwing shouted.

"Danny started it. Look what he did," Walter yelled, picking up his walkie-talkie. The antenna was **dangling** by a wire. "See? He breaks everything."

"I'm sure he didn't mean to," Mrs. Budwing said.

"Was an accident," Danny mumbled.

From downstairs, Mr. Budwing called to his wife, "We're going to be late!"

Mrs. Budwing gave her sons a kiss good-bye. "I set some dinner out in the kitchen. Dad and I shouldn't be too late."

"Can't you take him with you?" Walter whined.

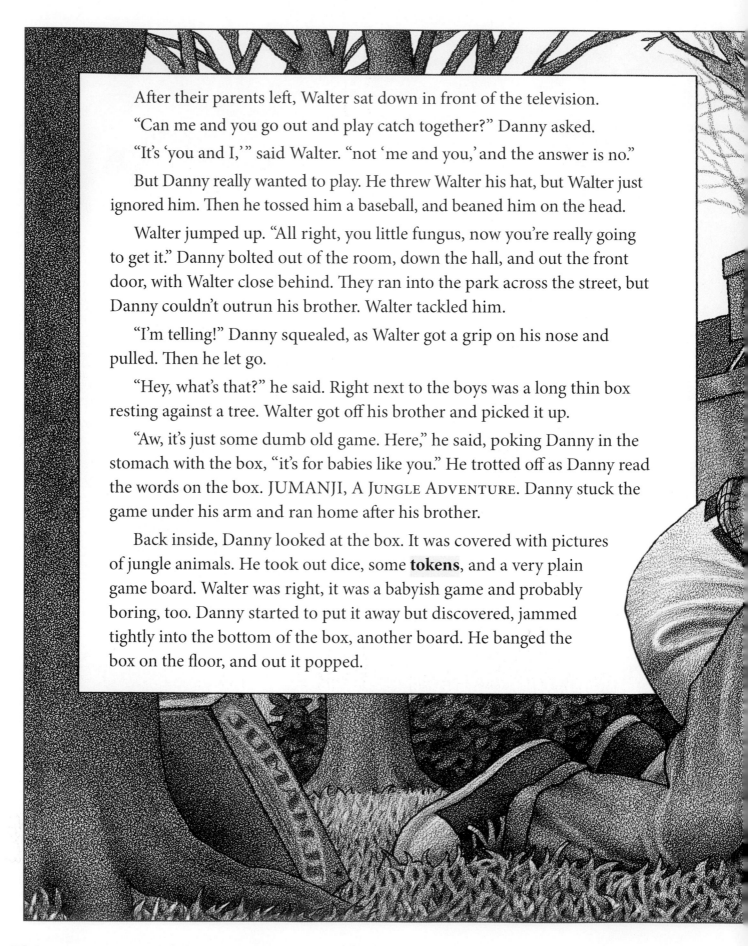

After their parents left, Walter sat down in front of the television.

"Can me and you go out and play catch together?" Danny asked.

"It's 'you and I,'" said Walter. "not 'me and you,' and the answer is no."

But Danny really wanted to play. He threw Walter his hat, but Walter just ignored him. Then he tossed him a baseball, and beaned him on the head.

Walter jumped up. "All right, you little fungus, now you're really going to get it." Danny bolted out of the room, down the hall, and out the front door, with Walter close behind. They ran into the park across the street, but Danny couldn't outrun his brother. Walter tackled him.

"I'm telling!" Danny squealed, as Walter got a grip on his nose and pulled. Then he let go.

"Hey, what's that?" he said. Right next to the boys was a long thin box resting against a tree. Walter got off his brother and picked it up.

"Aw, it's just some dumb old game. Here," he said, poking Danny in the stomach with the box, "it's for babies like you." He trotted off as Danny read the words on the box. JUMANJI, A Jungle Adventure. Danny stuck the game under his arm and ran home after his brother.

Back inside, Danny looked at the box. It was covered with pictures of jungle animals. He took out dice, some **tokens**, and a very plain game board. Walter was right, it was a babyish game and probably boring, too. Danny started to put it away but discovered, jammed tightly into the bottom of the box, another board. He banged the box on the floor, and out it popped.

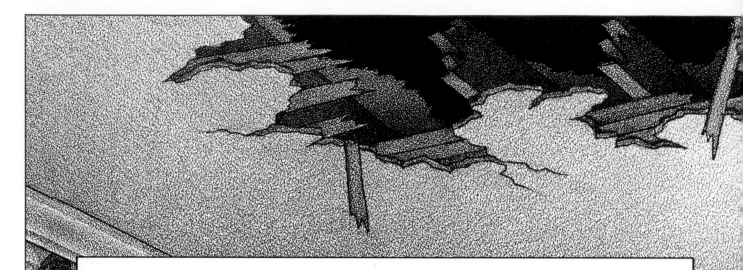

This board was more interesting. It showed flying saucers, rockets, and planets in outer space, with a path of colored squares leading from Earth to a purple planet called Zathura and back to Earth.

Danny put a token on Earth, then rolled the dice. After he'd moved along the path, something surprising happened. A buzzing sound came from the board and, with a click, a small green card popped out of the edge right in front of him. He picked it up and read, "**Meteor** showers, take evasive action."

"Hey, Walter," Danny started to say, "what does eva—" when he was interrupted by a noisy *rat-a-tat-tat* sound coming from the roof.

Walter looked up from the television. "Holy smoke," he said, "must be a hail storm!" "It's not hail!" shouted Danny, holding up the card. "It's meteors."

The noise grew louder, like a thousand golf balls bouncing off the roof. The room got so dark, Walter turned on the lights. Then—KABOOM—a rock the size of a refrigerator fell through the ceiling and crushed the television.

"See," Danny said. "I told you. Meteors."

Walter stared at the hole in the ceiling. "Okay," he agreed, "meteors. But how'd it get so dark so fast?" Through the hole he could see what was left of his parents' bedroom, and beyond that, a black, star-filled sky. "It looks like night up there."

"It's not night," said Danny. "It's outer space."

367

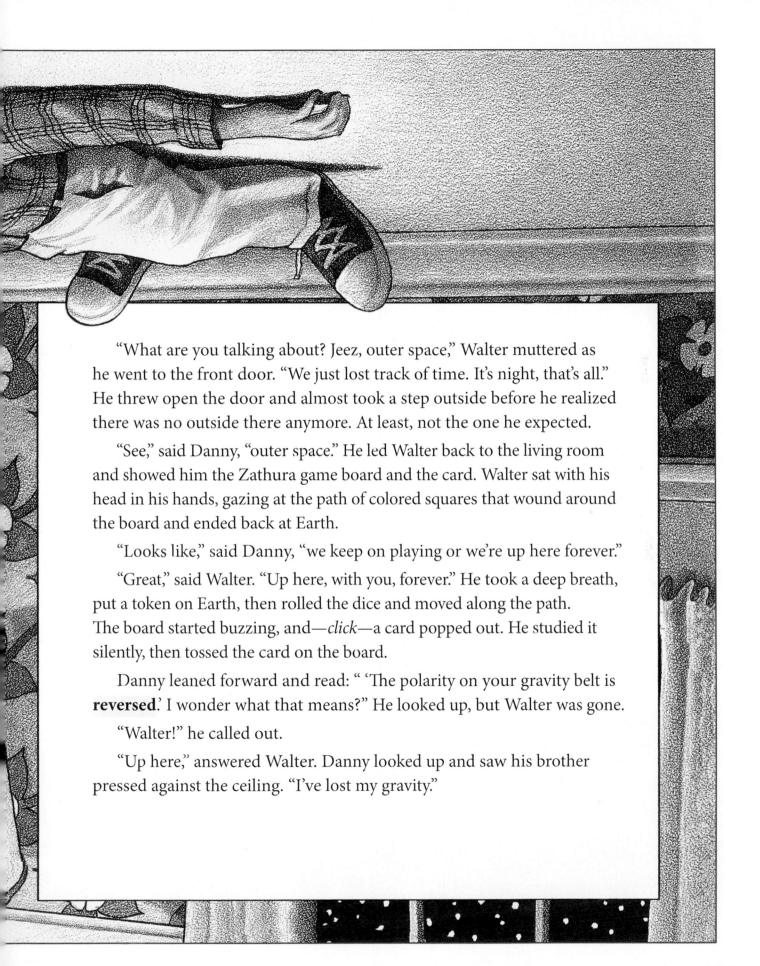

"What are you talking about? Jeez, outer space," Walter muttered as he went to the front door. "We just lost track of time. It's night, that's all." He threw open the door and almost took a step outside before he realized there was no outside there anymore. At least, not the one he expected.

"See," said Danny, "outer space." He led Walter back to the living room and showed him the Zathura game board and the card. Walter sat with his head in his hands, gazing at the path of colored squares that wound around the board and ended back at Earth.

"Looks like," said Danny, "we keep on playing or we're up here forever."

"Great," said Walter. "Up here, with you, forever." He took a deep breath, put a token on Earth, then rolled the dice and moved along the path. The board started buzzing, and—*click*—a card popped out. He studied it silently, then tossed the card on the board.

Danny leaned forward and read: " 'The polarity on your gravity belt is **reversed**.' I wonder what that means?" He looked up, but Walter was gone.

"Walter!" he called out.

"Up here," answered Walter. Danny looked up and saw his brother pressed against the ceiling. "I've lost my gravity."

"That's not all you're going to lose," Danny said nervously, because he could see that Walter was being pulled slowly toward the hole in the ceiling—and a lonely trip into outer space.

Walter realized it too and started clawing at the ceiling, but he couldn't keep himself from moving closer and closer to the hole.

Danny looked around. Lying next to the meteor was the cord from the shattered television. He tossed it to Walter, who knotted it tightly to his belt. Danny grabbed the end of the cord and tied his brother to the sofa.

Danny rolled the dice and moved his token along the path. *Click.* Out popped another card: "Your gyroscope is malfunctioning." Suddenly the house tilted. Everything in the room slid to one side, and Danny got buried under a mountain of furniture. He slowly dug himself out, clutching the game, only to find that Walter was floating back toward the hole in the ceiling.

Draw Conclusions
What purpose do you think a gyroscope serves on a space ship?

Danny tied him to the sofa again and handed up the dice. Walter rolled and got his gravity back, dropping to the floor with a thud. Danny moved his piece and handed him his card. " 'Your **robot** is **defective**,' " Walter read.

From the hallway came the sound of rattling metal and a steady *clank, clank, clank.* The boys stared at the doorway as a shiny silver robot stepped into view. He was having trouble walking on the tilted floor. His head **rotated** back and forth and seemed to freeze on Walter. The robot's eyes lit up and he spoke in an odd mechanical voice: "Emergency, emergency, alien life form. Must destroy." His clawlike metal hands snapped open and shut.

"Uh-oh," Danny whispered, "I think he's talking about you." Fortunately, when the robot stepped forward he missed the door, banged into the wall, and fell to the floor. He got up and did it again. And then again.

"Better hurry up and roll," said Walter, "before he makes it in here."

Danny rolled the dice and took his card: " 'You pass too close to Tsouris 3, gravity greatly increased.' "

The room began to level out, but something strange was happening to Danny. Walter looked at him. "Holy smoke," he said. Danny was getting shorter, and wider too. Soon he was about the shape and size of a large beach ball.

"Waaalter," he said in a low voice. "I feeeel verrrry heeeavy."

"Destroy alien life forms," the robot repeated from the hall as he picked himself up again. This time he made it through the door and headed for Walter.

Danny yelled to his brother, "Puuush meee!"

"What?" said Walter.

"Puuush meee," Danny yelled again. "Juuust puuush meee."

Walter bent down and gave his brother a shove. Danny rolled across the room and, like a giant bowling ball, knocked the robot over and flattened his legs. "Did I geeet hiiim?" asked Danny, who couldn't see because he'd rolled up against a wall and was upside down.

Walter pushed him back to the game board. "You sure did," he said, patting his brother's head. "You were terrific."

Walter picked up the dice and rolled. He took his card, and his hand trembled as he read, "'Zorgon pirate ship launches photon attack.'"

Through the window, the boys saw a spaceship. Two points of light shot from the ship and headed directly for the Budwing house. The first one hit the chimney and sent bricks falling into the fireplace. The second hit the upstairs bathroom. Water began dripping down from the hole in the ceiling.

Walter handed the dice to Danny, who had a hard time lifting his short, heavy arm. He rolled, and as Walter moved his token for him, he slowly returned to his normal shape. A card popped out. Danny read it silently. "This is bad," he said. "'Zorgon pirate boards your vessel.'"

The room shook as the spaceship banged up against the house. The boys heard footsteps on the roof. Through the opening in the ceiling they saw someone or something climb through the hole in the roof and enter the room above them. Danny and Walter moved to the hallway, standing behind the flattened robot. They held each other, too terrified to move. A humming sound came from their feet. They looked down and saw the robot's eyes light up.

He lifted his head, fixed his eyes on the hole in the ceiling, and spoke: "Alien life form, must destroy." His clawlike hands twitched but he couldn't get up.

Danny and Walter helped him to his feet. He **staggered** forward as the pirate's scaly tail and lizardlike legs swung down from the hole. The robot lifted one of his claws and snapped it sharply around the creature's tail.

The Zorgon howled, jerking himself back through the hole, with the robot still attached. He thrashed and wailed, banging against the walls overhead. Then, minus one arm, the robot dropped down through the hole. The boys heard the Zorgon scramble across the roof and saw the flash of his rockets as his ship sped away.

It seemed hopeless. The robot's eyes were dark again. They'd been playing almost three hours, and their tokens rested a galaxy away from Zathura and twice that far from Earth. "We're never going to make it," said Walter.

"Sure we are," answered Danny. He handed the dice to his brother. "Me and you, together. We can do it."

Walter cradled the dice in his hand and sighed. "'You and I,'" he said wearily. "'You and I.'" He looked at his little brother, who was grinning.

"That's right," said Danny. "Together."

Walter rolled the dice, a one and a two. He moved his token to the only black square on the board. The card popped out. "'You have entered a black hole,'" Walter read. "'Go back in time, one hour for each mark on the dice.'"

He jumped up and looked around the room. "You see any black holes?"

His brother pointed to the floor. A black spot was slowly spreading under Walter's feet, like a perfectly round puddle of ink. At first Walter thought he was sinking into it, but it was the hole that was rising. He tried to run but could not feel his feet. Then, as the hole rose higher, he couldn't feel his legs, either. "What's going on?" he cried.

Danny looked below the disklike hole. "Walter," he said, "the bottom part of you is gone." As the hole rose higher and higher, there was less and less of Walter, until only his head remained. Danny tried to pull on the hole to save what was left of his brother, but his hands passed through the blackness as if it were made of smoke. His chin dropped to his chest and he began to sob.

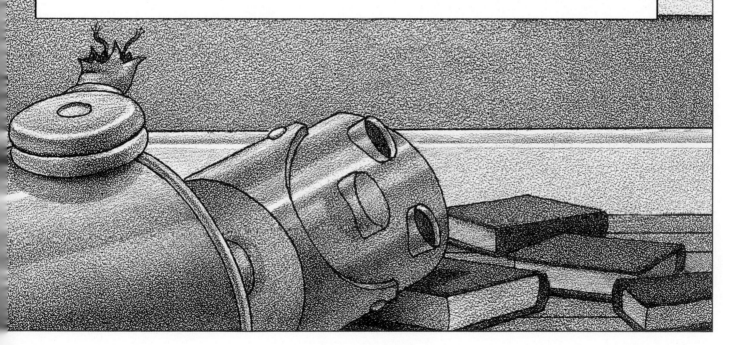

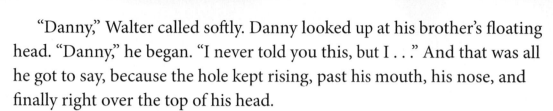

"Danny," Walter called softly. Danny looked up at his brother's floating head. "Danny," he began. "I never told you this, but I . . ." And that was all he got to say, because the hole kept rising, past his mouth, his nose, and finally right over the top of his head.

Walter was completely swallowed up, floating in empty darkness. He closed his eyes as he began to spin, plunging head over heels through pitch-black space. Then, *thud*, he landed hard on his knees. There was something in his arms, something wriggling around.

He opened his eyes and found himself back in the park by his house. He had an arm wrapped tightly around Danny's neck and a hand gripping the boy's nose. "I'm telling," Danny squealed.

Walter let go and fell back on the grass. He was dizzy, very dizzy. Danny jumped up and started to run, but stopped. "Hey," he said, "what's that?" He went to a tree and picked up a box resting against the trunk. He held the box out to Walter. "Look," he said, "it's some kind of game."

Walter grabbed it. "Hey, give it back," said Danny.

His big brother got to his feet. "You don't want to play this," he said. "Trust me, I tried it once." He went over to a trash can and jammed the box deep inside. "Come on," he said, "I've got a better idea. Let's go play catch."

Danny smiled. "You mean together, me and you?"

Walter put his arm around his brother. "Yeah, that's right," he said. "Me and you, together."

Draw Conclusions
What does Walter realize about the game Danny finds in the park?

Out of This World
with
Chris Van Allsburg

Chris Van Allsburg gets his ideas for stories when he sees a picture of something in his mind. Then he asks "What if...?" What if a boy went on a train that turned into the Polar Express? What if a game about outer space became real? Chris has been drawing since his college days. He calls his work "representational" (which means it's like real life), but he always puts a little mystery into the pictures. Because Chris has so many new ideas, he doesn't like to write sequels. However, kids do. Many of his fans have written sequels to his books.

Other books by Chris Van Allsburg:
Jumanji and *The Polar Express*

Author's Purpose
A fiction writer usually aims to entertain. Do you believe that is true for Chris Van Allsburg? Why or why not?

LOG ON Find out more about Chris Van Allsburg at **www.macmillanmh.com**

Comprehension Check

Summarize

Summarize the events that happened in *Zathura.* Use your own words and only include important information.

Think and Compare

1. Use your Conclusions Diagram to help you conclude what Walter would do if Danny brought home the game again. What evidence do you have for your conclusion? **Make Inferences and Analyze: Draw Conclusions**

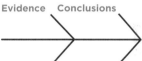

2. Reread page 381. What was Walter going to tell Danny before the black hole swallowed him? **Analyze**

3. If you were going on a space adventure during which you would be dodging **meteors**, aliens, and robots, would you choose Danny, Walter, or both to go with you? Explain your answer. **Evaluate**

4. A robot saves Danny and Walter from an alien. What do you think robots will do in the future? **Analyze**

5. Reread "Who Says a Robot Can't Think" on pages 358–359. What are the similarities and differences between Sylvia and the robot in *Zathura*? **Reading/Writing Across Texts**

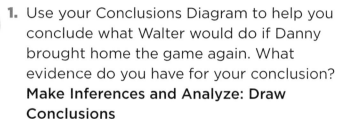

February 2

Robots Today & Tomorrow

by William Brackman
Dixon Daily Staff Writer

In 1939, millions of people flocked to the World's Fair in New York. Among the major attractions was a huge mechanical man named Elektro. Many visitors believed that a **mechanical** creature called a robot would do all kinds of work for humans in the future.

Today robots are used in many industries. A robot is any machine with moving parts that performs tasks on command. Most robots are used in factories. There they do tasks that are **repetitive**, or ones that are done in the same manner each time. Robots put parts together and move materials. They sometimes do work that is dangerous for humans. For example, they may work deep in the ocean or inside tanks filled with dangerous fumes. These robots are more than just moving mechanical parts because they actually seem to "think."

Thinking Machines

How can metal think? Robots are programmed to do certain jobs. A program is a set of computer instructions that tell the robot what to do. Complex robots do many things. In fact two complex robots are now on Mars, studying the planet.

These robots, called the Mars Exploration Rovers, have metal or plastic bodies that protect their mechanical parts. Computers in these robots act as their brains and cameras act as their eyes. These robots have sent photos and information about the surface of Mars back to Earth.

Future Robots

What will robots do in the future? One kind of robot will be able to recognize your voice and talk with you. It is being designed to be part companion and part security guard. Another robot will carry packages and open doors. It will walk forward and backward, turn easily without stopping, and climb stairs. It can also keep its balance on uneven ground.

The future for robots is **limitless**. They may clean our homes, fly airplanes, and maybe even help us learn. Robots are not meant to replace humans, but they are meant to make difficult tasks easier.

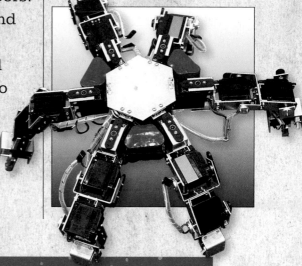

Connect and Compare

1. After reading the headline what facts did you expect to find in this article? Explain your answer. **Reading a Headline**

2. How do you think robots will help humans in the future? **Analyze**

3. Think about this article and *Zathura*. If the boys in *Zathura* could design a personal robot, what might it do? How might their robot be different from robots that are planned for the future? **Reading/Writing Across Texts**

 Science Activity

Do research about robots that have been used on recent space missions. Make a list of their special features and jobs.

 Find out more about robots at **www.macmillanmh.com**

Write a Diary Entry

Transition Words

Transition words in sentences can help you connect your ideas and make your writing flow more smoothly. Transition words can also help to show cause and effect.

The transition word "because" explains why Danny usually bothers Walter.

The phrase "as a result" helps connect my ideas.

Dear Diary

October 25

Dear Diary,

Tonight was the weirdest night of my life. As usual, Mom and Dad made me stay with Danny. I hate being left alone with him because he is such a pest! But tonight we weren't exactly alone.

First, our house was launched into space, where a meteor shower hit us. Then, I lost my gravity and, as a result, almost got sucked into outer space. Next, a robot appeared and started to make trouble.

At this point, I lost hope. Danny never did, though. He tried to make everything right. Finally, I woke up in the park. I was so happy when I realized Danny was with me, alive and well.

Your Turn

Write a diary entry from the point of view of a fictional character. Select an event from the story to describe in detail. Remember to tell about the event using the character's voice. Use the writer's checklist to check your writing.

Writer's Checklist

✓ **Ideas and Content:** Are the ideas I included those of the character?

✓ **Organization:** Does my description of the event unfold in a way that is easy to follow?

✓ **Voice:** Does the diary entry sound like the character is talking?

☑ **Word Choice:** Did I choose **transition words** that help to show cause and effect?

✓ **Sentence Fluency:** Did I start the sentences with words that show the order of events?

✓ **Conventions:** Did I use the correct verb forms and spell them correctly? Did I check my spelling?

Everybody Can Serve

by Belinda Cisneros

"Everybody can be great, because everybody can serve," said Martin Luther King, Jr. According to Dr. King, greatness is not inside a person. Greatness lies in what a person does for other people. Dr. King and many others like him spent their lives making the world a better place. He challenged all people to do the same. Think about your skills and the things you enjoy doing. Is there a way that you can share these skills and interests with another person? A community service project is a great way to learn how to be a leader and to help other people. It will also help you make new friends. Choose an adult to be your advisor. Then invite some friends or family members to plan a project together. Here are a few steps to follow for creating a community service project.

Step 1 Choose the Project

➡ Create a list of community issues that matter to you. Do you want to help younger students who are not doing well in school? Are you interested in working with the Special Olympics? Does your community have a recycling program?

Go On ▶

➡ Look over your lists. Are there already community groups that do the same thing? Are there families or schools that might be interested in helping? What materials will you need to do the project?

➡ Choose the project that you think will help your community the most and inspire the most interest.

Step 2 Plan the Project

➡ Create a schedule to help you manage the project. How long will it take to finish the project? How many days each week will you work on it? Where will the team meet?

➡ Decide what jobs need to be done. Assign each person to a specific job. Make sure that each person knows when his or her job needs to be completed. Mark these dates on your schedule.

➡ Contact any people or groups that might be able to help you. Local librarians can help you with your research.

Step 3 Begin the Project

➡ After the planning is done, it is time to get to work. No matter what precautions you take, problems may still occur. Don't get upset. Let the team members solve the problems as they happen. Make sure everyone feels that his or her ideas are respected. Most importantly, have fun!

Step 4 Document the Project

➡ As you work on the project, take photographs. Ask someone to put the pictures in order from beginning to end. Each member of the group can choose one picture and write a journal entry about it. Tell members to describe what is going on in the picture and to tell about their thoughts and feelings at the time.

Step 5 It's Time to Celebrate!

➡ Celebrate the completion of your project. Display the pictures and journal entries. Invite everyone who helped with the project. Your local newspaper or TV station may be interested in covering the event. This is a time to celebrate what makes people "great."

Go On ▶

Directions: Answer the questions.

1. **Which of the following would Dr. Martin Luther King, Jr., approve of the MOST?**

   A meeting new friends
   B helping members of the community
   C visiting Washington, D.C.
   D participating in a sports event

2. **Which of these activities could BEST be added to the diagram on page 389?**

   A selling lemonade at a baseball game
   B studying for a test
   C volunteering at a nursing home
   D cleaning your bedroom

3. **On page 390, what does the word** *precaution* **mean?**

   A being in a dangerous situation
   B not being afraid to take risks
   C avoiding problems after something happens
   D taking steps to prevent problems

4. **A group is choosing between two projects: bringing meals to the elderly and raising money for a new baseball field. Which project do you think the group should choose? Explain your choice.**

5. **Choose a community service project that you would like to do. Explain what the project is and how you would organize it. Use information from the selection to help you plan your project.**

Writing Prompt

Think about a time when you helped someone. Tell what happened and how you helped. Write a journal entry that is at least three paragraphs and include details.

STOP

CIVIL RIGHTS

Talk About It

What rights do you think all citizens of the United States should have? What does discrimination mean to you?

LOG ON Find out more about civil rights at **www.macmillanmh.com**

Vocabulary

scald	blurted
permission	clenched
autograph	chiseled
fare	spectacular

Homophones

Homophones are words that sound the same but have different meanings and spellings. For example, the word *fare* has a different meaning than the word *fair*.

Lunch Counter Encounter

by Ilysa Samuelson

Best buddies Joe and Paul loved to play baseball. They spent the morning of June 23, 1963, working on their swings and working up a sweat. It was a hot day and the Mississippi sun was doing its best to **scald** the boys with its hot rays. At about noon Paul started feeling hungry. He wanted to grab a burger from the drugstore on Center Street with Joe.

"Ummm, I'll ask my mom if I can go. I need her **permission**," Joe said. The situation was complicated for Joe. There were rules that would keep him from sitting with his friend because of the color of his skin.

Joe's parents and many other people were trying to change those rules. They listened to the speeches of Dr. Martin Luther King, Jr., a famous preacher who was trying to change unfair practices in many southern states. In Joe's house there was a picture of Dr. King with his **autograph** on the bottom.

"It's mighty hot," Joe's mother said. "Why don't you boys take the bus to the drugstore? I've got the bus **fare** right here."

"No, ma'am," Paul **blurted** out suddenly. "Bikes are fine!" He hated riding the bus with Joe. They would be forced to sit in the back.

When the boys reached Center Street, Joe started to get nervous.

"Dad told me about some trouble here last week," Joe said sadly. "I'll just wait outside."

"Not happening!" Paul said, as he grabbed Joe's arm and the two boys marched through the door. Paul's hand was **clenched** in a fist as they headed for two empty stools.

A man with a frown that looked like it was **chiseled** out of stone blocked their way. "Go around back if you're with *him*," he said pointing at Joe.

Before the boys could respond, a woman's voice interrupted the discussion.

"These boys will be joining me," the soft voice said. The man and the boys turned to see a woman in a wheelchair beside them. "Excuse us," she said smiling, as she moved her chair toward the man, intending to go forward.

Not wanting to appear rude to the woman, the man stepped aside.

Joe and Paul followed the woman to the stools. She parked beside them and talked steadily as they ordered and ate their lunch.

After the boys finished, the woman met them on the sidewalk outside. "Have a **spectacular** afternoon," she said. "Two friends like you, *that* shouldn't be a problem." Then she wheeled away. Joe and Paul never got her name, but they never forgot her either.

Reread for **Comprehension**

Story Structure
Character and Setting

A Character and Setting Chart can help you list important details about characters and settings. These two features are part of the story structure. Use your Character and Setting Chart as you reread "Lunch Counter Encounter" to figure out the characters' traits and information about where and when the story takes place.

Character	Setting

Comprehension

Genre

Historical Fiction tells a story in which fictional characters take part in actual events from the past.

Story Structure

Character and Setting

As you read, use your Character and Setting Chart.

Character	Setting

Read to Find Out

Why is 'Tricia Ann's "special place" different from other places in town?

Goin' Someplace Special

by Patricia C. McKissack
illustrated by Jerry Pinkney

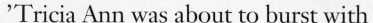

'Tricia Ann was about to burst with
excitement. Crossing her fingers and closing her eyes, she
blurted out her question. "Mama Frances, may I go to Someplace
Special by myself, today? Pretty please? I know where to go get off
the bus and what streets to take and all."

Although it had another name, 'Tricia Ann always called it
Someplace Special because it was her favorite spot in the world.

"Please may I go? Pretty please with marshmallows on top?"

"I don't know if I'm ready to turn you loose in the world,"
Mama Frances answered, tying the sash of 'Tricia Ann's dress.
"Goin' off alone is a mighty big step."

"I'm ready," the girl said, taking a giant leap across the floor.
"See what a big step I can make?"

Mama Frances chuckled, all the time studying her
granddaughter's face. "I trust you'll be particular, and remember
everything I've told you."

"I will, I will," 'Tricia Ann said, real confident-like. Suddenly,
her smile grew into a full grin. "So you're saying I can go?"

"I reckon . . . But you best hurry on 'fore I change my mind."

Pulling her pocketbook up on her shoulder, 'Tricia Ann blew her
grandmother a thank-you kiss. Then she rushed out the door and down
the sidewalk.

"And no matter what," Mama Frances called after her, "hold yo'
head up and act like you b'long to somebody."

At the corner a green and white bus came to a jerky stop and hissed. When the doors folded back, 'Tricia Ann bounded up the steps and dropped in the **fare** same as when Mama Frances was with her.

The girl squared her shoulders, walked to the back, and took a seat behind the Jim Crow sign that said: COLORED SECTION.

'Tricia Ann had seen such signs all her life. She recalled the first time she and Mama Frances had taken this bus ride, and her grandmother had told her, "Those signs can tell us where to sit, but they can't tell us what to think."

"I'm gon' think about Someplace Special." 'Tricia Ann said to herself and turned to look out the window.

Stop by stop the bus began to fill. At the Farmer's Market, people crowded on, carrying bags of fruit and vegetables. Mrs. Grannell, Mama Frances' friend from sewing club, climbed on board. As she inched her way toward the back, 'Tricia Ann noticed that there were no seats left behind the Jim Crow sign. So she stood up and gave Mrs. Grannell hers.

"It's not fair," she said glaring at the empty seats up front.

"No, but that's the way it is, honey," said Mrs. Grannell.

"I don't understand why—" she began. But by now the bus had reached 'Tricia Ann's stop in front of Capitol Square in the heart of downtown. The doors swung open and she hurried off.

"Carry yo'self proud," Mrs. Grannell called out the window as the bus pulled away.

Character

What does Mama Frances tell 'Tricia Ann about the sign on the bus? What does this tell you about the character of Mama Frances?

401

Holding her hat, 'Tricia Ann leaned back as far as she could to see Peace Fountain's magnificent water show. It made her dizzy to watch the sprays that shot into the air, but she liked the feeling and turned 'round and 'round with her arms outstretched. Then, giggling, she staggered on wobbly legs to a nearby bench.

Instantly, 'Tricia Ann leaped to her feet. On the bench was a sign that said: FOR WHITES ONLY.

Her face fell, and she wished for Mama Frances's strong hand to hold. "Silly signs," she muttered as she strutted away on sober legs.

At the edge of the square, she greeted Jimmy Lee, a street vendor. "What's got yo' face all clouded up like a stormy day?" he asked, handing 'Tricia Ann a free pretzel.

"Jim Crow makes me so mad!" she said. "My grandfather was a stonemason on Peace Fountain. Why can't I sit down and enjoy it?"

Jimmy Lee pointed to a sign in Monroe's Restaurant window. He said, "My brother cooks all the food they serve, but do you think we can sit at one of their tables and have a BLT and a cup of coffee together?" Then with a chuckle he whispered, "Not that I'd want to eat anything Jesse cooks. That man can't even now **scald** water."

The light changed and 'Tricia Ann carefully started across the street. "Don't let those signs steal yo' happiness," Jimmy Lee called after her.

'Tricia Ann pulled her shoulders back and fixed her thoughts on being inside that warm and welcoming place where there were no signs. Hurrying up Tenth Avenue, she passed the filling station, and stopped to buy a pop to wash down Jimmy Lee's pretzel.

At the second light, the Southland Hotel rose up in front of her, as **spectacular** as a palace. Mr. John Willis, the hotel's doorman, saw her. "I b'lieve an angel done slipped 'way from heaven," he said, smiling.

'Tricia Ann managed to smile back. Mr. John Willis always said the nicest things. "No, sir. It's just me."

"Your mouth is smiling, but your eyes aren't," he said. Just then a long white car with two police escorts pulled up in front of the hotel. A man with black shiny hair and shy eyes stepped out. Suddenly people were everywhere, screaming and begging for his **autograph**. 'Tricia Ann got caught in the crowd and swept inside.

Setting

What is the time and place of the story? What clues tell you this?

So often she'd wondered what it would feel like to walk on the royal carpet that covered the double-winding staircase, or to stand in the light of the chandelier that looked like a million diamonds strung together. Now, there she was—smack in the middle of the Southland Hotel's grand lobby.

Somebody pointed at her. "What is *she* doing in here?

It seemed as if the whole world had stopped talking, stopped moving, and was staring at her. The manager pushed his way to the front of the crowd. "What makes you think you can come inside? No colored people are allowed!" And he shooed the girl away with his arms.

'Tricia Ann backed out, shaking her head. "I-I didn't mean . . . ," She said, trying hard not to cry.

Hurrying past Mr. John Willis, 'Tricia Ann ran straight into the Mission Church ruins where Mama Frances often stopped to rest. There in the protection of the walled garden, the girl let the tears come. "Getting to Someplace Special isn't worth it," she sobbed. "I'm going home."

"My flowers have been watered already," came a voice above her. It was Blooming Mary, an elderly woman who took care of the garden with neither **permission** nor pay. Everybody said she was addled, but Mama Frances didn't agree. "Blooming Mary is a kind and gentle soul," she'd told 'Tricia Ann.

"You lost, child?" The woman asked.

Trying to steady her voice, 'Tricia Ann answered. "No, ma'am, I just wish my grandmother was here to help me get to Someplace Special."

"You can't get there by yourself?"

"It's too hard. I need my grandmother."

Blooming Mary nodded and thought on the matter.

Then she said, "I believe your granny *is* here, just as my granny is here with me even as I speak. Listen close. Tell me what you hear."

All 'Tricia Ann heard was the distant buzz of a bumblebee. What was Blooming Mary talking about?

But as she listened closer, she began to hear her grandmother's steady voice. "You are somebody, a human being—no better, no worse than anybody else in this world. Gettin' someplace special is not an easy route. But don't study on quittin', just keep walking straight ahead—and you'll make it."

'Tricia Ann recalled these words from many conversations they'd had in this quiet place. They were so comforting, she didn't feel alone anymore. She wiped her eyes and straightened her hat. "You were right, ma'am," the girl told Blooming Mary. "Mama Frances is here. And she wouldn't want me to turn back."

"So, you aren't lost after all," said Blooming Mary, giving 'Tricia Ann a bright orange zinnia.

"No, ma'am, I'm not." And saying good-bye, she headed, real determined-like, on her way.

Two blocks later 'Tricia Ann came to the Grand Music Palace, where a group had gathered for the matinee performance. As the girl approached, a little boy spoke to her. "Howdy, I'm Hickey and I'm six years old today. You comin' in?"

Before 'Tricia Ann could answer, an older girl grabbed his hand. "Hush, boy," she said through **clenched** teeth. "Colored people can't come in the front door. They got to go 'round back and sit up in the Buzzard's Roost. Don't you know nothing?" his sister whispered harshly.

Hickey looked at 'Tricia Ann with wide, wondering eyes. "Are you going to sit up there?"

"In the last three rows of the balcony? Why, I wouldn't sit up there even if watermelons bloomed in January. Besides, I'm going to someplace very, very special," she answered, and then 'Tricia Ann skipped away.

"I want to go where she's goin'" she heard Hickey say as his sister pulled him through the door.

At the corner 'Tricia Ann saw a building rising above all that surrounded it, looking proud in the summer sun. It was much more than bricks and stone. It was an idea. Mama Frances called it a doorway to freedom. When she looked at it, she didn't feel angry or hurt or embarrassed. "At last," she whispered, "I've made it to Someplace Special."

Before bounding up the steps and through the front door, 'Tricia Ann stopped to look up at the message **chiseled** in stone across the front facing:

PUBLIC LIBRARY: ALL ARE WELCOME.

PUBLIC LIBRARY: ALL ARE WELCOME.

411

Visit Someplace Special with
Patricia C. McKissack and Jerry Pinkney

Patricia C. McKissack based this story on her life growing up in Nashville, Tennessee. Like 'Tricia Ann, she couldn't go many places, but she could always go to the public library. Patricia wanted children to know that even though life sometimes seems unfair, love and determination often make things turn out all right. It was her teachers, she says, who started her on the road to books, reading, and the public library.

Jerry Pinkney started drawing by copying from comic books and magazines, just like his two older brothers. In junior high school, he sketched people he saw on the street, and has been drawing and painting ever since. Jerry has even drawn eleven postage stamps for the U.S. Postal Service. "I'd rather draw than do anything else!" he says.

Another book by Patricia
C. McKissack and Jerry Pinkney:
Mirandy and Brother Wind

Find out more about Patricia C. McKissack and Jerry Pinkney at **www.macmillanmh.com**

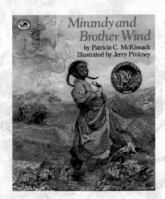

Author's Purpose

The author both shares information about life under Jim Crow and tells an entertaining story. Identify historic details.

412

Comprehension Check

Summarize

Use your Character and Setting Chart to help you summarize *Goin' Someplace Special*. Be sure your summary includes the most important information from the story.

Character	Setting

Think and Compare

1. How would the story be different if the author had set her story in the present instead of the past? **Story Structure: Character and Setting**

2. Reread page 410. How do you think the library was "a doorway to freedom"? **Critical**

3. How would you react to a law that denied you **permission** to sit in the front of a bus or enter a hotel lobby? **Analyze**

4. Explain what Mama Frances meant when she said that getting someplace special is not always easy. Do you agree or disagree with her opinion? Explain your answer. **Evaluate**

5. Reread "Lunch Counter Encounter" on pages 394–395. Compare Joe's experience at the drugstore to 'Tricia Ann's experience on the bus and in the hotel lobby. How are their situations the same? How are they different? Use evidence from both stories to support your answer. **Reading/Writing Across Texts**

Social Studies

Genre

An **Autobiography** is an account of events in a person's life that is written in that person's own words.

Text Feature

A **Time Line** is a diagram of several events arranged in the order in which they took place. A time line helps to organize information in an easy, visual way.

Content Vocabulary

unconstitutional
banned
boycott
segregation

by Ruby Bridges

Ruby Bridges was six years old in November 1960, and she was about to make history. A judge had recently ruled that it was unconstitutional for African American students to be banned from attending the same school as white students. Ruby Bridges was the first black student to attend William Frantz Elementary School in New Orleans. Here's an account in her own words of her first day at her new school and of the events that followed:

Once we were inside the building, the marshals walked us up a flight of stairs. The school office was at the top. My mother and I went in and were told to sit in the principal's office. The marshals sat outside. There were windows in the room where we waited. That meant everybody passing by could see us. I remember noticing everyone was white.

The artist Norman Rockwell painted this picture called *The Problem We All Live With.*

All day long white parents rushed into the office. They were upset. They were arguing and pointing at us. When they took their children to school that morning, the parents hadn't been sure whether William Frantz would be integrated that day or not. After my mother and I arrived, they ran into classrooms and dragged their children out of the school. From behind the windows in the office, all I saw was confusion. I told myself that this must be the way it is in a big school.

That whole first day, my mother and I just sat and waited. We didn't talk to anybody. I remember watching a big, round clock on the wall. When it was 3:00 and time to go home, I was glad. I had thought my new school would be hard, but the first day was easy.

When we left school that first day, the crowd outside was even bigger and louder than it had been in the morning. There were reporters and film cameras and people everywhere. I guess the police couldn't keep them behind the barricades. It seemed to take us a long time to get to the marshals' car.

Entering the school with U.S. Marshals

Marching Through History

SKILL Reading a Time Line

One way to review events from history is to organize them on a time line.

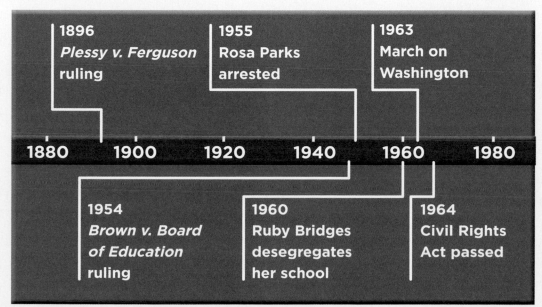

1896 *Plessy v. Ferguson* ruling	1955 Rosa Parks arrested	1963 March on Washington

1880 — 1900 — 1920 — 1940 — 1960 — 1980

1954 *Brown v. Board of Education* ruling	1960 Ruby Bridges desegregates her school	1964 Civil Rights Act passed

Later on I learned there had been protestors in front of the integrated schools the whole day. They wanted to be sure white parents would **boycott** the school and not let their children attend. Groups of high school boys, joining the protestors, paraded up and down the street and sang new verses to old hymns. Their favorite was "Battle Hymn of the Republic," in which they changed the chorus to "Glory, glory, **segregation**, the South will rise again." Many of the boys carried signs and said awful things, but most of all I remember seeing a black doll in a coffin, which frightened me more than anything else.

After the first day, I was glad to get home. I wanted to change my clothes and go outside to find my friends. My mother wasn't too worried about me because the police had set up barricades at each end of the block. Only local residents were allowed on our street. That afternoon I taught a friend the chant I had learned: "Two, four, six, eight, we don't want to integrate." My friend and I didn't know what the words meant, but we would jump rope to it every day after school.

My father heard about the trouble at school. That night when he came home from work, he said I was his "brave little Ruby."

The next day brave Ruby and her mother drove to school with the marshals. Here's more of Ruby's amazing story, in her own words:

When we finally got into the building, my new teacher was there to meet us. Her name was Mrs. Henry. She was young and white. I had not spent time with a white person before, so I was uneasy at first. Mrs. Henry led us upstairs to the second floor. As we went up, we hardly saw anyone else in the building. The white students were not coming to class. The halls were so quiet, I could hear the noise the marshals' shoes made on the shiny hardwood floors.

Mrs. Henry took us into a classroom and said to have a seat. When I looked around, the room was empty. There were rows of desks, but no children. I thought we were too early, but Mrs. Henry said we were right on time. My mother sat down at the back of the room. I took a seat up front, and Mrs. Henry began to teach.

I spent the whole first day with Mrs. Henry in the classroom. I wasn't allowed to have lunch in the cafeteria or go outside for recess, so we just stayed in our room. The marshals sat outside. If I had to go to the bathroom, the marshals walked me down the hall.

on the steps of William Frantz Elementary School

My mother sat in the classroom that day, but not the next. When the marshals came to the house on Wednesday morning, my mother said, "Ruby, I can't go to school with you today, but don't be afraid. The marshals will take care of you. Be good now, and don't cry."

I started to cry anyway, but before I knew it, I was off to school by myself.

Ruby Bridges finished the school year, and she returned in the fall. As years passed and Ruby continued in school, the fight for civil rights continued as well. In 1995 Ruby and Mrs. Henry decided to work together. Now they visit classrooms around the country, sharing what they have learned.

Ruby tells students that schools can bring people together. Ruby and Mrs. Henry are no longer a class of two.

Mrs. Henry and Ruby Bridges

Connect and Compare

1. Use the time line on page 415 to find how many years separate the arrest of Rosa Parks and the Civil Rights Act. **Reading a Time Line**

2. How is reading Ruby Bridges's own words different from reading about her experience from a secondary source? **Evaluate**

3. Think about "Through My Eyes" and *Goin' Someplace Special*. How are the experiences that Ruby Bridges and 'Tricia Ann went through similar? How are they different? Explain. **Reading/Writing Across Texts**

Social Studies Activity

Research a person involved in the civil rights movement. Write a summary of his or her life. Include a time line of important events in the life of this person.

 Find out more about civil rights at **www.macmillanmh.com**

Writer's Craft

Facts and Opinions

The first sentence, or lead, in a news article tells the most important fact. Details telling when, where, and why something happened appear later in the story. Include only **facts** and avoid words that show your **opinions**.

> My lead sentence presents the most important fact.

> After I wrote the lead, I presented only facts.

Write a News Article

Civil Rights Celebration

by Sunny C.

PHILADELPHIA, 2008 Students observed a special day of learning about the civil rights movement during the first civil rights celebration at Smith Middle School. The event was on February 20, after lunch in the auditorium.

The celebration began with a video about the 1963 March on Washington that showed Martin Luther King, Jr.'s famous "I Have a Dream" speech. The guest speaker, Mr. Ellis, who walked in the march, had many eyewitness stories. He talked about what it was like to grow up with segregation and of his involvement in the movement. There was also an art exhibit called "Heroes of Freedom," which covered the auditorium with colorful student drawings of famous leaders.

Students who attended the celebration said it was inspiring. Principal Thompson thanked the teachers, parents, and students who helped with the event. She said it was the perfect way to celebrate the victories and heroes of the civil rights movement.

Your Turn

Find an event happening in your school or community, like a play, that interests you. Attend this event and take notes of your observations. Write a news article telling others about it. Remember to grab your readers' attention with an interesting lead. Present important facts later in the article. Use the writer's checklist to check your writing.

Writer's Checklist

 Ideas and Content: Did I write about an event I attended in my school or community?

 Organization: Does my lead present the most important fact? Did I include enough supporting details in the rest of the article?

Voice: Did I state the **facts** and avoid **opinions**?

 Word Choice: Did I choose the right words?

 Sentence Fluency: Did I provide a variety of sentence types?

 Conventions: Did I check to be sure that all pronouns agree with their antecedents? Did I proofread for spelling errors?

419

ANIMAL DEFENSES

Talk About It

How do animals defend themselves when they are scared or threatened?

LOG ON Find out more about animal defenses at **www.macmillanmh.com**

Nosey and the Porcupine

by Susannah Heil

Nosey knew that she was supposed to stay in the yard, but today the gate was left open. Every time the puppy moved her head to the left, she caught a **glimpse** of the woods up the street. She enjoyed this brief peek at the forest. It reminded her of the time her owners took her there when they went for a jog.

For Nosey there was nothing as wonderful as dashing among the trees and sniffing the flowers. The woods were **secluded**, hardly visited by people from outside the neighborhood. Nosey didn't think it would be a problem if she went exploring for just a little while. After all, she was called Nosey for a reason. Her name described her usual, day-to-day **behavior**.

Today she would have to be especially quiet on this secret outing. Her neighbor, Mr. Garcia, was out fishing in the **arroyo**. Lucky for Nosey she slipped by her neighbor and headed toward the woods without **arousing** his attention.

Soon after Nosey arrived in the woods, a butterfly landed on her nose. She reached for it with her paw, but it flew away. Then Nosey spotted it again on a berry bush. When she was within striking distance, she jumped. The butterfly fluttered out of Nosey's reach once more, but it was too late for the puppy to stop. She landed directly on top of the berry bush with a crash. At first, she was **stunned** by the sudden fall. Then she was shocked to find herself face to face with a sleeping porcupine! The porcupine was **nestled** snugly under the bush.

The arrival of a noisy visitor caused the porcupine to wake up. Nosey wasn't afraid of the small porcupine. However, she *was* curious. She had never seen a porcupine before so she gently sniffed at it with her nose. By this time the porcupine had turned himself around. The quills on his tail were standing up, ready to be released. Suddenly Nosey found herself with a nose full of quills.

Nosey pawed at the quills, but they were firmly stuck. She had no choice but to head for home after this **unpleasant** experience. When Mr. Garcia saw her coming, he began to laugh. "Nosey," he said, "I see once again you've lived up to your reputation. You've had your nose exactly where it doesn't belong."

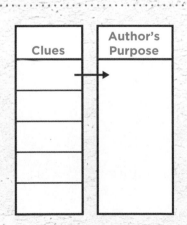

Reread for **Comprehension**

Evaluate
Author's Purpose

An author writes to inform, persuade, inquire, or entertain. An Author's Purpose Chart helps you evaluate the information in a story to figure out the author's purpose. Use your Author's Purpose Chart as you reread the selection to find the author's purpose.

Clues	Author's Purpose

Comprehension

Genre

Realistic Fiction tells an invented story that could have happened in real life.

Evaluate

Author's Purpose

As you read, use your Author's Purpose Chart.

Clues	Author's Purpose

Read to Find Out

What is the author's purpose for writing a story about Carlos?

Carlos and the Skunk

Award Winning Selection

written by
Jan Romero Stevens
illustrated by
Jeanne Arnold

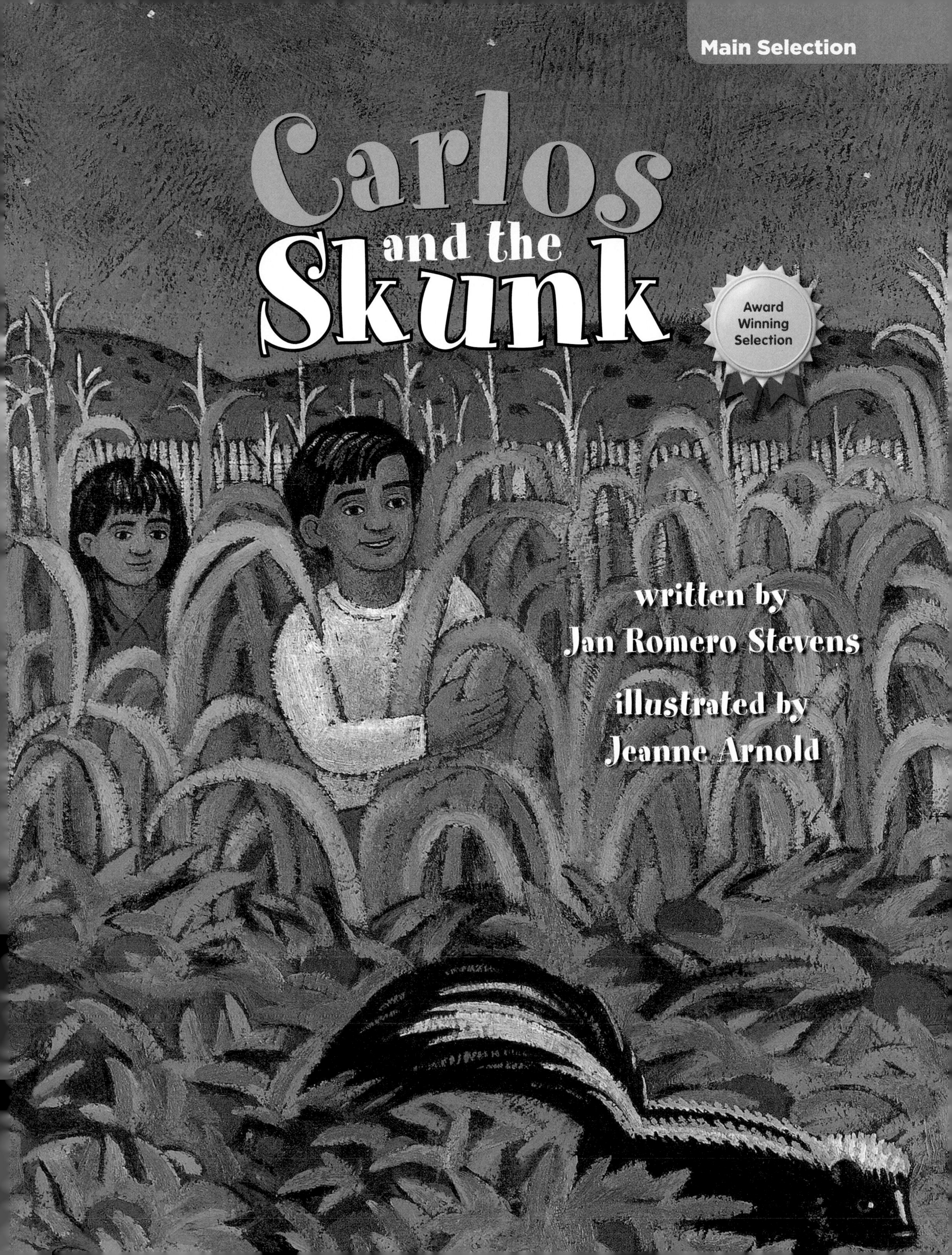

Carlos could not remember how long he and Gloria had been best friends.

When they were little, Gloria's mother would prop them up on old catalogs at the kitchen table while she strung red chiles together or rolled the dough for tortillas. If they were at Carlos's house, his mother would let them play in the garden while she sorted through the shiny green chiles, ripe red tomatoes, and sweet corn.

It seemed as if Carlos and Gloria were always together, but as they grew older, Carlos's feelings toward his friend started to change. He began gazing at himself in the mirror, combing his hair this way and that to see which looked better. He started showing off for Gloria, wanting her to notice how brave and smart he was becoming.

Carlos and Gloria lived in the fertile Española Valley **nestled** in the mountains of northern New Mexico. Their thick-walled adobe homes, with high tin roofs and matching gardens, were within walking distance from one another.

After school each day, Gloria and Carlos did their chores—weeding the garden, feeding the chickens, and doing their homework. After dinner, they were allowed to play.

One fall evening, when they were running through the cornfield playing hide and seek, they caught a **glimpse** of a striped skunk slinking through the shadows of the garden. The children had seen the skunk many times before. It had only two toes on its right front paw, and they had nicknamed it Dos Dedos (Two Toes).

Gloria feared the chance of **arousing** the skunk's anger and kept far away from it. But one afternoon, Carlos, wanting to impress Gloria, moved closer and closer until he could clearly see the narrow, single white stripe running from its head onto its tail.

"Carlos, you'd better be careful," whispered Gloria as Carlos inched along on his stomach toward the skunk.

"Gloria, don't worry. I know just how to catch a skunk," Carlos boasted. "You know what I heard? If you pick a skunk up by its tail, it can't spray you."

Gloria covered her mouth and giggled.

"Oh, Carlos," she said. *"No puedes creer todo lo que te dicen—*you can't believe everything you hear."

"But it's true," Carlos insisted to his doubting friend, and he became more determined than ever to prove himself right. He went to sleep that night still pondering over how to catch the skunk.

Author's Purpose
What do you think is the purpose in writing this scene? Why?

The next day, Carlos had planned to take Gloria fishing so he awoke early and got dressed. His mother prepared warm flour tortillas, fried eggs, and fresh salsa for breakfast. Salsa was a family tradition in Carlos's home. Made from tomatoes and green chiles grown in the garden, the salsa was spicy and tasty. Carlos spooned it on just about everything—from breakfast to dinner.

After breakfast, Carlos rushed outside to get his fishing pole and a can for worms. Rounding the corner of his house, he saw Gloria waiting for him by the gate. As they began walking down the road together, they saw Dos Dedos in the garden.

Qué suerte! (What luck!) thought Carlos. "I will catch Dos Dedos this time!"

Carlos gave no thought to what he might do with the skunk if he did catch it, but instead began creeping up behind it. He got closer and closer until he was inches away. For just a moment, Carlos hesitated, then winked at Gloria before he reached out and grabbed the tail. In an instant, the skunk's tail arched, and Carlos was sprayed from head to toe.

With a gasp, Carlos fell backward onto the ground. He was so **stunned** he hardly realized what had happened. He had never smelled such a strong odor. His eyes itched. He coughed and snorted and blew his nose. He did his best not to cry in front of Gloria.

Quite unconcerned, Dos Dedos disappeared down the side of an **arroyo**. And Carlos ran off to the river—leaving both Gloria and his fishing pole far behind.

Carlos chose a **secluded** spot and pulled off all his clothes as fast as he could. The smell of them was unbearable. He jumped into the stream and washed out his clothing, laying it out on a branch to dry in the sun. By afternoon his shirt and pants were dry, but the strong odor still lingered, especially on his shoes. He dressed and walked the long way home, climbing up and down the sides of the arroyos and stopping to gather piñon nuts. When he finally reached his house, he carefully took off his shoes and left them by the back door.

When his mother came into the kitchen, she noticed a strange smell, but before she could question Carlos, he slipped out the door and into the garden.

Carlos had heard that tomato juice helped to get rid of the smell of skunk, so he picked every ripe tomato he could find and sneaked into the bathroom. He squeezed the tomatoes into the bathtub and all over his hair, scrubbing himself as hard as he could with a washrag.

Beginning to think he smelled better, he crawled into bed and fell asleep quickly after his very **unpleasant** day.

The next morning was Sunday, and Mamá was up early, patting and shaping the dough for tortillas.

Dressed in his best shirt and pants, Carlos sat down at the table.

"Carlos, you look very nice for church this morning," said Mamá as she untied her flowered apron. "Where are your shoes?"

"They're outside, Mamá. I will get them when we leave," said Carlos, feeling uneasy.

Carlos's family walked to the church near their home. When they arrived, they squeezed into a bench near the back. Carlos was pleased that he was able to sit next to Gloria.

But a most peculiar thing happened in church that day.

As the choir began a hymn, some of the singers began to make strange faces and cover their noses with handkerchiefs. The priest, as he walked to the altar, sneezed loudly and cleared his throat.

The people in the first few rows of the congregation turned to each other with puzzled looks. The women began vigorously fanning their faces with their church programs. The children started squirming and pinched their noses. Little by little the strange **behavior** began working its way toward the back of the church.

Carlos couldn't figure out what was going on until he looked down at his feet. He was sitting next to an air vent for the church's heating system. The smell from his shoes, which he had forgotten to clean after being sprayed by Dos Dedos, was spreading through the heating ducts to the entire church.

"Papá, I think we better go home," whispered Carlos, hoping no one would realize he was the source of the terrible smell.

Several families began heading for the door. The priest dismissed the service early.

Embarrassed, Carlos pushed his way out of the church. He heard Gloria calling to him, but he bolted through the door, and ran all the way home. He untied his shoes, pulled them off, and left them on the back doorstep. Then he hurried to his room and shut the door.

Troubled over how he might rid himself of the strong-smelling shoes, Carlos stayed in his bedroom until his mother called him for dinner. While they were eating, his parents noticed he was unusually quiet but said nothing to him.

Finally, when dinner was over, Papá turned to Carlos.

"Carlos, I've noticed your shoes are looking a little small," said Papá, with a glance toward Mamá. "Isn't it time for a new pair?"

Carlos nodded, breathing a sigh of relief.

"Oh, *sí, sí,* Papá," he stammered. "My feet are getting too big for those shoes now."

The next day, Carlos and Papá drove to town. After trying on several pairs of shoes, Carlos chose a pair of heeled cowboy boots that made him appear much taller.

A few weeks passed and Carlos forgot about his encounter with the skunk. One evening, after a big dinner of pinto beans, rice, tortillas, and his favorite salsa, he decided to visit Gloria. He put on his new boots and took a good look at his hair in the mirror. As he was getting ready to leave, his father called him outside.

"I need your help," said Papá, and he pointed beneath the bushes alongside the house.

Carlos could just make out the shape of a small, black-and-white animal with three little ones that had made their home under the leaves.

"*Dios mío!*" ("Oh my goodness!") said Carlos. "What will we do?"

"It's no problem, Carlos," said Papá. "You know what I hear? You can catch a skunk if you pick it up by its tail. You go first."

Carlos's nose and eyes began to water just with the thought of it.

"Oh, Papá, *no puedes creer todo lo que te dicen*—you know you can't believe everything you hear," Carlos said, and he drew himself up a little taller, smoothed back his hair, and headed for Gloria's house.

Author's Purpose
What was the author's purpose in writing this story? Did the author write with a second purpose in mind?

Fresh Tomato Salsa

3 tomatoes, diced

¼ white or yellow onion, diced

2-3 scallions with green tops, chopped

1 medium clove garlic, minced

2 teaspoons vinegar

1 teaspoon vegetable or olive oil

3-4 sprigs of cilantro, chopped

1 roasted green chile or 2 serrano chiles, diced
(or 2 tablespoons canned green chile)

1 teaspoon salt

¼ teaspoon pepper

Mix all ingredients in a food processor, leaving salsa chunky, or stir by hand. Chill. Spoon over anything—eggs, beans, tacos—or use as a dip for tortilla chips.

Trading Tales with
Jan Romero Stevens and Jeanne Arnold

Jan Romero Stevens said there was nothing better than watching children enjoy her books, in both English and Spanish. Jan loved the Southwest and learned more about her Hispanic heritage by studying Spanish with her kids. To make the Carlos stories realistic, she based them on things that happened to her family and friends. Jan always enjoyed writing. Besides writing the "Carlos" series, Jan worked for newspapers and magazines as a reporter and editor.

Jeanne Arnold is an illustrator and a painter. Her work includes all three books in the "Carlos" series, as well as *When You Were Just a Little Girl* by B.G. Hennessy. Jeanne has spent time backpacking in the Southwest. This helps her capture the regional flavor of the "Carlos" books.

Other books by Jan Romero Stevens and Jeanne Arnold: *Carlos and the Carnival* and *Carlos Digs to China*

LOG ON Find out more about Jan Romero Stevens and Jeanne Arnold at **www.macmillanmh.com**

Author's Purpose

What clues help you to figure out the author's purpose for writing? How well did Jan Romero Stevens succeed in her purpose? Explain.

Comprehension Check

Summarize

Summarize the events of *Carlos and the Skunk*. Be sure the summary includes the most important information from the story.

Think and Compare

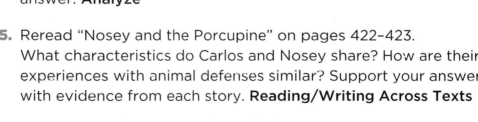

Clues	Author's Purpose

1. What was the Author's Purpose for choosing a skunk as the animal Carlos wants to catch? Use your Author's Purpose Chart to help explain your answer. **Evaluate: Author's Purpose**

2. Reread page 436 of *Carlos and the Skunk*. Explain why Papá asked Carlos if his shoes were too small. **Analyze**

3. Would showing off for a friend be worth suffering **unpleasant** consequences, such as being sprayed by a skunk? **Explain**

4. Explain why you agree or disagree with the advice, "You can't believe everything you hear." Include specific examples in your answer. **Analyze**

5. Reread "Nosey and the Porcupine" on pages 422–423. What characteristics do Carlos and Nosey share? How are their experiences with animal defenses similar? Support your answer with evidence from each story. **Reading/Writing Across Texts**

Animal Self-Defense

by Elle Wainwright

If you were a wild animal about to become someone's dinner, what would you do? Run? Hide? Fight? Animals may do any of these things when they feel threatened. Nature provides them with special weapons of protection.

Wild animals live dangerous lives. While they hunt for food, they must be careful not to be caught by another animal. To help them stay alive, animals have developed adaptations.

Hide and Seek

Some adaptations help animals hide. If an animal can remain unseen, it will be safe. Of course, an animal cannot really become invisible. However, it can seem to disappear by using **camouflage**. A baby deer can lie perfectly still in a bed of grasses and leaves. With its speckled fur, the little deer is almost invisible. A flounder swimming along the ocean shore is difficult to see. As it passes over sand, it turns a pale sandy color. When it swims over dark rocks, it turns dark. By changing its color, a flounder can avoid attacks by larger fish that would like to eat it. Some animals can hide without even moving! Both the **chameleon** and the octopus can quickly change their skin color and blend into the background.

Another kind of camouflage has to do with an animal's shape. Think of a bird hunting a butterfly for breakfast. The leaf butterfly has wings that resemble leaves. The bird is not looking for leaves to eat, so it will fly right past a leaf butterfly. A thornbug is another animal whose shape protects it from its enemies. Because thornbugs look like prickly thorns, their enemies stay away. There are also animals that change their shapes to hide. One inchworm stiffens up so that it is usually mistaken for a stick.

The octopus (above) and the chameleon (right) change color to blend into their surroundings.

443

What a Stink!

No one can forget the smell of a skunk. Skunks use their odor for self-defense. Have you ever wondered how skunks produce their smell?

These small animals have a physical adaptation that helps them protect themselves. They have two grape-sized sacs under the skin below their tails that hold a strong-smelling liquid. Skunks can shoot this powerful liquid spray and hit a target accurately from up to ten feet away.

How do skunks decide that it's time to get the jets firing? The distance of an enemy plays a big part in the decision. Skunks don't see well. When an enemy comes closer than four feet to a skunk, the skunk finally sees it. Then watch out! First, the skunk freezes. Then, it points its tail straight up as a warning. If the enemy doesn't go away, the skunk's tail bends over until it touches its back. Then the skunk turns around and squirts, stunning its enemy.

Skunks aren't the only animals that spray in self defense. Stinkbugs also spray a smelly liquid when threatened.

Catch Me if You Can!

What happens when a bird is surprised by a person or other animal it considers a threat? The bird flies away. Birds are one of many creatures that avoid danger by moving faster than their enemies. Some animals, such as zebras, travel in herds. If predators appear, the whole herd quickly flees. Most of the herd escapes. Only the slowest zebras get caught.

a herd of zebras

**What is that *smell*?
It might be a stinkbug.**

Ouch!

Would you touch a black-and-yellow-striped insect? Probably not because you know that yellow jackets can give you a painful sting. Animals that eat insects also avoid yellow jackets. They avoid an insect called a syrphid (SUHR-fuhd) fly even though it is harmless. Why? The syrphid fly fools insect eaters because it looks like a stinging wasp. Looking like something else, especially something unpleasant, is called **mimicry.**

Animals have developed many other amazing ways to stay safe. Take a look at the animals you find in your neighborhood, even the insects. How do they defend themselves against other animals that want to attack them?

A syrphid fly (left) fools its enemies by looking like a wasp (below).

Connect and Compare

1. How do the headings used in "Animal Self-Defense" engage the reader's attention? **Headings**

2. Of the adaptations you have read about, which kind of adaptation would you choose for yourself and why? **Evaluate**

3. If Carlos in *Carlos and the Skunk* had read the article "Animal Self-Defense," do you think he would have picked up the skunk? Why or why not? Explain your answer.
Reading/Writing Across Texts

Science Activity

Do research on an animal or insect that uses adaptations to survive. Write a magazine article describing how the animal defends itself against its enemies.

 Find out more about animal defenses at **www.macmillanmh.com**

Write a Scientific Observation

▼ **Writer's Craft**

Formal and Informal Language

When writers record scientific observations, they choose words that carefully describe what their five senses detect. Writers use **formal language** in scientific observations and avoid **informal language** that may show emotions.

When writing a scientific observation of a gray squirrel, I used formal language.

I chose exact words to describe the squirrel.

The Gray Squirrel

by Adam P.

I sat in a lawn chair in my backyard to begin my observation of a gray squirrel. It was five o'clock in the afternoon. The squirrel I watched was about 20 inches long. It had a dark gray back with splotches of brown. Its stomach was a silver color. It had a thick, bushy tail.

The squirrel was running across the lawn when I first saw it. It paused about ten yards away from me and made a clicking sound. Then it sat up on its hind legs. It held an acorn in its front paws and gnawed on it. The squirrel heard me sneeze and quickly climbed up an oak tree and disappeared into a hole.

Your Turn

Observe an animal of your choice. Write a paragraph in which you record your scientific observations. Remember to be precise and to use formal language in your descriptions. Choose words that describe what your senses detect. Use the writer's checklist to check your writing.

Writer's Checklist

✓ **Ideas and Content:** Did I observe the animal long enough to note plenty of details?

✓ **Organization:** Did I present my observations in a logical order?

✓ **Voice:** Did I use **formal language** and leave **informal language** and personal reactions out of my writing?

✓ **Word Choice:** Did I choose precise words to describe my observations?

✓ **Sentence Fluency:** Did my observations allow the reader to follow along at a steady pace?

✓ **Conventions:** Did I use subject and object pronouns correctly? Did I proofread for spelling errors?

Talk About It

What are the characteristics of a democratic form of government?

LOG ON Find out more about government at **www.macmillanmh.com**

Democracy

Vocabulary

compelled

presidential

disrespectful

unenthusiastically

succeed

preoccupied

Political cartoons
by Thomas Nast

PARTY ANIMALS

Were our country's two major political parties **compelled** to choose a donkey and an elephant as their symbols? Believe it or not, there was no pressure involved. Cartoons were behind both choices.

The donkey was first associated with Democrat Andrew Jackson's 1828 **presidential** campaign. Most of his opponents called him a donkey, intending to be **disrespectful**. But instead of taking the name as an insult, Jackson turned the tables on his opponents. He used the image of the strong-willed animal on his campaign posters. Later, newspaper cartoonist Thomas Nast used the donkey to represent the Democrats in his political cartoons. That's what made the symbol famous.

A Thomas Nast cartoon is also responsible for associating the elephant with Republicans. The Republicans lost the White House to the Democrats in 1877. Nast drew a cartoon of an elephant walking into a trap set by a donkey. The donkey was already a symbol for the Democrats. Nast chose the elephant as a symbol for the Republicans because elephants are intelligent but easily controlled. At the time, the Republicans reacted **unenthusiastically** to this image. But over time, they embraced it with enthusiasm and gave it new meaning.

Republicans today say the elephant is a good symbol because it is strong and dignified. Democrats take pride in the donkey because it is smart and brave.

 Find out more about political parties at **www.macmillanmh.com**

Presidential Succession

Who would take over if the President of the United States died, resigned, or was removed from office? The plan for who's next in line is known as presidential succession. It works like this: If for some reason the Vice President cannot serve, the Speaker of the House is next in line for the presidency, and so on down the line.

- ★ **Vice President**
- ★ **Speaker of the House**
- ★ **President Pro Tempore of the Senate**
- ★ **Secretary of State**
- ★ **Secretary of the Treasury**
- ★ **Secretary of Defense**
- ★ **Attorney General**
- ★ **Secretary of the Interior**

REMEMBER: An official cannot **succeed** to the presidency unless that person meets the Constitutional requirements for being president. Those are:

- ★ **Must be at least 35 years old**
- ★ **Must be a natural-born citizen of the United States**
- ★ **Must have lived in the United States for at least 14 years**

Lyndon B. Johnson is sworn in as President after the assassination of John F. Kennedy. Jacqueline Kennedy stands next to him.

the Great Seal of the United States

Aside from creating a new nation, what were three of our founding leaders **preoccupied** with? The answer: the Great Seal. Benjamin Franklin, John Adams, and Thomas Jefferson began designing the Great Seal in 1776. The Great Seal is printed on the back of the $1 bill and is used on certain government documents, such as foreign treaties. The bald eagle, our national bird, is at the center of the seal. It holds a banner in its beak. The motto on the banner says *E pluribus unum,* which is Latin for "out of many, one." This refers to the colonies that united to make a nation. In one claw the eagle holds an olive branch, a symbol of peace. In the other claw it carries arrows to symbolize war.

Comprehension

Genre

A **Nonfiction Article** in a newspaper or magazine presents facts and information.

Evaluate

Make Generalizations

A generalization is a broad statement that is made by combining the facts presented in a text with the reader's own prior knowledge.

Getting Out the VOTE

Who votes, who doesn't vote, and why?

WHO CAN VOTE?

ANYONE WHO IS:

 18 years of age

 a citizen of the United States who meets the residency requirements of his or her state

Voters wait in line to cast their ballots.

452

Poll workers for the 1980 presidential primaries

Before one national election, carpenter Robert Pike walked door to door in Las Vegas, Nevada, asking his neighbors to vote on Election Day. A famous musician gave a special concert just to encourage people to vote in her home state of Missouri. Across the nation volunteers made phone calls, sent e-mail reminders, even offered to drive voters to the polls, just to get as many people as possible to vote.

Why are they so **preoccupied** with this effort? Did they **succeed**? Believe it or not, only a little more than half of voting age Americans typically bother to vote in a **presidential** election. In 1996 voter turnout sank to 48.9%—the lowest figure since the 1920s. The highest voter turnout was in the election of 1960.

Excuses, Excuses!

People with illnesses, disabilities, and emergencies have good reasons for not voting. The rest—well, you be the judge. Here are the top reasons people gave for not voting in a recent presidential election.

1. No time off or too busy
2. Not interested
3. Ill, disabled, or had an emergency
4. Didn't like the candidates
5. Out of town
6. Other reasons
7. Forgot

453

Even in 1960 only about 63% of the people who were eligible to vote actually went to the polls. In other words, almost 40% of eligible voters did not feel **compelled** to exercise their right as citizens.

When we consider how hard Americans have fought for the right to vote, it seems **disrespectful** not to vote. It's puzzling that so many people stay away on Election Day.

African Americans gained the constitutional right to vote in 1870. But many African Americans were denied their lawful voting rights for nearly a hundred years after that. The states where they lived made

WHO VOTED IN 2004?

AGE	% WHO VOTED
18-29	17%
30-44	29%
45-59	30%
60+	24%

tricky rules designed to exclude them. The Voting Rights Act of 1965 put an end to this illegal practice.

Women weren't allowed to vote until 1920. Until 1971, Americans had to be at least 21 years old to vote. That year the voting age was lowered to 18. But young voters have responded **unenthusiastically** to elections since then. They have the worst turnout record of all. Political groups have responded by trying to register voters at rock concerts and many other places where young people go.

Voters cast their ballots in the 2000 presidential primary.

Think and Compare

1. What are two methods used to try to get people to vote on Election Day?

2. What generalization can you make about voters who are between the ages of 45 and 59?

3. If you were eligible to vote now, do you think you would vote or not? Explain the reasons for your answer.

4. Do you think the choice of vice-presidential candidate influences how most people vote? Do you think it should?

455

![Test Prep] **Test Strategy**

On My Own

The answer is not in the selection. Form an opinion about what you read for questions 4 and 5.

Moscow is a crowded city, but Russia is the "roomiest" country in the world.

WELCOME TO RUSSIA

St. Basil's Cathedral, Moscow

Stretching all the way across northern Asia and into Europe, Russia is by far the biggest country in the world. Its plains, mountains, and vast forests are rich with gold, coal, oil, timber, and other natural resources.

Throughout Russia's history, its rulers have often kept information about the country secret. No wonder former British Prime Minister Winston Churchill described Russia as "a riddle wrapped in a mystery."

In 1922 Russia became part of a group of countries called the Union of Soviet Socialist Republics (U.S.S.R.). The U.S.S.R. had a form of government called communism. In communist nations, the government owns all property and businesses. For almost 50 years after World War II, the U.S. and the U.S.S.R. were bitter enemies. That period is known as the Cold War, because the two enemies never fought with weapons, just words.

In 1991 the U.S.S.R. was dissolved, and Russia once again became an independent nation. It is no longer ruled by a communist government. As a result, relations between the U.S. and Russia have slowly improved.

Russia is known for its strong traditions in music, ballet, theater, and literature. Moscow is Russia's capital and largest city.

Directions: Answer the questions.

1. **Which of the following statements is true about Russia?**

   A It is a communist country now.

   B It is a small country.

   C It is rich in natural resources and culture.

   D Russia has been renamed the Soviet Union.

2. **How do you think the Cold War affected people in our country?**

   A Few people were able to travel to the U.S.S.R.

   B The U.S.S.R. was the biggest country in the world and the most respected.

   C Americans feared that the Cold War would become a real war.

   D Our cultural events were no longer being held.

3. **Which of the following statements can be made about a communist country?**

   A The government controls the economy.

   B It depends on natural resources to make money.

   C It prefers to fight wars with all its enemies.

   D It values culture more than business.

4. **Why do you think Russia was "a riddle wrapped in a mystery"?**

5. **Why is it important for countries around the world to work together? Explain your answer.**

Tip

Form an opinion.

Write to a Prompt

A student from a big city in the United States is going to spend the summer with relatives in a quiet Russian village. Write a one-page story about this character's experience.

I wrote about the way my problem was solved.

The Summer with Alexei

As the bus came to a stop, Tim knew this was going to be an unusual summer. He felt as though he had landed on Mars, but a sign with his name on it brought him right back down to Earth -- to Russia, to be exact.

The sign was held up by his cousin Alexei. Alexei's English wasn't very good, and Tim's Russian was even worse. Alexei took Tim back to his family's house. Inside there was no computer and no DVD player. The television received only three channels.

As Tim began thinking up excuses for returning home early, he heard a guitar. Alexei was playing, and he motioned to Tim to join him. Alexei began to play a popular American song, and the two boys ended up singing together all night long.

All summer Tim and Alexei sang songs in both English and Russian. Alexei even taught Tim how to play the guitar. It turned out to be a great summer after all.

458

Writing Prompt

You are traveling by train in Western Europe at night. In the morning you wake up to find you are on the wrong train. This one has traveled to Russia! You don't speak Russian. You don't know anyone there. You need to reach your original destination. Write a story about how you solve your problem.

Writer's Checklist

- ☑ Ask yourself, who will read my story?
- ☑ Think about your purpose for writing.
- ☑ Plan your writing before beginning.
- ☑ Use details to support your story.
- ☑ Be sure your story has a problem and a solution.
- ☑ Use your best spelling, grammar, and punctuation.

Talk About It

What is the most extreme weather experience you have had? What happened and what did you learn from it?

LOG ON Find out more about extreme weather at **www.macmillanmh.com**

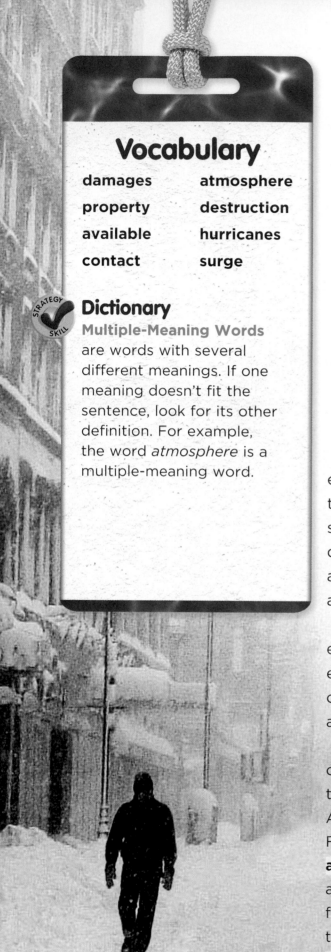

Vocabulary

damages	atmosphere
property	destruction
available	hurricanes
contact	surge

Dictionary

Multiple-Meaning Words are words with several different meanings. If one meaning doesn't fit the sentence, look for its other definition. For example, the word *atmosphere* is a multiple-meaning word.

THE EXTREME COSTS OF EXTREME WEATHER

by Eliana Rodriguez

Every now and then, nature provides examples of extreme weather. At these times the temperature, wind, water, and air pressure sometimes go wild. The result can be billions of dollars in **damages** to **property**. People's homes and belongings can be destroyed and people are sometimes hurt.

One government agency tracks the cost of extreme weather. Every year it lists each weather event that costs the United States a billion dollars or more. These facts can be obtained readily and are **available** to the public.

From May 1999 to May 2000 many incidents of extreme weather occurred. In May 1999, tornadoes ripped through Oklahoma and Kansas. A tornado is a violently spinning column of air. First, warm air makes **contact** with cool air in the **atmosphere** or surrounding air. Next, the warmer and cooler air stir together, spinning faster and faster. Finally, a tornado is born. The May 1999 tornadoes cut a 1.7 billion dollar path of ruin and **destruction**, killing 55 people.

Hurricanes are storms with heavy rain and strong winds, over 75 miles-per-hour, that grow stronger over warm oceans. In September 1999 a hurricane called Floyd hit North Carolina. When Hurricane Floyd hit land, its heavy rains lasted for two days. This rain caused a **surge** of water that rushed powerfully along North Carolina's coast. Twelve other states also had flooding. Floyd's price tag was 6.5 billion dollars and 77 people died.

By May of 2000, high temperatures and a drought in the western United States caused raging fires. Nearly 7 million acres burned and losses were more than 2 billion dollars.

Nature sometimes uses snow and ice to create extreme weather conditions. For example, blizzards are costly winter problems. A blizzard occurs when winds blow at 35 miles-per-hour, the temperature is 20°F or lower, and snow falls. One blizzard called the "Storm of the Century," howled along the east coast of the United States in March 1993. It cost more than 7 billion dollars and caused 270 deaths. Now that's extreme!

Reread for Comprehension

Text Structure
Description

Description is one way authors organize, or structure nonfiction text. A Description Chart will help you understand this text structure. Signal words like *first*, *next*, *finally*, or *for example* will alert you to descriptive facts. Use the Description Chart as you reread this selection.

Signal Words	Descriptive Facts

Comprehension

Genre

Informational Nonfiction
Presents facts about real people, things, places, or events.

Text Structure

Description
As you read, use your Description Chart.

Signal Words	Descriptive Facts
→	

Read to Find Out

How does a tropical storm become a category 5 hurricane?

Award
Winning
Author

HURRICANES

by **SEYMOUR SIMON**

Hurricanes are huge spinning storms that develop in warm areas around the equator. Hurricanes bring strong winds, heavy rains, storm surges, flooding, and sometimes even tornadoes. Coastal areas and islands are in the most danger during a hurricane, but even inland areas are at risk.

Hurricane season along the East Coast of the United States begins in June and continues until the end of November. The peak hurricane months are August and September. The East Coast averages about five hurricanes a year. Over other parts of the world, hurricanes happen year-round.

The word *hurricane* comes from people who lived in the Tropics in earlier times. The ancient Mayan people of South and Central America called their storm god Hunraken. An evil god of the Taino people of the Caribbean was called Huracan. Hurricanes are not really evil, but they can cause terrible **destruction** and great loss of life.

Hurricanes are one of three kinds of storms called tropical cyclones. Tropical means that the storms form over the warm waters of the Tropics near the equator. Cyclones are storms spinning around a calm center of low air pressure, which also moves. Cyclones spin counterclockwise in the Northern Hemisphere and clockwise in the Southern Hemisphere.

Tropical depressions are cyclones of clouds and thunderstorms that spin around a central area. They have steady wind speeds of 38 miles per hour or less.

Tropical storms are cyclones of heavy clouds and strong thunderstorms that spin at steady wind speeds of 39 to 73 miles per hour.

Hurricanes are the strongest tropical cyclones. They have steady winds of 74 miles per hour or higher. When these storms form over the North Atlantic, Caribbean Sea, Gulf of Mexico, or the west coast of Mexico, they are called hurricanes. In the North Pacific, these kinds of storms are called typhoons, and in the Indian Ocean they are called cyclones. In Australia, hurricanes are called willy-willies, after the word whirly-whirly.

Hurricanes are the only weather disasters that have been given their own names, such as Andrew, Camille, Floyd, Fran, Hugo, Irene, and Opal. In some ways all hurricanes are alike. But like different people, each hurricane has its own story.

Description
What characteristics does the author list about hurricanes?

All hurricanes form in the same way. They begin life in the warm, moist **atmosphere** over tropical ocean waters. First, the atmosphere gathers heat energy through **contact** with ocean waters that are above eighty degrees Fahrenheit to a depth of about two hundred feet. Next, moisture evaporating from the warm waters enters the atmosphere and begins to power the infant hurricane.

The growing hurricane forms bands of clouds and winds near the ocean surface that spiral air inward. Thunderstorms form, heating the air further and forcing the winds to rise higher into the atmosphere and the spinning to increase. Because of their power, hurricanes can easily last more than a week and may strike Caribbean islands days before whirling north and east into the United States.

Hurricane forecasts estimate when the eye will pass over a particular location. But even a small hurricane has damaging winds and rains that may arrive many hours before the eye.

One of the worst hurricanes in the United States in terms of **property** damage was Hurricane Andrew. Andrew became a tropical storm in the southern Atlantic Ocean on August 17, 1992. At first, Andrew was a small storm with winds of about 40 miles per hour. But the storm rapidly gained strength over the warm waters, and wind speeds reached 155 miles per hour. Andrew was a category 5 hurricane by the time it passed over the Bahamas and began heading east toward Florida.

STRATEGY SKILL

Description
Which signal words in the first paragraph alert you to an upcoming list of descriptive facts?

Andrew hit the coastline of southern Florida on August 24. It was moving quickly and dropped about seven inches of rain across the state. Even more rain would have fallen had it been moving slowly. Storm tides reached seventeen feet along Biscayne Bay.

Wind speeds started to decrease over land, but Andrew quickly reached the warm waters in the Gulf of Mexico, where it regained 120-mile-per-hour winds. Then Andrew turned and slammed into the shoreline of Louisiana on August 26.

Andrew left a path of destruction in its wake. Damages totaled more than $25 billion. Thousands of people had lost their homes. More than a million people had been evacuated. But fewer than fifty-five people died, because of early hurricane warnings.

Weather forecasters at the National Hurricane Center were able to give a twenty-one-hour advance warning of Hurricane Andrew. This made it possible for people to flee dangerous low-lying places along the coast and go to safer spots inland.

Forecasters need to find where a hurricane is developing and how strong it is. At one time this was possible only when people saw the storm from a ship or from land. Nowadays forecasters use satellite images, airplanes, radar, and computers to track a hurricane.

Weather satellites orbit the earth at an altitude of nearly twenty-two thousand miles over the equator. The satellites send back images day and night of bands of clouds and early signs of a tropical storm. To get accurate readings of wind speed and pressure, pilots and scientists fly right through a hurricane into its eye.

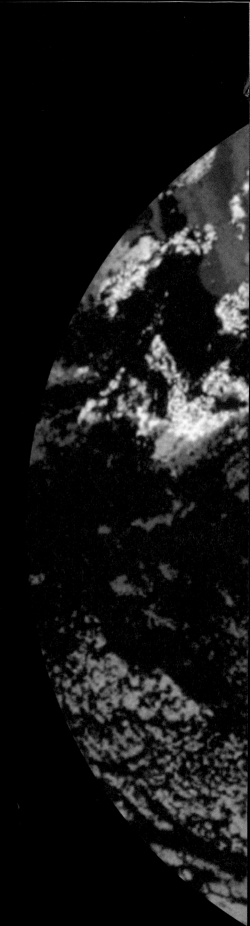

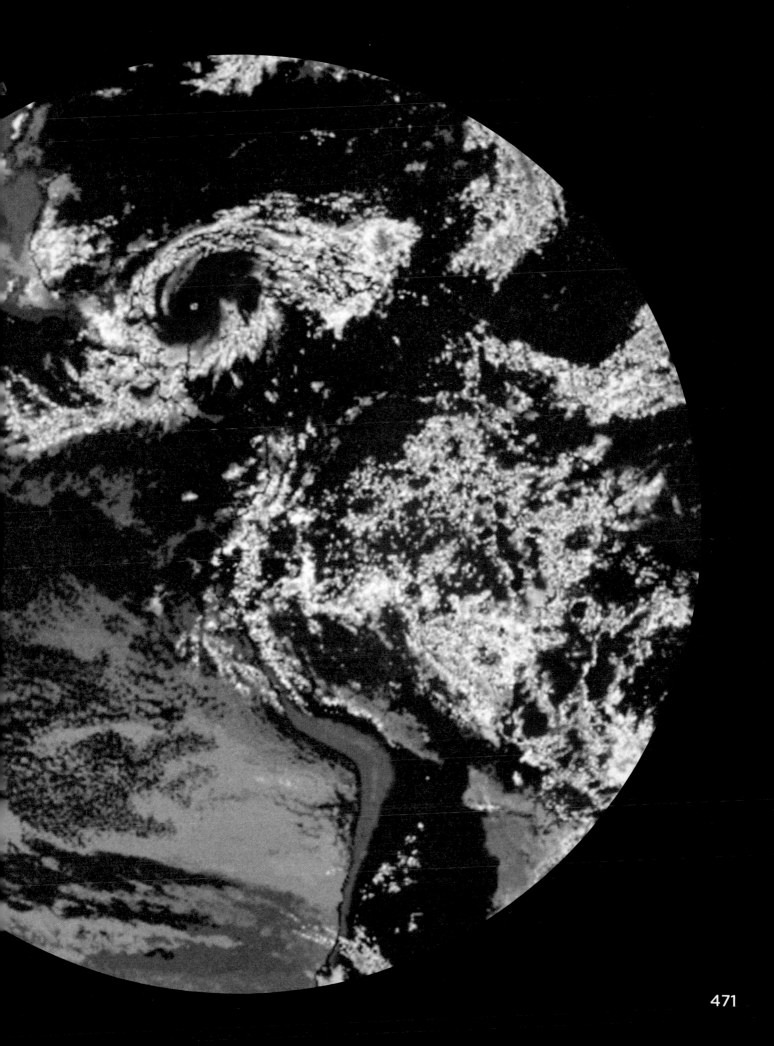

When a hurricane gets close to the coast, it is pictured on land-based weather radars. Doppler radars show wind speeds and location and quickly detect changes. The National Hurricane Center takes the information from radars and other sources and uses computers to help forecast the path, speed, and strength of hurricanes.

Hurricane and storm warnings are broadcast over radio and television and are also **available** on the Internet. National Oceanic and Atmospheric Administration (NOAA) Weather Radio broadcasts warnings, watches, forecasts, and other weather information twenty-four hours a day. These radio stations cover all the states, coastal waters, Puerto Rico, and United States Pacific territories.

A hurricane or a flood *watch* is usually given within thirty-six hours of an approaching storm. During a watch, it's important to prepare and decide what you and your family are going to do during the storm. A hurricane or a flood *warning* is usually given within twenty-four hours for a particular area. During a warning, listen to local radio or television stations for safety instructions.

National Weather Service (NWS) radios are specially equipped to give you immediate news about tropical hurricanes and floods. Regular NWS programs send out a special tone that turns on these radios in the listening area when there is an emergency. The radios can be connected to lights, computers, even bed shakers so that everyone can get the information.

Because of early warnings, the number of hurricane-related deaths has decreased in the United States in recent years. But hurricanes still remain a danger along the Atlantic coast and the Gulf of Mexico.

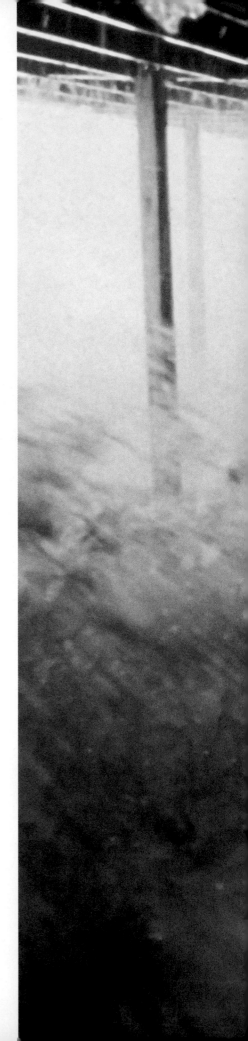

473

Scientists think that, potentially, the most dangerous place in the United States during a hurricane is New Orleans. That's because a storm **surge** could cover the low-lying city with twenty feet of water. Southwest Florida from Tampa Bay to the Everglades National Park is also dangerous, because the area is also very close to sea level.

If you are ever caught in a hurricane, it's important to know what to do. The first thing to remember is to listen closely to the radio, television, or NOAA Weather Radio for official bulletins. Follow instructions and leave immediately with your family if told to do so.

Only stay in a house if you are not ordered to leave. Stay away from windows and doors during the storm. During the worst of the storm, lie on the floor under a table or another sturdy object. Make sure you have a battery-driven portable radio and keep listening for storm information. Keep on hand at least a three-day supply of water and food that won't spoil.

Even after a hurricane passes by, conditions outside may still be dangerous. Here are some tips for you and your family.

- Keep listening to the radio for updates on flooding and highway conditions. Wait until an area is declared safe before going back into it.

- Stay away from moving water. Rapidly moving water even less than a foot deep can sweep you away. If you see water flowing across a street, turn around and go another way.

- Don't play in flooded areas. They are dangerous. The water may also be electrically charged from downed or underground power lines.

- Use a flashlight for emergency lighting. Don't use a candle or a flame indoors if the power goes off.

- Use bottled or stored water for drinking and cooking. Use tap water only when local officials say it is safe.

- Use the telephone only for emergency calls. If someone needs to be rescued or helped, call the police or local officials.

By preparing ahead and listening to the radio and following instructions, everyone can be much safer during a hurricane.

People are now much more aware of hurricanes than they were twenty-five years ago. When a hurricane threatens the United States, it becomes big news on television and radio. Even people who live in the middle of the country and will never experience a hurricane at home are interested in what's happening during the storm.

Along the East Coast, hurricanes are a fact of life. But nowadays forecasts, combined with timely warnings about hurricane dangers, are saving lives. The more we learn about hurricanes, the better our chances of coming through them safely.

Talking Up a Storm with Seymour Simon

Seymour Simon has written over 200 books, but he still calls himself a teacher. He started by teaching in a classroom, but now reaches more kids through his books. First, Seymour picks a topic he loved as a child. "Interests don't change," he says. "Kids still love spectacular things." After that, he researches and writes and rewrites the story until the explanations and descriptions are perfectly clear. Seymour wants his books to open up new worlds to the reader, not just answer questions. Then, when the books come out, he is back in the classroom, talking again to students and teachers.

Other books by Seymour Simon: *Storms* and *Volcanoes*

 Find out more about Seymour Simon at **www.macmillanmh.com**

Author's Purpose
Would you say that the author believes it is important to study extreme weather? What details from the selection help you to know?

Comprehension Check

Summarize

Use your Description Chart to help you summarize *Hurricanes.* Be sure to include descriptive facts, characteristics, and important details in your summary.

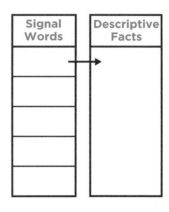

Signal Words	Descriptive Facts
→	

Think and Compare

1. Use the descriptive details on page 467 to describe tropical depressions, tropical storms, and hurricanes. Include facts and characteristics about each kind of storm in your description. **Text Structure: Description**

2. Reread the tips on page 475. Why should you stay inside until the area is declared safe after a hurricane? **Analyze**

3. Decide why you would or would not like to be a pilot or scientist who flies through the eyes of **hurricanes** to measure wind speed. Explain your answer. **Analyze**

4. Why are people who will never directly experience hurricanes interested in these storms? **Evaluate**

5. Reread "The Extreme Costs of Extreme Weather" on pages 462–463. Compare the damage and injury caused by Hurricane Floyd with the damage and injury caused by Hurricane Andrew that is described in *Hurricanes*. **Reading/Writing Across Texts**

Poetry

Free Verse Poems are written without a traditional rhyme scheme or meter.

Literary Elements

Personification is when human characteristics are given to animals, objects, or ideas.

Imagery is the use of descriptions to create vivid pictures in the reader's mind.

Onomatopoeia is a word that sounds like the action or object it describes.

Suspense

by Pat Mora

Wind chases itself
Around our house, flattens
          wild grasses
with one hot breath.
          Clouds boil purple
               and gray, roll
and roil. Scorpions
dart
          under stones. Rabbit eyes peer
From the shelter of mesquite.
               Thorny silence.

> The wind "chases itself" is an example of *personification*.

> The poet uses imagery with the words "Clouds boil purple and gray."

My *paisano*, the road runner
        paces, dashes into the rumble,
races from the *plink, plink*
        splatter into his shadow,   leaps
                at the crash   flash
splash,
        sky rivers rushing into arroyos and
Thirsty roots of prickly pears,
                        greening cactus.

"Plink, Plink" is an example of *onomatopoeia*.

Connect and Compare

1. List another example of imagery from this poem. Describe the picture that this example paints in your mind. **Imagery**

2. What effect does the use of the present tense have in this poem? **Analyze**

3. Compare and contrast the storm in the poem to the information in *Hurricanes*. How are the storms different? How are they the same? Use information in each text to explain your answer. **Reading/Writing Across Texts**

LOG ON Find out more about poetry at **www.macmillanmh.com**

479

Writing a Magazine Article

I wanted to discuss important facts about global warming and how it might cause extreme weather.

I used a serious tone throughout my article.

Global Warming and Extreme Weather

by Robert L.

Are you tired of hearing about long droughts, blazing fires, roaring floods, and huge hurricanes? Global warming and extreme weather seem to go hand in hand. That's why we're experiencing more and more serious storms.

Smoke pouring from our cars and factories is partly to blame. Carbon monoxide is a gas found in this smoke. It creates a hot-air blanket around Earth. If too much carbon monoxide is released into the atmosphere, Earth becomes warmer and severe weather can occur.

Scientists are working to find ways to reduce the amount of carbon monoxide that is released into the atmosphere. One solution is the development of new products that are more fuel efficient. Another solution is for each of us to do our part. We can slow global warming by thinking about the future and using energy sources more responsibly.

Your Turn

Choose a weather topic that interests you. Write a descriptive magazine article about it. Remember to take good notes as you do your research. Add details to the facts in your notes. Be sure to maintain an appropriate tone in your article. Use the writer's checklist to check your writing.

Writer's Checklist

 Ideas and Content: Did I choose a weather topic that interests me? Did I research it fully?

 Organization: Does each paragraph of my article have a clear main idea?

 Voice: Did I use an appropriate **tone** in my article?

Word Choice: Did I choose words that will appeal to my audience?

 Sentence Fluency: Do descriptive details make some of my sentences longer and more interesting?

 Conventions: Did I use hyphens correctly? Did I proofread for spelling errors?

TRICKSTER TALES

ANANSI AND COMMON SENSE

A Stage Play Adapted from a Jamaican Folktale

by Trey Reeves

Characters

ANANSI	NARRATOR	LITTLE GIRL

Stage is bare except for a tall tree on one side and the edge of a river on the other.

ANANSI (*is sitting by the **riverbank** thinking.*)

NARRATOR: Anansi the spiderman was greedy for power and wealth. One day he decided he could get these things by gathering all the common sense in the world.

ANANSI: (*snapping his fingers*) That's it! If I have all the common sense, people will come to me with their problems. The **wares** I sell will be bits of advice! I will make so much money that I will need to hire a **treasurer** to be in charge of my finances.

NARRATOR: So Anansi set out to gather every bit of common sense in the world. As he found it, he stuffed it in a large hollow fruit called a calabash. When he thought he had found every bit of common sense, Anansi closed the calabash with dry leaves.

ANANSI: I will hide this stack of precious **merchandise** at the top of the island's tallest tree!

(**LITTLE GIRL** *enters and sits by the riverbank.*)

NARRATOR: Anansi tied a rope to the neck of the calabash. Then he tied the two ends of the rope around his neck. The calabash hung against his stomach.

(**ANANSI** *tries to climb the tree, falls down, tries again.* **LITTLE GIRL** *watches him and laughs.*)

ANANSI: *(whirling around toward the riverbank)* Who's there?

LITTLE GIRL: You need a teacher to **educate** you. Don't you know that heavy **burdens** are best carried on your back?

NARRATOR: Anansi didn't value her helpful tip and showed no **appreciation**.

ANANSI: Useless calabash! *(ripping the calabash from his neck)* The day I filled you was a sad and **unfortunate** day indeed! *(flinging the calabash against the tree, so that it breaks open)*

NARRATOR: When the calabash broke, little pieces of common sense were scattered everywhere. That is why today everyone has at least a little bit of common sense.

Reread for **Comprehension**

Evaluate
Author's Purpose
Authors write to entertain, persuade, or inform. An Author's Purpose Chart helps you identify clues to the author's purpose for writing the story. This helps you evaluate the selection as you read it. Reread "Anansi and Common Sense" and use your Author's Purpose Chart to find the author's purpose.

Clues	Author's Purpose

Comprehension

Genre

A **Play** is a story told through dialogue that is intended to be performed.

Evaluate

Author's Purpose

As you read, look at your Author's Purpose Chart.

Clues	Author's Purpose

Read to Find Out

What purpose did the author have for writing this play?

THE CATCH OF THE DAY

A TRICKSTER PLAY

Award Winning Author

written by Angela Shelf Medearis

illustrated by Wendy Born Hollander

487

CHARACTERS

THE GRIOT (STORYTELLER)

GROUP OF CHILDREN

CHILD ONE

CHILD TWO

THE FISHER

THE BASKETMAKER

THE BAKER

THE WOMAN WITH THE FRUIT

THE FARMER WITH SOME YAMS AND CORN

THE MAN WITH THE BAGS OF RICE

The **GRIOT** stands in the center of a **GROUP OF CHILDREN** who are seated on the ground. A **GRIOT** is an African storyteller and keeper of the history of the family and the village. It is early evening and time for the nightly story. It is a common practice in Africa to tell stories in the evening to pass on oral history, carry on traditions, instruct and **educate** the village children, and to entertain. The **GRIOT** and the **CHILDREN** are off to one side of the stage. All the action for the play takes place center stage.

GRIOT: *(loudly)* Jambo, children! Hello!

CHILDREN: Jambo!

GRIOT: I am a Griot, the keeper of the history of my West African tribe, a storyteller, and a teacher. I have a special story to share with you about a tricky fisher and a bridge made out of a log. When I am ready to begin, I'll clap my hands once. When you are ready to listen, you'll clap your hands twice. *(The GRIOT claps once.)*

CHILDREN: *(Clap their hands twice.)*

GRIOT: And now it's time for our story. One day a hungry fisher set out to catch some fish to sell at the village market. He came to a wooden log bridge crossing the river.

FISHER *(walking past GRIOT and standing center stage)*: I will cross this bridge to the other side of the river. I know a place on that side of the river that is usually a good place to fish. After I catch the fish, I will sell them at the market. Then I will have lots of money to buy a good basket, some cloth, and maybe some bread, yams and other good things to eat.

GRIOT: The fisher crossed the bridge. Well, it wasn't really a bridge. It was only an old log that stretched from one side of the river to the other. The log bridge had been used by everyone in the village for many, many years. It was the only way to get across the river. Even more important, it was the only way to get from the village to the market.

FISHER: I think I have a nibble! Yes! This is it! *(pulls up fishing line)* Nothing!

Author's Purpose
What is the author's purpose in having the Griot narrate the trickster play?

GRIOT: The fisher tossed his line into the river again and again. He got more and more hungry. And as the blazing sun beat down, it got hotter and hotter.

CHILD ONE: Did he catch anything?

FISHER *(pulling in fishing line)*: Nothing!

GRIOT: That's right. Nothing! All that morning, he tried. The fisher pulled out lures with feathers on them and lures with insects on them, but he didn't catch anything. Then he tried using wiggly worms. Still, he didn't catch anything. He continued to try with all of his might to catch some fish.

CHILD TWO: Did he ever catch anything?

FISHER *(pulling in fishing line)*: Nothing!

GRIOT: Right again. Nothing! The sun continued to burn down upon the poor fisher. And he was very hungry! He felt he would die of hunger if he didn't catch something soon.

FISHER *(pulling up his fishing line and shaking his head sadly)*: My plan was to cross the log bridge and catch lots of fish on this side of the river. I wanted to sell the fish at the market and buy a good basket, some bread, and other good things to eat! But I didn't catch any fish.

CHILD ONE: So he can't buy a basket.

CHILD TWO: Or bread.

GRIOT: Or other good things to eat. And he was very, very hungry.

FISHER: I'm hungry, hungry, hungry! I can't believe this turn of events! My great-grandfather was a fisher, and my grandfather and my father before me! My family has fished in this very river for generations. It is how we always have earned a living. If I can't catch any fish, I must think of another way to get the things I need.

GRIOT: The poor fisher was about to return to his home. He had one foot on his side of the log bridge when he saw someone starting out on the other side of the log bridge. It was a basketmaker with a load of baskets.

FISHER *(waving and stepping back onto the riverbank)*: Jambo!

BASKETMAKER *(calling to the fisher on the other side of the river)*: Jambo! How are you today, Fisher? Did you catch anything?

FISHER *(sadly)*: No, I didn't catch a single fish today.

BASKETMAKER: That's too bad. I'm sorry, but I don't have time to talk. I must hurry to the market so that I can sell my baskets.

GRIOT: Suddenly, the fisher thought of a way he could get a basket.

FISHER *(holding up his hands in warning)*: Stop! Don't try to cross the bridge.

BASKETMAKER: What is wrong with it?

FISHER: I think the recent rainstorms must have loosened it. If I don't hold this log in place it will fall into the river and no one will be able to get to the market.

BASKETMAKER: That's nonsense! I just crossed this bridge two days ago! Besides, you got across!

FISHER: I risked my life crossing this bridge. Besides, I'm an excellent swimmer. If I fall in, I can always swim to safety. But out of the goodness of my heart, I decided to wait here so I could warn people who try to cross about the danger they face.

BASKETMAKER: I don't believe you! I'm going across. I don't care what you say.

FISHER: As you wish, but remember, you've been warned.

GRIOT: As the basketmaker starts to cross, the fisher secretly shakes the log with his foot when the basketmaker isn't looking.

BASKETMAKER (loudly): Oh no! The bridge is falling! Help! I'm going to fall in the river!

FISHER (waving his arms wildly): Quick! Turn back! You'll never make it across. I told you that it was too dangerous!

BASKETMAKER: (running back to the bank she started from): What should I do? I have to get to market to sell my baskets! This log is the only way to cross the river.

FISHER: I know what you should do! I'll hold on tightly to this end of the log while you cross. But, dear lady, I think that you are carrying too many baskets. You must leave some behind or you will fall into the waters below.

BASKETMAKER: You are right. If I carry all these heavy baskets across the bridge, I might fall into the river. Thank you, my friend! I will leave two baskets on this side of the river for you. Please pick them up when you return here on your way home.

FISHER: Oh, I couldn't do that.

BASKETMAKER: Please, it is a token of my **appreciation**.

FISHER: No, no, no!

BASKETMAKER: Yes, yes, yes!

FISHER: Well, if you want me to have them, how can I refuse? I will hold the log with all of my strength while you cross over. Careful now! Steady! Slowly, slowly, slowly . . . safe!

GRIOT: The basketmaker thanked the fisher and hurried off to market, never realizing that she had been tricked. Two of her nicest baskets were now left behind on the bank for the fisher.

FISHER: Now I have two beautiful baskets. But I'm still hungry, hungry, hungry! I must get something to eat! Wait, I think I hear somebody coming.

GRIOT: It was a weaver with a load of beautiful, multicolored, Kente cloth. The weaver made the Kente cloth especially for the king and it was very valuable.

WEAVER (loudly): Jambo!

FISHER (loudly): Jambo!

GRIOT: It occurred to the fisher that he could get some of the weaver's beautiful Kente cloth in the same way he had gotten baskets.

FISHER (*holding up both hands and calling to the weaver on the other side of the river*): Stop! Don't try to cross the bridge.

WEAVER: What is wrong with the bridge?

FISHER: I'm holding the log so that it won't fall into the river.

WEAVER: But I've always used this bridge to go to market. I have some Kente cloth I'm going to sell to the king's **treasurer**. I must hurry if I'm going to get to the market in time. You got across safely and so will I.

FISHER: I'm warning you! I barely made it across, and the basketmaker just risked her life crossing the bridge to get to the market.

WEAVER: Oh no! What happened to the basketmaker? Why, there are some baskets on the ground here! Did the basketmaker drop them when she fell into the river?

FISHER (*slowly and sadly with one hand over his heart*): Well, all I can say is that the basketmaker is no longer here with us.

WEAVER (*sadly*): How **unfortunate**! The poor, poor woman! But I must get to the market no matter what. I know what I'll do. I will run across the log bridge very quickly! That's how I'll get across safely!

GRIOT: The weaver adjusted the bundle of cloth on his head and tried to run across the bridge. As soon as he reached the middle of the log, the fisher secretly shook it with his foot.

WEAVER (*loudly, swaying back and forth in the middle of the log*): Help! Help! I'm falling!

FISHER (*gesturing wildly*): Go back before you fall in! You'll never make it all the way across! It's much too dangerous!

GRIOT: The fisher stopped shaking the log. The weaver ran back to the side of the riverbank where he started his journey, grateful to be alive.

WEAVER: Did you see that? I almost fell in! What am I going to do now? I must get across the bridge so I can get to the market!

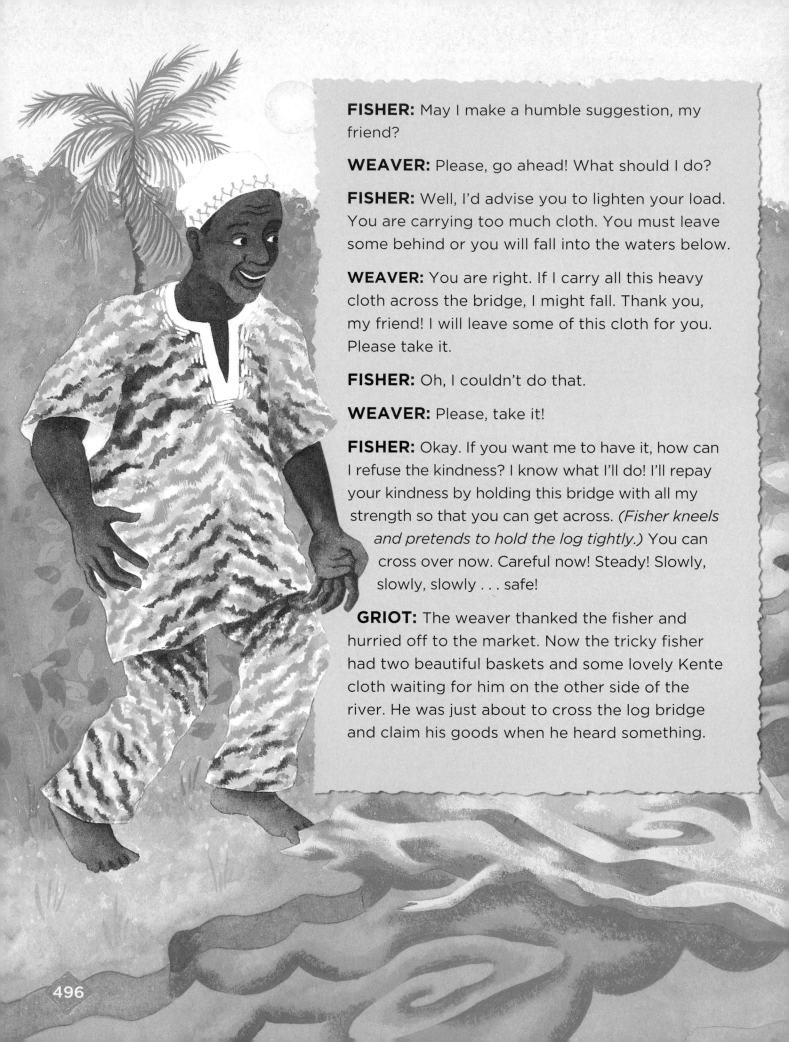

FISHER: May I make a humble suggestion, my friend?

WEAVER: Please, go ahead! What should I do?

FISHER: Well, I'd advise you to lighten your load. You are carrying too much cloth. You must leave some behind or you will fall into the waters below.

WEAVER: You are right. If I carry all this heavy cloth across the bridge, I might fall. Thank you, my friend! I will leave some of this cloth for you. Please take it.

FISHER: Oh, I couldn't do that.

WEAVER: Please, take it!

FISHER: Okay. If you want me to have it, how can I refuse the kindness? I know what I'll do! I'll repay your kindness by holding this bridge with all my strength so that you can get across. *(Fisher kneels and pretends to hold the log tightly.)* You can cross over now. Careful now! Steady! Slowly, slowly, slowly . . . safe!

 GRIOT: The weaver thanked the fisher and hurried off to the market. Now the tricky fisher had two beautiful baskets and some lovely Kente cloth waiting for him on the other side of the river. He was just about to cross the log bridge and claim his goods when he heard something.

FISHER: Someone is coming down the path! Jambo!

ALL: Jambo!

GRIOT: It was a baker with a stack of bread, a farmer with a basket of yams, a woman with a basket of fruit, and a man with several bags of rice. The fisher thought he could get some food in the same way he had gotten baskets and Kente cloth. He figured if his trick worked with the basketmaker and the weaver, it would work on the baker with the bread, the farmer with the yams, the woman with the fruit, and the man with the rice, as well.

FISHER (*holding up both hands and calling across the river*): Stop! Don't try to cross the bridge.

FARMER: What is wrong with the bridge?

FISHER: I'm holding the log so that it won't fall into the river.

BAKER: I thought you were fishing.

FISHER: Well, I had every intention of fishing on this side of the river. But, when I tried to cross the bridge I noticed that it was very shaky. I barely made it across with my life. I decided to stay here and warn everyone of the danger.

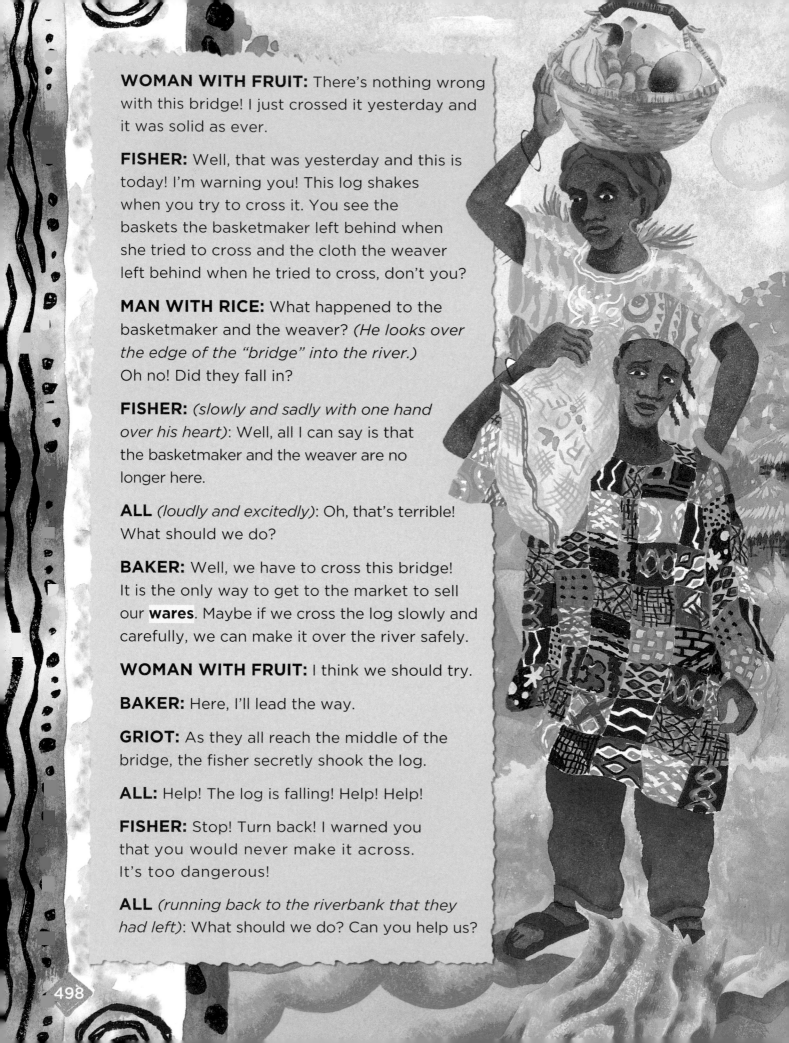

WOMAN WITH FRUIT: There's nothing wrong with this bridge! I just crossed it yesterday and it was solid as ever.

FISHER: Well, that was yesterday and this is today! I'm warning you! This log shakes when you try to cross it. You see the baskets the basketmaker left behind when she tried to cross and the cloth the weaver left behind when he tried to cross, don't you?

MAN WITH RICE: What happened to the basketmaker and the weaver? *(He looks over the edge of the "bridge" into the river.)* Oh no! Did they fall in?

FISHER: *(slowly and sadly with one hand over his heart)*: Well, all I can say is that the basketmaker and the weaver are no longer here.

ALL *(loudly and excitedly)*: Oh, that's terrible! What should we do?

BAKER: Well, we have to cross this bridge! It is the only way to get to the market to sell our **wares**. Maybe if we cross the log slowly and carefully, we can make it over the river safely.

WOMAN WITH FRUIT: I think we should try.

BAKER: Here, I'll lead the way.

GRIOT: As they all reach the middle of the bridge, the fisher secretly shook the log.

ALL: Help! The log is falling! Help! Help!

FISHER: Stop! Turn back! I warned you that you would never make it across. It's too dangerous!

ALL *(running back to the riverbank that they had left)*: What should we do? Can you help us?

FISHER: You are carrying too much food. You must leave some of it behind or you will fall into the waters below. Now, put some of your **merchandise** down and cross the log in single file, one at a time. I will hold this log with all my strength while you go across one by one.

BAKER: Perhaps he is right, my friends. If we carry these heavy **burdens** across the bridge, we might fall into the river. Let's leave some of our food behind so that we can safely reach the other side.

FISHER: Good thinking! Now, come across! I will hold the bridge for all of you. Careful now! Steady! Slowly, slowly, slowly . . . safe!

GRIOT: The baker with the loaves of bread, the farmer with the basket of yams, the woman with the fruit, and the man with the bags of rice all slowly crossed the bridge while the fisher held the log. Once they safely reached the other side, they all thanked the fisher, then hurried off to the market.

The fisher waited until they were down the road and out of sight. Then he danced and skipped across the log bridge. He picked up the bread, the yams, the fruit, the bags of rice and the cloth and put everything into the baskets that the basketmaker had left behind for him.

FISHER: Now I have a beautiful basket, some bread, some lovely Kente cloth, some yams, fruit, and a few bags of rice. I'm going to have a good dinner and I won't be hungry, hungry, hungry anymore.

GRIOT: The fisher danced all the way home, thinking about the sumptuous meal he would enjoy that evening.

CHILD ONE: What a tricky fisher! He made everyone think that the bridge was too dangerous to cross!

CHILD TWO: That's how he tricked them into leaving all the food, the baskets and the cloth.

GRIOT: You're right! But remember, even a trickster gets tricked. When the basketmaker, the weaver, the baker, the farmer, the woman with the fruit, and the man with the rice returned from the market and discovered that there was nothing wrong with the bridge, they decided to teach the fisher a lesson.

CHILD ONE: What did they do?

CHILD TWO: Yes, please tell us!

GRIOT: The very next day the basketmaker, the weaver, and all the other people the fisher had tricked met in the village.

BASKETMAKER (smiling): I know how we can play the same trick on the fisher that he played on us.

WOMAN WITH FRUIT: How?

WEAVER: Yes, tell us!

BASKETMAKER: In the next village my brother knows someone who makes his living as a fisher. I will travel there with my horse and cart today, and buy some fish from him. Tomorrow meet me by the river early in the morning. Bring a bucket with you.

MAN WITH RICE: A bucket? Why?

BASKETMAKER: You will see.

GRIOT: And so the basketmaker traveled to the next village and came home later that day with more fish than any one person could eat. The next morning she met the woman with the fruit, the weaver, the baker, the farmer, and the man with the rice on the side of the river closest to the village.

BASKETMAKER:
The fisher crosses to this side of the river every morning to try his luck. Here, each of you put two fish in your bucket, and fill it with water from the river. I have made a fishing pole from this branch. Ah, and just in time. Here comes the fisher now. *(loudly)* Jambo!

ALL: Jambo! Jambo!

FISHER: Jambo, my friends! What are you all doing?

BASKETMAKER: Why, fishing, of course. It's a great day for it! We have each caught more fish than we can eat!

FISHER: Fishing?! But that's my job!

BASKETMAKER: Come now! The fish in the river are for everyone to catch!

WOMAN WITH FRUIT: Yes, and can I help it if these fish are so eager to be caught, they jumped from the river right into my bucket? *(She shows the fisher the fish in her bucket.)*

WEAVER: Mine, too! *(He shows the fisher his bucket.)*

FISHER: I'm coming over there to join you! I didn't catch any fish yesterday.

BASKETMAKER: Wait, Fisher! You remember the bridge is loose. I had better help you to get across, but you shouldn't risk it unless you are a very good swimmer. It may be even more unsteady than it was yesterday.

FISHER: Oh . . . yes. That's very kind of you. I *am* an excellent swimmer and a person with a good sense of balance.

GRIOT: The fisher walked to the edge of the river toward the log bridge. He knew he had to pretend that the log bridge was loose. The basketmaker kneeled down to hold the bridge. As the fisher walked across, the basketmaker began to shake the log with her hand.

FISHER (*excitedly*): What are you doing? I'll fall into the river!

BASKETMAKER (*pretending to be concerned*): Oh, my! The bridge is so loose! I don't think I can control it! Careful now! Steady! Slowly, slowly, slowly . . . Oops!

GRIOT: The basketmaker shook the log so hard that the fisher fell into the river.

BASKETMAKER: Oh, my! I guess the log is even looser than it was yesterday. Sorry, Fisher!

GRIOT: As the fisher floated in the river, a fish swam right by his nose! He was annoyed at the trick played on him but he knew he couldn't say anything. Clearly the others had discovered that the log bridge hadn't been loose and that the fisher had tricked them the day before. Back on the riverbank, the woman with the fruit, the weaver, the farmer, the basketmaker, and the man with the rice just laughed and laughed. And later that day they ate a fine fish dinner!

CHILD ONE: Ha ha! I guess the fisher learned his lesson!

GRIOT: Yes! We will all hope he never tries to trick anyone again! (*He claps his hands once.*) That tricky story was fun! Now my time is done!

Author's Purpose
What is the author's purpose in writing this play? Did the author write with a second purpose in mind?

TELLING STORIES WITH ANGELA SHELF MEDEARIS

ANGELA SHELF MEDEARIS'S father was in the Air Force, so she moved a lot when she was growing up. One of the first things Angela did after moving to a new place was check out the library. She loved reading books, and she loved talking to the librarians. Angela writes because she likes to learn about life and make people laugh. "I enjoy that wonderful feeling you get when you have a great idea and can't wait to get started at it," she says. Angela also writes cookbooks and books about her African-American heritage.

Other books by Angela Shelf Medearis: *The Singing Man* and *Dare to Dream: Coretta Scott King and the Civil Rights Movement*

LOG ON Find out more about Angela Shelf Medearis at **www.macmillanmh.com**

Author's Purpose
What features in the text tell you that this is a play and that the author intends for it to be performed? Might she have had another purpose?

Comprehension Check

Summarize

Summarize *The Catch of the Day.* Be sure to present the events in the order in which they happened.

Think and Compare

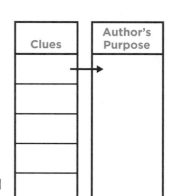

Clues	Author's Purpose

1. Authors sometimes have more than one purpose for writing a particular selection. What was the author's main reason for writing this play? Use your Author's Purpose Chart to explain your answer. **Evaluate: Author's Purpose**

2. Reread the Weaver's lines on page 495 and the Fisher's lines that follow. Why didn't the Fisher give specific answers to the Weaver's questions? **Critical**

3. Would you have participated in the trick to get back at the Fisher. Why or why not? **Analyze**

4. Can playing tricks on a trickster, like the Fisher, be an effective way to get them to stop fooling others who are **unfortunate**? Explain your response. **Evaluate**

5. Reread *Anansi and Common Sense* on page 484–485. Is the author's purpose the same or different in that play as in *The Catch of the Day*? Use examples from the selections. **Reading/Writing Across Texts**

Language Arts

Fables are stories that are meant to teach a lesson, often through the actions of animals that act like people.

SKILL ✓

Literary Elements

The **Moral** of a fable is the lesson it illustrates, which the reader can apply to his or her life.

Metaphor is a type of figurative language that compares two different things or actions to show a likeness between them without using "like" or "as."

The FOX and the Crow

retold by Mei Kirimoto

A ravenous crow kept a watchful eye on a family eating a picnic lunch.

"I can't believe that they will eat the entire quantity of food," thought the hungry crow.

While waiting for the family to finish, the crow took a dip in the pond to pass the time. The crow loved to admire herself. She was attractive and spent a long time looking at her reflection in the water. In her enthusiasm over her own loveliness, she did not notice that the family had eaten and gone.

However, when her stomach grumbled, she remembered how hungry she was and quickly flew back to the picnic spot. There she found that the family had left behind a big piece of cheese. She clamped the cheese in her beak and flew to a branch in a birch tree to enjoy her snack.

Just then a fox appeared. The fox lifted his long nose and smelled the piece of cheese. "Where could the cheese be?" said the tricky fox to himself. "I must investigate. I'm very hungry today."

He soon spotted the crow with the cheese.

The fox knew the crow quite well. He looked up at her and graciously said, "Why, Miss Crow, don't you look lovely! The sun shines gloriously on your feathers. Your beauty is a ray of sunlight on a gloomy day."

The fox saw that the crow was puffing up with each line of praise, so he continued. "Your feathers are of the finest polished ebony. Ah, if only I could hear your sweet voice. Certainly it's as magnificent as your feathers."

The crow immediately wanted to prove that she did indeed have an impressive voice. She opened her beak and began to sing *Caw, Caw, Caw* with tremendous volume. As she sang, the cheese fell to the ground.

> **This metaphor compares beauty to a ray of sunlight.**

Faster than a blinking eye, the triumphant fox scooped up the cheese and ate it.

"Dear Miss Crow," said the fox as he licked his lips, "your voice may be lovely, but you should think before you act."

MORAL: *Do not trust someone who gives too much praise.*

> **The moral teaches a lesson.**

Connect and Compare

1. Give an example of the use of metaphor in the fable. Explain your choice. **Metaphor**

2. What does the fox know about the crow that allows him to trick her? **Analyze**

3. Think about "The Fox and the Crow" and *The Catch of the Day.* How are the fable and the play similar? How are they different? **Reading/Writing Across Texts**

 Find out more about fables at **www.macmillanmh.com**

Writer's Craft

Precise Words
Good writers use **precise words** to convey meaning. In an interview, writing questions that contain precise words will help the interview subject give clear responses.

I interviewed my best friend, Maria.

I used precise words to ask about a particular story.

Write an Interview

by Elsa T.

Q: What stories do you find most inspiring?

A: The stories that inspire me the most come from Brazil. I like the trickster tales.

Q. Can you summarize the tale that explains why bats sleep during the day?

A: Yes, that's the tale about a little bat who steals sleep from a lizard. The selfish lizard wants sleep all for himself. The bat tricks him and shares sleep with the whole world. As a reward, the moon shines its brilliance so the bat can sleep during the day and play at night.

Q: I love that story. Why do you like to tell stories?

A: They help me to remember Brazil, and I like to share my family's culture with others.

Your Turn

Does anyone in your family like to tell stories? Interview this person about why stories are important. If no one in your family is a storyteller, interview a librarian at your local library. Prepare your questions beforehand. Use the writer's checklist to check your writing.

Writer's Checklist

✓ **Ideas and Content:** Did I choose the best person to interview?

✓ **Organization:** Did I present what I learned from the interview in a way that makes sense?

✓ **Voice:** Will the readers feel as though I am talking respectfully to the person I interviewed?

☑ **Word Choice:** Did I choose **precise words** that will be easy for my readers to understand?

✓ **Sentence Fluency:** Did I use a variety of sentence types? Will readers want to keep reading?

✓ **Conventions:** Have I used apostrophes and possessives correctly? Did I check my spelling?

Thomas Alva Edison, Inventor

by Robert Cohen

The next time you enjoy a movie, you might want to thank Thomas Alva Edison. You could thank him, too, when you turn on a light or use a battery-powered toy. This famous inventor is responsible for at least 1,000 inventions we use everyday.

Edison was born in Milan, Ohio, in 1847. He began working when he was 12 years old. He sold newspapers and food to people on trains headed for Detroit, Michigan. When he was 15, he saved the son of a man who ran the railroad station. The young boy had wandered onto the train tracks with a train approaching. Edison was able to pull the boy out of the way in the nick of time.

Go On ▶

That turned out to be one of the most important events in Edison's life. As a reward the boy's father taught Edison how to use a telegraph. Afterward Edison began to work for Western Union Telegraph Company. He became fascinated with the telegraph and began working to improve it and other mechanical devices.

Edison's first invention was the stock ticker, which recorded the purchase and sale of stocks. Over the next fifty years, he invented a motion-picture camera and made improvements to the electric light bulb. His favorite invention, however, was the phonograph. Edison discovered that he could record sound on cylinders coated with tinfoil. He made a machine that had two needles. One of the needles recorded sound, and the other one played the sound back. When Edison talked into the mouthpiece, the sound vibrations created by his voice made indentations on a cylinder, which were then recorded. The first words he recorded were "Mary had a little lamb."

Not everything Edison worked on was a success, however. He also had a few failures. Take, for instance, Edison's interest in cement. He started the Edison Portland Cement Co. in 1899. He wanted to make everything out of cement, including furniture, pianos, and houses. Concrete cost a great deal of money at the time, and the idea never took off. He also worked on machines to process iron ore, which were never successful either.

Edison believed in working long hours, and sometimes he worked more than twenty hours a day. He said "Genius is one percent inspiration and 99 percent perspiration." He set a goal in 1876 to have one major invention every six months, and he came very close to that goal. During his life Edison applied for and received more than 1,093 patents, the most ever issued to one person. He enjoyed designing new things, but he also wanted people to actually use them.

Edison's successes make our everyday lives easier. To honor Edison, President Herbert Hoover ordered all electric lights dimmed for one minute on October 21, 1931, a few days after Edison's death.

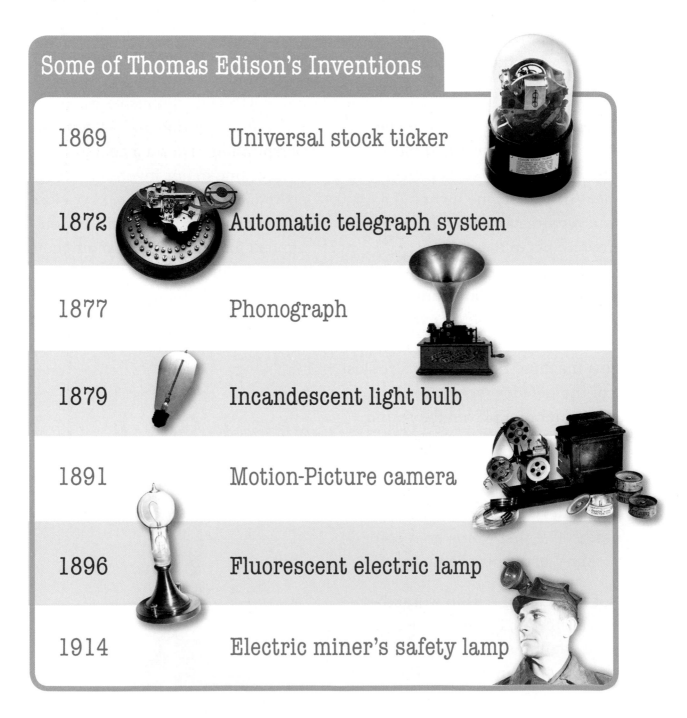

Some of Thomas Edison's Inventions

Year	Invention
1869	Universal stock ticker
1872	Automatic telegraph system
1877	Phonograph
1879	Incandescent light bulb
1891	Motion-Picture camera
1896	Fluorescent electric lamp
1914	Electric miner's safety lamp

Go On ▶

Directions: Answer the questions.

Tip

Skim for clues.

1. **An important event in Edison's boyhood was**

   A   inventing a motion-picture camera.
   B   working at a cement plant.
   C   saving someone's life.
   D   winning a fortune.

2. **Reread the time line on page 512. During which decade was the phonograph invented?**

   A   1860s
   B   1870s
   C   1880s
   D   1890s

3. **Why might you want to thank Thomas Edison?**

   A   He was a great writer.
   B   He invented many of the things we use every day.
   C   He told funny stories.
   D   He started an art museum.

4. **Based on what you have read in the selection, would you have enjoyed working with Thomas Edison? Explain why or why not.**

5. **How did Edison make everyday life easier? Use details from the selection in your response.**

Writing Prompt

Write a news article about one of Edison's inventions. State what the invention is, when it was created, and what it does. Include reasons why the invention is important.

STOP   513

NORTH
POLE

SOUTH
POLE

Talk About It

What images come to mind when you think about the North and South Pole? Why would it be exciting to explore these places?

LOG ON Find out more about the North and South Pole at **www.macmillanmh.com**

ICE
and More
ICE

by Tamika Washington

Vocabulary

frigid	expedition
treacherous	labor
triumph	dismantled
uninhabited	abandon

Word Parts
By breaking down an unfamiliar word into parts, such as the **Root**, the **Prefix**, at the beginning of the word and the **Suffix**, at the end of the word you can figure out its definition. For example, *uninhabited (un-inhabit-ed)* means "not lived in."

People often think of the North and South Poles as similar frozen wastelands. They are both places with **frigid** temperatures and few people. However, the North and South Poles are not much alike.

The North Pole has no land, only thick sheets of ice. Temperatures rarely go above 32°F, which is the freezing point for water. Most of the time, the thermometer stays below zero. Winter temperatures as low as -30°F are common.

Despite such **treacherous** conditions, people tried for many centuries to reach the North Pole. Then about 100 years ago, two men were able to **triumph** over this tough environment. Robert Peary and Matthew Henson reached the North Pole on March 8, 1909. It was not an easy trip.

There are few things more dangerous than crossing the Arctic on foot. Explorers can face many problems: freezing temperatures, sudden storms, even starvation. Most of the area is **uninhabited** by people. Few people can live in such a harsh place.

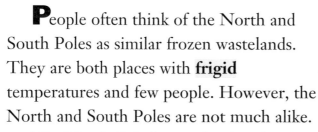

One might think that with freezing temperatures for most of the year, the ice pack would be thick and hard. However, this is not true in the Arctic. The movement of ocean currents under the ice causes constant changes on the surface. Sometimes the ice breaks apart, opening lanes of water called "leads." Anyone who falls into a lead can drown or freeze to death in minutes.

Peary, Henson, and the other members of their **expedition** ran into this problem constantly. They learned to move in packs of three or four men, so that if something happened a member of the team would be nearby to help. Henson once slipped into a lead and was rescued just in time by his Eskimo assistant, Ootah.

Another time, four members of Peary's team became trapped on an ice island. The island was formed when leads opened around their igloo in the middle of the night. One of the men woke up just in time, or they would have floated out to sea.

The men built igloos each night to protect themselves from the wind while they slept. An igloo is a small hut made of hard, packed snow. Cutting the blocks in the freezing cold was back-breaking **labor**. Sometimes the wind was very strong, and it would **dismantle** the igloos before morning.

Some members of Peary's team gave up and turned back. But Peary and Henson refused to **abandon** their expedition. Their hard work paid off. They became the first people to reach the North Pole!

Reread for **Comprehension**

Generate Questions
Problem and Solution

A Problem and Solution Map helps you ask questions to figure out problems and solutions in a selection. Reread "Ice and More Ice" and use your Problem and Solution Map to identify problems the writer presents and the actions that are taken to solve them.

| Problem |
| Attempts → Outcomes |
| → |
| → |
| Solution |

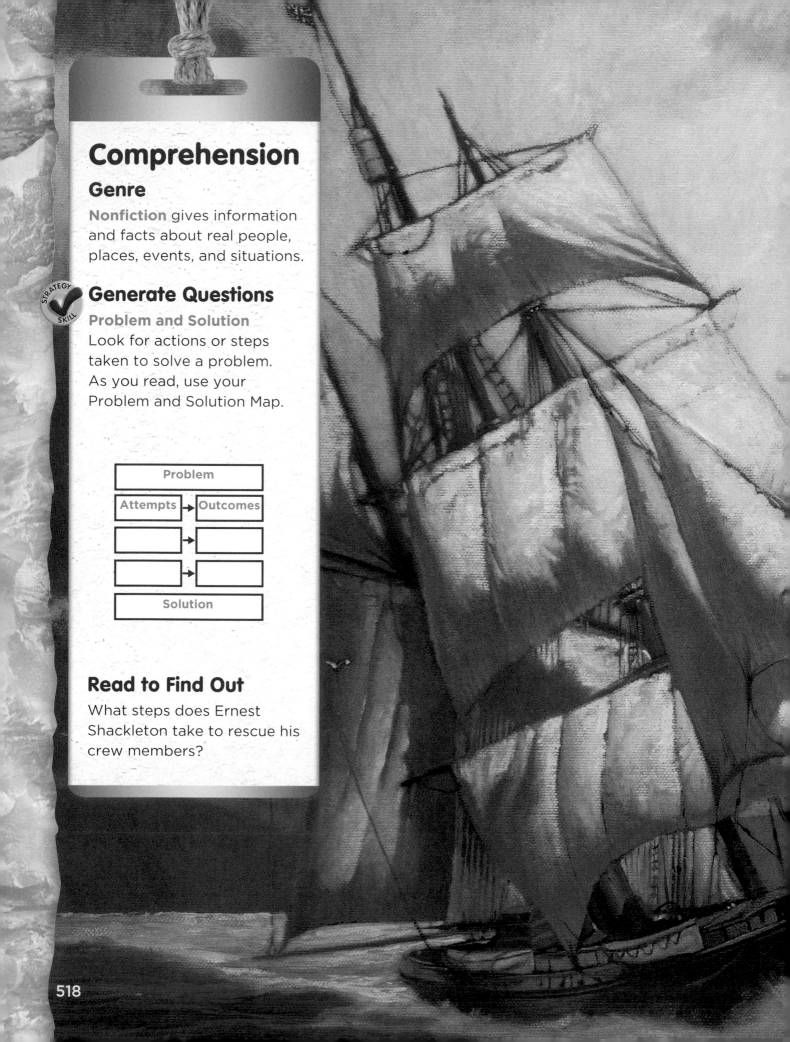

Comprehension

Genre

Nonfiction gives information and facts about real people, places, events, and situations.

Generate Questions

Problem and Solution
Look for actions or steps taken to solve a problem. As you read, use your Problem and Solution Map.

Problem

Attempts	→	Outcomes
	→	
	→	

Solution

Read to Find Out

What steps does Ernest Shackleton take to rescue his crew members?

Spirit of Endurance

Award Winning Selection

by Jennifer Armstrong
illustrated by William Maughan

When Ernest Shackleton was young, he fell in love with books and adventure. At 16 he set off to sea to explore the world. His most famous adventure took place in Antarctica in January of 1915. On Shackleton's third expedition to Antarctica, the **frigid** waters on the Wedell Sea that borders Antarctica froze over. Shackleton's ship, the *Endurance*, became stuck in the ice. Shackleton's goal was to be the first explorer to trek 1,500 miles across the **treacherous** continent. Would he and his crew **triumph**? Or would the ice prove to be too much?

519

The weather outside *Endurance's* cozy cabins was terrible. Furious winds howled across the ice. Blizzards drove snow into drifts against the sides of the ship. Sometimes the wind was so fierce that it pressed the ice floes against *Endurance*. The ship's wooden timbers squeaked eerily as the pressure grew stronger. The force of the ice was so great that Shackleton began to worry that *Endurance* would be seriously damaged. What if they were forced to **abandon** the ship?

One night in July, at the height of a winter storm, the pressure grew stronger than ever. Shackleton shared his fears with the captain, Frank Worsley.

"If the *Endurance* does have to, well, get left behind, we will manage, somehow," Worsley said to the Boss.

Shackleton replied, "We shall hang on as long as we can. It is hard enough on the men as it is. Without a ship in which to shelter from these blizzards, and in this continuous cold—" He broke off and paced the cabin. He didn't want to think about it. But as commander of the **expedition**, Shackleton had to prepare for the worst.

The members of the Endurance *expedition, photographed as the ship sailed south. Shackleton is in the center, in the hat and buttoned white sweater. Second-in-command Frank Wild is standing behind Shackleton's left shoulder. Next to Wild is the captain of* Endurance, *Frank Worsley (in the white sweater and seaman's cap).*

Frank Hurley (left) and the ship's meteorologist (weatherman), Leonard Hussey, play chess during a night watch.

The ice continued to press against *Endurance* through August and September. On some days, it rammed the ship so sharply that it knocked books and tools and equipment off shelves and made the masts tremble like twigs. The men were becoming frightened and jumpy. Each time the ship let out a squeak or groan from its straining hull, they held their breath.

The crew **dismantled** the dogloos and brought all the animals back on board because they were afraid that the ice would break up under the dogs. One day in October, the ice pressed nonstop against the sides of *Endurance*, pushing the ship over on its port side. Everything that wasn't fastened down crashed onto the decks. For several terrifying minutes, the men thought the ship was done for.

But the pressure stopped, and *Endurance* settled back into place. They were safe—for now.

Then, in the third week of October, the pressure started up again and continued without relief. *Endurance* groaned and creaked as the ice squeezed from all sides. The timbers began to buckle and snap. Water began leaking into the hold.

Endurance photographed at night in August 1915—the depth of the Antarctic winter. The ship is covered with frost, making it white against the inky sky.

The crew took turns at the pumps, trying to keep the water out, but it was no use. On October 27, Shackleton looked around at the ship, which was being crushed like a nut in a nutcracker before his eyes.

"She's going, boys. I think it's time to get off," he said.

Then the crew of *Endurance* abandoned ship—in the middle of the frozen sea.

Luckily, the destruction of *Endurance* happened in slow motion. This gave the crew plenty of time to unload food and equipment. As the ship continued to break up, the pile of gear on the ice grew larger: suitcases, books, clocks, sleeping bags, guns, crates of flour and sugar, clothes, lifeboats, diaries, axes, scrap lumber, toothbrushes, buckets—everything that could be taken off the ship was removed. The crew worked without a break. Their survival would depend on saving everything that might come in handy.

Finally, exhausted, they pitched their tents and crawled inside to sleep. Meanwhile, the timbers and rigging of *Endurance* snapped and crashed onto the deck of the dying ship.

While the rest of the men slept, Shackleton held a conference with his second-in-command, Frank Wild, and with the skipper of *Endurance*, Frank Worsley. With no way to communicate with the outside world, they were completely on their own. If they were going to survive, they would have to rescue themselves.

They came up with a plan: they would drag their three lifeboats, filled with food and equipment, across the ice to Paulet Island. It was 346 miles away. When Shackleton told the men in the morning what lay ahead of them, they reacted calmly. They trusted his leadership. If he said they would walk 346 miles, then that was what they would do.

Problem and Solution

What kind of plan does Shackleton devise after his crew abandons the *Endurance*? Do you think it will be successful? Why or why not?

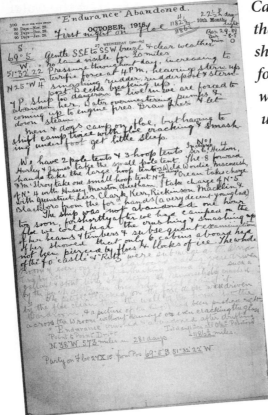

The dogsleds, each loaded with 900 pounds of gear, went in the lead. The drivers struggled to hack a path through the jumbled ice field with axes and shovels. Behind came the three boats, pulled in stages by fifteen men in harness. They dragged one boat forward a quarter of a mile, left it, and returned for the second boat. When the third boat was hauled up to join the other two, they began dragging the first boat again.

But it was torture. The surface of the ice was broken and uneven, and the men sometimes sank to their knees in freezing slush while the snow swirled down onto them. After two hours of backbreaking **labor**, they were only a mile from *Endurance*. At this rate, they would never reach Paulet Island. The floe they were on was solid: they would set up camp and stay put.

Ocean Camp was to be their home for the next two months. They returned to *Endurance* for more equipment and food. With lumber rescued from the ship, they built a cookhouse to hold an oil stove.

Then they settled in to wait. Shackleton knew that the ice they were camped on was drifting north and would carry them to the open ocean. Eventually, they would need to take to the lifeboats. Once the ice drifted into warmer waters, it would not be stable enough to camp on. Their only hope of rescue lay across the water. So the carpenter worked on improving the boats and making them more seaworthy.

The Antarctic spring was under way now, and temperatures sometimes climbed into the thirties, which seemed almost tropical to the men. They continued to hunt, to exercise the dogs, and to keep themselves busy with books and card games and chores. Just keeping their gear dry in slushy Ocean Camp was a steady job.

Slowly, the ice drifted away from Antarctica. Large cracks appeared on their ice floe. The surface became soft. November 21 brought an unforgettable event: the broken, twisted wreck of *Endurance* finally slipped through the ice and sank forever. In December, Shackleton decided they should move again, hoping to narrow the distance between themselves and Paulet Island.

But the going was tough: it still took three days to cover seven miles. After two more days of backbreaking effort, it looked as though they were stuck. The ice was mush and unstable. They couldn't go back. They couldn't go forward. They would have to make another camp.

They called this one Patience Camp, and patience was what they needed. The year 1915 was drawing to a close and the new year was before them.

Dragging one of Endurance's *lifeboats across the ice.*

What lay ahead? Shackleton couldn't be sure. The drift of the ice was haphazard. Sometimes they were carried north, sometimes east or west.

The months of February and March dragged by.

By early April, the ice floe that Patience Camp sat on was alarmingly small, and leads of open sea surrounded them. Killer whales spouted in the water as they hunted seals. The men could feel the rise and fall of the ocean lifting their floe, and some of them began to feel seasick.

On April 8, Shackleton gave the order: "Launch the boats!"

Thousands of birds circled overhead as the crew shoved the boats off the ice. Sitting on their gear and their last crates of food, the men bent to the oars. Waves crashed against icebergs. The three boats picked their way through the maze of ice, pulling north toward the open ocean.

As the light faded, they began looking out for an ice floe to camp on. Shackleton soon spotted one. Luckily, a large seal was sleeping on it, and the men quickly killed it and cooked it for dinner. Then they pitched their tents and tried to get some rest.

Launch the boats! The crew, with their provisions, crowd into three small lifeboats . . . and set off for Elephant Island . . .

The next days were filled with danger and hard work. Once they left the shelter of the ice pack, the violence of the open ocean met them like a hurricane. Waves broke over the tiny, crowded lifeboats, and howling winds and sleet lashed the men's faces. The temperature sank. The men could hear ice crackling on their clothes and on the sails that now filled with wind. Sleep was out of the question. They were low on drinking water and short on food. The men were beginning to break.

Shackleton feared that the boats would become separated or that some of the men would die of exhaustion. But ahead of them, somewhere, lay a tiny, rocky islet called Elephant Island. If they could make that, they would be able to rest.

At the limit of their strength, the men saw Elephant Island between tattered rags of mist. They had been in the boats for seven days, climbing giant waves, trying to keep from freezing—seven days with little sleep, little food, no water. When at last they landed, the men fell to their knees on the shore, weeping and laughing.

It was the first time in almost a year and a half that they had stood on solid ground.

Elephant Island was solid ground, but it was also **uninhabited**, and winter was approaching. They would not just wait for a ship to come along and rescue them—it might never happen.

After three days of much needed rest, Shackleton announced that he would take the best boat, the *James Caird*, and sail back to South Georgia Island, over 800 miles away, to get help. He would take Captain Worsley, for his sailing skills; the carpenter, Harry McNeish, in case the boat needed repairs on the way; and three other men. After he reached the whaling station, he would return to rescue the crew.

McNeish reinforced the boat. The men collected fresh water from a glacier on the island. They made the *James Caird* as seaworthy as possible. On April 24, 1916, the *James Caird* shoved off.

For more than two weeks, Shackleton and his five-man crew sailed across the stormiest ocean in the world, facing 100-foot waves, bitter temperatures, and hurricane-force winds. The twenty-two-foot boat was often covered with ice, and the men had to crawl across the decking while the boat heaved and pitched to chop the ice away.

They slept in shifts, crawling into the bow to grab what rest they could. Worsley navigated the best he knew how, although conditions were terrible. In order to calculate their position, he had to be able to see the sun at noon—and with the stormy weather, that was possible only four times. If they lost their way and missed South Georgia Island, they would be headed out into the vast Atlantic Ocean, and that would mean certain death. The men were constantly drenched with salt water and spray as waves broke across the boat. They ached with cold.

Shackleton kept them going with hot meals and drinks—six times a day. Lighting their little camp stove on the bucking boat was tricky, and the moment their cocoa or stew was ready, they put the stove out to save fuel. They learned to eat and drink their meals scalding hot and let the food warm their numbed bodies.

If Shackleton feared they wouldn't make it, he never let on. Day after day he sat at the tiller, scanning the horizon. And with Worsley's almost miraculous skill with compass and sextant, the battered boat and its exhausted crew reached the island on the seventeenth day.

There was just one problem: they had landed on the southwest side of the island, and the whaling station was on the northeast side. The boat was too damaged to risk sailing it around in the stormy waters. But the interior of the island was blocked by a range of jagged mountains and glaciers. They would have to cross it on foot.

Two of the men were completely broken down and a third would have to stay and look after them. That left Shackleton, Worsley, and second officer Tom Crean to make the hike across South Georgia Island.

Problem and Solution

Once the men landed safely on South Georgia Island, what was the next big problem they faced? How did they overcome it?

The voyage of the James Caird. Only twenty-two feet long, the boat has two masts and three small sails and is steered by a rope yoke attached to the rudder. Worsley calculates the Caird's position by sighting the sun through an instrument called a sextant. The cutaway shows the cramped space below, where one man sleeps in the bow and two prepare a meal using a camp stove.

Their mountaineering equipment wasn't the best gear they could have wished for on a climb such as this one. They had an ax and fifty feet of rope. They studded the soles of their boots with nails for a better grip on the icy peaks. They rested for several days. Then, with food for three days and a small camping stove, they set out, crossing the first snowfield by moonlight.

Months of poor nutrition and inactivity had left them in no shape for a rugged hike. But as the Boss said long afterward, "The thought of those fellows on Elephant Island kept us going all the time.... If you're a leader, a fellow that other fellows look to, you've got to keep going. That was the thought which sailed us through the hurricane and tugged us up and down those mountains."

South Georgia Island had never been crossed before. There were no trails, no clue which passes led to safety and which ones led to sheer drops. The men rested and cooked quick meals, and pushed on. The Boss didn't dare let them stop to sleep, fearing that they might lose the will to continue. On they trudged, hour after hour, through the first night and a day, then another night. By the next morning, they were haggard, exhausted, and trembling with cold, but they were within sight of the eastern coast.

Faintly, from far below, came the sound of the seven o'clock whistle at the whaling station. They had reached safety at last.

Back on Elephant Island, the rest of the crew had no idea of the Boss's triumph. Once the *James Caird* had disappeared from view, the twenty-two remaining members of the expedition set to work. Frank Wild, in charge, decided on the first task. Antarctic winter was sweeping up from the South Pole, and they would have to shelter themselves from it.

They scavenged the beach for rocks and built a low foundation. Then they took the two remaining boats, the *Dudley Docker* and the *Stancomb Wills*, and turned them upside down over the stones. The tattered canvas sails were lashed across the boats, and the chinks in the walls were stuffed with moss to keep out the wind. They rigged a chimney from some small sheets of metal and installed the blubber stove. When they were done, they had a crude hut to wait out the winter in.

The first storms came quickly. While the winds howled outside their cabin, the men kept each other company. A popular pastime was listing their favorite foods—after a steady diet of seal meat and penguin, the men dreamed of fresh fruit, cakes, and roast beef. The hours passed slowly. The days passed slowly. The weeks passed slowly. Camp Wild was a dreary place.

There were jobs to do: ice had to be chipped off the glaciers and melted for drinking water. There were penguins and seals to hunt.

And there was an operation to be performed. Percy Blackborrow's feet had frozen on the boat journey to Elephant Island, and gangrene had sct in. Now the toes on his left foot were dead and black and had to be amputated. There were few medical supplies left. But the expedition's doctors, James McIlroy and Alexander Macklin, performed the surgery by the light of a seal oil lamp.

Outside the hut, the winds screamed over the cliffs of Elephant Island. Sea ice crowded the shore. They knew Shackleton could not return until the winter was over.

Camp Wild. The Dudley Docker *and the* Stancomb Wills *have been overturned and covered with sails to make a hut, where the remaining members of the crew wait for Shackleton to return with a rescue ship.*

Rescue! Shackleton returns to Elephant Island to bring home his men. In the background is the Yelcho, *the ship that Shackleton borrowed from the Chilean government for the rescue attempt.*

Wild tried to keep the men optimistic. Every morning, he rolled up his sleeping bag and said to the men, "Get your things ready, boys. The Boss may come today."

But as the months went by, they began to wonder if "today" would ever come.

When Shackleton, Worsley, and Crean walked into the whaling station on May 20, they looked like wild men. They were in rags, their faces black from oily smoke, and their hair and beards long and matted. Dogs barked in alarm as they staggered to the station manager's house.

"Who are you?" asked the manager.

"My name is Shackleton," the Boss replied.

There was stunned silence. No one had expected to see Shackleton alive, let alone see him come walking down from the peaks of South Georgia Island. But when the Boss told their story, they were treated as heroes.

The three weary men were given hot baths and hot food, and allowed to sleep. As soon as they awoke, Shackleton began arranging a rescue party. Worsley set out in a boat with some of the whalers to pick up the men on the other side of the island.

A steamer was outfitted to make for Elephant Island, and Shackleton left at once. But the weather and the ocean were against him. He was forced to turn back for South Georgia Island. Twice more he tried, but the cruel Atlantic winter was too brutal.

June and July went by, and Shackleton was desperate to get his men. At last, in August, he took a Chilean ship called the *Yelcho* and made once more for Elephant Island.

On August 30, George Marston, the expedition artist, was keeping lookout at Camp Wild. On the horizon, he saw the smoke of a ship's funnel. "SHIP HO!" he yelled.

The *Yelcho* steamed into the bay, and a boat was lowered over the side. It was Shackleton. "Are all well?" he shouted as soon as he was near enough.

"YES!"

The men crowded around the Boss as he landed, shaking his hand. "We knew you'd come back," one said to him.

They had all survived. Shackleton had returned to take them home.

EXPLORING WITH JENNIFER ARMSTRONG AND WILLIAM MAUGHAN

JENNIFER ARMSTRONG always felt like a writer, even when she thought about becoming an archeologist. She says, "I always had a good imagination and loved making up stories. It just seemed natural to me that I would become an author." When she was researching this book, Jennifer went on an unusual field trip to Antarctica. There she saw seals sunbathing, penguins squealing, and Shackleton's winter "house" still standing a century later. Luckily Jennifer ate her own food instead of the canned food left behind by Shackleton. After surviving the South Pole, Jennifer returned home to New York.

Another book by Jennifer Armstrong:

Shipwreck at the Bottom of the World

WILLIAM MAUGHAN is both an accomplished artist and a teacher. His art has appeared in books and magazines as well as on television and in the movies. When William isn't drawing about Shackleton's heroic trek, he is teaching art to his students—and learning from them at the same time. "Every teacher will admit they learn more from their students than their students learn from them," William says. William lives in California with his wife and seven children.

LOG ON Find out more about Jennifer Armstrong and William Maughan at **www.macmillanmh.com**

Author's Purpose

What is Jennifer Armstrong's opinion of Ernest Shackleton? Tell how you know. How do all the facts in the selection serve as clues to the author's perspective on the explorer?

Comprehension Check

Summarize

Write a summary of *Spirit of Endurance* using your Problem and Solution Map. Be sure to identify the major problems that Shackleton and his men faced, and explain how they solved them.

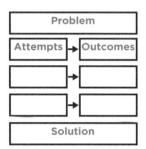

Problem	
Attempts →	Outcomes
→	
→	
Solution	

Think and Compare

1. Why do you think the author chose a problem and solution structure to tell Shackleton's story? **Generate Questions: Problem and Solution**

2. How would you describe Shackleton's crew? Use evidence from the story. **Analyze**

3. What would you name a ship that was about to set out on a long and dangerous **expedition** like Shackleton's? **Apply**

4. Describe the characteristics of a strong leader like Shackleton. Tell why such qualities are important for leaders. **Analyze**

5. Reread "Ice and More Ice" on pages 516–517. Imagine that Shackleton's journey would have taken him to the North Pole instead of to the South Pole. How do you think the search for help for his crew might have been different? Use evidence from both selections to support your answer. **Reading/Writing Across Texts**

THE Bottom OF THE World

by Mary Ann Williams

It may be hard to believe that any part of today's Earth has gone unexplored. People have traveled to almost all of nature's mysterious places. However, the **continent** of Antarctica has held onto many of its secrets.

One reason people have stayed away is the continent's harsh environment. A huge obstacle for explorers is the ice that surrounds the continent. Even during the summers, 95 percent of Antarctica is covered with ice. In addition to ice, it is surrounded by dangerous waters that are hard to navigate. This might explain why centuries went by before explorers, who traveled by ship, were able to reach the unknown continent.

People must also overcome Antarctica's intense weather. During the winter Antarctica remains dark and cold around the clock. The inner part of the continent is the coldest place on Earth with temperatures below –126°F. High winds blow almost continuously and blizzards are frequent. Blowing snow sometimes combines with low clouds to create "whiteouts." During a whiteout, the sky and the ground blur together and people cannot tell which way is up.

Despite all these obstacles, countries have now established permanent scientific stations where scientists live and work on the continent. Slowly, the last secrets of Antarctica are being revealed.

Modern-day adventurer Jennifer Owings Dewey is one person trying to solve some of Antarctica's mysteries. She went to Antarctica for four months.

During her trip she kept a journal, a daily record of **observations** and events. Most people keep journals as a way to remember the details of their daily lives.

Journal Entries

Here are two entries from Dewey's journal. Notice that journal entries are dated and written from a first-person point of view.

November 12

For millions of years Antarctica, the fifth largest continent, has been in the grip of an ice age. It is the windiest, coldest, most forbidding region on earth, and I am heading straight for it.

"Goodbye, America," I whisper as the airplane heaves off the ground with a shuddering roar. "See you later."

November 24th Palmer Station Antarctica

– is five and a quarter million square miles; it's larger than Europe.

– has no native human population.

– contains two thirds of the planet's fresh water in the form of glaciers.

– receives less than two inches of snow or rain in a year (precipitation at the South Pole is barely measurable).

– has no land-based predators (other than humans).

– has one hundred million penguins in residence.

– is a world park, a continent devoted to science, a vast outdoor laboratory.

– has freezing temperatures that keep anything from rotting, even old shacks built by early explorers.

– has ice up to three miles thick, covering ninety-eight percent of the land; in winter the **volume** of ice doubles along the edge of the continent.

– has bedrock that is depressed two to three thousand feet by the weight of the ice.

– has only one mammal, the Weddell seal (named for an early explorer), that lives there all year long.

– has only two flowering plants: Antarctic hair grass (*Deschampsia antarctica*) and Antarctic pearlwort (*Colobenthos subulatus*).

Letters

Letters are another way for a person to share experiences and feelings. Here is part of a letter that Dewey wrote home just after she arrived in Antarctica.

November 18th Palmer Station

Dear T.,

Palmer Station is a group of insulated metal buildings, housing fifty people comfortably. The station was built on Anvers Island. You don't know you're on an island because permanent ice fills the gap between Anvers and the mainland.

We learn the rules the first night: no travel alone, except to climb the glacier behind Palmer, flagged with poles to show the safest way up. We sign out when leaving, giving a departure hour and an estimated time of return. We are given walkie-talkies and check with "base" every hour. If we're half an hour off schedule, someone comes looking, unless a storm blows in. If it's too dangerous for anyone to come after us, we are expected to wait out the bad weather.

The sunscreen they pass out is "the only kind strong enough." We are ordered never to forget to use it.

Tomorrow we learn about the zodiacs, small rubber boats with outboard motors. I'm excited about what comes next, and sleepy.

    Much love,

    Mom

Young Weddell seal sunning on the beach

Gentoo parent feeding chicks

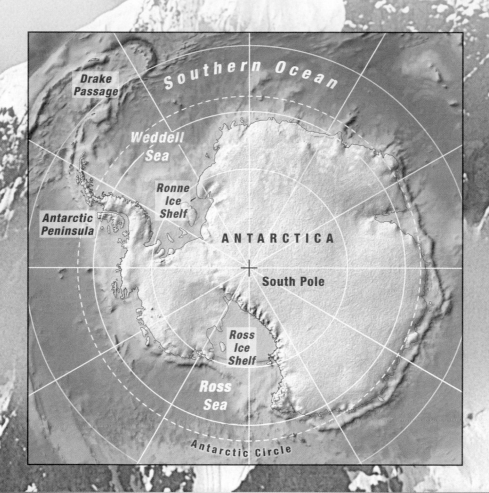

Drake
Passage

Southern Ocean

Weddell
Sea

Ronne
Ice
Shelf

Antarctic
Peninsula

ANTARCTICA

South Pole

Ross
Ice
Shelf

Ross
Sea

Antarctic Circle

Connect and Compare

1. Think about the experiences Dewey recorded. What is the value of keeping a journal? **Reading a Journal**

2. If you had the opportunity, would you choose to travel to Antarctica? Support your answer with information from the article. **Evaluate**

3. Think about *Spirit of Endurance* and this article about a modern-day trip to Antarctica. How are the two trips alike, and how are they different? **Reading/Writing Across Texts**

Geography Activity

Research another explorer of Antarctica. Mark the route of the explorer's journey on a map of Antarctica.

LOG ON   Find out more about Antarctica at **www.macmillanmh.com**

Writer's Craft

Beginning, Middle, and End

Writers use a good **beginning, middle, and end** so readers can follow the points being made. For a speech of introduction, choose facts that will grab the reader's attention at the beginning and hold it until the end.

I included interesting points about Dr. Robert Ballard in my speech.

I ended by welcoming Dr. Ballard.

Write an Introduction Speech

Introducing Dr. Robert Ballard

by Whitney O.

I am honored to introduce our guest today, Dr. Robert Ballard. He explores the deep seas. You might know him from one of his most famous discoveries, the wreck of the R.M.S. Titanic. Dr. Ballard has been on more than 100 deep-sea expeditions and has made countless other discoveries.

At the bottom of the Mediterranean Sea, Dr. Ballard and his team found an amazing, ancient fleet of Roman ships from the first century B.C. He also discovered volcanoes under the sea near California. Because they are so hot, he named them black smokers.

Dr. Ballard reminds people that explorers are still important in today's world. Join me in welcoming our country's most passionate oceanographer.

Your Turn

What famous person would you invite to your school? Choose someone whom you admire. Then prepare a speech to introduce this person to your fellow students. Remember to write a good beginning, middle, and end when you are describing this person and his or her accomplishments. Use the writer's checklist to check your writing.

Writer's Checklist

☑ **Ideas and Content:** Did I choose a person whom I truly admire?

☑ **Organization:** Does my speech build in energy, with a good **beginning, middle, and end**?

☑ **Voice:** Can the reader tell how much I admire this person?

☑ **Word Choice:** Did I choose the most precise adjectives possible?

☑ **Sentence Fluency:** Did I use a variety of sentence types?

☑ **Conventions:** Did I capitalize all proper nouns and adjectives? Did I proofread for spelling errors?

FANTASTIC FOODS

Talk About It

What is the most interesting fruit or vegetable that you have ever seen or tasted?

LOG ON Find out more about fantastic foods at **www.macmillanmh.com**

Juanita and the Cornstalk

by Sandra Garcia

Little rain had fallen in the small Mexican village of Tula. Juanita and her mother had planted seeds in the spring. With a **shortage** of rain, nothing grew. "Take the donkey to the market and sell her," Juanita's mother said. "We need the money." Juanita tied a rope to the donkey and led her toward the marketplace.

On the way Juanita met a sad merchant. "It would be a great kindness if you would sell that fine donkey to me," said the merchant. "I need help carrying my goods to the market. Unfortunately, I have only these magic corn seeds to trade. Plant the seeds in the ground. They do not need any water. Soon you will have giant cornstalks in your field." Juanita was happy to help the merchant. She made the trade and hurried home.

When Juanita's mother heard her story, she became upset and **bedlam** broke out. "How could you have been so foolish?" she yelled. She tossed the corn seeds out the window and went to bed. Juanita felt like an **outcast** even though she was going to sleep in her own house.

The sun that **reflected** off the glass of the window the next morning woke Juanita. She was surprised to find a giant cornstalk outside her window. The stalk reached so high into the sky that Juanita could not see the top.

She decided to climb the stalk to see how high it grew. Soon she developed a **strategy** for climbing and her plan helped her reach the top.

Above the clouds Juanita spotted Quetzalcoatl, the Toltec god of **civilization**. This leader of cultured life was sitting in a **traditional** rocking chair that had been passed down from generation to generation.

Quetzalcoatl welcomed her with a warm smile. "Hello, Juanita. I'm happy to have a visitor after all these years. I'm lonely. I would like to visit Earth again."

"I've got an idea, but it's full of detail and quite **complex**," Juanita said. "Why don't you turn yourself into a small creature that I can put in my pocket?"

"Why, little one, that's a brilliant thought! I'll give myself wings so that I can fly back here when I get tired. Let me give you some gold coins for your kindness."

After carrying Quetzalcoatl down to Earth, Juanita hurried home with the gold coins. Juanita hoped that this time her mother might understand how good things can happen when a kind act is repaid.

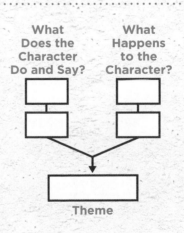

Reread for Comprehension

Make Inferences and Analyze Theme

A Theme Chart helps you make inferences and analyze information so you can determine the overall idea the author wants to tell in a story. Use your Theme Chart as you reread "Juanita and the Cornstalk" to identify the theme in the story.

545

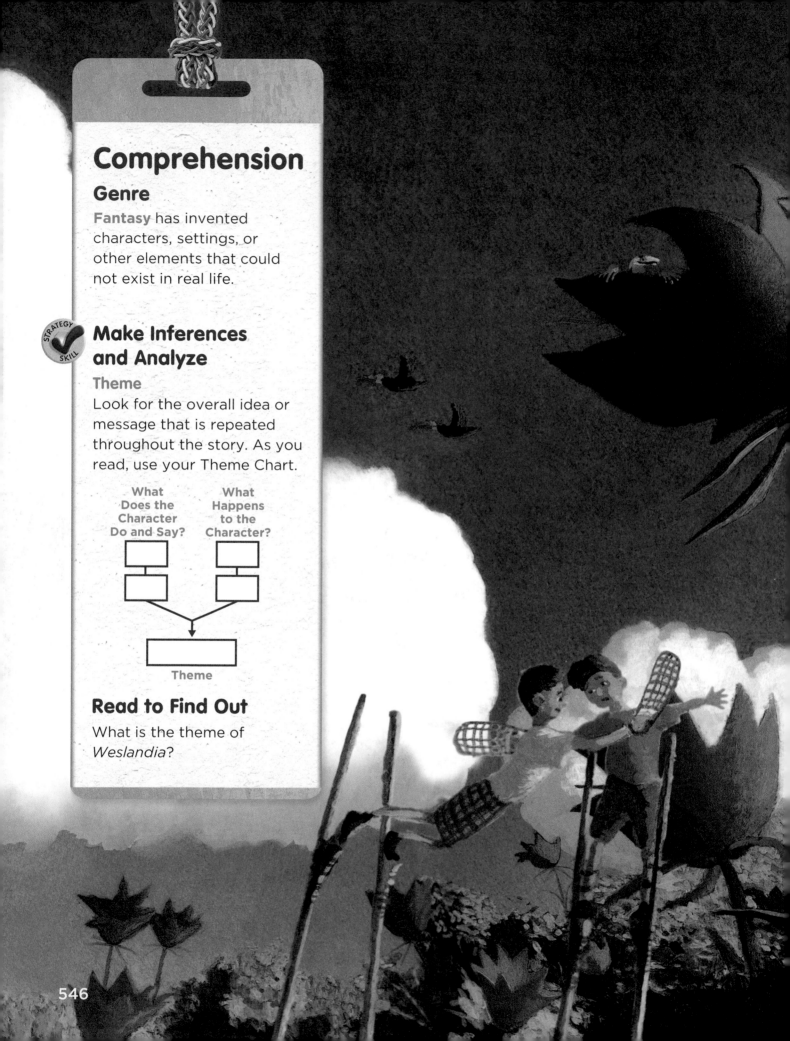

Comprehension

Genre

Fantasy has invented characters, settings, or other elements that could not exist in real life.

Make Inferences and Analyze

Theme

Look for the overall idea or message that is repeated throughout the story. As you read, use your Theme Chart.

What Does the Character Do and Say?	What Happens to the Character?
▢	▢
▢	▢

Theme

Read to Find Out

What is the theme of *Weslandia*?

546

Weslandia

by Paul Fleischman
illustrated by Kevin Hawkes

Award
Winning
Selection

"Of course he's miserable," moaned Wesley's mother. "He sticks out."

"Like a nose," snapped his father.

Listening through the heating vent, Wesley knew they were right. He was an **outcast** from the **civilization** around him.

He alone in his town disliked pizza and soda, alarming his mother and the school nurse. He found professional football stupid. He'd refused to shave half his head, the hairstyle worn by all the other boys, despite his father's bribe of five dollars.

Passing his neighborhood's two styles of housing—garage on the left and garage on the right—Wesley alone dreamed of more exciting forms of shelter. He had no friends, but plenty of tormentors.

Fleeing them was the only sport he was good at.

Each afternoon his mother asked him what he'd learned in school that day.

"That seeds are carried great distances by the wind," he answered on Wednesday.

"That each civilization has its staple food crop," he answered on Thursday.

"That school's over and I should find a good summer project," he answered on Friday.

As always, his father mumbled, "I'm sure you'll use that knowledge often."

Suddenly, Wesley's thoughts shot sparks. His eyes blazed. His father was right! He could actually *use* what he'd learned that week for a summer project that would top all others. He would grow his own food crop—and found his own civilization!

The next morning he turned over a plot of ground in his yard. That night a wind blew in from the west. It raced through the trees and set his curtains snapping. Wesley lay awake, listening. His land was being planted.

Five days later the first seedlings appeared.

"You'll have mighty **bedlam** on your hands if you don't get those weeds out," warned his neighbor.

"Actually, that's my crop," replied Wesley. "In this type of garden there are no weeds."

Following ancient tradition, Wesley's fellow gardeners grew tomatoes, beans, Brussels sprouts, and nothing else. Wesley found it thrilling to open his land to chance, to invite the new and unknown.

The plants shot up past his knees, then his waist. They seemed to be all of the same sort. Wesley couldn't find them in any plant book.

"Are those tomatoes, beans, or Brussels sprouts?" asked Wesley's neighbor.

"None of the above," replied Wesley.

Fruit appeared, yellow at first, then blushing to magenta. Wesley picked one and sliced through the rind to the juicy purple center. He took a bite and found the taste an entrancing blend of peach, strawberry, pumpkin pie, and flavors he had no name for.

Theme
What message do you think the author wants to get across in the conversations between Wesley and his neighbor?

Ignoring the shelf of cereals in the kitchen, Wesley took to breakfasting on the fruit. He dried half a rind to serve as a cup, built his own squeezing device, and drank the fruit's juice throughout the day.

Pulling up a plant, he found large tubers on the roots. These he boiled, fried, or roasted on the family barbecue, seasoning them with a pinch of the plant's highly aromatic leaves.

It was hot work tending to his crop. To keep off the sun, Wesley wove himself a hat from strips of the plant's woody bark. His success with the hat inspired him to devise a spinning wheel and loom on which he wove a loose-fitting robe from the stalks' soft inner fibers.

Unlike jeans, which he found scratchy and heavy, the robe was comfortable, **reflected** the sun, and offered myriad opportunities for pockets.

His schoolmates were scornful, then curious. Grudgingly, Wesley allowed them ten minutes apiece at his mortar, crushing the plant's seeds to collect the oil.

This oil had a tangy scent and served him both as suntan lotion and mosquito repellent. He rubbed it on his face each morning and sold small amounts to his former tormentors at the price of ten dollars per bottle.

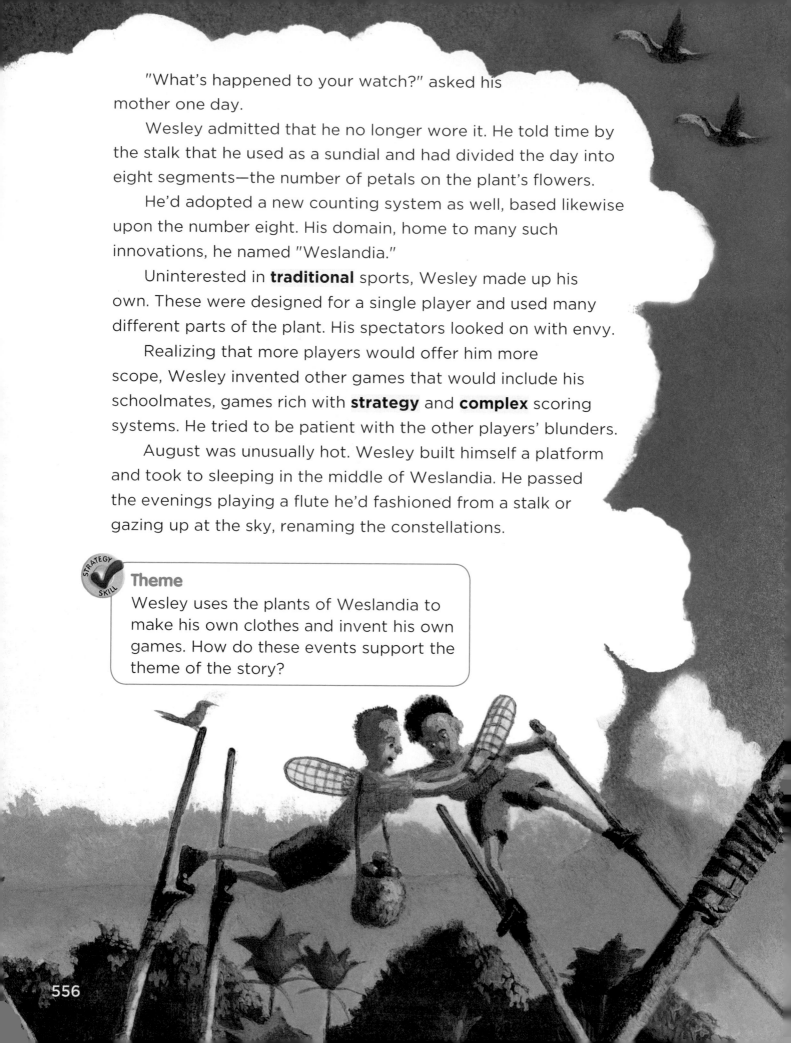

"What's happened to your watch?" asked his mother one day.

Wesley admitted that he no longer wore it. He told time by the stalk that he used as a sundial and had divided the day into eight segments—the number of petals on the plant's flowers.

He'd adopted a new counting system as well, based likewise upon the number eight. His domain, home to many such innovations, he named "Weslandia."

Uninterested in **traditional** sports, Wesley made up his own. These were designed for a single player and used many different parts of the plant. His spectators looked on with envy.

Realizing that more players would offer him more scope, Wesley invented other games that would include his schoolmates, games rich with **strategy** and **complex** scoring systems. He tried to be patient with the other players' blunders.

August was unusually hot. Wesley built himself a platform and took to sleeping in the middle of Weslandia. He passed the evenings playing a flute he'd fashioned from a stalk or gazing up at the sky, renaming the constellations.

Theme
Wesley uses the plants of Weslandia to make his own clothes and invent his own games. How do these events support the theme of the story?

His parents noted Wesley's improved morale. "It's the first time in years he's looked happy," said his mother.

Wesley gave them a tour of Weslandia.

"What do you call this plant?" asked his father. Not knowing its name, Wesley had begun calling it "swist," from the sound of its leaves rustling in the breeze.

In like manner, he'd named his new fabrics, games, and foods, until he'd created an entire language.

Mixing the plant's oil with soot, Wesley made a passable ink. As the finale to his summer project, he used the ink and his own eighty-letter alphabet to record the history of his civilization's founding.

In September Wesley returned to school . . .

He had no **shortage** of friends.

Meet Weslandia Creators
Paul Fleischman and Kevin Hawkes

Paul Fleischman, like Wesley, created his own world while he was growing up in California. Paul and his friends invented their own sports, ran a newspaper, and created their own alternative universe. His vivid imagination comes from his father, Sid Fleischman, who also wrote books. Often he would ask Paul to help him with the plot of a story. Words and imagination come naturally to Paul. "They were as much fun to play with as toys," he said.

Other books by Paul Fleischman: *Joyful Noise: Poems for Two Voices* and *Seedfolks*

Kevin Hawkes says he learned how to draw by practicing, practicing, and practicing some more. As a child he drew pictures and used modeling clay to mold sculptures, such as a life-size sculpture of a mountaineer. Today Kevin makes a "dummy" book for each book he illustrates. These first sketches help him create the unique images that bring stories like *Weslandia* to life.

LOG ON Find out more about Paul Fleischman and Kevin Hawkes at **www.macmillanmh.com**

Author's Purpose
How is Weslandia different from real life? Do you think the author wrote this fantasy story mainly to entertain? Why or why not?

560

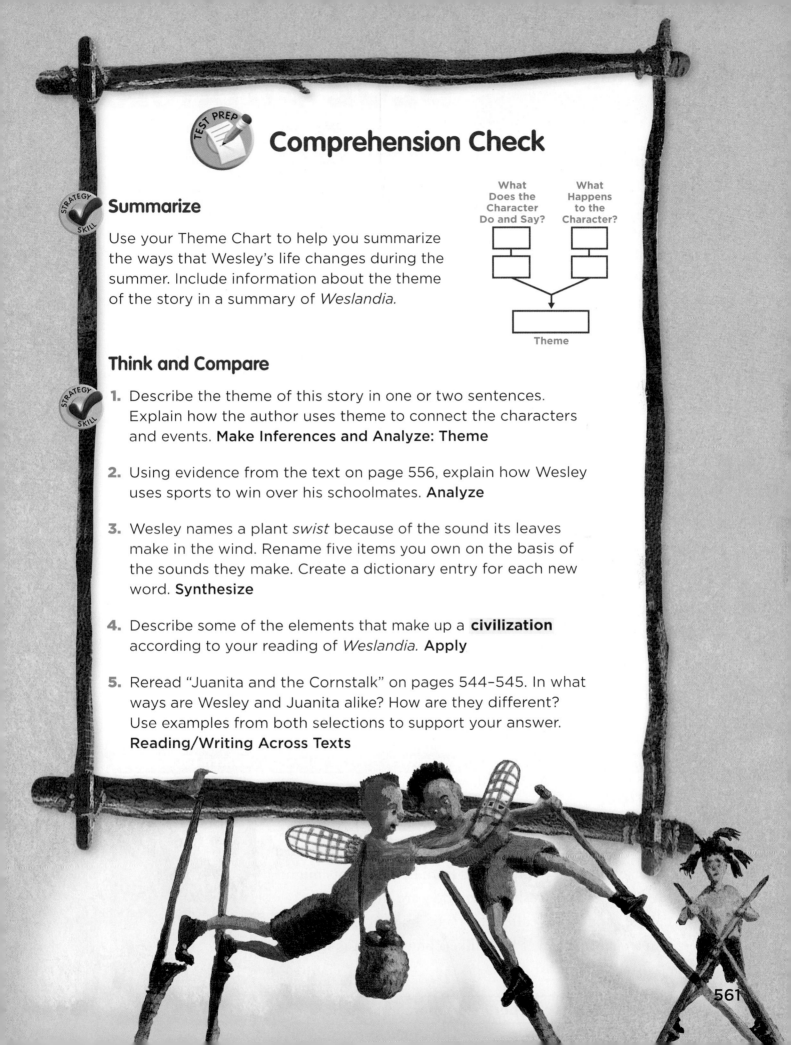

Comprehension Check

Summarize

Use your Theme Chart to help you summarize the ways that Wesley's life changes during the summer. Include information about the theme of the story in a summary of *Weslandia*.

What Does the Character Do and Say?	What Happens to the Character?
☐	☐
☐	☐

Theme

Think and Compare

1. Describe the theme of this story in one or two sentences. Explain how the author uses theme to connect the characters and events. **Make Inferences and Analyze: Theme**

2. Using evidence from the text on page 556, explain how Wesley uses sports to win over his schoolmates. **Analyze**

3. Wesley names a plant *swist* because of the sound its leaves make in the wind. Rename five items you own on the basis of the sounds they make. Create a dictionary entry for each new word. **Synthesize**

4. Describe some of the elements that make up a **civilization** according to your reading of *Weslandia*. **Apply**

5. Reread "Juanita and the Cornstalk" on pages 544–545. In what ways are Wesley and Juanita alike? How are they different? Use examples from both selections to support your answer. **Reading/Writing Across Texts**

Science

Genre

Online Encyclopedia Entries contain information about real people, living things, places, situations, or events.

Text Features

A **Hyperlink** is an electronic connection within text on a Web page that provides direct access to other documents or information.

A **Key Word** is a specific word that helps you find information when searching the Internet. It is often typed into a search box.

Content Vocabulary

flukes   crossbreeding
hybrids

BLUE POTATOES AND SQUARE WATERMELONS

by Omar Naid

Visit the produce section of any large supermarket. You may be astonished by the variety of unusual fruits and vegetables. Square watermelons, blue potatoes, and purple cauliflower attract shoppers' attention. Some plants are unusual because they are grown in special ways. For example, square watermelons grow inside square glass cases. The result is a specially shaped melon that is easy to cut and store in the refrigerator.

Some plants, called **flukes**, result from odd, sudden changes that happen only once. Other plants are "designed" when they are seeds.

Here are two online encyclopedia articles to help you learn more about how these unusual plants come about.

Address: http://www. example.com   **go**

Home   **Browse**   **Newsletters**   **Favorites**   **Search** hybrids

Hybrids

| This is a Key Word. |

Hybrids are new plants created by scientists. They are a combination of two different "parent" plants that form a whole new kind of plant. Foods from hybrid plants might taste better or stay fresher when they are shipped. For example, a new fruit called the pluot is a cross between a plum and an apricot. It looks like a plum, but it is sweeter and firmer than most plums.

| This is a hyperlink to more information. |

Address: http://www. example.com | go

Home | Browse | Newsletters | Favorites | Search crossbreeding

Crossbreeding

Crossbreeding is when two plants of the same kind are combined to create a better plant. A farmer might crossbreed a small, sweet tomato with a large but tasteless tomato to create a large, sweet tomato, which will provide delicious slices that fit better on sandwiches. Farmers must use plant selection, which means choosing the plants with qualities that people want and then growing more of these plants.

The next time you go to the supermarket and see a square watermelon or pluot, remember how much work went into producing it.

TOMATO
CROSSBREEDING

Connect and Compare

1. How would you find more information about the pluot? **Hyperlinks**

2. What type of produce would you like to improve? How could you find out more about how to improve it? **Synthesize**

3. Think about "Blue Potatoes and Square Watermelons" and *Weslandia*. How is the process of growing produce different in each story? **Reading/Writing Across Text**

 Science Activity

Research a plant that is a hybrid. List the traits of this hybrid and compare and contrast it to the two parent plants using a Venn Diagram.

 Find out more about new produce at **www.macmillanmh.com**

563

Writer's Craft

Mood

Writers use dialogue to reveal a character's personality, thoughts, and feelings. Dialogue also shows the conflict between characters. Writers use precise words to reinforce the **mood** established by the dialogue.

I used precise words to reinforce the mood established by the dialogue.

I showed the characters' feelings with dialogue.

Write a Play

The Four Eaters

by Mary W.

Setting: The school cafeteria during lunch.

Jorge: (tasting a french fry) Mia, you aren't eating. Consider the french fry, so tender on the inside, so crispy on the outside.

Mia: (frowning) They're too greasy. I hate grease.

Todd: (stuffing his face with a handful of fries) Who has time to notice? I'm starving! Hey, Mia, if you aren't eating any can I have them? (Mia slides her tray over to Todd.)

Kelli: Mia, we're not supposed to trade food. Todd, don't you think about the importance of nutrition? I'm not sure about the vitamin content of those fries.

Todd: (mouth full) The whaaaa?

Jorge: Nutrition? It's about taste! (takes another bite)

Kelli: Don't you guys ever think about anything but your stomachs? This food should come with a warning label.

Mia: Yeah. It should say: "Eat at your own risk."

Your Turn

Write a play so that you can practice using dialogue. Choose a theme that has something to do with food. Plan to use strong characters with unique personalities. Make sure that the words you choose for each character fit that character's personality. Remember that the best way to show conflict between characters is through what they say to each other. Use the writer's checklist to check your writing.

Writer's Checklist

✓ **Ideas and Content:** Did I choose a theme about food that interests me?

✓ **Organization:** Does the conversation among the characters flow easily from person to person?

✓ **Voice:** Did I choose words for each character that those characters would really use when speaking?

☑ **Word Choice:** Did I choose precise words that help to reinforce the **mood**?

✓ **Sentence Fluency:** Do the sentences in the dialogue among characters flow smoothly?

✓ **Conventions:** Did I punctuate my play properly? Did I check spelling?

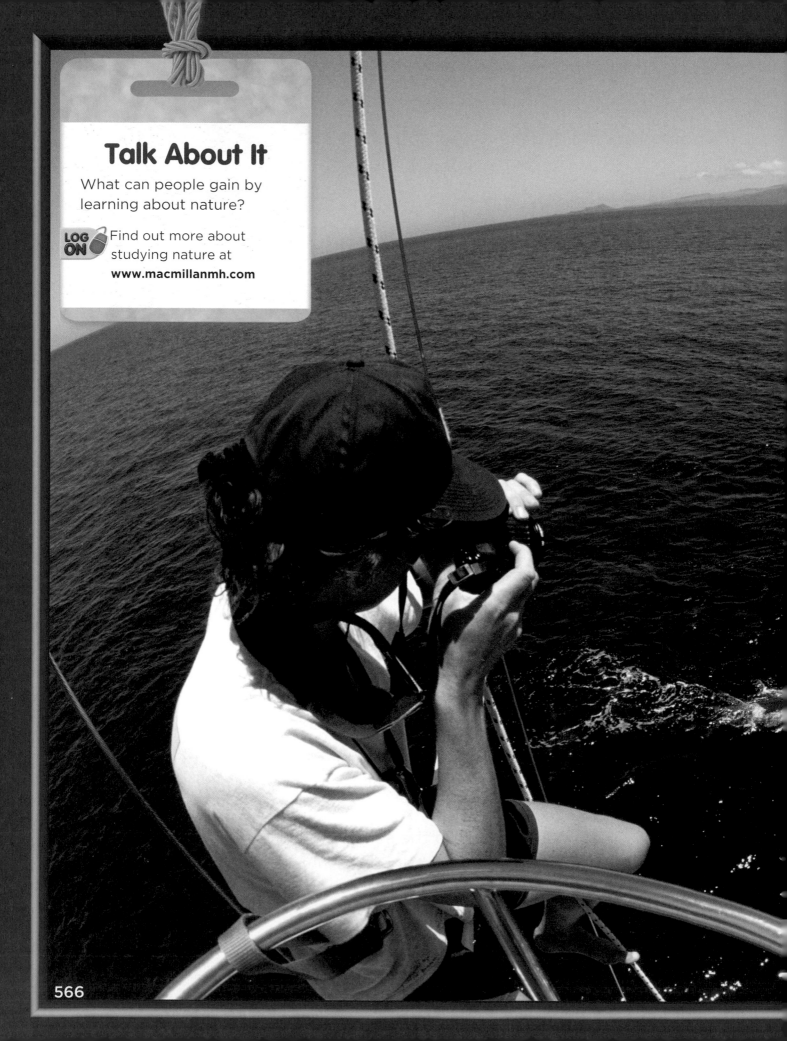

Talk About It

What can people gain by learning about nature?

LOG ON Find out more about studying nature at **www.macmillanmh.com**

Learning from Nature

Vocabulary

instill

combined

naturalist

vacant

diverse

Paul Cox collects a vine from high up in a banyan tree in Samoa.

The Healing Power of Plants

Even as a kid in Utah, Paul Cox was wild about plants. He built a greenhouse and collected weird, insect-eating plants.

Cox studied to become an ethnobotanist (eth•no•BOT•uh•nist). This, he explains, "is someone who loves plants and people and studies the relationship between them." Cox is most interested in how to use plants for healing.

When he won an important science award, Cox decided to use the money to "go live with native healers to learn from them." He, his wife, and their four kids moved to a remote village in Samoa, an island nation in the South Pacific. They lived for a year in a hut without running water or electricity.

Cox studied how the people of Samoa use plants to treat illness. One tree he learned about from a native healer could someday be used to make a valuable drug. If so, "the [native healer's] whole village will share the riches," says Cox. The leafy kingdom of plants is full of such treasures. Cox's work and the knowledge of native healers may ultimately lead to medicines that save many lives.

Teaching "EARTHKEEPING"

All the earthkeepers pitched in to help build an outdoor seating area and nature trails.

For more than 27 years, Joseph Andrews has tried to **instill** a love of nature in his students. "I try to tie nature into every subject," he explains. Andrews teaches a **combined** fourth- and fifth-grade class at Jones Lane Elementary School in Gaithersburg, Maryland.

One year his students helped build an outdoor classroom for the school. There students can enjoy a view of a meadow and stream while they learn. Language arts, social studies, and Earth science all come to life in the outdoor classroom. Sometimes the students read poetry and Native American tales. At other times they simply listen to the sounds of nature and hope to catch a glimpse of the deer and foxes that make their homes near the school.

"Mr. Andrews calls us his earthkeepers," says fifth-grader Emmanuel Maru. Andrews says giving students that title helps them understand that they have an important role in helping to protect the environment.

THE "BIODIVERSITY" MAN

Edward Osborne Wilson was a **naturalist** from the start. As a child growing up in Alabama and northern Florida, he loved to study nature. He made his first important scientific discovery when he was 13. In a **vacant** lot in Mobile, Alabama, he found the first known U.S. colonies of fire ants. Starting as an entomologist—a scientist who studies insects—E.O. Wilson went on to become one of the most respected scientists in the world. He is most well known for making the world aware of the importance of biodiversity. "Bio" means "life." "Diversity" comes from the word "**diverse**," which means "different from one another." Biodiversity describes the complex web of life, with many different plant and animal species, that is necessary to keep Earth healthy.

LOG ON Find out more about biodiversity at **www.macmillanmh.com**

A Historic Journey

Comprehension

Genre

A **Nonfiction Article** in a newspaper or magazine presents facts and information about real people, places, and events.

Make Inferences and Analyze

Cause and Effect
A cause is what makes something happen. An effect is the thing that happens.

How did the leaders of the Lewis and Clark expedition make history as both explorers and scientists?

IN 1803, President Thomas Jefferson asked Captain Meriwether Lewis to explore a huge area of North America known as the Louisiana Purchase. The United States was about to buy this land from France. The effect of this purchase was to double the size of the United States territory, but very little was known about it. Jefferson hoped it included a water route between the Mississippi River and the Pacific Ocean that would help U.S. trade.

Besides learning about the geography of the Louisiana Purchase, Lewis was ordered to report on the people, plants, and animals that inhabited this vast territory.

Meriwether Lewis

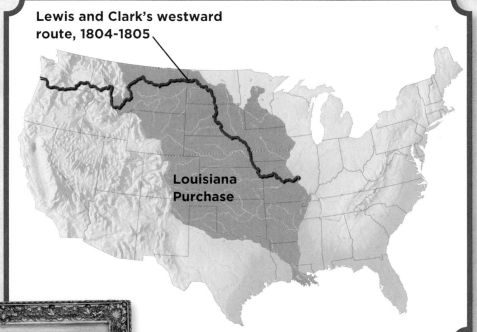

Lewis and Clark's westward route, 1804-1805

Louisiana Purchase

William Clark

Accompanying Lewis on this adventure was Captain William Clark, Lewis's best friend. During their historic journey, each of these two army captains would prove to be an excellent **naturalist**. They kept superb maps and diaries of everything they saw and learned. They were the first to write about many Native American tribes who lived in the territory. Their **combined** efforts produced descriptions of the **diverse** plant and animal life in the territory—122 kinds of animals and 178 kinds of plants.

Barking Squirrels or Ground Rats?

The expedition started in May 1804. Lewis and Clark led a 33-member team out of St. Louis, Missouri. That September, the team set eyes on an endless sea of little animals that French members of the team called *petite chiens*—French for "little dogs." Plans for future travel were halted until these creatures could be thoroughly investigated. Lewis called them "barking squirrels." Clark preferred to call them "ground rats." The name we now know—"prairie dogs"— came later. The team even captured a live prairie dog and sent it back to President Jefferson in Washington.

Prairie dog

William Clark's diagram of the Handsom Falls on the Missouri River

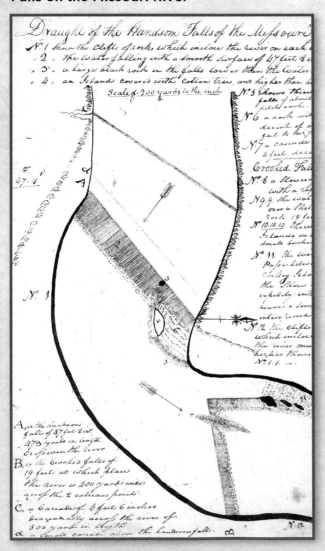

Where Do the Buffalo Roam?

The Missouri River from St. Louis to what is now North Dakota was already well-traveled by trappers and traders. But Lewis and Clark collected a trove of new plant and animal specimens from the area. They also created a detailed map of the route.

The farther north Lewis and Clark and their team traveled in the summer of 1804, the more buffalo they saw. By fall, however, the immense herds were starting to move south toward their wintering grounds. A few months later, feasts of fresh buffalo were just pleasant memories. Thankfully, the explorers enjoyed the hospitality of two Native American tribes, the Mandan and Hidatsa. Mule deer replaced buffalo as a source of meat for the explorers.

In 1805 the expedition paddled northwest on the Missouri River toward Montana. There Lewis and Clark found less open prairie. The land was broken up by shallow gullies and streams. It was dotted

with bushes and scrubby trees. The rugged landscape of western North Dakota amazed and challenged the expedition. They crossed the Badlands—a harsh, nearly **vacant** area of rolling hills and little vegetation—and moved onto the plains. Here the explorers spotted wondrous sights. Meriwether Lewis wrote this in his journal on September 16, 1805: ". . . vast herds of buffalo, deer, elk, and antelopes were seen feeding in every direction as far as the eye of the observer could reach."

Keeping Track While Making Tracks

More than 500 days and 4,000 miles after they had set out, Lewis and Clark reached the Pacific. Clark—who was a horrible speller—wrote in his journal "Ocian view! O! the joy!"

Lewis and Clark never found the water route that Jefferson hoped they would, but they became the first U.S. citizens to explore the Midwest and West—the endless Great Plains, the jagged Rocky Mountains, and the glittering Pacific. They took the time to write down in their journals everything they saw each day.

Perhaps the greatest effect of the Lewis and Clark expedition was the opening of U.S. territory west of the Mississippi River to other explorers and to settlers. Thanks to the courage, endurance, and keen observation skills of Lewis and Clark, we can look back today and see the land as it was then. The record of their journey helps to **instill** in Americans today the same sense of wonder and adventure they must have felt more than two hundred years ago.

Think and Compare

1. What caused Jefferson to send Lewis and Clark on their expedition?

2. According to this selection, what was the most important result of the Lewis and Clark expedition?

3. Do you think you would have liked to have been part of the Lewis and Clark expedition? Why or why not?

4. What common theme can you find among all of these selections? What are the individuals in each selection interested in?

Lewis and Clark camped near here in what is now Montana. The Rocky Mountains are in the distance.

573

Test Strategy

On My Own

The answer is not in the selection. Form an opinion about what you read.

Model of a morphing-wing plane

DESIGNED by NATURE

Like birds, airplanes have wings and tails that are necessary for flight. It seems natural that the design of airplanes would be inspired by the bodies of birds. Engineers are still trying to make airplanes do as many things in flight as birds can do.

Just spend a little time on a beach watching seagulls, and you'll recognize the challenge. A seagull swoops over the sand, suddenly changes direction, pauses in midair, drops earthward, lands, and takes off again—all in just a few seconds. An airplane can't do that. Scientists don't yet understand how birds are able to make certain kinds of movements in the air.

Understanding how birds perform their aerial feats is one step in the effort to improve the design of aircraft.

The hope is to make aircraft more efficient and maneuverable—able to change direction easily. Someday this research may produce an airplane with wings that are dramatically different from the wings we see today. Another possibility: airplane wings that can actually morph, or change shape, in flight.

The design of this 1928 airplane was based on an owl in flight.

Go On ▶

Directions: Answer the questions.

1. **Engineers who design airplanes are inspired by birds because**

    A   migrating birds can sometimes interfere with air travel.

    B   they want to build airplanes that make similar movements.

    C   they want to find a way to keep birds away from certain areas.

    D   they want to design sturdier wings for aircraft.

2. **Among the things a seagull can do that an airplane can't do are**

    A   fly fast and carry cargo.

    B   raise and lower landing gear in flight.

    C   take off and land on a runway.

    D   pause in midair and change direction suddenly.

3. **Someday airplanes may have wings that can**

    A   flap like the wings of birds.

    B   change color in flight.

    C   change shape in flight.

    D   move up and down in flight.

4. **What new uses can you think of for airplanes that have wings like birds?**

5. **Airplanes have changed over the years, from ones with simple, box-shaped wings to supersonic jets. How important is flight today? Should airplanes continue to change? Explain your answer.**

Tip

Form an opinion.

Write to a Prompt

The selection "The Healing Power of Plants" tells about ethnobotanist Paul Cox, who studies how native healers use plants as medicines. Should modern doctors be required to learn about methods used by native healers? Write a one-page persuasive essay giving your opinion on this question.

I used facts and reasons to support my argument.

We Know Better

I do not believe modern doctors should have to learn about methods used by native healers. The reason is simple: Now we know better.

We have made so many advances in medicine that native healers really don't have anything valuable to teach us. They don't have the benefit of high-tech machines. Modern doctors do. Native healers don't have college classes to learn chemistry and biology. Doctors who have taken those classes are already way ahead of native healers.

Native healers may know how to use plants to make a person feel better. But doctors don't need plants when the best, most effective medicines are available to them and their patients.

Doctors prescribe medicines that have been tested by the government. How would we know if a medicine made from plants by a native healer is safe? That's the strongest argument of all to stick with modern medicine. It's as simple as this: We know better.

Writing Prompt

"Teaching Earthkeeping" is about Joseph Andrews, a teacher who tries to instill a love of nature in his students. Do you believe schools should spend money and time instilling a love of nature in students? Write a one-page persuasive essay giving your point of view on this question.

Writer's Checklist

☑ Ask yourself, who is my audience?

☑ Think about your purpose for writing.

☑ Choose the correct form for your writing.

☑ Form an opinion about the topic.

☑ Use reasons to support your opinion.

☑ Be sure your ideas are logical and organized.

☑ Use your best spelling, grammar, and punctuation.

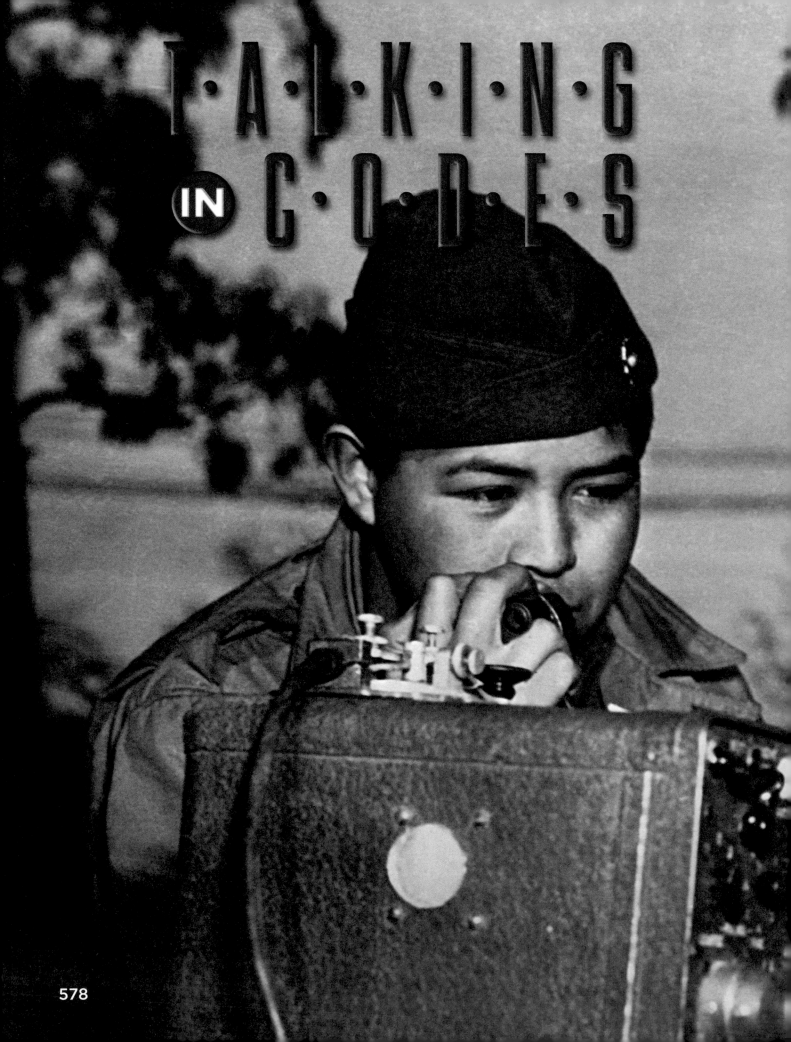

T·A·L·K·I·N·G
IN C·O·D·E·S

Talk About It

Name some different kinds of codes. What are some situations in which you might want to talk in code?

Find out more about codes at **www.macmillanmh.com**

Rita, the Storyteller

by Nina Gabriel

My friend Rita is excited about her new baby sister. She stood in the busy hospital **corridor** watching the baby sleep as people passed by.

Rita's new sister is the newest member of the Meskwaki tribe. Some members of this tribe have never lived on a **reservation**, land set aside for Native Americans by the United States government. Meskwaki are proud of their own traditions, especially storytelling.

The Meskwaki pass on their stories to the very young. Rita loves telling stories. She is very excited to tell her new sister a true story she learned from the elders. It is about the brave Meskwaki code talkers of World War II.

In 1941, twenty-seven men from the Meskwaki tribe **enlisted** in the army because they wanted to fight for their country. From this group eight men were chosen for a secret mission. They became code talkers who used their native language to send secret messages.

Before the code talkers, U.S. troops were not able to move around safely. The enemy was able to understand the messages sent to the troops. The United States turned to the Meskwaki because members of this tribe had their own language that few outsiders understood. They could pass on important information without the enemy knowing what was being said.

The group of eight code talkers was sent to North Africa. During an **invasion** some of these code talkers entered enemy territory. The mission took place at night when the **shield** protecting them was darkness. They used walkie-talkies to tell the **location** of the enemy. The position of the enemy was said in code. This information was passed to other code talkers back at camp.

The code was never broken during World War II. The code talkers helped the United States win the war. However, they got little recognition.

When Rita first told me this story, I felt sad. The eight code talkers should be heroes! Rita saw how my shoulders **sagged** down from my disappointment. My forehead was **creased** as I frowned.

"Don't worry!" she smiled. "In Meskwaki culture we pass down stories about our heroes. The code talkers will never be forgotten."

Reread for Comprehension

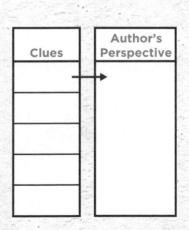

Generate Questions
Author's Perspective

An Author's Perspective Chart helps you ask questions to determine an author's opinion or point of view. Use your Author's Perspective Chart as you reread "Rita, The Storyteller" to find the author's perspective.

Clues	Author's Perspective

Comprehension

Genre

Historical Fiction tells a story in which fictional characters take part in actual historical events from the past.

Generate Questions

Author's Perspective

Look for clues that reveal the author's point of view. As you read, use your Author's Perspective Chart.

Clues	Author's Perspective

Read to Find Out

How does the author feel about the Navajo language?

The Unbreakable Code

by Sara Hoagland Hunter ◆ illustrated by Julia Miner

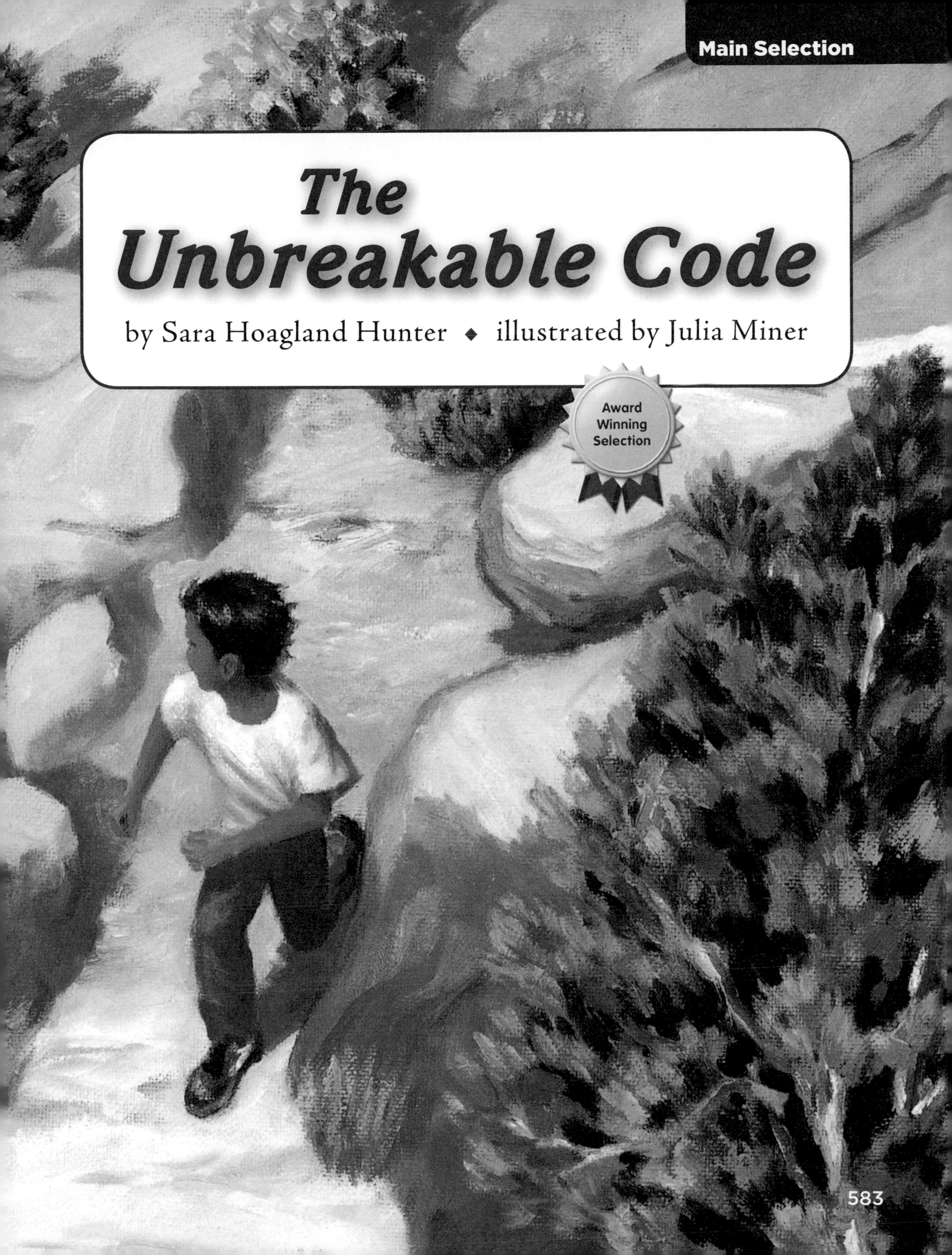

Award Winning Selection

John raced up the trail, sending pebbles skidding behind him. When he reached his favorite hiding place, he fell to the ground out of breath. Here between the old piñon tree and the towering walls of the canyon, he felt safe. The river full of late-summer rain looked like a silver thread winding through his grandfather's farm land. They would be looking for him now, but he was never coming down.

His mother had married the man from Minnesota. There was nothing he could do about that. But he was not going with them. He closed his eyes and rested in the stillness. The faint bleat of a mountain goat echoed off the canyon walls.

Suddenly a voice boomed above him: "Shouldn't you be packing?"

John's eyes flew open. It was his grandfather on horseback.

"Your stepfather's coming with the pickup in an hour."

"I'm not going," John said.

"You have to go. School's starting soon," said Grandfather, stepping down from his horse. "You'll be back next summer."

John dug his toe deeper into the dirt. "I want to stay with you," he said.

Grandfather's soft, brown eyes disappeared in the wrinkles of a smile. John thought they were the kindest eyes he had ever seen.

"You're going to be all right," Grandfather said. "You have an unbreakable code."

"What's that?" asked John.

Grandfather sat down and began to speak gently in Navajo. The sounds wove up and down, in and out, as warm and familiar as the patterns of one of Grandmother's Navajo blankets. John leaned against his grandfather's knee.

"The unbreakable code is what saved my life in World War II," he said. "It's the Navajo language."

John's shoulders **sagged**. Navajo couldn't help him. Nobody in his new school spoke Navajo.

"I'll probably forget how to speak Navajo," he whispered.

"Navajo is your language," said his grandfather sternly. "Navajo you must never forget."

The lump in John's throat was close to a sob. "You don't know what it's like there!" he said.

His grandfather continued quietly in Navajo. "I had to go to a government boarding school when I was five. It was the law.

"They gave me an English name and cut my hair off. I wasn't allowed to speak my language. Anyone who spoke Navajo had to chew on squares of soap. Believe me, I chewed a lot of soap during those years. 'Speak English,' they said. But Navajo was my language and Navajo I would never forget.

"Every summer I went home to herd the sheep and help with the crops. I cried when the cottonwoods turned gold and it was time to go back.

"Finally, one night in the tenth grade, I was working in the kitchen when I heard a bulletin on the school radio: 'Navajo needed for special duty to the Marines. Must be between the ages of seventeen and thirty-two, fluent in English and Navajo, and in excellent physical condition.'

"Just before lights out, I snuck past the bunks and out the door towards the open plain. I felt like a wild horse with the lasso finally off its neck. Out in the open, the stars danced above me and the tumbleweeds blew by my feet as I ran. The next day, I enlisted."

"But you weren't seventeen," said John.

"The reservation had no birth records," Grandfather said with a grin. "Two weeks later I was on a bus headed for boot camp with twenty-eight other Navajos. I stared out the window into the darkness. I was going outside of the Four Sacred Mountains for the first time in my life."

"Were you scared?" asked John.

"Of course," said his grandfather. "I didn't know where I was going or what our mission was. Most of all, I didn't know how I would measure up to the people out there I had heard so much about."

"How did you?" asked John, chewing his fingernail.

His grandfather began to laugh. "We were known as the toughest platoon at boot camp. We had done so much marching at boarding school that the drills were no problem. Hiking in the desert of California with a heavy pack was no worse than hauling water in the canyon in midsummer. And I'd done that since I was four years old.

"As for the survival exercises, we had all gone without food for a few days. A Navajo learns to survive.

Author's Perspective
What clues reveal how the author feels about the Navajo platoon?

"One weekend they bused us to a new camp in San Diego. On Monday we were marched to a building with bars on every window. They locked us in a classroom at the end of a long, narrow **corridor**. An officer told us our mission was top secret. We would not even be allowed to tell our families. We were desperately needed for a successful **invasion** of the Pacific Islands. So far the Japanese had been able to intercept and decode all American messages in only minutes. This meant that no information could be passed between American ships, planes, and land forces.

"The government thought the Navajo language might be the secret weapon. Only a few outsiders had ever learned it. Most importantly, the language had never been written down, so there was no alphabet for the Japanese to discover and decode.

"He gave us a list of more than two hundred military terms to code. Everything had to be memorized. No trace of the code could ever be found in writing. It would live or die with us in battle.

"When the officer walked out of the room, I looked at the Navajo next to me and began to laugh. 'All those years they told us to forget Navajo, and now the government needs it to save the country!'

"We were marched every day to that classroom. We were never allowed to leave the building. We couldn't even use the bathroom by ourselves. Each night, an officer locked our notes in a safe.

"The code had to be simple and fast. We would have only one chance to send each message. After that, the Japanese would be tracing our **location** to bomb us or trying to record the code.

"We chose words from nature that would be easy to remember under fire. Since Navajo has no alphabet, we made up our own. 'A' became *wollachee*." "Ant?" asked John in English.

Grandfather nodded.

"'B' was *shush*."

"Bear," said John.

"'C' was *moasi*. 'D', *be*. 'E', *dzeh*." His grandfather continued through the alphabet. Each time he named the Navajo word, John answered with the English.

"We named the aircraft after birds. The dive-bomber was a chicken hawk. The observation plane was an owl. A patrol plane was a crow. Bomber was buzzard.

"At night we would lie in our bunks and test each other. Pretty soon I was dreaming in code.

"Since we would be radiomen, we had to learn all kinds of radio operations. We were taught how to take a radio apart and put it together blindfolded. The Japanese fought at night, so we would have to do most of our work in complete darkness. Even the tiniest match flame could be a target.

"When the day came for the code to be tested in front of the top Marine officers, I was terrified. I knelt at one end of a field with our radio ground set. The officers marched towards me. Behind a building at the other end of the field, another code talker sat under military guard waiting for my transmission. One officer handed me a written message:

"'Receiving steady machine gun fire. Request reinforcements.'

"It took only seconds for me to speak into the microphone in Navajo code. The officer sent a runner to the end of the field to check the speed and accuracy of the message. The Navajo at the other end handed him the exact message written in English before he even came around the corner of the building! They tested us over and over. Each time, we were successful. The government requested two hundred Navajo recruits immediately. Two of our group stayed behind to train them. The rest of us were on our way."

"Tell me about the fighting!" said John.

Suddenly Grandfather's face looked as **creased** and battered as the canyon walls behind him. After a long pause he said, "What I saw is better left back there. I would not want to touch my home or my family with those pictures.

"Before we invaded, I looked out at that island. It had been flattened and burned. 'Let this never happen to a beautiful island again,' I thought. I just stayed on the deck of the ship thinking about the ceremonies they were doing for me at home. We invaded at dawn.

"I almost drowned in a bomb crater before I even got to shore. I was trying to run through the water and the bullets when I felt myself sinking into a bottomless hole. My eighty-pound radio pack pulled me straight down. I lost my rifle paddling to the surface.

"On the beach, it was all I could do just to survive. I remember lying there with gunfire flying past my ears. A creek that ran to the beach was clear when I first lay there. By noon it was blood red.

"The worst were the fallen soldiers I had to run over to go forward. I couldn't even stop to say I was sorry. I just had to run over them and keep going.

"I had to move through the jungle at night, broadcasting in code from different locations. One unit needed medical supplies. Another needed machine-gun support. I had just begun broadcasting to another code talker. 'Arizona! New Mexico!' I called. The next thing I knew, an American soldier behind me was yelling, 'Do you know what we do to spies?'

"'Don't shoot!' I said. 'I'm American. Look at my uniform.' He didn't believe me. He had just heard the foreign language. He had seen my hair and my eyes. Japanese spies had been known to steal uniforms from fallen soldiers.

"One of my buddies jumped out of the bushes right at that moment and saved my life."

"How did you stay alive the rest of the time?" asked John.

"My belief was my **shield**," Grandfather answered.

He drew a ragged wallet from deep inside of his shirt pocket. "Inside of this, I carried corn pollen from the medicine man. 'Never be afraid,' he said. 'Nothing's going to touch you.' And nothing ever did. More than four hundred code talkers fought in some of the bloodiest battles of World War II. All but a few of us survived.

"The Japanese never did crack the code. When they finally discovered what language it was, they captured and tortured one poor Navajo. He wasn't a code talker and couldn't understand the message they had intercepted. He told them we were talking about what we ate for breakfast. Our code word for bombs was 'eggs'.

"Six months before the war ended, Navajo code talkers passed more than eight hundred messages in two days during the invasion of Iwo Jima.

"When the American flag was raised on top of Iwo Jima's mountain, the victory was announced in code to the American fleet. 'Sheep-Uncle-Ram-Ice-Bear-Ant-Cat-Horse-Itch' came the code."

John tried to spell out the letters.

"Suribachi?" asked John.

"Yes," said Grandfather. "Mount Suribachi.

"When I came home, I walked the twelve miles from the bus station to this spot. There weren't any parades or parties.

"I knew I wasn't allowed to tell anyone about the code. I looked down at that beautiful canyon floor and thought, 'I'm never leaving again.'"

"But why did you leave in the first place?" asked John.

His grandfather lifted him gently onto the horse. "The answer to that is in the code," he said. "The code name for America was 'Our Mother.' You fight for what you love. You fight for what is yours."

He swung his leg behind John and reached around him to hold the reins.

"Keep my wallet," he said. "It will remind you of the unbreakable code that once saved your country."

John clutched the wallet with one hand and held the horse's mane with the other. He wasn't as scared of going to a new place any more. His grandfather had taught him who he was and what he would always have with him. He was the grandson of a Navajo code talker and he had a language that had once helped save his country.

Author's Perspective
How does the author feel about the Navajo code talkers? How can you tell?

Decoding the Facts about Sara Hoagland Hunter and Julia Miner

Sara Hoagland Hunter was a teacher and a journalist before she combined her interests and started her own company. Today she writes and produces books as well as videos, scripts, and albums for children. For this book Sara interviewed the "code talkers." She found them kind and strong, and she felt privileged to be able to tell their story.

Julia Miner became interested in illustrating this book when her college classmate Sara Hoagland Hunter told her about the idea. They made several trips to Arizona to meet with actual code talkers, which helped them capture the spirit of the Navajo code talkers' experience. Besides illustrating children's books, Julia is an architect and writer. Often she travels to different countries for inspiration for her illustrations.

 Find out more about Sara Hoagland Hunter and Julia Miner at **www.macmillanmh.com**

Author's Purpose

This selection is historical fiction. Which parts of the story are based on real events? How well does the author inform readers about those events? Explain.

Comprehension Check

Summarize

Understanding an author's perspective can help you organize ideas and make judgments about the piece you are reading. Use your Author's Perspective Chart to help you write a summary of *The Unbreakable Code*.

Clues	Author's Point of View

Think and Compare

1. Use the Author's Perspective Chart to describe how the author feels about the Navajo code talkers. Explain how the story would change if the author felt differently about the subject. **Generate Questions: Author's Perspective**

2. Reread page 594. What is Grandfather's belief? How was it like a **shield** during the war? **Analyze**

3. Describe why you would or would not like to have been a Navajo code talker. Explain your answer. **Apply**

4. Grandfather says that "You fight for what you love." Explain why you agree or disagree with his statement. Include examples from your experience in your answer. **Evaluate**

5. Reread "Rita, the Storyteller" on pages 580–581. In what ways are Rita's and John's family histories and traditions similar? In what ways are they different? Use examples from both selections to support your answer. **Reading/Writing Across Texts**

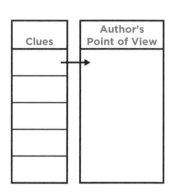

599

Poetry

A **Cinquain** is a five-line stanza poem. The first line has two syllables. The next lines have four, six, eight, and two syllables respectively.

Literary Elements

Consonance is the repetition of identical end consonant sounds in a series of words.

Symbolism is the use of concrete objects to represent or express abstract concepts, qualities, or ideas.

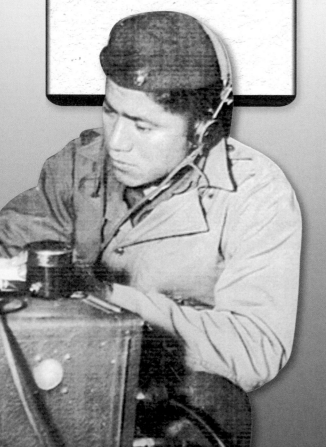

Navajo Code Talkers
Five Cinquains
by Mary Willie

Uncle
Remembers how
He and fellow fearless
Navajo Code Talkers saved lives
And hope.

Try to
Imagine this:
Dangerous night with stars
Cold stars different from the ones
Back home.

Secrets
We sent kept safe
In this ancient language.
No enemies could understand
Secrets.

The repetition of the end sound "t" in *sent* and *kept* is an example of consonance.

This code
Bold invention,
Created for wartime
By brave soldiers, who marched in lines
Like ants.

Soldiers
Guarded the Flag.
The word *America*
Whispered in code as "our mother"
Kept safe.

The words "our mother" symbolize the soldiers' feelings about America.

Connect and Compare

1. Find another example of consonance in one of the cinquains. **Consonance**

2. How does the poet feel about the Code Talkers? **Analyze**

3. Compare these cinquains to *The Unbreakable Code*. What details from both texts give you clues about how the Navajo felt about fighting in World War II? **Reading/Writing Across Texts**

 Find out more about cinquains at **www.macmillanmh.com**

Write to Compare and Contrast

A Comparison of Two Story Characters

by Pearl N.

I found three similarities between the characters in *Weslandia* and *The Unbreakable Code*.

I used the transitions "as a result" and "finally" between paragraphs.

Wesley, the main character in *Weslandia*, is similar to the grandfather in *The Unbreakable Code*. Wesley is a creative person who doesn't feel like he fits in with kids his own age. Similarly, as a young boy, the grandfather felt that he did not fit in at boarding school. Both Wesley and the grandfather seem most happy when they are pursuing their own goals.

As a result, Wesley changes his life by creating his own civilization. The grandfather changes his life by joining the Marines.

Finally, language is important to both Wesley and the grandfather. Wesley creates a new alphabet and the grandfather uses the Navajo language to affect history.

Your Turn

Choose two characters to compare and contrast. They can be from the same story or from two different stories. Write a compare and contrast essay. Be careful to organize it so that the points are easy to follow. Include transitions between paragraphs. Use the writer's checklist to check your writing.

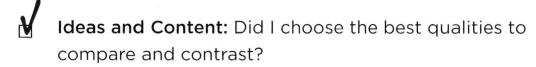

Writer's Checklist

✓ **Ideas and Content:** Did I choose the best qualities to compare and contrast?

✓ **Organization:** Can the reader easily follow the traits I am comparing and contrasting?

✓ **Voice:** Does my personality show through where I want it to?

☑ **Word Choice:** Did I use words that signal **transitions** between paragraphs?

✓ **Sentence Fluency:** Did I rewrite any sentences that sounded awkward? Does my writing flow smoothly?

✓ **Conventions:** Did I use *more* and *most* correctly? Did I check my spelling?

Talk About It

What are some words that come to mind when you think about whales? How many different kinds of whales do you know about?

LOG ON Find out more about whales at **www.macmillanmh.com**

WHALES

605

A Song for Makaio

by Tamira Jackson

Long ago, near the islands now called Hawaii, lived a young girl named Makaio. She loved to swim and listen to the whales sing. The ocean could be dangerous, but Makaio did not mind the challenge. During the winter months, she bravely **ventured** into the water. Every day Makaio would float for hours, listening to the whale songs.

She always looked wiser when she **emerged** from the waves and walked onto the beach.

Though others could see her, Makaio could not see them. She was blind. Her other senses were unusually strong as a result. In fact, Makaio was the only one who could hear the whales sing.

Makaio said she could recognize each whale by his voice. She did not think it was strange or **unreasonable** to spend so much time listening to whales.

Whenever a new whale joined the group, Makaio would know. The newcomer would sing a different song. Gradually over several winters, the other males would start singing the new whale's song. The **attraction** that pulled Makaio towards the whales had to do with how they respected each other and the kindness they showed each other.

Makaio lived a long life. During her lifetime many of her whale friends died. Each time this happened, Makaio would have a sad look in her eyes. The islanders would **inquire** about what had happened. Makaio would answer simply, "One of my whale friends has died. I miss his voice."

She never wanted to have long **discussions** about it.

One night during her eightieth winter, Makaio did not return to the village. The islanders searched the beach. There they found a whale **sprawled** out on the shore. Next to him was Makaio. Her eyes seemed to be **focused** on the whale's long body spread awkwardly on the sand.

When the villagers reached her, Makaio spoke softly. "The voice of my very first whale friend has gone. It is time for me to go now, too. Do not be sad. Remember the whales' lessons: Learn from others. Always accept newcomers." With those words, Makaio died.

To this day people still try to understand the mystery of whale songs. Perhaps Makaio told us their secret many centuries ago.

Reread for **Comprehension**

Generate Questions
Summarize

A Summary Chart helps you answer questions about what happens at the beginning, middle, and end of a story. Use your Summary Chart as you reread "A Song for Makaio" to summarize the important ideas in the selection.

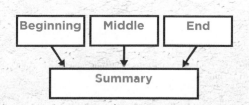

Comprehension

Genre

Realistic Fiction has real-life settings, well-developed characters, and realistic problems and solutions.

Generate Questions

Summarize
As you read, use your Summary Chart.

Beginning	Middle	End

Summary

Read to Find Out

How does Ana Rosa's community come to appreciate her talents?

The Gri Gri Tree
from
The Color of My Words

by Lynn Joseph
illustrated by Marla Baggetta

Award Winning Selection

No one had to point out that I was different from everyone else in our village. It was clear from the first day I began climbing the gri gri tree and staying up there for hours.

"What's wrong with your daughter?" neighbors asked Mami.

"She's not right in her head," they answered themselves, when Mami only shrugged her shoulders.

Papi would say, "Nothing wrong with sitting in a tree. It's the same as sitting on a porch except it's higher."

Roberto would climb up with me sometimes but he got bored quickly and swung down, yelling like a monkey. Angela shook her head at me and said I would never be a real *chica*, because *chicas* do not climb trees when they are twelve years old.

Not even Guario understood, although he tried. He asked me once what I did up there. That was more than anyone else had **ventured** to **inquire**.

I told him I looked around.

609

He asked if I didn't think I was wasting a lot of time, when
I could be doing something to prepare for my future such as
studying English.

Guario always had his mind on the future. Sometimes I think
that he was tormented by all of us who didn't particularly care what
tomorrow was going to bring. And really, what was there to know—
either it would rain or it would not. But it was definitely going to be
hot and Mami was going to cook and Papi was going to sit on the porch
and the radio was going to play *merengues* all day. That was for sure.

Besides, I already knew what I wanted to do in my future. I wanted
to be a writer, but only Mami knew that. If I told Guario, he would
say I was **unreasonable**. If I told anyone else, they would laugh. But
in my gri gri tree, I could be anything I wanted to be—even a writer
with words for everything I saw from my leafy green hideout.

I could see the ocean glittering silver in the sunlight. I could see
people trudging along the dusty road from Sosúa; some balancing
buckets of water on their heads. I could see boys playing baseball in
the schoolyard with a tree branch bat and a rubber band ball. I could
see the river, meandering over rocks, hungry for rain. Far off in
Puerto Plata, I could see Mount Isabel de Torres, a green giant with
misty white curls dancing 'round her head.

I could see the sleepy lagoon and the sad little homes of the
lagoon people. I could see the birds that flew past my gri gri, their
ruby-and-gold velvet feathers shimmering on their tiny bodies. I
could see the rainbows that glowed in the sea-sky after a rain passed.
I could count the sunset roses in Señora Garcia's backyard. I could
see my teacher climbing the hill near her house, and I could see Papi
sitting on our porch, nodding off to sleep.

Then one day I saw something that I had never seen before and I was so scared that I almost fell out of the tree. There I was looking at the sea when suddenly out of it rose a giant monster, tall and black and covering the sun with its shadow. Before I could scream, the monster fell back into the sea.

I scrambled down the tree quickly and ran toward my house, shouting "Papi, there's a monster in the sea!"

Papi woke from his siesta. "*¿Qué pasa?*"

"A monster," I repeated. "A giant sea monster and it's coming this way!"

I shouted inside the house. "Mami, come quick. There's a monster in the sea. I saw it."

Mami came outside and Angela followed her. They were drying their hands from washing the lunch dishes.

Everyone looked at me as if I were crazy.

"It's true," I said, jumping up and down.

Mami made me sit down and describe exactly what I saw. Before I had finished, Angela shouted my news to her best friend walking by. Then Papi waved over some of his domino-playing *amigos* and told them what I saw from on top of my gri gri tree.

Soon our porch was surrounded with people all asking me to tell my story again.

When I had told it for the fourth time, Señor Garcia, the *colmado* owner, began to laugh.

"You must have fallen asleep in the tree and had a bad dream, *cariño*," he said.

"No," I replied, shaking my head. "I saw it."

But his words had relieved everyone's fears of a sea monster. "Yes," they agreed. "You must have imagined it."

"No, you idiots," I wanted to shout. "I didn't imagine anything." But I kept quiet because Mami and Papi would not like it if I shouted at the neighbors and called them idiots. That was for sure.

As everyone sat down on the porch to share a drink and talk about my sea monster, I slipped away and ran to my gri gri tree. I heard Mami calling me, but I pretended I didn't hear and climbed up the tree fast. I needed to find out if what I had seen would come back again.

I sat down on my usual branch and tucked a few leaves away from my eyes. Then I stared at the sea. I looked so hard and for so long that its blueness filled up my eyeballs and I had to blink a lot so I wouldn't go blind.

The afternoon faded into evening and the sea's blueness turned gray. I watched and waited. My stomach made grumbling noises but I covered them with my hand.

Then, just as I began to think that maybe I had imagined it after all, I saw a splash of white water. The splash of water rose up, up until it was high in the air like a magic fountain.

"It's a volcano," I whispered. I remembered that my teacher had told us how many of the Caribbean islands had been formed by volcanoes that rose out of the sea.

I gasped. Maybe I was seeing the beginning of a brand-new island right next to the República Dominicana. As I kept on looking, a black shape **emerged** out of the fountain of water. It rose and turned, as if doing a dance, and that's when I saw the gleaming white throat of the sea monster.

It hovered in between heaven and ocean for a few seconds and then fell back into the water with a splash that sprayed salt drops as high as the pearl-pink clouds.

My heart beat furiously and I steadied myself so I wouldn't fall down from the tree. I was right. I had not imagined anything. There really was a sea monster out there. But this time I didn't rush down to tell anyone.

What would the people do, I wondered. Would they try to find it? Or maybe to kill it? Somehow, although I didn't know why, I could tell that the sea monster was not dangerous. It just wanted to swim and splash and jump out of the sea the same way I jumped over the waves.

I climbed down the tree and went home. The first thing I wanted to do was eat, but people were all over the porch talking wildly. "We saw it, Ana Rosa," they shouted. "We saw that big sea monster of yours."

Mami was passing around a plate of *dulces*, the sweet milk candy that I love. She must have just made them because they were still warm and soft.

Children were carrying huge plates filled with different foods that their mothers had made. Angela was directing them to put the food here or there on our big table. I saw plates piled high with *arroz con pollo*, *plátanos fritos*, and *batatas fritas*.

Señor Garcia apologized over and over to me. About a hundred people were gathered on our porch, in the yard, and along the roadside, talking about the sea monster.

"The tourist high-season is coming," said Señor Rojas, who owned a Jeep that he rented to tourists. "We can't let anyone know we have a sea monster hanging around Sosúa Bay."

"But why not?" asked Señora Perez, who sold paintings on the beach. "It could be a tourist **attraction**. Plenty people may decide to come here just to see it."

Half the folks whispered, "He's right." And the other half said, "She's the one who's right."

Summarize
Summarize what happened after the narrator went home.

It looked as if we were going to have a big debate on our porch just like the ones that take place when it is a presidential election year. The way everyone was carrying on, soon we would be having people writing *merengues* about the sea monster and there would be sea monster fiestas all over the place just like during elections.

I shook my head and just listened to everyone as I ate a plate heaped high with food. That poor sea monster, I thought.

Then the people began to make a Plan. When Dominicans get together and decide to make a plan, watch out, because there are plans, and then there are Plans, and this was definitely a PLAN!

The first thing the people decided was that someone had to keep watch over this sea monster. Well, everyone looked around to see who would volunteer. That's when we knew the PLAN would not work because no one wanted to do something so stupid as to go down to the sea and watch for the sea monster.

It was Angela who got the bright idea that since I saw it first, I could keep watch over it from my gri gri tree. Everyone turned to me and nodded their heads.

"Finally, a good reason for her to be up there all the time," I heard Señora Garcia whisper.

Papi was looking at me and nodding his head, proud that his daughter was selected for such an important job. I said, Okay, I would do it.

Then the PLAN continued. Half the people wanted to make signs and announce that Sosúa Bay had a new visitor and it was a one-of-a-kind sea monster. The other half of the crowd shook their heads and said, No, it was too obvious.

"We must be subtle about a delicate matter like this," said Señora Perez. "We must make up a wonderful story about this sea monster, give it a name, make it a friendly monster, and then tell the world. Otherwise all we will do is scare everyone away from this side of the island."

She had a point. A story about the sea monster was much better than a big billboard with an arrow pointing "This way to Sea Monster of Sosúa Bay!"

The idea of it all made me giggle. Wait until Guario came home and heard all this. I could hardly wait for him to return from the restaurant.

"Well," said Señor Rojas, "what will we name the sea monster?"

"And who knows how to write a story about it anyway?" asked Señor Garcia.

Señora Perez shrugged her shoulders. "I don't know how to write too good, but we could make up something."

Then Mami, who was usually quiet during these kinds of **discussions**, spoke up loud and clear. "Ana Rosa would be the best person to write a story about the sea monster."

I was shocked. This wasn't the same Mami who worshiped silence.

People began to shake their heads. "A child to do something so important?" they whispered.

"Yes," said Mami. "Let us give her a notebook to write in and she will write us a story about the sea monser. If we don't like it, someone else can try."

The way Mami said it, so definite and firm, made people nod their heads in agreement. "Well it doesn't hurt to let her try," they said.

So Señor Garcia went and brought back a notebook from his *colmado*. Mami gave it to me and her hands were cold like the river.

While the grown-ups stayed up late on the porch talking and drinking and eating, I went inside and began to write a story about the sea monster. First I tried to give him a name. But I couldn't think of a good one. So instead I thought about what he looked like. Then I imagined what he must feel like living all alone in the sea, different from all of the other sea creatures.

The fish and animals in the ocean were probably afraid of his huge size and his big nose and long, swishing tail. And they probably didn't want to play with him. Maybe they whispered about how strange he looked. But the sea monster wanted a friend. Deep down, I understood exactly how the sea monster must feel.

I began to write. I wrote page after page in the notebook the people had given to me. When I was finished, it was almost midnight. I went to the porch. Everyone was still there laughing and talking and some were dancing to the music on the radio.

Children were asleep on their mothers' and fathers' laps. Some of the bigger children were **sprawled** out on a blanket on the floor and the *merengue* music was a background lullaby for them.

 Summarize
What kind of plans do the villagers make to publicize the sea monster, and how do these plans lead to the narrator's story?

When the people saw me, they got quiet. Someone turned off the radio. Some woke the children on their laps. Papi moved from his chair and put his arms around my shoulders. He led me to the front of the porch.

Then everyone watched me and waited. I stood there trembling, holding that notebook with my story close to my heart. I knew right then that this was it. The whole world would find out about me.

I stopped thinking. I just started to read. I did not look at anyone, not Papi, or Mami or Angela. I read and read until I turned to the last page of the story. There the other sea creatures invite the lonely sea monster to a big underwater fiesta, even though there is no one else like him around, and even though he is so big that he knocks over many of them with his big nose and tail.

"And the sea monster is so happy that he leaps out of the ocean, sending sparkling waves all around him in a giant ring of light."

I looked up then and I saw many things at once. I saw Papi sitting on the edge of his chair, strange and silent. I saw Mami with her hands folded and her head bowed as if praying. I saw the neighbors smiling and nodding their heads. Then I saw Guario, who must have walked up to the edge of the porch while I was reading.

It was Guario's face I **focused** on. He was smiling. My big strong brother who worried about our future, my serious Guario who almost never smiled, suddenly let out a loud whoop and grabbed me up. He spun me around and around.

"Little sister, I am buying you a new notebook every month no matter what!" he shouted.

I closed my eyes so I wouldn't start crying there in front of all the neighbors. Guario always kept his promises. I would be able to write down everything now, everything I thought or dreamed or felt or saw or wondered about. I was so happy I thought I would leap as high as the sea monster.

Then, in the background, I heard clapping. The people had stood up from their chairs and were clapping for me.

I heard shouts of how great my story was and people congratulating Papi and kissing Mami's cheeks telling them how lucky it was that I was so smart. I heard Mami saying it had nothing to do with luck. I grinned and went over to her. She put her arms around me and squeezed my shoulders.

"You're going to write many stories, remember, *cara*?" She whispered in my ear. It was the happiest night of my life.

We all forgot about the sea monster until the next day.

Over the radio, a news broadcast announced that one of the humpback whales making its way to Samaná Bay for the annual winter mating season had gotten sidetracked in Sosúa.

"But Samaná Bay is only a two-hour drive from here," said Papi.

"Well, the poor whale doesn't know how to drive," Mami teased.

For two weeks our humpback whale jumped and frolicked about in Sosúa Bay until finally heading east to Samaná to join the other three thousand humpbacks that go there every winter.

But while he was in Sosúa, I watched him every day from my gri gri tree. The beautiful black-and-white sea monster had helped me to make my dream come true. I loved the whale. And I named him Guario.

A Whale of a Time with
Lynn Joseph and Marla Baggetta

Lynn Joseph grew up in Trinidad, an island in the West Indies. While growing up Lynn was good with words and loved learning. Today she combines both passions in her two jobs. Besides being an author, Lynn is a lawyer in New York City. Her talent with words comes in handy by allowing her to make her case in court and on paper. Lynn has two sons and a new home in the Dominican Republic.

Other books by Lynn Joseph:

A Wave in Her Pocket: Stories from Trinidad

The Mermaid's Twin Sister: More Stories from Trinidad

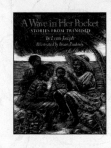 

Marla Baggetta is an artist and illustrator whose work has appeared nationally in galleries, books, advertisements, and magazines. She graduated from art school in Pasadena, California. She lives with her husband and two sons in West Linn, Oregon.

LOG ON Find out more about Lynn Joseph and Marla Baggetta at **www.macmillanmh.com**

Author's Purpose
Although the author's main purpose in writing *The Gri Gri Tree* is to entertain, realistic fiction includes true-to-life details. What details here are realistic?

Comprehension Check

Summarize

Use your Summary Chart to help you summarize "The Gri Gri Tree." When you prepare your summary, be sure to include only important events and details.

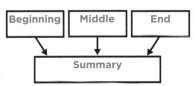

Beginning	Middle	End

Summary

Think and Compare

1. Summarize what you know of Ana Rosa's story about the sea monster. Explain why the author did not include Ana Rosa's story within "The Gri Gri Tree." **Generate Questions: Summarize**

2. Reread the last three paragraphs on page 622. Explain what everyone will find out about Ana Rosa. **Analyze**

3. The gri gri tree is a special place for Ana Rosa. Describe a place that is special to you. Explain what it is about this place that makes it special. **Apply**

4. Ana Rosa's brother is always **focused** on "what tomorrow was going to bring." Do you think people should consider what might await them in the future? Why or why not? **Evaluate**

5. Reread "A Song For Makaio" on pages 606–607. How is Ana Rosa like Makaio? How do others react to each of these characters? Use details from both selections to support your answer. **Reading/Writing Across Texts**

Science

Genre

Informational Nonfiction provides information about real people, living things, places, situations, or events.

Text Feature

Graphs are diagrams that show the relationships among objects. They make it easy to compare different amounts or sizes.

Content Vocabulary

mammals
traits
organisms
carnivores

The LARGEST Creature on Earth

by Yolanda Robertson

What is the largest animal that ever lived on Earth? Do you think it is a dinosaur? Guess again! It's the blue whale, and it is still on Earth today. A blue whale can grow to be as long as a nine story building turned on its side. The blue whale is so vast that its heart alone weighs about 1,000 pounds and is about the size of a small car.

The blue whale is just one kind of whale. There are many members of the whale family, including porpoises and dolphins. All of these animals belong to the family of sea creatures called Cetaceans. The name *Cetacean* comes from the Latin word *cetus*, meaning large sea animal, and from the Greek word *ketos* meaning sea monster.

Despite living in water, whales are not enormous fish. Like human beings, whales are **mammals**. All mammals share common **traits**, such as using lungs to breathe air and nursing their young. Mammals are warm-blooded, have a heart with four chambers, and have hair. They generally live on land, but whales and manatees are two mammals that spend their entire lives in the water. Unlike humans who use their noses to breathe, whales breathe air through blowholes on top of their heads. There are two main groups of whales— baleen whales and toothed whales. Each has special traits.

Big Whales, Bigger Whales!

Reading a Graph

You can use this graph to compare the weights and lengths of four kinds of whales.

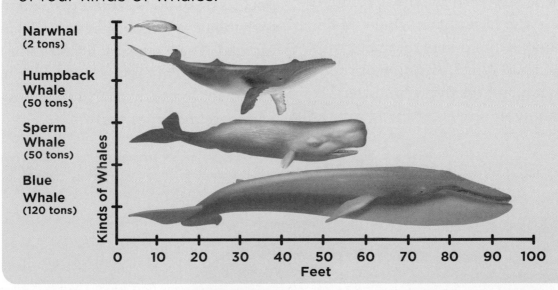

Narwhal (2 tons)

Humpback Whale (50 tons)

Sperm Whale (50 tons)

Blue Whale (120 tons)

Kinds of Whales

0 10 20 30 40 50 60 70 80 90 100

Feet

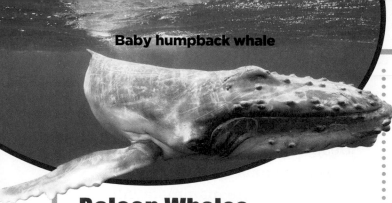
Baby humpback whale

Baleen Whales

Baleen whales have two blowholes. Instead of teeth they have baleen plates or comb-like structures that strain food from the water. These enormous whales have hundreds of baleen plates. The largest baleen whale is the blue whale. Similar to an enormous vacuum cleaner, a blue whale will suck in and eat up to 8,000 pounds per day of tiny, shrimp-like **organisms** called krill.

Like all other whales, baleen whales live in pods, or small groups. These whales also "sing" to each other. Many whales communicate by singing. The blue whale's songs are the loudest, even louder than a jumbo jet. Scientists think the baleen whale with the most complex songs is the humpback whale. Male humpbacks make very distinct types of clicks and whistles. Some of their songs can last for thirty minutes. You can even buy recordings of humpback whale songs. However, female humpback whales do not sing. One theory scientists have is that males are probably using this whale music to court female humpback whales.

Toothed Whales

A toothed whale has one blowhole and many teeth. The largest of the toothed whales is the sperm whale. Its brain alone weighs up to 20 pounds and is the largest of any animal. Sperm whales are **carnivores**, and they eat about 2,000 pounds of food a day. Their favorite food is the giant squid, but they also eat fish and octopus.

Two other toothed whales that are much smaller than the sperm whale are the porpoise and the dolphin. A quick look at these three creatures makes it difficult to believe that they are related, but a close study will reveal shared traits. One thing that sperm whales, dolphins, and porpoises all do is "fluking." Fluking is the way in which these whales dive for food. They start by lifting their tails into the air. This helps them pick up speed so that they can plunge down and feed in deeper waters.

Fluking tooth whale

Unicorn or Whale?

The strange-looking narwhal is a toothed whale that lives in the Arctic Ocean. The male narwhal is known for its long tooth, called a tusk, which looks like a long, pointed broomstick. The narwhal's special tooth grows out of the front of its head and can be up to ten feet long. Years ago, before they knew about narwhals, some people thought these tusks came from unicorns.

Scientists know about more than 80 kinds of Cetaceans, and they believe that there may be more types of whales that have not yet been discovered. So the next time you are at the ocean, watch for whales. Maybe you'll discover a new breed of Cetaceans!

Male narwhal with tusk

Connect and Compare

1. Look at the graph on page 629. What are the differences in weight and length between blue and sperm whales? **Reading a Graph**

2. Based on the information in the article, how is the mouth structure of baleen whales suited for their diet of krill? **Analyze**

3. Think about "The Largest Creature on Earth" and *The Gri Gri Tree*. How do you think Ana Rosa would have described a fully grown blue whale? How do you think it would compare to the description given in "The Largest Creature on Earth"? **Reading/Writing Across Texts**

Science Activity

Research three or four whales not mentioned in the article and make a bar graph that compares the weights of each type of whale.

Find out more about whales at **www.macmillanmh.com**

Writer's Craft

Figurative Language

Writers choose the words of a poem carefully to paint a picture for the reader. They often use **figurative language**, including personification, to describe the sights, sounds, and even smells of a scene.

I used personification when I wrote that dolphins dance and dash.

I described the dolphin as a surfer.

Dolphin Watching

by Manny S.

I watched a dolphin jump so high
It nearly touched the cloudless sky.
And when it came back to the sea,
Its foamy splash delighted me.

Today I watched a dolphin dance.
Its leaps put me into a trance.
Sunlight sparkled on the sea's waves,
Like gleaming gems from distant caves.

Today I watched a dolphin dash.
Its dorsal fin moved like a flash.
It skimmed through waves of white
and green.
No better surfer have I seen.

Your Turn

What fascinates you about a body of water? Is it the water itself or the creatures living in it? Choose something about an ocean, lake, or other body of water to describe in a poem. Make every word count as you describe a scene or a creature. Use the writer's checklist to check your writing.

Writer's Checklist

☑ **Ideas and Content:** Did I choose **figurative language** to help the reader see what I am describing?

✓ **Organization:** Does my poem build in energy, pulling the reader along?

✓ **Voice:** Does my poem include my feelings?

✓ **Word Choice:** Did I select colorful words that have a strong visual appeal?

✓ **Sentence Fluency:** Does my poem have a pleasing rhythm when it is read aloud?

✓ **Conventions:** Did I use irregular adjectives correctly? Is every word spelled correctly?

Test Strategy

Author and Me
The answer is not always directly stated. Think about everything you have read to figure out the best answer.

The Work of Giants

by Ming Chen

The Transcontinental Railroad

Today you can board a plane in St. Louis and arrive in San Francisco about four hours later. You might even sit and enjoy a movie while traveling. However, two hundred years ago, that same trip took many weeks. The journey was uncomfortable and often dangerous. Travelers had to cross mountains, rivers, and canyons. They had to face the blazing heat of the deserts and freezing temperatures as they crossed mountains. Many people dreamed of ways to make the trip easier and faster. Their dream was to build a railroad connecting East and West.

Not everyone shared that dream, however. Horace Greeley, editor of the New York Tribune, said, "It is perfect insanity, or the next step to it, for anyone to indulge in further discussion about . . . a railroad from the Mississippi to the Pacific Coast . . . ." Many Americans agreed with him. The difficulties in building a transcontinental railroad seemed too great.

Go On ▶

The Dream Takes Shape

The dreamers won over those who doubted, and plans were drawn for a railway connecting East and West. This was not an easy task. The first problem was deciding on the route. Senators from the North and the South argued for the railway to pass through their states. When the Civil War began, however, the Southern senators left Congress and the Northerners took charge of the plan.

Getting from Here to There

The next problem was getting materials to California. The process took many months. Everything had to be shipped from New York, around South America, and then to San Francisco. From there all materials had to be put on smaller boats for the 120-mile trip to Sacramento, California.

Once the materials and machines were in place, workers had to be hired. Thousands were needed, yet only hundreds could be found. The Civil War and the California gold rush took most men away from railroad work. If not for workers who came from China, the railroad would never have been built.

The Work Begins

In 1863 work on the railroad finally began. The Union Pacific started building west from the Mississippi River. The Central Pacific moved east from Sacramento. At first construction was slow. Crews had to drill through solid rock in places. They had to build bridges across rivers and ravines.

While some workers finished the track, other workers were building the rail cars. One news reporter wrote from the Union Pacific Railroad shop in Omaha, Nebraska:

The lumber used is of three kinds, oak, ash and pine, all brought from Chicago and cut into proper lengths and thicknesses for the object designed. The material is first run through the plainer, which smooths it; from there to the saw and again to the plainer;

then to the . . . machines, till it is at last ready for men employed for framing and bolting the car on the trucks which rest on the rails, extending through the whole length of the building. When the car is finished, it is transferred to the painting department, receives its different coats and stripes, and is then run back to the drying room. In this department there are three hundred and fifty hands employed . . . and the average wages of the men is about $3.50 each per day . . . .

All the problems were finally solved. Six years later the two crews met in Promontory, Utah. Through a great deal of money, the backbreaking work of thousands, and many risks, a railroad linking the East and West coasts of North America became a reality.

Building the Transcontinental Railroad truly was a heroic effort. William Tecumseh Sherman, a famous Civil War general, wrote in a letter to his brother: "If it is ever built, it will be the work of giants."

> ## Railroad
> Engine
> Fierce and smoky,
> Roaring, belching, slashing
> Slicing up the grassy prairie
> Wild beast

Go On ▶

Directions: Answer the questions.

Tip

You have to think about the entire selection to choose the best answer.

1. **What is the theme of the selection?**

   A The Transcontinental Railroad should not have been built.

   B Building the Transcontinental Railroad took tremendous effort.

   C The problems in building the Transcontinental Railroad were minor.

   D Important people with money made the Transcontinental Railroad possible.

2. **Which of these BEST describes the viewpoints of the poet and the author of the selection?**

   A Both believe that the work on the railroads was a positive influence.

   B The author thinks the railway is great, and the poet does not.

   C Both writers are angry about the hardships of working on the railroad.

   D The poet thinks the work was worthwhile, but the author does not.

3. **What does the word *construction* mean on page 635?**

   A moving from one place to another

   B taking something apart

   C the act of building something

   D the process of clearing land

4. **The news reporter's account of the railroad shop is an example of a primary source. Why do you think it is included here?**

5. **Why was the building of the railroad called the work of giants? What challenges did the railroad workers face? Use details from the selection to support your answer.**

Writing Prompt

Write a speech to persuade people to work on the railroad. Include the benefits and hardships workers will have to face. Your speech should be at least three paragraphs long.

STOP 637

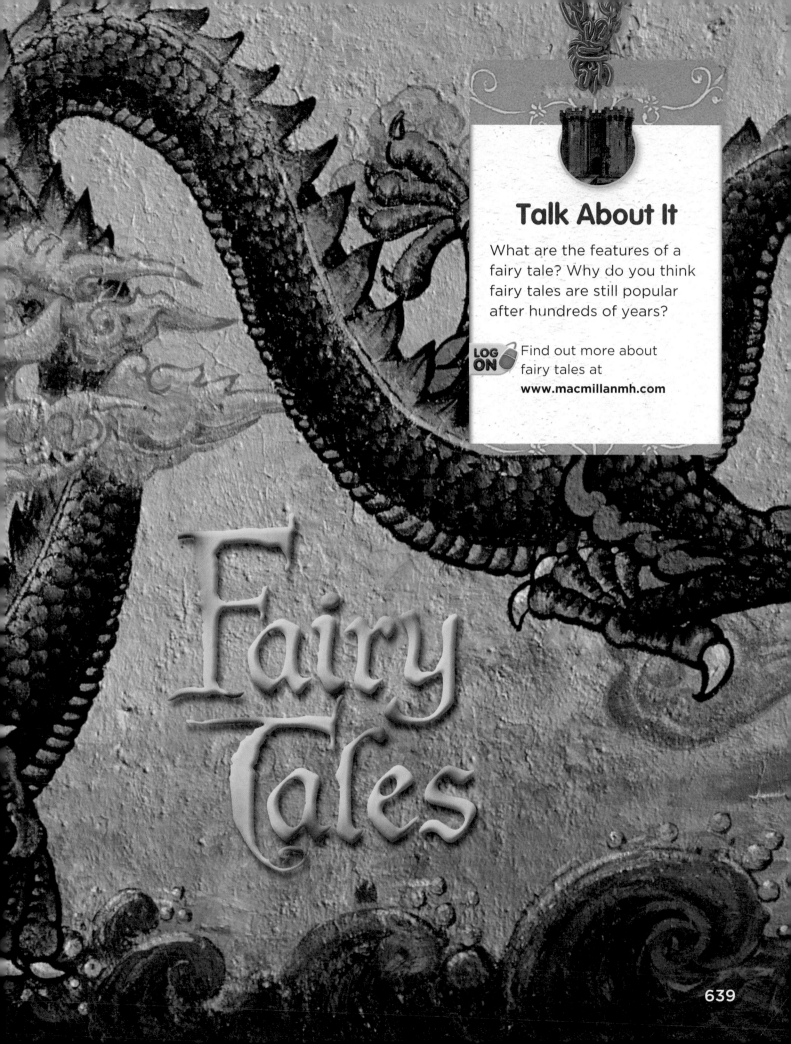

Talk About It

What are the features of a fairy tale? Why do you think fairy tales are still popular after hundreds of years?

LOG ON Find out more about fairy tales at **www.macmillanmh.com**

Fairy Tales

A Real Princess

by Tonya Schaeffer

Once upon a time there was a prince named Vincent. He was about to turn 30 years old. This was an important age. If he didn't marry a princess by his birthday, the king's advisors would **dismiss** him from the court. They would send the prince away, and he would never be able to become king.

Prince Vincent's **intentions** did not include losing the crown. However, over the years, he had broken the heart of every princess from kingdoms near and far. Now he felt **despair** at finding a real princess to wed. Prince Vincent had lost all hope.

"What will I do?" he asked his mother. "It's not my fault that there are no princesses left."

The queen rolled her eyes. "It's your fault you've treated so many princesses so badly," she snapped back.

Just then a young lady approached the castle. Her **bridle** had broken. The harness would not go over her horse's nose.

The girl entered the great hall after she **descended** from the great staircase. She introduced herself as Princess Araya from Zelnorm. When Prince Vincent saw her torn and muddy clothes, he sighed. "This cannot be the princess who will solve my problem," he said to his mother. "In fact, I doubt she's a princess at all," he said.

The queen thought for a moment. "I know how to find out," she said. "However, if it turns out she *is* a princess, you must promise to marry her."

"Done!" Prince Vincent said. He was sure his mother was wrong.

Now the queen had a plan. First, she asked a servant to **accompany** Araya to the dining room. There the princess was fed rare **delicacies** from faraway lands prepared by the royal chef. Then the queen gave orders to get the best room ready.

"I want seven feather-filled mattresses on the bed," she demanded. "Place a small pebble at the bottom of the pile. Only a true princess will be able to feel it."

The next morning the queen asked Araya how she had slept.

"I didn't sleep at all!" Araya said. "I saw a homeless mother and child standing by the castle gate, so I took them two mattresses. When I saw other needy townfolk nearby, I gave away the other mattresses. My father, King Paul, will repay you."

The queen was speechless. Prince Vincent, however, was not. He finally saw the real beauty of Princess Araya and asked her to be his wife. She **consented** to his request, and the two of them became the kindest rulers in all the land.

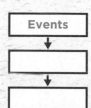

Reread for Comprehension

Summarize
Sequence
A Sequence Chart helps you summarize information by listing events or actions in the order that they take place. Use your Sequence Chart as you reread "A Real Princess" to figure out the sequence of events.

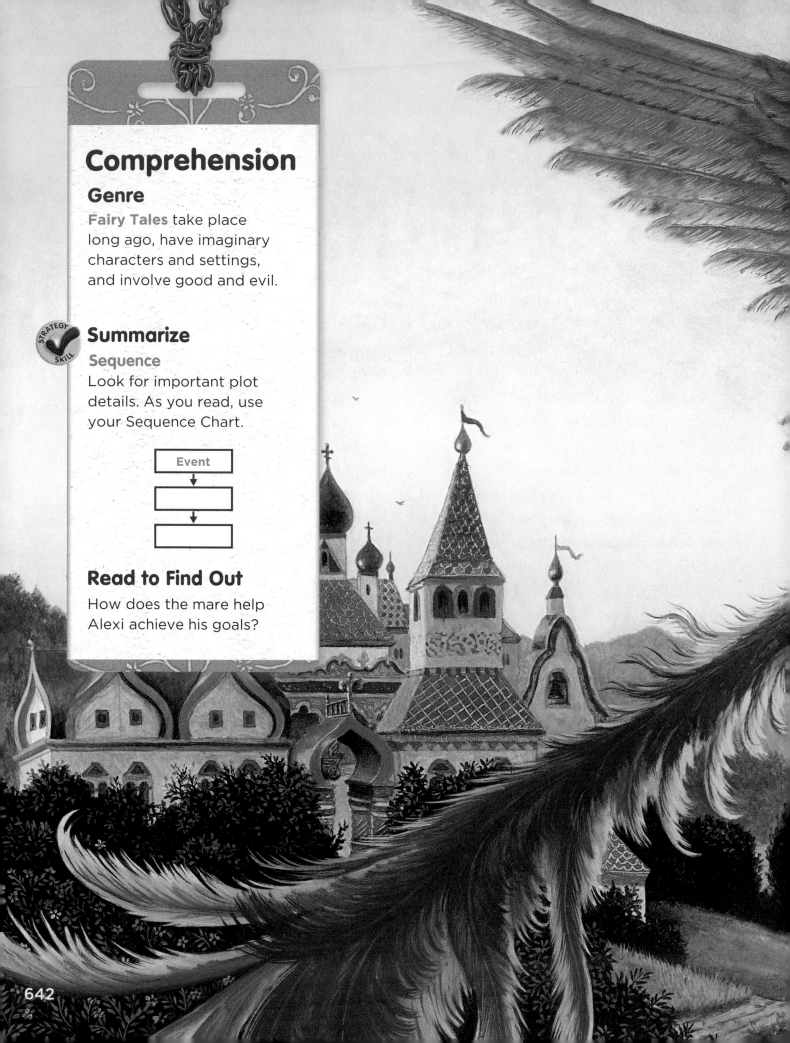

Comprehension

Genre

Fairy Tales take place long ago, have imaginary characters and settings, and involve good and evil.

Summarize

Sequence

Look for important plot details. As you read, use your Sequence Chart.

Event

Read to Find Out

How does the mare help Alexi achieve his goals?

The Golden Mare, the Firebird, and the Magic Ring

by Ruth Sanderson

Award Winning Selection

Once upon a time, in a place where magical beasts still roamed the earth, a young man named Alexi left home to seek his fortune and perhaps to find an adventure or two as well.

Alexi was an excellent huntsman, but after traveling for a week he had found neither work nor adventure. One evening, as night **descended** and the moon arose, he made camp at the edge of a glade.

A noise of hoofbeats in the forest startled Alexi. Thinking it a herd of deer or some other game, the lad readied his bow. Yet the young hunter did not loose his arrow, for the beast that appeared in the clearing was too

wondrous to shoot. It was a golden mare with a silvery-white mane that streamed around her and sparkled in the moonlight.

The Golden Mare stood and gazed at the huntsman, who pointed an arrow at her heart.

"Hold, fair sir, do not shoot," said the mare, to the astonishment of the lad. Alexi lowered his bow and slowly approached the remarkable mare.

"I am at your service for sparing my life," she said. "What is your desire?"

Alexi told the mare he sought work and adventure.

"The Tsar of this region could use another huntsman," said the horse. "Tomorrow I will take you to his palace. If he hires you, I promise to serve you well."

The next morning Alexi fashioned a rough **bridle** with a bit of rope, mounted the Golden Mare, and set off for the palace of the Tsar.

The Tsar hired the young man at once, so impressed was he by Alexi's mount. He offered Alexi a princely sum for the mare.

"Thank you, sire," said Alexi, "but I'm afraid she'll allow no rider but me." Annoyed that his offer was declined, the Tsar ordered a saddle and a real bridle put on the horse, but not one of his men could stay on the Golden Mare's back.

The Tsar glowered at Alexi, for he usually got what he wanted. "I trust that you will serve me *quite* well," he said coldly, not wanting to **dismiss** him in case he turned out to be a good huntsman.

In just a few weeks, Alexi became first among the Tsar's huntsmen, for he was a good shot and the Golden Mare was swift at the chase. As luck would have it, there came a day that Alexi spied no game but rode on and on until it began to grow dark. He was about to turn the mare around when he noticed something glowing brightly on the path ahead. It was a golden feather, bright as a flame, and Alexi knew it must be a feather from the great Firebird.

"I will take this prize to the Tsar," said Alexi. "Then perhaps he will look upon me with favor."

The Golden Mare was protective of her kind master. "If you take the Firebird's feather, you will surely learn the meaning of fear," she warned. But so confident was Alexi that he did not heed her words and presented the feather to the Tsar the very next day.

Sequence
What events in the story lead Alexi to a position as a huntsman with the Tsar?

As the Tsar greedily took the feather, he saw a way to rid himself of this insolent huntsman, whose horse was a constant reminder of what he could not have.

"You bring me a mere feather!" bellowed the Tsar. "If you are so clever, bring me the whole bird, or I'll have your head brought in on a platter!"

Alexi left the throne room in **despair** and went to the Golden Mare's stall.

"Do not worry," said the Golden Mare. "Ask the Tsar to have a hundred sacks of maize scattered at midnight upon the open field on the hill. I will see to the rest."

The Tsar agreed to Alexi's request, and at midnight his men scattered one hundred sacks of maize on the field. Alexi took the saddle and bridle off the Golden Mare and she wandered loose in the field. Then he hid in the branches of a huge oak tree that stood at the top of the hill. All night they waited.

As the first golden rays of dawn lit the sky, from the eastern edge of the world the Firebird came flying, wings aflame with the reflected light of the sun.

The mighty bird landed in the field and began to eat the maize. As the Golden Mare grazed nearby, she wandered closer and closer to the Firebird. When the bird was close enough, the mare placed a hoof upon its tail, pinning it to the ground. The Firebird tried in vain to fly away, but the mare held fast. Alexi jumped from the tree, tied the struggling bird securely with rope, and placed it carefully in a sack.

The Tsar was amazed to see Alexi bearing the mythical Firebird. He ordered a huge, ornate cage built for the magnificent bird. People came from miles around to see the captive Firebird, and all the neighboring tsars were quite jealous of his prize possession. Alexi, however, felt sorry for the bird and wished he had never seen its feather shining in the forest path.

Alexi remained the Tsar's best huntsman and brought him much profit. But no matter how well Alexi did, he could not please the Tsar, for the Golden Mare still obeyed Alexi alone.

A few weeks later, the Tsar called Alexi to him.

"Since you seem to have a talent for impossible tasks, I have another one for you," said the Tsar. "In a distant eastern land, Yelena the Fair sails in her golden boat upon the Lake of the Sun. Find her and bring her back to be my bride. It will mean your death if you fail."

With a heavy heart, Alexi went to the Golden Mare, certain that this new task was hopeless. "Ask the Tsar for a brocaded tent and all sorts of sweetmeats and **delicacies**," the mare said, "and I will take you to her."

The Tsar supplied Alexi with a beautiful tent and fine foods, which Alexi packed into saddlebags upon the Golden Mare's broad back.

As they set out, it seemed to Alexi that the mare's feet barely touched the ground, so swiftly did she run. For seven days and nights she ran, through green forests, past waterfalls, up and down mountains, until on the eighth morning she stopped.

Silhouetted against the blazing sunrise, the boat of Yelena the Fair sailed upon the Lake of the Sun.

Alexi set up the tent and arranged rugs and cushions inside along with the fancy foods he had brought. Then he sat inside and waited for Yelena the Fair. Before long the boat sailed closer and closer to the shore until finally she lowered sail and landed upon the beach. Stepping out lightly, the maiden approached the regal-looking tent and saw the feast that Alexi had laid out.

Yelena and Alexi had a merry time, eating and talking of many things.

"My master the Tsar is rich and powerful, and famous, too," Alexi boasted. "And he has in his possession the legendary Firebird. Perhaps you would accept the Tsar's invitation to be an honored guest at his palace."

Yelena the Fair was so impressed by Alexi's persuasive words and gracious manner that she agreed to **accompany** him. When Alexi lifted the beautiful young maiden upon the Golden Mare's back, he felt a pang of guilt for not mentioning the old Tsar's true **intentions** to make her his wife.

The Tsar was astonished to see Alexi coming through the palace gates with Yelena the Fair.

"My bride!" he exclaimed.

Yelena the Fair was not pleased and quickly realized that Alexi had brought her there under false pretenses. She looked from the old Tsar to the young huntsman who had trapped her.

"I will marry no man," she said to the Tsar, "without my grandmother's wedding ring. It lies under a stone at the bottom of the Lake of the Sun."

"Well," said the Tsar, gesturing impatiently to Alexi, "what are you waiting for? Go at once and fetch the ring!"

When Alexi was alone with the Golden Mare, he said, "I do not wish to fetch Yelena's wedding ring for the Tsar, for then she, too, would be a captive like the Firebird."

"I will retrieve it then," said the Golden Mare. "Whatever happens, do not worry, for it is a magic ring and can grant its wearer any one wish."

When she reached the Lake of the Sun the mare stamped her hoof three times on the sand. A huge crab crawled out of the water.

"At the bottom of the lake there is a ring under a stone," said the Golden Mare. "Please get it for Yelena the Fair, for she has need of it."

Patiently the Golden Mare waited on the shore while the crab called together all the creatures that crawled on the lake's bottom to search for the ring. After some time he emerged with ring in claw. Delicately the Golden Mare took the ring in her teeth and then fairly flew back to the palace stables, where Alexi awaited.

Alexi presented the ring to the Tsar, who gave it at once to Yelena the Fair.

"You have your ring," he said. "Now let the wedding bells be rung! Let the feast be prepared!"

"Wait," said the shrewd maiden, who saw the remorse in Alexi's eyes. "I cannot marry a man as old as you, for you are surely four times my age."

"But what can I do about that?" asked the Tsar.

"Indeed, you can do something…with my help," said Yelena. "Prepare a cauldron of boiling water, and with my magical power I will turn it into the Water of Youth. If you bathe in it you will become young again."

The Tsar ordered the cauldron prepared, and soon the water bubbled and steamed.

"Let us first test this miracle," said the Tsar slyly. "You, Alexi, will be the first to enter the pot. Guards, seize him!" The Tsar's men held Alexi fast. He remembered the Golden Mare's words about the ring and hoped that they were true, for now he knew the meaning of fear.

Yelena the Fair approached the cauldron and passed her hand several times over the boiling water. Silently, she made a wish and dropped the magic ring into the cauldron.

"It is ready," she said.

At the Tsar's signal, the guards flung Alexi into the boiling liquid. He sank below the surface once, twice, and after the third time he rose like a shot and leaped from the cauldron. He was in perfect health and unharmed by the scalding water. No one but Yelena noticed the golden ring on his little finger.

Hoping to be as young and as strong as his huntsman, the Tsar jumped into the cauldron. At the same instant, Alexi made a wish on the magic ring, for he did not desire the Tsar's death.

Sequence
What key events in the story lead up to the moment when Alexi is flung into the boiling water?

To everyone's surprise, Alexi reached into the cauldron and lifted out a little baby, smiling and unharmed. The Tsar was indeed young again!

Since the Tsar was now too young to rule, the people made Alexi the Tsar in his place. And Yelena the Fair **consented** to become his bride. So she did marry the Tsar after all. And as for the baby Tsar, he was given a new name and raised as their own child.

As his first official act as Tsar, Alexi ordered the release of the Firebird, for such a bird did not belong in a cage. In a joyful blaze of light it flew to its home in the eastern sky. The Golden Mare ran free once more, but she continued to advise Alexi until the end of his days.

Once Upon a Time with Ruth Sanderson

Ruth Sanderson could usually be found reading books about horses in the library where her grandmother worked. This led to her second passion: drawing. On Saturday mornings in the fourth grade, Ruth started a class to teach her friends how to draw. It's no surprise that when Ruth grew up, she went to art school and became a writer and illustrator of children's fantasy and fairy tale books. Ruth is married and has two daughters.

Other books by Ruth Sanderson: *Papa Gatto* and *Crystal Mountain*

 Find out more about Ruth Sanderson at **www.macmillanmh.com**

Author's Purpose

Ruth Sanderson entertains readers with this tale. In what ways is *The Golden Mare, the Firebird, and the Magic Ring* informative as well?

Comprehension Check

Summarize

Use your Sequence Chart to summarize *The Golden Mare, the Firebird, and the Magic Ring*. Keeping track of the order of events can help you better understand the story.

Event

Think and Compare

1. Describe how the story would be different if the author changed the sequence of events. **Summarize: Sequence**

2. Reread page 653. Why does Alexi feel guilty about persuading Yelena the Fair to visit the Tsar? **Analyze**

3. If the Golden Mare were to **accompany** you throughout your life, what might you ask her to help you do? Explain. **Synthesize**

4. The Tsar only thinks about himself. How do selfish people create difficult situations? Explain your answer. **Evaluate**

5. Reread "A Real Princess" on pages 640–641. Explain the similarities and differences between Alexi's and Prince Vincent's situations. Use details from both selections in your answer. **Reading/Writing Across Texts**

Social Studies

Informational Nonfiction gives information and facts about a topic.

Text Feature

A **Venn Diagram** shows the similarities and differences between two things.

Content Vocabulary

versions
identity
transforms
elements

A *Tale* Told Around the *World*

by Lateesha Gray

People all over the world enjoy fairy tales. Some fairy tales may be popular in only one country, but others are told around the globe. For example, the story of Cinderella has more than 500 **versions**. In most versions a kind young girl is the main character and other characters include a cruel stepmother and her equally cruel daughters, a fairy godmother, and a prince.

The plot is similar in all of the tales. The young girl is forced to do household chores, then someone grants her wish and helps her attend a celebration, such as a ball. At the ball the girl's beauty attracts a powerful man who falls in love at once. The girl's true **identity** is kept secret so the man must search all over the land for her.

The French Cinderella

The French writer Charles Perrault wrote the Cinderella tale that most of us know. Cinderella, or Cendrillon, is very beautiful, and her stepsisters are ugly and jealous. Cinderella is forced to do the most difficult chores. One day the prince invites all of the women in the kingdom to a ball. Cinderella almost does not go, until a fairy godmother appears and helps Cinderella. The fairy godmother waves her wand and **transforms** Cinderella's ragged dress into a beautiful gown.

Cinderella also wears glass slippers. The transformation will wear off at midnight so she must be sure to leave before then. As she is leaving the ball, Cinderella loses a slipper and the prince looks all over the kingdom for her. The prince finds her and marries her. At the end of the story, Cinderella forgives her stepmother and stepsisters and asks them to come live with her.

Venn Diagram

Reading a Venn Diagram

In a Venn diagram, differences are written in the left and right ovals. The similarities are written in the center section.

French Version
- Glass slipper
- Fancy ball
- Prince
- Fairy godmother
- Stepmother and stepsisters nice to her later

Cinderella Stories
- A kind young girl is treated badly
- Evil stepmother, stepsisters
- Receives help that transforms her
- Must be home at a certain time
- Loses slipper
- Powerful man searches for unknown girl
- Man marries girl

Chinese Version
- Gold slipper
- Festival
- King
- Talking fish
- Stepmother and stepsister never see her again

The Chinese Cinderella

In the Chinese version, Yeh-Shen also has an evil stepmother and stepsisters. Her only friend is a beautiful fish with golden eyes. Her stepmother later kills the talking fish and cooks it for dinner. However, Yeh-Shen learns that the fish's bones are magical and hides them. The bones later help her dress in fine clothing for a festival. While rushing to leave the festival to be home by a certain time, she loses a gold slipper. A king buys the slipper and searches for its owner. When he meets Yeh-Shen, he is struck by her beauty and falls in love. Yeh-Shen's stepmother and stepsisters are forbidden to see her.

The Egyptian Cinderella

An Egyptian version of *Cinderella* is based on the actual marriage of a slave girl and the pharaoh, or ruler, of ancient Egypt. In this version Rhodopis, a servant girl from Greece, is teased by other servants in the household. Her only friends are the animals along the river. She often sings and dances for them. One evening she loses a slipper, and a falcon snatches it. The falcon flies over the pharaoh's throne and drops the slipper. The pharaoh searches his kingdom for the woman whose foot fits the slipper. When he finds Rhodopis, he falls in love and she becomes his queen.

THE NATIVE AMERICAN CINDERELLA

Some Native American tales echo many of the **elements** of *Cinderella*. One famous tale tells about a young maiden whose hands and face are burned from tending a fire. Like the European Cinderella, she is usually left out of events and feels as though she does not belong. This story, however, uses the setting and customs of the Algonquian nation to tell this tale. A Zuni version features talking turkeys that help the girl. The setting for that tale is a village in the southwestern United States.

Connect and Compare

1. Look at the Venn diagram on page 663. What are two details from the French Cinderella story that are different from details in the Chinese version? **Reading a Venn Diagram**

2. Why do you think the story of Cinderella is so popular around the world? **Analyze**

3. Think about *The Golden Mare, the Firebird, and the Magic Ring*. In what ways is the story similar to that of *Cinderella* and *Yeh-Shen*? **Reading/Writing Across Texts**

Social Studies Activity

Make a Venn diagram that compares and contrasts a Cinderella tale from another culture to the Cinderella story you know.

 Find out more about Cinderella tales at **www.macmillanmh.com**

Writer's Craft

Voice

In an eyewitness account, writers describe the important events they see and how they feel. They use appropriate words to show **voice**. That way, readers feel as if they were there.

Write an Eyewitness Account

First Steps

by Natsu Y.

I shared my own thoughts about my little brother's first steps.

I expressed how happy and proud I felt.

I witnessed something very important and unexpected the day my little brother, Toshi, turned 11 months old.

We were in the living room after dinner. Toshi was standing up, holding on to the coffee table. He does that well. I sat on the floor a few yards away. Toshi has never walked before. He was never able to balance himself without the coffee table.

"Come on, Toshi! Walk over to me!" I called. I thought he would never do it. I had been calling to him for over a month, but he wouldn't move from behind that table.

Toshi stared at me, smiling and bouncing. Suddenly, he put his arms straight out and started walking right toward me. I couldn't believe it! One, two, three, four steps, then plop. My little brother had taken his first steps, and they were right to me!

Your Turn

What interesting or important event have you witnessed? Write an eyewitness account about how you felt, and describe the event in detail. Use the writer's checklist to check your writing.

Writer's Checklist

 Ideas and Content: Did I choose to describe an event that was important to me?

 Organization: Can the reader tell how the event unfolded before me?

☑ **Voice:** Did I share the emotions I felt as I witnessed the event? Did I choose words that show **voice**?

 Word Choice: Did I use vivid words to describe the details of what happened?

 Sentence Fluency: Did I use a variety of sentence types?

 Conventions: Did I use adverbs correctly? Did I proofread for spelling errors?

CAMPING OUT

Talk About It

Have you ever been camping? How is camping out different from living at home?

LOG ON Find out more about camping at **www.macmillanmh.com**

THE ★★★ BEST ★★★ FOURTH OF JULY

by Lateesha Gilbert

Sunday, July 5

Dear Mom and Dad,

I hope you had a great Fourth of July. You can imagine what a big deal it was here at Camp Freedom. With a name like that, the camp really went all out to celebrate!

For weeks every cabin was working on a Fourth of July skit. Since all the girls in my cabin are super funny, our counselor **guaranteed** the other cabins we would have the funniest skit in camp. At first we were pretty casual about working on it. Then the days went by and no one had come up with a good idea. Our counselor, Jean, started getting worried. Finally, she decided she should **supervise** us and our ideas more closely. She went from cracking jokes with us to being bossy. We all felt **frustrated**. She kept telling us what to do and she would not listen to our ideas. In the end, we did a skit about the founder of the camp, Fannie Freedom. Hardly anyone laughed.

After the skits we had a cookout, complete with those yummy chocolate, marshmallow, and cracker things. Arranging everything on sticks involved a lot of **coordination**. The ingredients were sticky and hard to manage. I didn't poke my stick all the way through each marshmallow. As I would **ease** the stick into the fire, the marshmallows would fall off. I am surprised the fire didn't go out from all the marshmallows that fell in.

Later that day the counselors took us to the top of Lookaway Mountain. The **scenery** was amazing from up there. The hard part was we had to carry a large **bundle** of blankets tied together with some string. The big surprise at the end of the day was a fireworks display, which lit up the entire sky. On the way back to camp, Jean apologized to us for not listening to our ideas. We told her that we had fun anyway.

By the way, thank you for the package you sent me. Everything was really great. The jelly beans melted and **fused** together, but don't worry. That didn't affect the taste. My bunkmates and I ate them for a late night snack on July Fourth, and everyone agreed they were still delicious!

Love you all,
Lateesha

Reread for Comprehension

Monitor Comprehension
Make Judgments

A Judgments Chart helps you judge whether or not a character's actions are a good idea. This will help you monitor your comprehension or understanding of the character and the story. Use your Judgments Chart as you reread "The Best Fourth of July" to make judgments about Jean's actions.

Action	→	Judgment
	→	
	→	
	→	
	→	

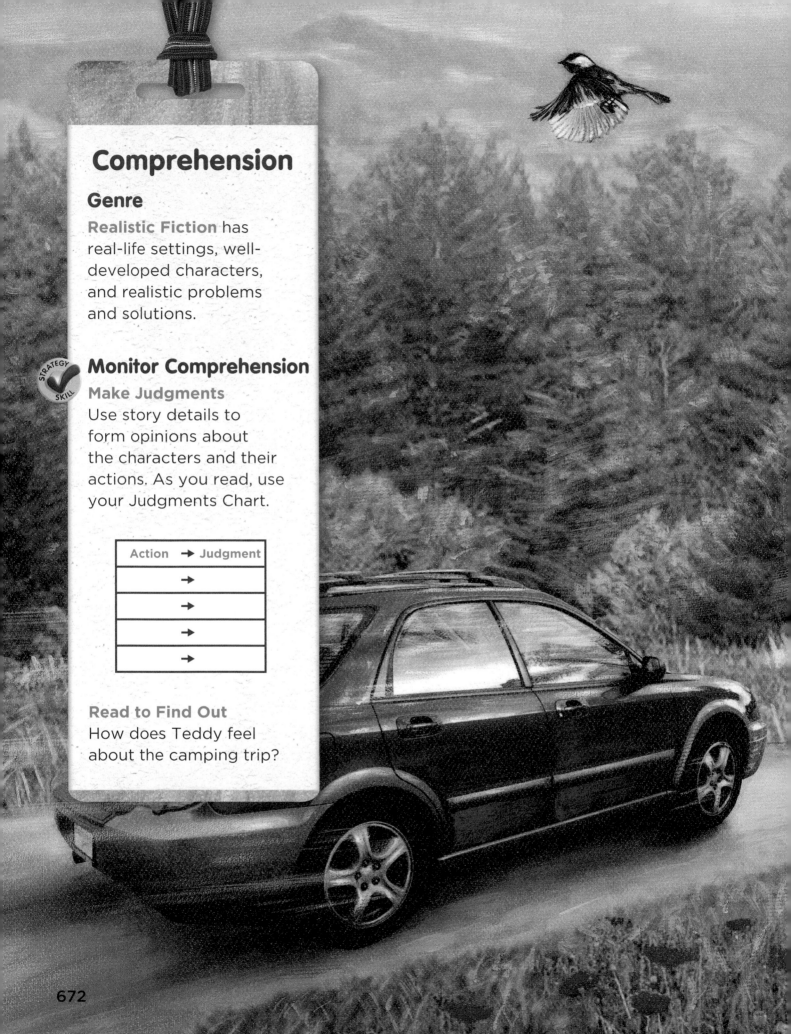

Comprehension

Genre

Realistic Fiction has real-life settings, well-developed characters, and realistic problems and solutions.

Monitor Comprehension

Make Judgments
Use story details to form opinions about the characters and their actions. As you read, use your Judgments Chart.

Action	➔	Judgment
	➔	
	➔	
	➔	
	➔	

Read to Find Out
How does Teddy feel about the camping trip?

SKUNK SCOUT

by Laurence Yep

Award Winning Author

illustrated by Winson Trang

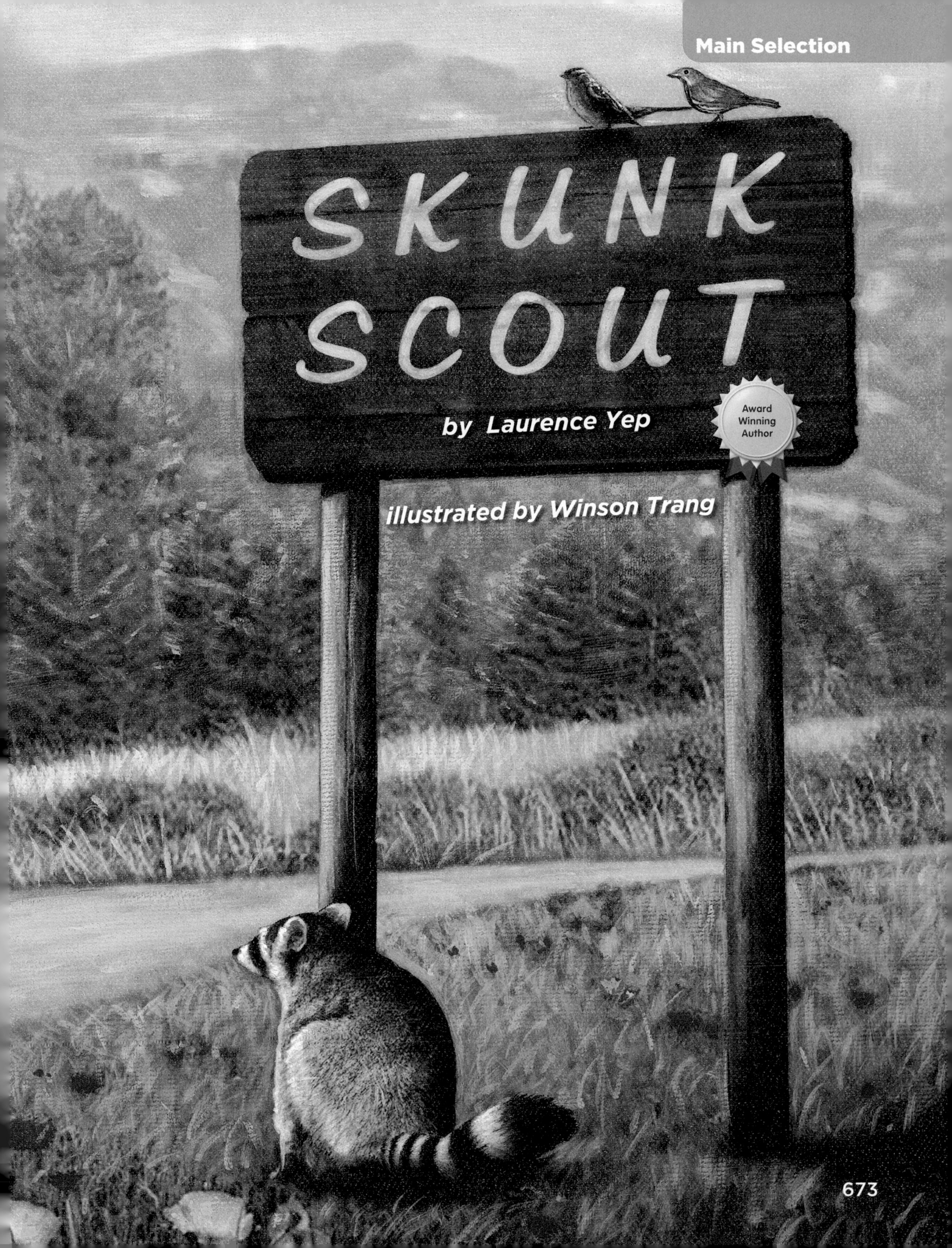

Teddy lives in San Francisco's Chinatown and loves city life. When Teddy reluctantly accepts an invitation to go camping with his Uncle Curtis and little brother Bobby, he has no idea what adventures Mother Nature has in store for them.

Mount Tamalpais kept growing bigger and bigger as we drove along. I thought some of the skyscrapers in San Francisco had been big, but they were toys compared to it.

You wouldn't think anyone could miss something that huge, but our uncle did. "Look, boys. That hawk's diving!" I thought he had told us everything possible about hawks, but he began spouting more.

"Oh, too bad," Bobby said. "He missed. I wonder what he was going for?"

The hawk wasn't the only one that needed better aim. As we shot past the exit, I leaned over the back of my uncle's seat. "Unh, Uncle Curtis, you should have turned back there."

Bobby rattled his map as he examined it. "Really?"

"Bobby you're supposed to be the navigator," I sighed.

"I'm sorry," Bobby said.

"How could you miss the sign?" I asked. "It's as big as a car."

"Now, now, no harm." Uncle Curtis shrugged. He left the freeway the first chance he got and then reentered the freeway, heading south.

Bobby leaned against his shoulder strap. "We'll get it this time."

But just as we got near the correct exit, Uncle Curtis suddenly twisted in his seat. "There's a rabbit!" he cried, pointing.

"Where?" Bobby asked, craning his neck.

As we shot past, I moaned, "We missed it again."

Uncle Curtis glanced into the rearview mirror. "Man, that came up faster than I thought."

I put a hand on his shoulder. "Okay. This time, no hawks. No rabbits. Just exit signs. Okay?"

Uncle Curtis gave a thumbs-up. "Got you."

"And don't you dare say anything except navigation stuff," I warned Bobby.

This time we got off at the right exit. I began to wonder how Uncle Curtis found his own bathroom at home. Maybe Aunt Ethel put up signs.

Make Judgments
Do you think Teddy's actions on this page are appropriate? Why or why not?

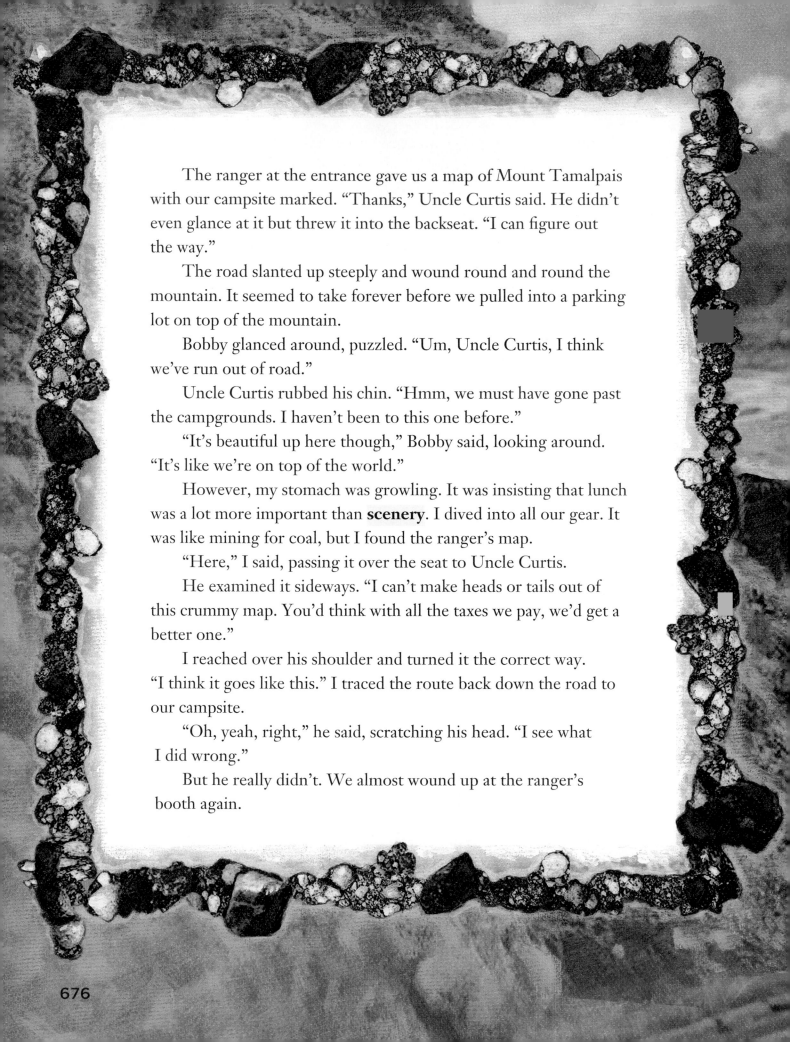

The ranger at the entrance gave us a map of Mount Tamalpais with our campsite marked. "Thanks," Uncle Curtis said. He didn't even glance at it but threw it into the backseat. "I can figure out the way."

The road slanted up steeply and wound round and round the mountain. It seemed to take forever before we pulled into a parking lot on top of the mountain.

Bobby glanced around, puzzled. "Um, Uncle Curtis, I think we've run out of road."

Uncle Curtis rubbed his chin. "Hmm, we must have gone past the campgrounds. I haven't been to this one before."

"It's beautiful up here though," Bobby said, looking around. "It's like we're on top of the world."

However, my stomach was growling. It was insisting that lunch was a lot more important than **scenery**. I dived into all our gear. It was like mining for coal, but I found the ranger's map.

"Here," I said, passing it over the seat to Uncle Curtis.

He examined it sideways. "I can't make heads or tails out of this crummy map. You'd think with all the taxes we pay, we'd get a better one."

I reached over his shoulder and turned it the correct way. "I think it goes like this." I traced the route back down the road to our campsite.

"Oh, yeah, right," he said, scratching his head. "I see what I did wrong."

But he really didn't. We almost wound up at the ranger's booth again.

If Uncle Curtis was good at one thing, it was making up alibis. I guess he'd had a lot of practice from getting lost all the time. "They really ought to mark the campsite better," he grumbled.

"Well, we're getting to see a lot of the mountain," Bobby said. He was always trying to find the silver lining.

Big deal. I would rather have had a meal. "Let me help," I said. I took the map from Uncle Curtis. "Just drive slowly."

I managed to get us to the parking lot of the campgrounds. Tents dotted the slope under the trees like a rag quilt.

"It's crowded," I said. With a little luck, someone would have taken our reserved spot.

"But none of them are on the Fun Express," Uncle Curtis insisted. When he had parked, he took the map from me and jumped out of the car. "This way, boys, for the beginning of your great adventure."

We followed him up a dirt trail from the parking lot to a patch by some trees. Uncle Curtis stopped. "This is it," he declared, folding the map into neat little squares. "The great outdoors!"

As I kicked at one of the many rocks on the ground, I didn't see what was so great about it. "Isn't fun supposed to be less lumpy?"

My parents are always scolding me about being so messy. However, they should have seen Mother Nature. There were all these pebbles and leaves littering the dirt. I would have tidied up a little, especially for paying guests.

Satisfied, Uncle Curtis surveyed the site. "All this fresh air! It's **guaranteed** to make you feel so tired, you won't notice any rocks."

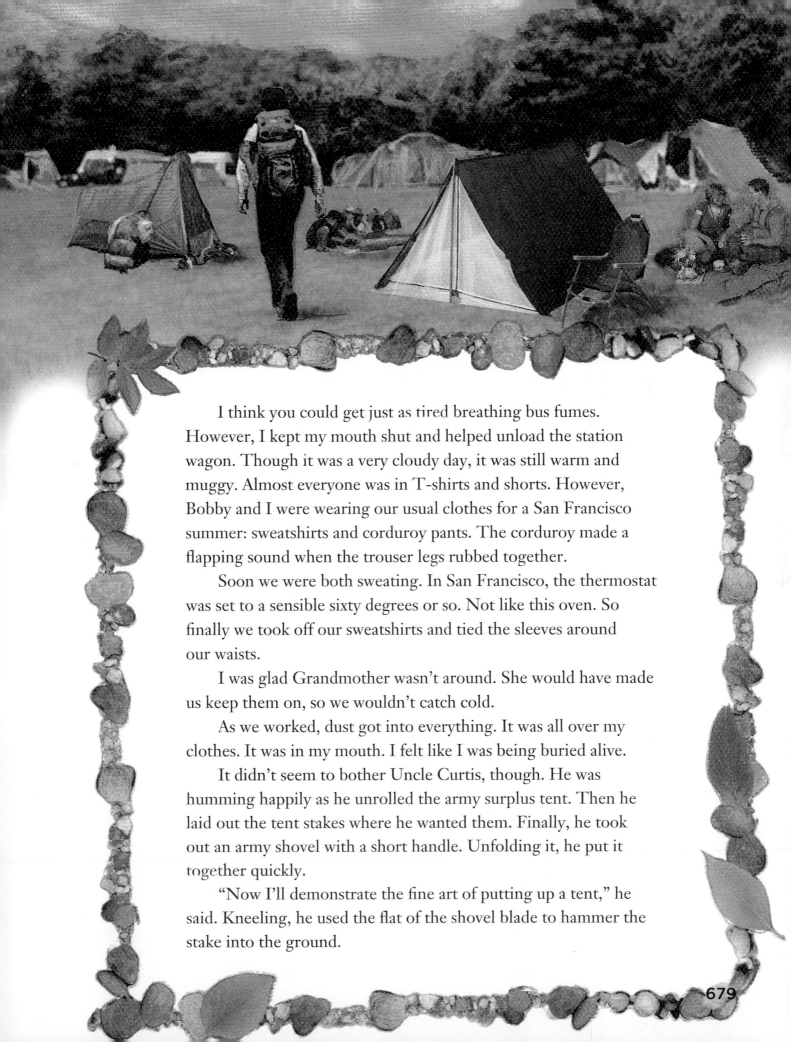

I think you could get just as tired breathing bus fumes. However, I kept my mouth shut and helped unload the station wagon. Though it was a very cloudy day, it was still warm and muggy. Almost everyone was in T-shirts and shorts. However, Bobby and I were wearing our usual clothes for a San Francisco summer: sweatshirts and corduroy pants. The corduroy made a flapping sound when the trouser legs rubbed together.

Soon we were both sweating. In San Francisco, the thermostat was set to a sensible sixty degrees or so. Not like this oven. So finally we took off our sweatshirts and tied the sleeves around our waists.

I was glad Grandmother wasn't around. She would have made us keep them on, so we wouldn't catch cold.

As we worked, dust got into everything. It was all over my clothes. It was in my mouth. I felt like I was being buried alive.

It didn't seem to bother Uncle Curtis, though. He was humming happily as he unrolled the army surplus tent. Then he laid out the tent stakes where he wanted them. Finally, he took out an army shovel with a short handle. Unfolding it, he put it together quickly.

"Now I'll demonstrate the fine art of putting up a tent," he said. Kneeling, he used the flat of the shovel blade to hammer the stake into the ground.

"Me next," Bobby said eagerly.

"You want to try everything, don't you?" Uncle Curtis grinned but he surrendered the shovel.

I knew my little brother, so I stepped back. Bobby thought that energy could always make up for lack of **coordination**. Uncle Curtis, though, made the mistake of staying close to **supervise**. He almost lost a kneecap when Bobby whacked at the tent stake and missed.

"Easy there," Uncle Curtis warned as he stumbled back.

Most of the time I try to get someone else to do all the work. But I saw another chance to prove I was just as good as my little brother.

"Let me have a turn," I said, holding out my hand.

I guess Uncle Curtis figured Bobby could take forever. "Let Teddy do that. You help me get the tent ready."

"But I want to do it," Bobby complained.

Uncle Curtis rubbed his head. "The sooner we set up camp, the sooner I can show you around. Isn't that what's really important?"

Bobby grudgingly handed the shovel to me and helped Uncle Curtis unroll the tent itself.

The ground was a lot harder than it looked. But lifting all those boxes in the store had given me muscles. So I hammered away until I got the stakes in.

It took all three of us to put up the tent. I still thought it leaned a little when we were done.

Uncle Curtis inspected the tent ropes carefully. He acted as though they were the cables holding up the Golden Gate Bridge. Finally, though, he nodded his head in approval. "That looks good."

When we had stowed our gear inside, I said, "I'm hungry. Let's eat."

"We've gotten used to eating Spam," Bobby explained.

"When you ride the Fun Express, you dine first class," Uncle Curtis boasted as he went over to the ice chest in the shadow of a big tree. He squatted down and undid the lid's clasps. "I brought hot dogs and hamburgers. I'll make you boys a feast." When he raised the lid, fog rolled out around him.

Bobby and I jumped back. "What's wrong?" my brother asked.

"It's just the dry ice." I laughed. I was enjoying my moment of triumph.

Uncle Curtis fanned his hand over the chest to help blow away some of the fog. "Boy, Teddy, I know this is one batch of meat that's not going to spoil."

White ribbons crept out of the chest and down the sides while Uncle Curtis carefully lifted out a big parcel wrapped in pink butcher paper.

He lost his grin though. "It's like a glacier."

I poked at the package in his hands. It was cold enough to make my body and hands ache. Through the paper, I traced the shape of hot dogs. "They feel like rocks."

Uncle Curtis lifted out the other package and hefted it over his shoulder like a shot put. "The hamburger's like a lump of coal, too."

I wasn't going to let this ruin my achievement. "Let's set them out," I urged. "Part of one of these packages will thaw out and we can have that."

So Uncle Curtis placed both packages out on a rock. "You boys have to get some firewood anyway. Just pick up the dead wood lying around. We're not allowed to chop down any trees."

"Right away," Bobby said, heading out.

"Wait for me, oh, fearless leader," I muttered, and wandered off after Bobby. "Just how much wood do you need to cook food anyway?" I asked the researcher. "I don't think we can carry back a log."

"The books didn't say," Bobby said, "but on television they always seem to use the wood about this thick." He held his fingers apart about six inches.

In the movies, there's always dead wood lying around, but all we could gather were twigs.

Disgusted, I looked at the handful I had. "This isn't even enough for a broom."

Bobby held up his own. "The other campers must have picked the mountain clean."

When we returned, Uncle Curtis stared at the handful of twigs. "That's okay for kindling. But where are the branches?"

"This is all we could find," I confessed helplessly.

Uncle Curtis rubbed the back of his neck. "I was counting on using firewood."

I saw a column of smoke rising a short distance away. "Maybe someone has spare firewood?"

"I'll borrow some. Nature lovers always share with one another. It's the code of camping," Uncle Curtis said. Suddenly he slapped himself. "Ow. Darn mosquitoes."

Apparently, there were other creatures besides humans having a meal. "I guess it's time to use my birthday gift," I said.

I went back to the tent. Something rustled in the brush nearby, but the bushes were too small for a bear to hide behind. So I went inside and got the mosquito repellent.

I can't say it did much good. Even as I sprayed my arm, a mosquito flew right through the mist to land on it. "This stuff just makes us tastier to the mosquitoes," I said.

I was hot, sweaty, being eaten alive, and hungry. So hungry that even Spam would have tasted good.

I poked each package in disappointment. "They're still like ice."

Bobby turned the packages over on the rock. They each clonked against the stone. "Darn dry ice." **Frustrated**, he picked up the package and dropped it against the rock. It landed with a loud crack. I thought there was a fifty-fifty chance that either the rock or the meat had broken.

Uncle Curtis grabbed a package under either arm. "We'll defrost the meat as we cook it. What's the menu for today, boys? Hot dogs or hamburgers?"

Bobby punched cheerfully at the air. "Hot dogs!"

I guess the dry ice hadn't been such a good idea, after all. Sulking, I jammed my hands in my pockets. "I'll settle for anything that isn't part of the polar ice cap."

Uncle Curtis put the hamburger into the chest and snapped the clasps shut. "You boys bring the buns and mess kits. I'll bring the hot dogs."

The cooking area was an open space. A row of stoves had been built from stones and metal grills.

Uncle Curtis went over to a table where some campers were eating.

He came back with half a bag of charcoal. "Ten dollars for this," he complained. "Fellow lovers of nature, my eye."

"Well, maybe it's the membership fee to the club," I said.

Uncle Curtis shot me a dirty look as he poured charcoal from the bag into the pit beneath the metal grill. Without lighter fluid, it took a little work and a lot of fanning and blowing before the coals caught.

As the coals slowly turned red, we began to set our stuff out on a nearby picnic table.

The previous cooks had not bothered to clean the grill. Uncle Curtis, though, had brought a spatula. He used it to scrape the metal bars.

In the meantime, we unwrapped the paper. The hot dogs were **fused** together into a lump the size of a football. No matter how hard we tried, we could not break them apart.

"Wait." Bobby proudly opened his borrowed mess kit and took out a fork. When he tried to pry a hot dog off, the tines bent.

We still hadn't freed any hot dogs by the time the coals were ready. By now, Uncle Curtis was too impatient to be careful. Lifting the mass of hot dogs, he set the whole fused lump on the grill. "I'll pry them off as they defrost." Water began dripping onto the coals with loud hisses. As steam rose around the hot dogs, Uncle Curtis straightened the tines of the fork. Carefully he worked at one of the hot dogs. "Almost…almost," he muttered.

With a plop, the hot dog fell through the grill and onto the coals. In no time, it was as black as a stick of charcoal. By the time this had happened to three more hot dogs, I tried to use a stick to **ease** them out of the coals.

Uncle Curtis shoved me back. "They're dirty."

"I don't care," I admitted. "I'm hungry."

"And they're half raw, too." He threw them into a trash can.

Make Judgments
Was Uncle Curtis right to throw the hot dogs away?

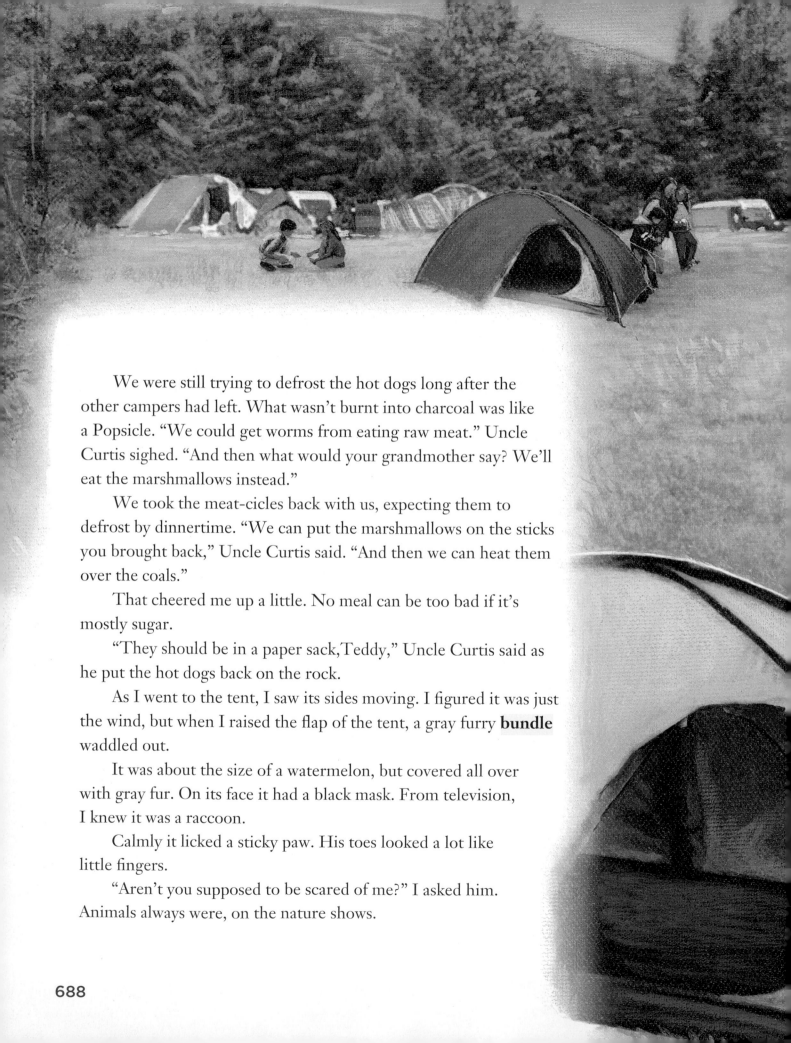

We were still trying to defrost the hot dogs long after the other campers had left. What wasn't burnt into charcoal was like a Popsicle. "We could get worms from eating raw meat." Uncle Curtis sighed. "And then what would your grandmother say? We'll eat the marshmallows instead."

We took the meat-cicles back with us, expecting them to defrost by dinnertime. "We can put the marshmallows on the sticks you brought back," Uncle Curtis said. "And then we can heat them over the coals."

That cheered me up a little. No meal can be too bad if it's mostly sugar.

"They should be in a paper sack, Teddy," Uncle Curtis said as he put the hot dogs back on the rock.

As I went to the tent, I saw its sides moving. I figured it was just the wind, but when I raised the flap of the tent, a gray furry **bundle** waddled out.

It was about the size of a watermelon, but covered all over with gray fur. On its face it had a black mask. From television, I knew it was a raccoon.

Calmly it licked a sticky paw. His toes looked a lot like little fingers.

"Aren't you supposed to be scared of me?" I asked him. Animals always were, on the nature shows.

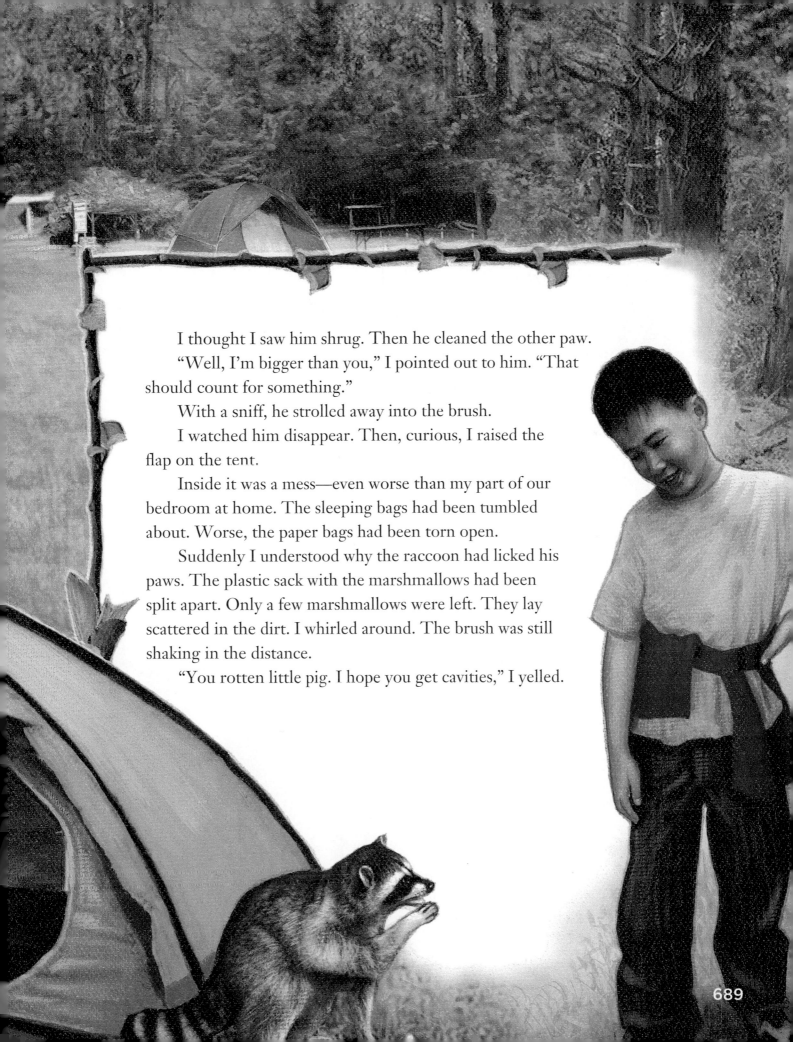

I thought I saw him shrug. Then he cleaned the other paw.

"Well, I'm bigger than you," I pointed out to him. "That should count for something."

With a sniff, he strolled away into the brush.

I watched him disappear. Then, curious, I raised the flap on the tent.

Inside it was a mess—even worse than my part of our bedroom at home. The sleeping bags had been tumbled about. Worse, the paper bags had been torn open.

Suddenly I understood why the raccoon had licked his paws. The plastic sack with the marshmallows had been split apart. Only a few marshmallows were left. They lay scattered in the dirt. I whirled around. The brush was still shaking in the distance.

"You rotten little pig. I hope you get cavities," I yelled.

Going Camping with Laurence Yep and Winson Trang

Laurence Yep got bit by the writing bug at his California high school. A teacher challenged his entire class to send their essays off to a national magazine. Laurence did, and soon after that he sold his first story. He was paid a penny a word! His advice to young writers: "Writing only requires one step to the side and looking at something from a slightly different angle." Laurence still lives in California with his wife.

Other books by Laurence Yep:
Dragonwings and *Dragon's Gate*

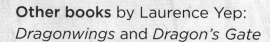

Winson Trang is a book illustrator. He has illustrated many stories, especially those focused on Asian-American subjects. This is the second time he has worked with Laurence Yep. The first book they both worked on was *Child of the Owl*. Winson currently lives in Los Angeles with his wife and son.

Author's Purpose

Why is *Skunk Scout* considered to be realistic fiction? What are some details that Laurence Yep uses to make the story true-to-life as well as entertaining?

LOG ON Find out more about Laurence Yep and Winson Trang at **www.macmillanmh.com**

Comprehension Check

Summarize

STRATEGY SKILL

Use your Judgments Chart to help you summarize the chapter from *Skunk Scout*. The actions of the two brothers and their uncle while they were camping will help you organize your summary.

Action	→	Judgment
	→	
	→	
	→	
	→	

Think and Compare

STRATEGY SKILL

1. Describe how your opinions about the characters might change if the story were told by Bobby instead of Teddy. **Monitor Comprehension: Make Judgments**

2. Reread pages 678–679. What can you tell about Teddy's life at home? Use details from the story in your answer. **Analyze**

3. Would you enjoy going on a camping trip with Uncle Curtis? Explain why or why not. What **gear** would you bring with you? **Analyze**

4. Do you think it is important to preserve our national parks? Explain your answer. **Evaluate**

5. Reread "The Best Fourth of July" on pages 670–671. Compare and contrast the camping experiences that Teddy and Lateesha had. Use details from both stories to support your answer. **Reading/Writing Across Texts**

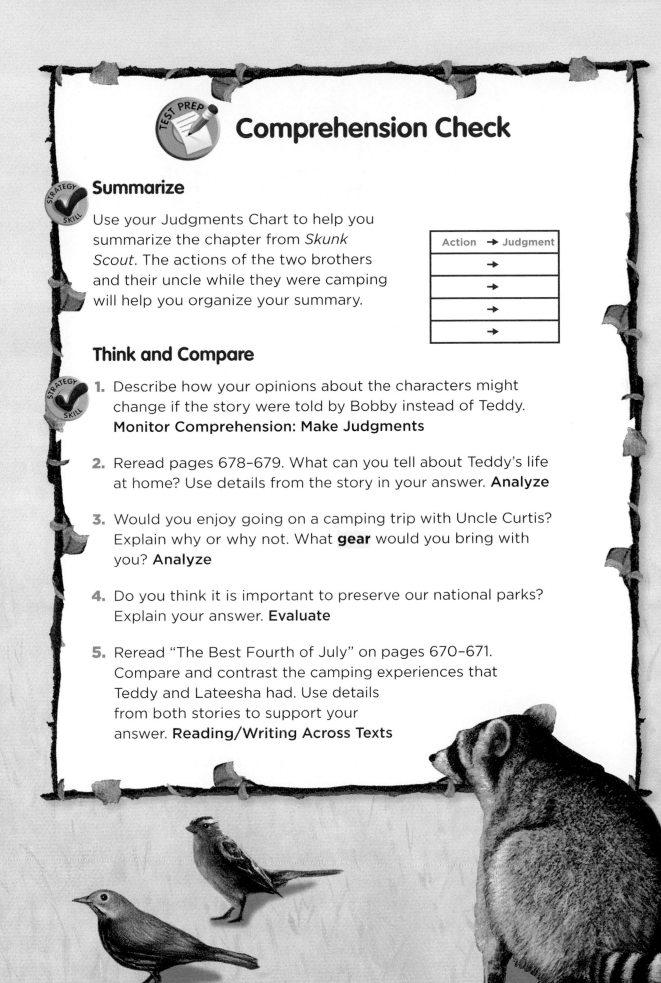

Our National Parks

by Tanya Sumanga

Among the greatest treasures of the United States are its national parks. These parks contain an amazing variety of natural wonders, including plants, wildlife, rock **formations**, **geysers**, and waterfalls. More than 50 national parks attract visitors every year. Some parks are quite large. Big Bend National Park in west Texas encompasses more than 800,000 acres of the Chihuahuan Desert along the United States–Mexico border. Famous for its many different environments, the park offers sharp contrasts in wilderness scenery. The Rio Grande curves through the park in a big bend, creating deep canyons. Rugged mountains, a desert plain, and unusual rock formations make up the park's landscape. Big Bend is noted for its rare forms of animal and plant life, such as roadrunners and prickly pears.

10 Largest National Parks
in the lower 48 States (as of 1997)

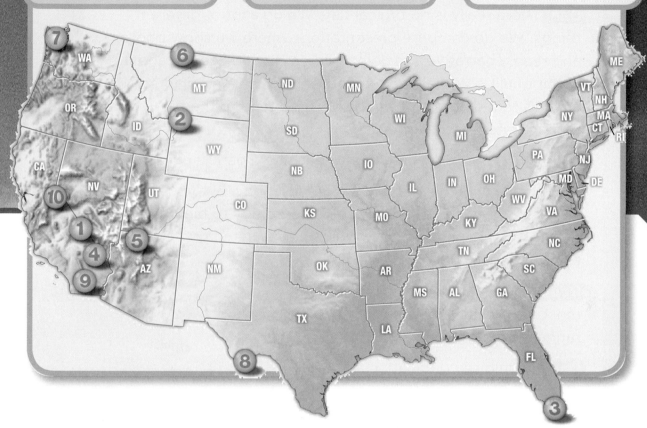

1 Death Valley National Park
California

2 Yellowstone National Park
Wyoming

3 Everglades National Park
Florida

4 Mojave National Preserve
California

5 Grand Canyon National Park
Arizona

6 Glacier National Park
Montana

7 Olympic National Park
Washington

8 Big Bend National Park
Texas

9 Joshua Tree National Park
California

10 Yosemite National Park
California

Archaeologists have found and studied pictographs (painted art) and petroglyphs (carved art) on rock walls and artifacts here that are nearly 10,000 years old. They reveal information about early Native American cultures and what life may have been like long ago.

The people who take care of national parks and who guide visitors through the parks are known as park rangers. Park rangers at Big Bend tell visitors how the area has changed over thousands of years.

People who like working outdoors and respect nature often become park rangers. Many park rangers enjoy reading about nature and studying the sciences.

Our reporter interviewed Dan Levitt, a park ranger who works at Big Bend National Park.

Reporter: What are the kinds of things you have to do when you are a park ranger? Do you give talks about the park? What is the typical day for a park ranger like?

Dan: There really is no typical day. We do a lot of different things. We do campfire presentations where we show photos and read a narrative. I'm doing one on the Rio Grande and its water quality. We talk about water, the earth, and plants and animals found here in the park. We also tend to the park trails and operate visitor centers.

Reporter: What did you study to become a park ranger?

Dan: I have a bachelor's degree in geography, but you can study anything from geology to paleontology to biology. I got my start by volunteering at various parks. Here I find that I use all the science courses I've taken.

Reporter: What would be the most important qualities for a ranger to have?

Dan: I would say dedication, understanding your duties, being loyal to the park, and wanting to help visitors.

Park Ranger Dan Levitt

AMAZING NEW BUG SPRAY!

Are you tired of being a breakfast, lunch, and dinner for bugs when you're camping?

Then use 100% natural "Chase Away Bug Spray!" It is guaranteed to work during your ENTIRE camping trip!

Created exclusively for park rangers, this is the first time it is being offered to the public at the low, low price of $19.95.

"'Chase Away Bug Spray' is the only bug spray I trust!" says Junior Park Ranger Charles "Chipper" Cruz.

Connect and Compare

1. Reread the interview on page 694. What do you think made Dan Levitt want to become a park ranger? What qualities does he think a park ranger should have? **Reading an Interview**

2. Do you think it is important to preserve national parks? Why or why not? **Analyze**

3. Think about "Our National Parks" and *Skunk Scout*. Do you think either of the boys or Uncle Curtis would make a good park ranger? Use examples from the texts to explain your answer. **Reading/Writing Across Texts**

Science Activity

Choose a national park, and research some interesting facts about its geography, and its plant and animal life. Write a two paragraph summary of your research.

 Find out more about national parks at **www.macmillanmh.com**

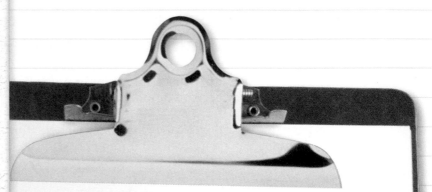

Writer's Craft

Time-Order Words

In giving directions, writers use **time-order words** such as *first, next, then,* and *finally.* These sequence words help the reader follow the steps in the correct order.

I started the directions for making my favorite recipe with a list of required items.

I used a sequence word for each step in the process.

How to Make a Veggie Delight

by Michelle Z.

Plan to make this delicious dish when the campfire coals are hot. First, gather a 12-inch piece of heavy-duty aluminum foil, pre-cut vegetables, water, butter, salt, and pepper.

Next, fold each piece of foil in half horizontally. Press flat and fold the sides shut. Rub the inside of the pocket with butter. Then, fill it with the vegetables until it is about two-thirds full. Sprinkle with salt and pepper and dot with more butter. Next, pour in about a tablespoon of water.

Close the top shut, and get an adult to place the pocket on the hot coals. Let it cook for 15 minutes on each side. Finally, enjoy your Veggie Delight!

Your Turn

Write a how-to paragraph telling the reader how to complete a process. You might explain how to make a healthful snack, play a game, or complete a task. Remember that sequence words help the reader complete the steps in the proper order. Use the writer's checklist to check your writing.

Writer's Checklist

☑ **Ideas and Content:** Did I write about something that I know how to do?

☑ **Organization:** Did I present the steps in the right order?

☑ **Voice:** Did I use an instructional tone rather than a conversational tone?

 ☑ **Word Choice:** Did I use **time-order words** to help the reader understand when each step should be done?

☑ **Sentence Fluency:** Did I use simple, easy-to-read sentences?

☑ **Conventions:** Did I use adverbs like "more" and "most" correctly? Did I check my spelling?

Talk About It

How do our physical abilities and health affect the quality of our lives?

 Find out more about physical fitness at **www.macmillanmh.com**

Improving Lives

Vocabulary

elementary

physical

rigid

interact

wheelchair

THE NEW GYM

At Riverside School in Miami, Florida, gym class isn't always held in the gym. In fact, it isn't even always held on land. One option available to kids at Riverside is an **elementary** course in sailing taught on real sailboats on Biscayne Bay.

Thanks to a terrific new **physical** education movement, gym class is no longer just about traditional team sports. The idea is to help kids find activities they'll enjoy so

much that they'll stay active for the rest of their lives. The fun activities include yoga, cycling, martial arts, dance, kickboxing, in-line skating, using treadmills, and even sailing and kayaking. The goal is to teach children sports and physical activities that they can enjoy outside of school.

Advocates of the "new" gym class point to studies that show kids are less active than ever before. They believe that children's natural boundless energy isn't being channeled into healthy activities for a lifetime. One in four kids gets no physical education in school at all. Kids' general activity level is at its highest in tenth grade but then slowly declines all the way into adulthood. That's what the new movement is designed to change.

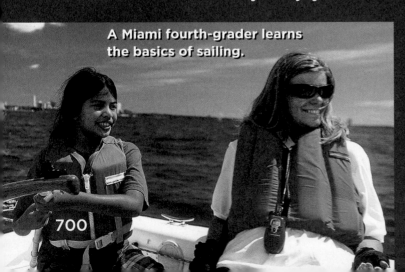

A Miami fourth-grader learns the basics of sailing.

Satellite Guidance for the Blind

Pocket-size GPS guide

Before leaving her apartment, Carmen Fernandez, a blind woman living in Madrid, Spain, used to carefully memorize her route. If she didn't, she would get lost. But a new device using GPS (Global Positioning Satellite) technology frees her from such a **rigid** routine.

Using the gadget's Braille keypad, she punches in her destination. As she walks, the device calls out directions to her. "Now I can walk home by any route," Fernandez says. "I've learned so much about my own neighborhood."

While the current technology cannot guarantee total accuracy, it already grants a new level of freedom for the visually impaired. It allows them to **interact** more directly with their surroundings and their neighbors. "Soon I'll be giving directions to the taxi driver," says Fernandez.

THE SECOND OLYMPICS

Every two years men and women from around the world come to compete at the Olympic Games. However, this is not the only time a gold medal is up for grabs. After the Olympics come the Paralympics.

The Paralympics are just like the Olympics, but these games are for athletes with physical disabilities. A Paralympic athlete may use a **wheelchair** or get around with the help of a guide dog in everyday life. Athletes who share a particular disability compete to win medals and set world records. Paralympians want others to see them as world-class athletes whose disabilities do not hold them back.

LOG ON Find out more about the Paralympics at **www.macmillanmh.com**

Canada's team at the 2002 Winter Paralympic Games

A Dream Comes True

Why do ALL kids need a place to play?

Comprehension

Genre

A **Nonfiction Article** in a newspaper or magazine reports on real people, places, and events.

Monitor Comprehension

Persuasion

Persuasion is a method of convincing others that they should believe something or feel a certain way about a subject.

Most kids love recess, but for Hannah Kristan, it was her least favorite part of the school day. "I never got to do anything except sit there," she recalls.

Hannah was born with a disease that kept the bones in her back from forming properly. She uses a **wheelchair**. Sadly, for kids like her, most playground equipment is off limits. In fact, Hannah is one of 5 million kids in the United States who cannot use traditional playground equipment because of some type of disability.

Paint panel

Talk tube

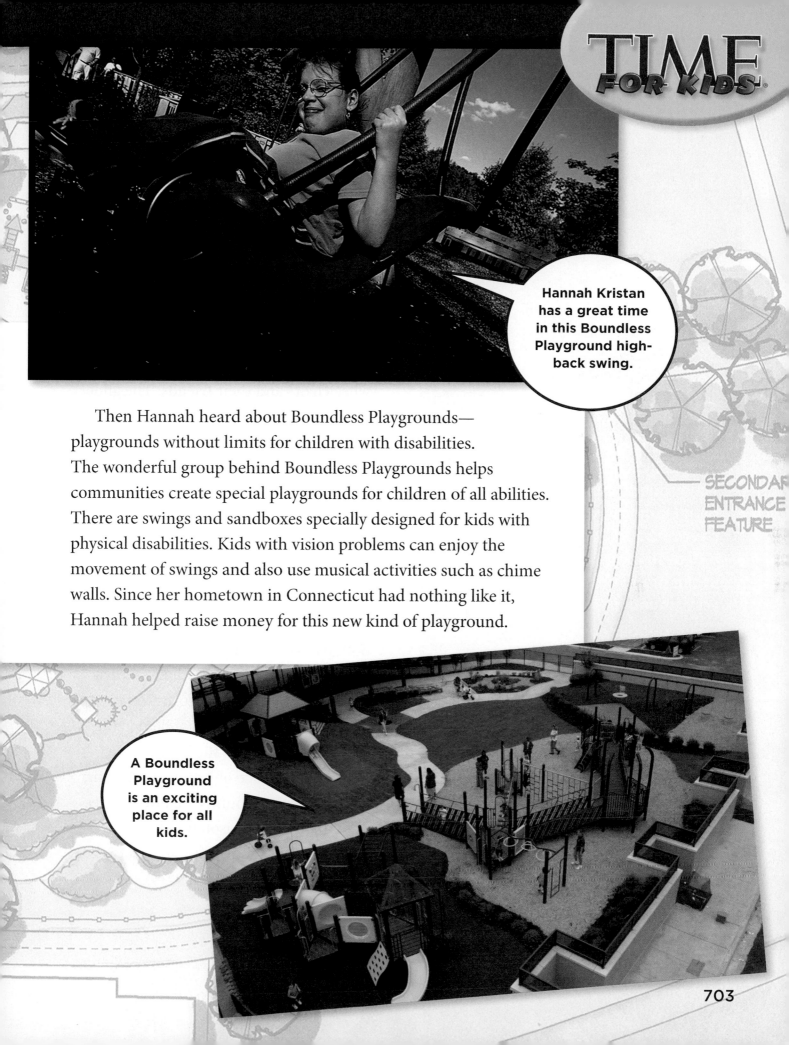

Hannah Kristan has a great time in this Boundless Playground high-back swing.

Then Hannah heard about Boundless Playgrounds—playgrounds without limits for children with disabilities. The wonderful group behind Boundless Playgrounds helps communities create special playgrounds for children of all abilities. There are swings and sandboxes specially designed for kids with physical disabilities. Kids with vision problems can enjoy the movement of swings and also use musical activities such as chime walls. Since her hometown in Connecticut had nothing like it, Hannah helped raise money for this new kind of playground.

SECONDARY ENTRANCE FEATURE

A Boundless Playground is an exciting place for all kids.

703

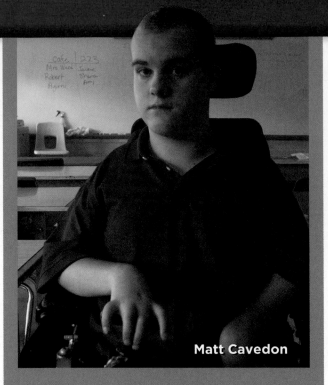

Matt Cavedon

NEW EXPERIENCES

Matt Cavedon designed a swing especially for Boundless Playgrounds, but his commitment didn't stop there. In a speech he gave in 2004, Matt, then 15 years old, described an experience he had at the grand opening of a Boundless Playground in Rhode Island:

"A girl our age [15 years old] was swinging, laughing, and crying all at once. Her mom explained that it was the girl's first time on a swing! Is this a small thing? Not for her! Not for her mom! Not for the kids without disabilities who came up to her to say congratulations! I wonder how many of those kids had just talked to a person with a disability for the first time. I wonder how many will choose to interact with people who have different abilities because of that experience."

The inspiration for Boundless Playgrounds was a playground created by Amy Jaffe Barzach. It is named Jonathan's Dream in honor of her son. Jonathan's Dream and many Boundless Playgrounds around the country have a glider swing that can be used by kids who use wheelchairs and their friends. The glider swing at Jonathan's Dream was designed by Matthew Cavedon, who wasn't even 10 years old at the time. Matthew was motivated because he uses a wheelchair himself and wanted to be able to have fun at playgrounds with other kids, regardless of their **physical** abilities or disabilities.

The **elementary** idea behind Boundless Playgrounds is that play is both part of the joy of childhood and an important way for children to learn about the world. Kids who are kept away from playgrounds are denied this enjoyment as well as the learning. Far from being a place of happy excitement, traditional playgrounds are often places of humiliation and isolation for those who can't join in the fun.

Amy Barzach and friends at Jonathan's Dream, the playground she designed and named for her son

Contrary to some **rigid** ideas about what a playground for children with special needs should be like, a Boundless Playground is every bit as colorful and challenging as a traditional playground. That's why it is inviting and fun for all children. And for Hannah, Matthew, and other kids like them, a playground like this is also a dream come true.

STRATEGY SKILL ✓

Think and Compare

1. What "dream" has come true for kids in this selection?

2. How does Matt Cavendon persuade his audience that Boundless Playgrounds are worthwhile?

3. According to this article, what do kids miss out on when they can't play at a playground?

4. Why do you think "The New Gym" was included in this section along with the other articles about health and fitness?

PROFILE *of a* PARALYMPIAN

Jennifer Howitt may use a wheelchair, but she isn't sitting out life. Since being paralyzed after breaking her back in a hiking accident at age nine, she has developed into one of the country's top young disabled athletes.

Howitt competed in the 1998 World Athletic Championships in track and field and went to the 2000 Sydney Paralympics as the youngest member of the 12-person U.S. women's wheelchair basketball team. Although the team finished in fifth place, "I was on an emotional high," says Howitt. "It was pretty inspirational. If the entire world can come together to celebrate sport and disability, then it is really possible for us, as a planet, to work out all our problems."

Howitt is committed to changing the world in positive ways. She has coached young paraplegic athletes, traveled extensively, and attended Georgetown University in Washington, D.C., where she studied international politics. She hopes "to show young girls with disabilities that they can achieve whatever they want. A disability doesn't get in the way of anything. Maybe you'll have to adapt your goal, but you can always achieve it," Howitt says.

Go On ▶

Directions: Answer the questions.

1. Which of the following best describes Jennifer's attitude?

    A   committed to achieving goals

    B   able to play basketball

    C   sitting out life

    D   paralyzed

2. What does Jennifer believe about disabilities?

    A   People with disabilities live in Washington, D.C.

    B   Disabilities should not keep a person from achieving his or her goals.

    C   People always need wheelchairs.

    D   You can help the entire world.

3. Jennifer believes that having a disability

    A   is a handicap in many areas of life.

    B   is not an obstacle to achieving one's goals.

    C   can keep someone from traveling as much as they'd like.

    D   prevents someone from becoming a good athlete.

4. Other than excelling as an athlete, what are some of Jennifer's other achievements?

5. How would you describe Jennifer's attitude toward her disability and her future? Use details from the article in your response.

Tip

Look for information in more than one place.

Write to a Prompt

"The New Gym" tells about a new approach to gym class. The goal is to help kids find an activity to keep them active into adulthood. Imagine your school is considering such a program. Write an editorial for the school paper designed to persuade school administrators to approve or reject this kind of program.

Working Out

I agree strongly with the proposal to introduce yoga and skateboarding as activities in gym class. I believe these activities would make gym class more exciting for many students.

The purpose of school is to give our brains AND our bodies a workout. Many students find the usual choice of team sports and track and field events boring and uninspiring. Instead of joining the rest of the class, they sit off on the sidelines. They are missing an opportunity to improve their health.

If we added these new types of activities as part of our gym program, more students would be motivated to "get up and GO!" They might start to take the idea of physical fitness more seriously. This could lead to healthful exercise habits that will stay with them for the rest of their lives.

I summed up my point in the last paragraph.

It just seems obvious. Let's expand what we offer in gym class. Everyone will benefit from the change!

Writing Prompt

Your youth group has decided to take on a community service project, but you need community approval first. Write a persuasive editorial for your town's newspaper describing the project and making a strong argument for why it is a good project for the community.

Writer's Checklist

- ☑ Ask yourself, who is my audience?
- ☑ Think about your purpose for writing.
- ☑ Choose the correct form for your writing.
- ☑ Form an opinion about the topic.
- ☑ Use reasons to support your opinion.
- ☑ Be sure your ideas are logical and organized.
- ☑ Use your best spelling, grammar, and punctuation.

BALLOON FLIGHT

Talk About It

Nowadays people can travel quickly by plane to almost any part of the world. Why do you think people still like to go up in hot-air balloons?

LOG ON Find out more about balloon flight at **www.macmillanmh.com**

The Science of Hot-Air Balloons

by Enriquez Mera

Since the first hot-air balloon was **launched** in 1783, few things have changed about how they fly. However, some new differences have made ballooning a safer activity enjoyed by many people worldwide.

In the past hot-air balloons were always made out of linen and paper. Today most are made of nylon. Long pieces of nylon, called *gores*, are stitched together to create the balloon. Balloonists use nylon because it is a thin and light material. Also, it cannot be damaged by heat.

Heat is the basic ingredient needed for ballooning. As air becomes hotter, tiny **particles** of matter move faster and faster. As the balloon fills with warmer particles, it begins to rise. This is because the air inside is lighter than the **dense** air surrounding the balloon. It is the warmer air particles that allow the balloon to float above the cooler air.

How the air is heated to **inflate** the hot-air balloon has changed a great deal since the early days of ballooning. Back in 1783 fire from damp straw and wool heated the air as the balloon remained **anchored** to the ground. Usually, a brave man or woman and a **companion** would climb into the basket, cut the line, and soar into the air.

Now balloonists use propane—the same gas used in most outdoor grills—instead of straw. For hot-air balloons, it is piped from a tank to metal tubes. Once there, a small fire heats up the tubes and the propane. When the propane flame is released, it creates hot air that fills the inside of the hot-air balloon.

Besides propane, another gas that could be used is **hydrogen**. Hydrogen is a gas that has no odor, color, or taste and burns very easily. One advantage of hydrogen gas is that it does not need to be heated. However, hydrogen is expensive, so it is mostly used for balloons during **scientific** studies. These are studies designed to gather information that will help scientists.

Whether for science or sport, more people than ever are taking to the air in balloons.

Reread for **Comprehension**

STRATEGY SKILL

Monitor Comprehension
Make Generalizations

A Generalizations Chart helps you make broad statements that describe ideas or events. This will help you monitor your comprehension or understanding of what you read. To make generalizations, combine key facts from the text and your prior knowledge. Use your Generalizations Chart as you reread "The Science of Hot-Air Balloons."

Information from Text	
Prior Knowledge	
Generalization	

Comprehension

Genre

Nonfiction gives information and facts about real people, places, events, and situations.

Monitor Comprehension

Make Generalizations

As you read, combine information from the text with prior knowledge. Use your Generalizations Chart.

Information from Text	
Prior Knowledge	
Generalization	

Read to Find Out

How has the invention of ballooning been useful?

Up in the Air:
The Story of Balloon Flight

by Patricia Lauber

Award
Winning
Author

Saturday promises to be fair, with no high winds, no storms. It's a perfect day for ballooning. Members of the balloonist club turn out early and set to work. Fans blow air into the balloons. Tongues of orange flame shoot out of roaring gas burners, heating air to make the balloons rise. The balloons **inflate** and stand up. Pilots climb into their baskets, the ground crews let go of the ropes, and it's up, up, and away.

A balloon floats along, silent as a cloud, until a pilot turns on the burners to heat air inside and gain altitude. Balloons cannot be steered. They travel only where the winds carry them. By changing altitude, though, a pilot may find a different wind, going in a different direction. A chase crew follows on land to bring balloonists and balloons home at journey's end.

Today thousands of people in many parts of the world belong to balloon clubs. Their sport was invented more than 200 years ago by a handful of people who willingly risked their lives flying the balloons they had built.

As the balloons fill with hot air, they stand upright. They are ready to soar away, carrying pilots and passengers in big baskets called gondolas.

MONTGOLFIER BALLOON. Ascent of a Montgolfier balloon from Paris, c. 1864: engraving from an English newspaper.

The Story of Ballooning

People have always dreamed of soaring like a bird or floating like a cloud. Over several hundred years a few people thought they knew how to do this. They theorized that a certain kind of big balloon might lift them up. The balloon would be lighter than the air around it, and it would float in air as a boat floats in water. But no one managed to make such a balloon until 1783 when two French brothers built and **launched** the world's first hot-air balloon. Their names were Joseph and Etienne Montgolfier.

The World's First Balloon Flight

Hot smoky air rising from a fire had given Joseph Montgolfier an idea. Perhaps such air would make a balloon rise. Using small balloons Joseph found that it did.

After many experiments the brothers built a balloon that was about 30 feet across and 38 feet tall. It had a wooden frame at the base and was made of linen backed with paper. On June 5, 1783, near the city of Lyons, France, the Montgolfiers built a huge fire of damp straw and wool. Hot air poured into the base of the balloon. As a small crowd watched in amazement, the balloon stirred, swelled, and finally rose upright.

Eight men were holding the balloon down. At a signal they let go. It rose some 6,000 feet into the air and stayed aloft for ten minutes, landing gently in a nearby vineyard. This was the world's first public balloon flight.

The Montgolfiers mistakenly thought smoke, not hot air, made a balloon rise. They used damp fuel to create dense smoke which escaped in flight.

Professor Charles' hydrogen balloon came to a bad end when attacked by pitchforks and dragged through the mud.

A Lighter-than-Air Balloon

Meanwhile in Paris, Professor Jacques A. C. Charles had designed a lighter-than-air balloon. He filled his balloon with a newly discovered gas called **hydrogen**, which weighed much less than air.

On August 27, 1783, Professor Charles launched his balloon at 5 P.M. As a crowd watched, it rose 3,000 feet and disappeared into the clouds.

Forty-five minutes later the balloon came down outside a village 15 miles away. The villagers, who had never heard of such a thing as a balloon, thought a monster had fallen out of the sky. As it bounced toward them, they attacked it with pitchforks. When at last the monster lay still, men tied it to a horse's tail and dragged it through the mud to make sure it was dead.

Now there were two ways to send balloons aloft: with hot air and with hydrogen. The fires were messy and dangerous, but hydrogen took a lot of time to make. Nevertheless, most of the early flights were made with hot-air balloons.

Professor Jacques A. C. Charles

Make Generalizations
What generalization does the author make about early balloon flights?

The king and queen of France watched the launching of the first balloon passengers.

722

The First Passenger Balloons

The first passengers to go up in a balloon were a trio of animals—a duck, a rooster, and a lamb. On September 19, 1783, they traveled in a wicker basket, or gondola, attached to a balloon. After a short flight, the air in the balloon cooled and the passengers drifted safely to Earth. Their flight showed that it was possible to breathe while floating a few thousand feet above Earth.

It was now time for humans to risk ballooning. A daring young French chemist was the first. On October 15, 1783, François Pilâtre de Rozier went up 100 feet. He was **anchored** to the ground by a long rope called a tether. His balloon carried a big metal pan under its mouth. A fire in the pan sent hot air into the balloon. The flight was a success. After that de Rozier made many tethered flights to find out how much straw and wool he needed to burn for each hour he stayed in the air.

By November 21, de Rozier was ready to make the first untethered flight. A huge crowd gathered to watch. The giant balloon filled, and at 1:54 P.M., de Rozier and a **companion** were up, up, and away. When the balloon was 200 feet in the air, the pair took off their hats and bowed to those below. Then they sailed off over Paris. The travelers flew for 25 minutes and covered about five miles before landing in a field outside the city.

Spectators watch de Rozier and his companion as they take flight in a hot-air balloon.

Blanchard and
Jeffries were
saluted by boats
near the English
and French coasts.

724

Daring Balloonists

Between 1783 and 1785, many men, and some women, went up in balloons. Some went for sport. Others, more daring, wanted to do what no one had done before. Jean-Pierre Blanchard was one of these. Blanchard wanted to cross the English Channel from England to France.

On January 7, 1785, the wind was blowing in the right direction over the cliffs of Dover. Blanchard and his American friend John Jefferies filled their balloon with hydrogen, climbed in, and set off for France.

The first half of the trip went smoothly, but then the balloon began leaking gas. The water came closer and closer. To lighten the load, they threw everything overboard—their bags of sand, food and drink, anchors. They were still sinking. Finally they stripped and threw their clothes overboard, saving only their cork life jackets.

The weather changed. The air grew warmer, heating the gas. The balloon rose, and they sailed over the French coast, landing in a forest where they were soon rescued.

On January 9, 1793, Blanchard made the first flight in North America, taking off from Philadelphia and carrying out **scientific** experiments at 5,000 feet. He brought back sealed bottles of air that showed there was less oxygen at that height than at sea level. He also measured his heartbeat and found it was faster. At sea level it beat 84 times a minute; at 5,000 feet it beat 92.

In the years ahead, daring balloonists would keep setting records, but the chief discoveries were made in 1783, when a handful of people who dreamed of flying up, up, and away, made the dream come true.

On June 4, 1784, Marie Thible, an opera singer, became the first woman to make a balloon flight. She sang an aria while floating over Lyons, France.

Make Generalizations
The author makes a generalization that all the chief discoveries in balloon flight were made in 1783. Do you agree? Why or why not?

A balloonist uses a gas heater to warm the air.

Why a Balloon Rises and Floats

When you place a block of wood in water, it takes up space, pushing some of the water aside. As the wood pushes against the water, the water pushes back. This upward force is called *buoyancy*. Buoyancy is the force that keeps things afloat.

A hot-air balloon rises and floats in an ocean of air for the same reason that the block of wood floats in water. It has buoyancy.

Like all matter, air is made of tiny **particles** called molecules. When air is heated, its molecules spread out and move faster. When the air inside a balloon is heated, some of the molecules inside the balloon are forced out. The air inside becomes thinner, or less **dense**. It weighs less than before, but it takes up the same amount of space. As a result, the air inside the balloon weighs less than an equal amount of outside air. Buoyancy carries the balloon up.

Some gases are lighter than air because the molecules themselves are less dense. One of these is hydrogen, the lightest gas known. However, it is a dangerous gas that can burn and explode. That is why balloonists today use helium, which is slightly heavier but does not burn or explode. Helium is the gas used in party balloons.

The Science Behind Hot-Air Balloons

Air inside weighs less than air outside, so the balloon is carried up by buoyancy.

Air is made of tiny particles called molecules.

When air inside a balloon is heated, some of the molecules are forced out.

Balloons Then and Now

In the centuries since 1783, balloons have found many uses in both war and peace. Many balloonists have competed to soar the highest or to make the longest voyage. Here are a few important events.

1860s:
In the Civil War, Union troops, like the French Army before them, used balloons to spy behind enemy lines to see how battles were going.

1900s: The early 1900s brought the dirigible, or blimp. Made of several balloons, it was fitted with motors and propellers that let the pilot steer. A cabin on the underside held more than 100 people on Atlantic crossings.

1875: Three French scientists, exploring the atmosphere, soared to 25,000 feet in a balloon. The men took bottles of oxygen with them, but when the balloon landed only one scientist had survived.

1932:
The man who invented a way to travel safely high into the atmosphere was a Swiss named Auguste Piccard, who built a ball-shaped aluminum gondola. Sealed inside with oxygen tanks, he safely reached a height of 54,000 feet.

1961: Brave men kept going higher and higher. Two U.S. Navy officers, Malcolm D. Ross and Victor Prather, Jr., went up 113,740 feet in an open gondola to test space suits for astronauts.

Present day: Planes have long been the way to travel by air, but you often see a dirigible carrying a TV crew above a football game or other sports event.

1999: Others had crossed the oceans, but Bertrand Piccard (grandson of Auguste) and Brian Jones were the first to balloon non-stop around the world, covering 30,000 miles in 20 days. Their balloon was a cross between a hot-air balloon and a gas balloon.

Every day: Hundreds of small weather balloons explore the atmosphere and transmit their findings to Earth.

Up, Up, and Away with Patricia Lauber

Patricia Lauber says she was probably born wanting to write but had to wait until she had gone to school to learn a few things. She has been writing happily ever since and has produced about 125 books. Many are about things in the natural world, such as volcanoes, dinosaurs, and planets. Patricia loves doing the research for these books because she is always learning something new. Filled with enthusiasm about a new subject, she shares what she has learned by writing books. Patricia Lauber lives in Connecticut with her husband and their two cats, Beemer and Meetoo.

Another book by Patricia Lauber:
Living with Dinosaurs

LOG ON Find out more about Patricia Lauber at **www.macmillanmh.com**

Author's Purpose

This nonfiction piece informs and explains. Identify text features that convey information.

Comprehension Check

Summarize

Making generalizations will help you organize information and summarize it more effectively. Use your Generalizations Chart to help you summarize *Up in the Air*.

Information from Text	
Prior Knowledge	
Generalization	

Think and Compare

1. Describe a few characteristics of a modern–day balloon ride. What clues in the article help you make these generalizations? **Monitor Comprehension: Make Generalizations**

2. Reread page 723. Why do you think the first balloon passengers were animals? Include facts from the selection in your answer. **Analyze**

3. Hot-air balloons transformed life over 200 years ago. Think about a recent **scientific** invention that has affected you. Identify the invention and tell how it has changed your life. **Evaluate**

4. People risked their lives to fly in hot-air balloons. How has their commitment to science contributed to the modern world? **Explain**

5. Reread "The Science of Hot-Air Balloons" on pages 712–713. Compare and contrast the different ways hot-air balloons are able to fly. Use details from each selection in your answer. **Reading/Writing Across Texts**

Poetry

Haiku is an unrhymed form of Japanese poetry that is three lines long. The first line has five syllables; the second line, seven syllables; the third line, five syllables.

Literary Elements

A **Simile** is a comparison of two essentially unlike things that uses the words *like* or *as*.

A **Metaphor** is a comparison of two essentially unlike things that does *not* use the words *like* or *as*.

Hot-Air Balloon Haiku

by Rita Bristol

Balloon, so high up.
A big, bright, bouncing bubble
Too buoyant to burst.

This is an example of a metaphor.

What a strange flower!
With petals as white as sheets.
A bee sleeps within.

732

What do clouds feel like
Floating above the balloon
As it takes you far?

It floats like freedom
In the hazy August light
Soon, though, it will land.

This is an example
of a simile.

Connect and Compare

1. Find another example of metaphor in one of the other haiku. **Metaphor**

2. How do these four haiku help readers get a stronger sense of seeing or being in a hot-air balloon? **Analyze**

3. What is the difference between the information in these haiku and the information presented in "Up in the Air"?
Reading/Writing Across Texts

LOG ON Find out more about haiku at **www.macmillanmh.com**

733

Write to Explain How Something Works

Rearrange Ideas
Writers have to know how something works to explain it clearly. They use everyday examples and sometimes need to **rearrange ideas** to explain complicated concepts more clearly. As you revise, you may want to move a sentence or paragraph.

I carefully arranged the ideas in my explanation about how helium-filled balloons float.

I used an example from everyday life.

How a Helium Balloon Floats

by Tamara E.

Have you ever wondered why the balloons we blow up with air from our lungs don't float up in the air? Balloons filled with helium from a tank float easily. Why is this? Think about what it means to float in a swimming pool. A 2-liter bottle filled with sand will sink to the bottom. However, that same bottle filled with air will float.

The same thing happens with the balloons you blow up yourself. The air inside the balloon is not lighter than the air outside, so it sinks. Helium gas actually weighs less than air, so helium balloons float up to the sky.

Your Turn

Write a short essay telling how something works. You might explain something you already know about. Or, you might decide to do research to find out how something works. As you write your explanation, remember that it has to make sense to anyone who will read it. Rearrange ideas if necessary. Use the writer's checklist to check your writing.

Writer's Checklist

✓ **Ideas and Content:** Did I select a topic that I can explain to others?

☑ **Organization:** Did I **rearrange ideas** so that they fit together well?

✓ **Voice:** Did I make my explanation clear by using examples from everyday life?

✓ **Word Choice:** Did I use common words instead of complex, scientific terms?

✓ **Sentence Fluency:** Did I use prepositions to help my sentences and paragraphs flow well?

✓ **Conventions:** Did I use commas correctly after introductory words? Did I proofread my spelling?

Talk About It

If you could be a scientist, what would you study? What do you think the scientist in this photograph is doing?

LOG ON Find out more about scientists at **www.macmillanmh.com**

Scientists at Work

Vocabulary

specimens	scoured
erupted	biology
murky	research
dormant	observer

Word Parts

Some words have **Greek** or **Latin Roots**. If you know the meaning of a root, you can figure out a word's definition. For example, *bio-* means "life," so *biology* means "the study of living things."

Dr. Priscilla C. Grew, GEOLOGIST

by Josh Taylor

Dr. Priscilla C. Grew is a well-known scientist in the field of geology, the study of Earth's rocks. As a geologist, Dr. Grew looks at a lot of **specimens** to learn how Earth has changed in the past 4.5 billion years.

A good time and place to look for these changes is after a volcano has **erupted**. Afterward, the air becomes dark and **murky** from ash. When the ash settles, it blankets the land. Sometimes a volcano can release hot lava as well. When hot lava spills out, the ground becomes an excellent place to study how new rocks and minerals are formed. This is especially true for the ground near a **dormant** volcano because the area surrounding such a volcano has not changed in a very long time.

Areas affected by earthquakes are another good place to find a geologist. Early in her career, Dr. Grew helped many people in California lower the chances of getting harmed during major earthquakes. Then Dr. Grew moved to Minnesota where she became the first woman to be named state geologist. She and her team searched all over the state for minerals in the soil. Once they were found, they were **scoured** clean and prepared for studies that Dr. Grew would perform.

After leaving Minnesota, Dr. Grew became the first female director of the University of Nebraska State Museum. Visitors to the museum learn about geology, earth science, and **biology**. They enjoy the displays of rocks and fossils.

During her life and career, Dr. Grew has tried to connect the world of rocks and soil to people's needs. By helping people to be safer during earthquakes and looking for important minerals in the soil, Dr. Grew connects her **research** to the real world. All this makes Dr. Grew more than an **observer**. She is a hands-on scientist who is making a difference.

Dr. Priscilla C. Grew

Reread for **Comprehension**

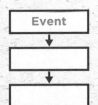

Summarize
Sequence

A Sequence Chart helps you summarize information by listing events or actions in the order that they take place. Use your Sequence Chart as you reread "Dr. Priscilla C. Grew, Geologist" to figure out the sequence of events in Dr. Grew's career.

Event
↓
↓

Comprehension

Genre

Nonfiction gives information and facts about real people, places, events, and situations.

Summarize

Sequence

Look for clues that indicate the order of events. As you read, use your Sequence Chart.

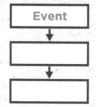

Event

Read to Find Out

What events influenced Dennis's career in science?

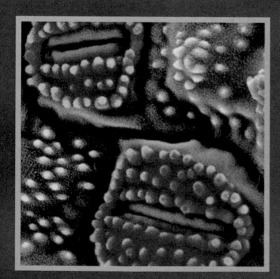

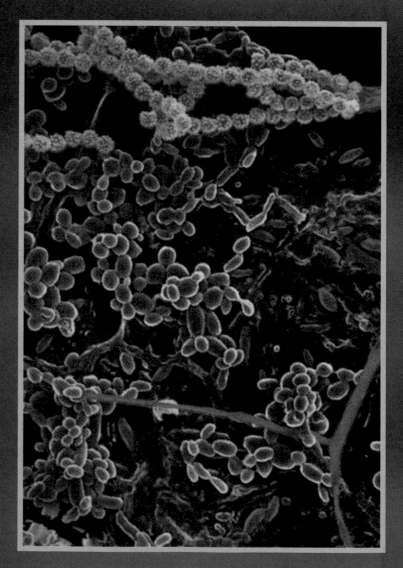

Hidden Worlds

Looking Through a Scientist's Microscope

by Stephen Kramer
photographs by Dennis Kunkel

Becoming a Scientist

Dennis Kunkel grew up in the Iowa countryside, where cornfields stretched for miles in all directions. Dennis helped tend the flowers and vegetables in the family garden. He went on weekend fishing trips with his parents and his sisters, and he took care of the family pets. Dennis loved nature and being outdoors, but he did not know that someday he would become a scientist.

Then Dennis received a gift that changed his life. "When I was ten years old, my parents gave me a microscope for Christmas," he recalls. "It came with a set of prepared slides—things like insect legs, root hairs, and tiny creatures called protozoans. As soon as I unwrapped the microscope, I forgot about my other presents and tried to figure out how to use it."

Dennis working at one of his microscopes

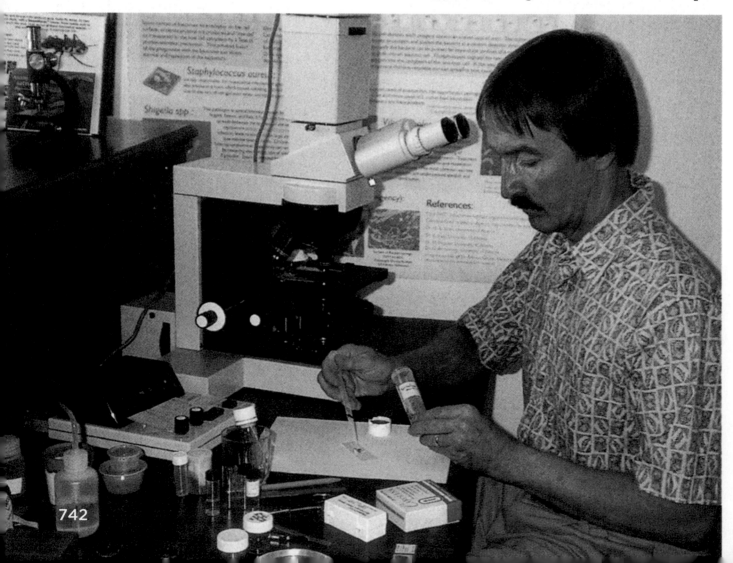

When Dennis looked at pond water with his first microscope, he saw these kinds of simple plants. They are green algae. Above: *Volvox*. Right: *Micrasterias*.

The prepared specimens that came with the microscope were dead. Dennis quickly discovered that it was more fun to observe things that were alive and moving, so he began to take collecting trips. One of Dennis's first trips was to a pond about a mile and a half from his house. "I started hiking down there with my little collecting bottles and bringing back water samples to look at under my microscope," he explains. "I couldn't wait to get home from school in the afternoon so I could go to the pond. Before long I was looking at all kinds of fascinating creatures."

743

Dennis used his microscope to look at anything he could fit under its lenses. He examined insects, soil samples, and parts of plants. He looked at fur from his pets and seeds from nearby fields. Dennis made drawings of the things he observed, and he spent many hours reading about them.

After Dennis graduated from high school, he enrolled in a junior college in his hometown. A **biology** teacher there encouraged his love of science and microscopes. Dennis often worked in the science lab after school, using microscopes to study the things he collected.

Then Dennis transferred to the University of Washington, in Seattle. Finally he could learn and do things he had dreamed about. "I had the chance to work in labs with good microscopes," explains Dennis. "I spent hours speaking with professors and students about science. I had dreamed of exploring and learning about undersea life like Jacques Cousteau, but until I left Iowa I had never even seen the ocean. While I attended the University of Washington, I learned how to scuba dive. It was thrilling to go underwater to observe and collect the plants and animals I wanted to study."

**Dennis examines leaves
with two young scientists.**

STRATEGY SKILL

Sequence
What clue words does the author use to indicate the time order of events in Dennis Kunkel's life?

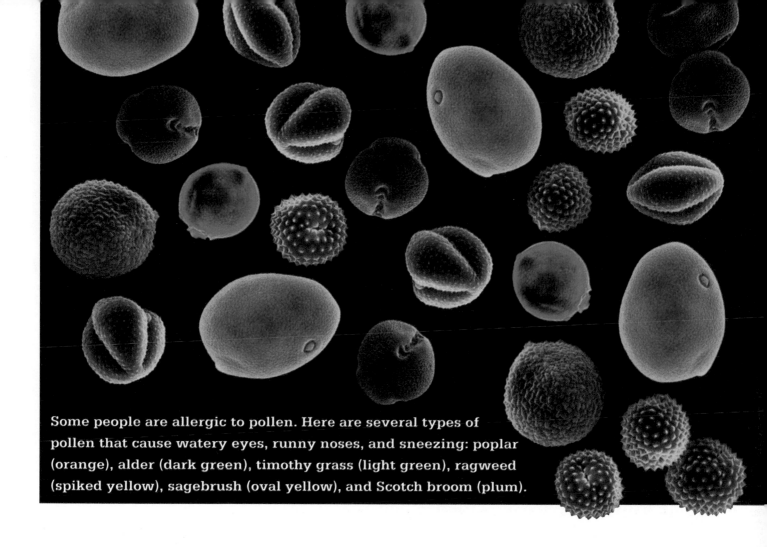

Some people are allergic to pollen. Here are several types of pollen that cause watery eyes, runny noses, and sneezing: poplar (orange), alder (dark green), timothy grass (light green), ragweed (spiked yellow), sagebrush (oval yellow), and Scotch broom (plum).

In graduate school, Dennis began to use the science department's electron microscopes for his own **research**, studying tiny living things called cyanobacteria. But Dennis also used the microscopes to help other scientists. He helped one of his professors study and classify pollen grains from different kinds of flowers. He helped a fellow graduate student examine wood with an electron microscope to learn about how plant cells deposit minerals and create "hard" wood. He helped other students with their studies of algae, fungi, and flowering plants.

After eight years of graduate work—including thousands of hours of research and work with microscopes—Dennis earned a Ph.D. in botany, the study of plants. Although Dennis was finishing his schooling, he was just beginning a lifetime of scientific learning and discovery.

Dennis worked on research projects at the University of Washington and the University of Hawai'i for about twenty-five years. Now he does much of his work in his home on the island of O'ahu, Hawai'i.

Working as a Scientist

Scientists are explorers. They usually make discoveries by asking questions and then trying to answer them. Some scientists find their answers in laboratories, surrounded by equipment and instruments. Others travel to natural areas to find their answers. Dennis's work has taken him to mountains, rainforests, deserts, caves, beaches, and into the sea.

Whenever Dennis goes on field trips, he takes along collecting boxes and bottles. When he returns to the lab, the boxes and bottles are usually full of interesting **specimens**: algae, lichens, mushrooms, seeds, leaves, insects, bark, soil, and flowers. Dennis has explored hidden worlds in places ranging from the blast zone of a volcano to the dust balls underneath people's beds!

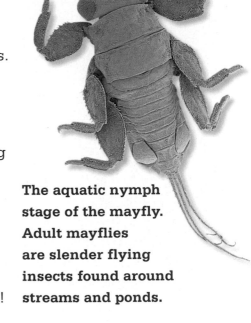

The aquatic nymph stage of the mayfly. Adult mayflies are slender flying insects found around streams and ponds.

A butterfly's proboscis, the coiled mouthpart it uses to sip nectar.

Dennis and the scientific team collect water samples.

Mount St. Helens

In 1980, a **dormant** volcano called Mount St. Helens **erupted** in Washington State. The blast from the eruption flattened huge forests of tall trees. Floods of boiling mud and water from melting snow **scoured** riverbeds. The countryside was covered with a thick layer of ash for miles around.

Some of the first people allowed to visit the blast zone were biologists, scientists who study living things. They were stunned by the destruction. One of the first things they wanted to know was whether any living things had survived.

A team of scientists from the University of Washington made plans to study the lakes and streams of the blast area. Since Dennis was an expert on algae, the simple plants found in lakes and streams, he was invited to help with the study. The scientists traveled to a camp set up on the north side of Mount St. Helens. Twice a day, a helicopter flew them into the blast zone. All they could see, for miles in every direction, were dead trees blanketed by a heavy layer of ash.

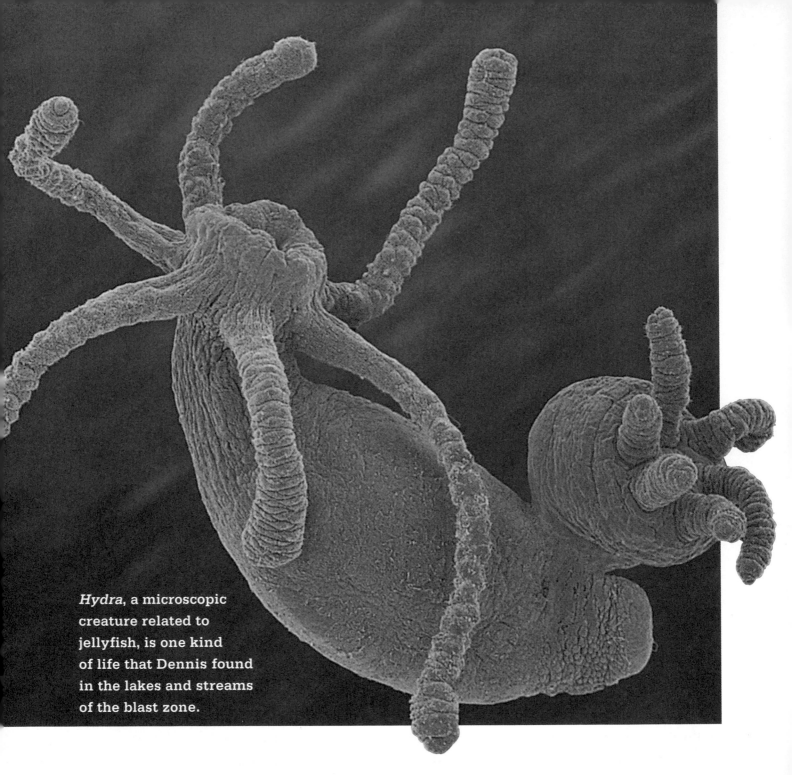

Hydra, a microscopic creature related to jellyfish, is one kind of life that Dennis found in the lakes and streams of the blast zone.

The scientists were thrilled because they had never explored the area around an active volcano so soon after this type of eruption. But no one knew when the mountain might erupt again. In fact, no one even knew for sure whether it was safe to land a helicopter in the blast zone. Some pilots thought the ash stirred up by the whirling helicopter blades might choke the engines. So Dennis and the other scientists weren't allowed to land in the study area on the first few trips. They had to collect their water samples while the helicopter was in the air!

As Dennis and the team crisscrossed the blast zone in the helicopter, they kept their eyes open for water. When they spotted a lake or pond that had survived the blast, the pilot flew the helicopter into position. As the helicopter hovered over the **murky** gray water, Dennis lowered collecting bottles on ropes. The bottles had triggers so Dennis could open them at different depths. This allowed him to collect some water samples from near the surface and others from deep in the lakes.

The first water samples the scientists collected showed that some of the lakes were completely dead. Nothing had survived the heat, gases, and choking ash of the eruption.

Just a few weeks later, Dennis used microscopes to look at new water samples he had collected from the same lakes. He was amazed to see algae, protozoans, and bacteria living in the water. Within several months, small crustaceans—animals that feed on algae and bacteria—began to reappear in some of the lakes.

Dennis and the other scientists kept careful records of the kinds of living things that returned to the lakes and when they reappeared. They identified the kinds of algae, protozoans, bacteria, and crustaceans they found. Later, Dennis and the team also discovered that frogs and fish were returning to some of these lakes, apparently carried in by surrounding streams. Their studies helped other scientists understand what happens to life in lakes when a nearby volcano erupts—and how living things eventually return to areas where all life was destroyed.

***Vorticella,*
**a single-celled
protozoan**

Sequence

List the different life forms that developed in the dead lakes near the volcano in the order that they appeared.

How to Become a Scientist

Here is Dennis's advice for students who think they might like to become scientists:

*Become an **observer**.* One of the most important things you can do to become a good scientist and microscopist is practice being a careful observer. Find a comfortable chair and put it in the middle of your garden, yard, or a park. Sit in the chair for ten minutes or thirty minutes or an hour. Watch the insects that fly past or land on the plants. Look at the shapes of leaves and stems and branches. Listen to the sounds of buzzing bees and chirping crickets. See if you can find a sight or smell or sound that surprises you. Use a loupe or magnifying glass to look closely at interesting objects.

Dennis and graduate student examine a South African clawed frog.

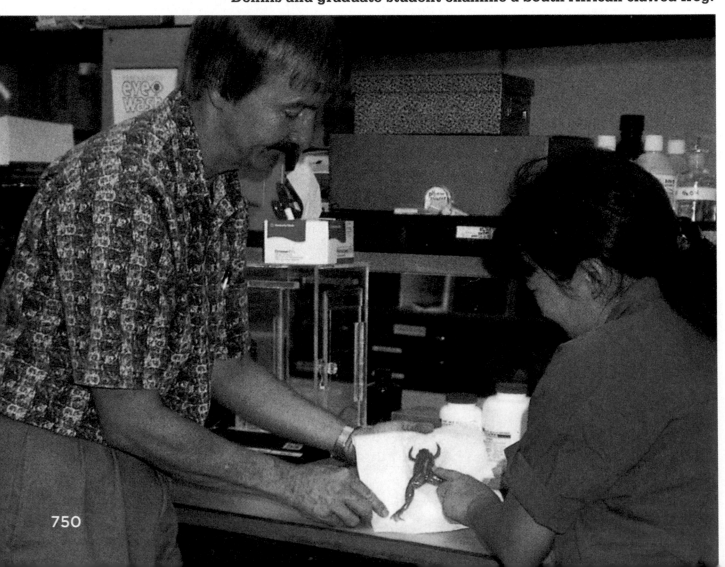

Dennis looking closely at a fern leaf

Learn everything you can about a topic that interests you.
Suppose you'd like to explore flowers by using a microscope. Go
to the library and check out some flower books. See what you can
find on the Internet. Pick some flowers and carefully take them
apart. Use a loupe or a magnifying glass to see how everything fits
together. The more you know about flowers from reading about
them and observing them, the more you'll understand when you
begin looking at them with a loupe or a microscope.

Ask for help from a knowledgeable person. After you've learned
everything you can on your own, ask someone else to help with
questions you still have. Maybe there's someone at a nearby
school or museum who knows about insects, spiders, algae, moss,
or something else you'd like to learn about. If you don't have a
microscope of your own, maybe a teacher would help you look at
some specimens with a school microscope.

*Find a scientist to talk to or find a place where scientific research
is being done.* If you still want to learn more, you may be able to
find a scientist to talk to at a nearby college, university, or research
station. Write a letter or an e-mail message to the scientist,
explaining what you're interested in. Ask if you can schedule a
time to visit. Most scientists are happy to talk to students who
share their passion for science.

Under the Microscope with Stephen Kramer and Dennis Kunkel

Stephen Kramer is an author and teacher. When he is not writing about avalanches or following Dennis Kunkel into a volcano, he is teaching fifth graders. Both of his careers focus on a love of science and teaching. He especially enjoys teaching children different scientific facts about bats, rainforests, or machines. Stephen lives in Vancouver, Washington, with his wife and their two sons.

Another book by Stephen Kramer:
Tornado

Dennis Kunkel is often found looking at fleas, bacteria, and blood cells under his microscope. He has made large contributions to the science world with what he has witnessed through his lens. Dennis loves the new information his microscope unveils because he appreciates the beauty of what is missed by the naked eye. Dennis's research and pictures have appeared in magazines, museum exhibits, and even movies.

 LOG ON Find out more about Stephen Kramer and Dennis Kunkel at **www.macmillanmh.com**

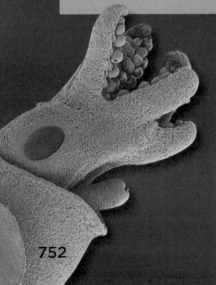

Author's Purpose

How can readers tell that Stephen Kramer respects scientists greatly? Give examples from the text, headings, or photos.

Comprehension Check

Summarize

Use your Sequence Chart to summarize important information from *Hidden Worlds: Looking Through a Scientist's Microscope*.

Think and Compare

1. Describe the steps Dennis thinks are important in becoming a better scientist. **Summarize: Sequence**

2. Reread page 749. Why do you think Dennis looked for living things after the eruption of Mt. St. Helens? Include facts from the selection in your answer. **Analyze**

3. Explain how you would practice becoming a careful **observer**. Include where you would choose to observe and what you might see, smell, hear, and touch. **Evaluate**

4. What effect do scientists like Dennis Kunkel, Albert Einstein, and others, have on the world? Explain your answer. **Analyze**

5. Reread "Dr. Priscilla C. Grew, Geologist" on pages 738–739. Compare and contrast Dr. Grew's experiences with Dennis Kunkel's career. Use details from both selections in your answer. **Reading/Writing Across Texts**

Mountain of FIRE:
A Native American Myth

retold by Grace Armstrong

Long ago when the world was new, there was one land and one people. All lived together by the great river in peace, worked well, and were happy.

Into this world were born two brothers who grew up quarreling. They argued over who was stronger and who had better land to work. Soon all the people had taken sides. The Great Spirit, Sahale, saw this quarreling and decided to end it.

> **This simile, comparing the voice to thunder, is an example of _figurative language_.**

In a voice like low, rumbling thunder, Sahale called the brothers together and gave each one an arrow for his bow. He said, "Wherever your arrow falls, that will be your land, and there you will be a chief." The first brother shot his arrow high in the air, and it landed to the south of the great river. He went there with his people, and they became known as the Multnomahs. The second brother shot his arrow into the air and it landed north of the river. There he went with his people, who became known as the Klickitats.

The brothers lived with their people in peace for some time. As time passed though, envy began to cause quarrels. "The Klickitats have better land," some said. "The Multnomahs have more beautiful land," others cried. Sahale heard this bickering that seemed to grow like a storm and was unhappy with the two tribes. When violence threatened, Sahale stopped it by taking away all fire, even the sun, just as the autumn winds, cold, and snow were beginning.

Only one in all the land still had fire. She was Loo-Wit, an old, wrinkled woman with gray hair and quiet ways. She had stayed apart from all the quarrels. After the people had suffered and seemed to have mended their ways, Sahale asked Loo-Wit if she would like to share her fire with them. "For doing this," he told her, "you may have anything you wish."

"I wish to be young and beautiful," she said.

"Then that is what you will be," Sahale said.

Sahale led Loo-Wit to a great stone bridge over the river that joined the two lands. The people arrived at the bridge, led by their chiefs, to find the most beautiful woman they had ever seen. She began to give them fire. Loo-Wit kept the fire burning all day until fire was restored to all the people.

This was not to be the end of the quarreling. During this day the two chiefs had both fallen in love with Loo-Wit and wanted her for a wife. Loo-Wit could not choose between them, and once again, fighting erupted.

The two brothers refused to compromise or work on a solution. Because the brothers were unyielding in their positions, Sahale angrily changed the brothers into mountains. The chief of the Klickitats was turned into the mountain known today as Mount Adams. The chief of the Multnomahs was turned into the mountain known today as Mount Hood.

The use of the mountains, which are rock hard and immovable, represents the brothers' stubborness and is an example of *symbolism*.

Loo-Wit, her heart broken over this, lost her desire to be young and beautiful. Sahale, in his pity, also changed her into a mountain, and placed her between the two brother mountains. She was allowed to keep inside her the fire she had shared with the people.

Because Loo-Wit was beautiful, her mountain was a beautiful cone of dazzling white. Today she is known as Mount St. Helens.

Loo-Wit wants to remind humans to care for Earth and for each other. When she is unhappy, she will awaken as she did in the 1980s.

Once her anger passes, though, the ground heals and plant and animal life have a chance to flourish once again.

Connect and Compare

1. What do you think of Sahale's decision to turn the quarreling brothers into mountains? What do mountains symbolize? **Symbolism**

2. What elements make this a myth? What would you choose to write a myth about? **Evaluate**

3. Compare the ways in which the narrator of "Mountain of Fire" and the scientists of *Hidden Worlds* view the eruption of Mount St. Helens. What is the value of having different versions of events? **Reading/Writing Across Texts**

 Find out more about myths at **www.macmillanmh.com**

757

Writer's Craft

Beginning, Middle, and End

Using a good **beginning, middle, and end** makes an essay about problem solving easy for readers to understand. State the problem in the beginning, and explain the solution in the middle and end.

The Problem of Hole #13

by Mary A.

I explained my problem to readers at the beginning of my essay.

My three best friends and I play miniature golf every Friday night. Hole #13 is an annoying problem for me. Every time, it takes me ten frustrating strokes to finish Hole #13.

My dad suggested I attack the problem in a scientific way. He said I should do research, make observations, and experiment to solve my problem.

I explained my solution with a good middle and end.

First, I did some research. I went to the library and found a book that showed me a better way to putt. Next, I made careful observations. I studied the technique my friends used as they played Hole #13. I saw how they aimed the first shot so that the ball skipped a few inches from the hole. Finally, I experimented on my own and practiced for hours. The next Friday night I used what I had learned. It worked! I improved my score and the problem of Hole #13 was solved.

Your Turn

What problem have you recently solved for yourself? Write an essay that explains the problem and the steps you took to solve it. Remember to describe the steps using a good beginning, middle, and end. Use the writer's checklist to check your writing.

Writer's Checklist

✓ **Ideas and Content:** Did I describe a problem that I solved on my own?

☑ **Organization:** Did I present the steps I took to solve the problem using a good **beginning, middle, and end**?

✓ **Voice:** Can the reader tell that I worked hard to solve the problem and that I feel proud of my efforts?

✓ **Word Choice:** Did I use clear, precise words to help the reader understand my solution?

✓ **Sentence Fluency:** Did I combine some ideas to create longer, more interesting sentences?

✓ **Conventions:** Is my essay punctuated correctly? Did I check my spelling?

National Parks: Our National Treasures

by Carlos M. Spinoza

Where can you go to experience the great outdoors as it was 200 years ago? Fresh air, sparkling lakes, untouched land, and breathtaking scenery are all there for you to enjoy in this country's national parks. There are almost 400 national parks in the United States. One of them may be near your home town. Each park is special, and each park has a story. Where did the idea to protect special parkland originate? It all started with Yellowstone National Park.

Yellowstone National Park

Trappers who had been out West told stories about bubbling mud and steamy springs that gushed hot water and steam. In the East these stories sparked people's interests. Adventurers set out to find the places that inspired such stories. In 1871 one such adventurer, Ferdinand Hayden, led a group to explore the area that would become Yellowstone National Park. Thomas Moran and William H. Jackson also joined this group. Moran was an artist and Jackson was a photographer. When they arrived they found land that had been formed by a volcano. The volcano had erupted more than 640,000 years earlier. The ash covered the western United States and some of the Midwest and Mexico. Old Faithful and other hot springs amazed the visitors. The stories they had heard seemed to be true!

Go On ▶

Moran and Jackson captured the beauty of Yellowstone in paint and on film. Moran became so well known for his watercolor sketches of Yellowstone that people started calling him Thomas "Yellowstone" Moran. Along with Jackson's black-and-white photographs, Moran's watercolor paintings were later used to persuade Congress that Yellowstone needed protection.

Thomas Moran,
*Grand Canyon of the
Yellowstone Park,* 1872

The National Park Service

President Ulysses S. Grant thought that protecting natural areas was such a good idea that in 1872 he made Yellowstone the first national park.

He said that Yellowstone would be "set apart as a public park . . . for the benefit and enjoyment of people."

Yellowstone paved the way for the National Park Service (NPS). The NPS began in 1916. Writer Wallace Stegner said, "National parks are the best idea we ever had. Absolutely American . . . . they reflect us at our best . . . ." Congress asked the NPS to conserve national treasures "for the enjoyment of future generations." The NPS now takes care of more than 84 million acres of land in the United States.

Stephen T. Mather was the NPS director from 1917 to 1929. He said:

> *The parks do not belong to one state
> or to one section . . . . The Yosemite,
> the Yellowstone, the Grand Canyon
> are national properties in which
> every citizen has a vested interest;
> they belong as much to the man
> of Massachusetts, of Michigan, of
> Florida, as they do to the people
> of California, of Wyoming,
> and of Arizona.*

Answer Questions

The Antiquities Act

In 1906 the Antiquities Act gave the President the power to grant further protection to national parks and other special places. These areas may be valuable because of their beauty or because they are important to history or science. They might contain structures or lands that should be left untouched. The number of places protected by the Antiquities Act has increased over the years. Now these areas can be found on public or private land. Congress also provides for such things as national lakeshores and rivers.

The National Parks and You

Visiting a national park is like traveling back in time. You can view land that looks much as it did when the United States established itself as a nation. You can see natural waterfalls in Yosemite National Park. You can gaze at the sculpted rock of Grand Canyon National Park. You can learn how animals and plants live together in their natural environment at Joshua Tree National Park. If history is your passion, you can explore important events in America's past by visiting Gettysburg National Military Park. Similarly, by visiting the Clara Barton or Frederick Douglass National Historic Sites, you can learn about people who helped make this country great.

These places, events, and people helped write the American story. By learning about them, you can begin to understand and appreciate your own special place in this country's continuing story.

Arches National Park, Utah

Directions: Answer the questions.

Tip

You have to think about the entire selection to choose the best answer.

1. Why are parks called national treasures?

A   They were found by accident.

B   They are operated by the President.

C   They contribute to the nation's economy.

D   They preserve untouched natural areas for all people to enjoy.

2. What is the BEST reason for learning about national parks?

A   to help plan a career

B   to see where artists painted famous pictures

C   they will all be gone one day

D   to find out about the nation's history and natural wonders

3. Why might the National Park Service want photographers and artists to visit their parks?

A   to create postcards

B   to develop on-site art schools

C   to show why we need to continue to protect the parks

D   to compare their work with that of writers

4. How is visiting a national park like traveling back in time?

5. Do you agree with Wallace Stegner that the national parks are a great idea? Should national parks be protected? Use details from the selection to support your response.

Writing Prompt

Your friend is coming to visit. Write directions for your friend on how to get from school to your home. Include details such as landmarks and street signs.

Glossary

What Is a Glossary?

A glossary can help you find the **meanings** of words in this book that you may not know. The words in the glossary are listed in **alphabetical order**. **Guide words** at the top of each page tell you the first and last words on the page.

Each word is divided into syllables. The way to pronounce the word is given next. You can understand the pronunciation respelling by using the **pronunciation key**. A shorter key appears at the bottom of every other page. When a word has more than one syllable, a dark accent mark (ˊ) shows which syllable is stressed. In some words a light accent mark (ˊ) shows which syllable has a less heavy stress. Sometimes an entry includes a second meaning for the word.

Guide Words

First word on the page   Last word on the page

Sample Entry

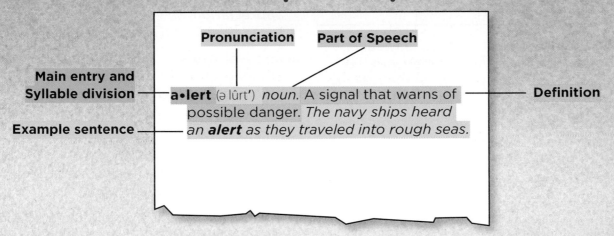

Pronunciation   Part of Speech

Main entry and
Syllable division

Example sentence

a•lert (ə lûrt′) *noun.* A signal that warns of
possible danger. *The navy ships heard
an **alert** as they traveled into rough seas.*

Definition

Pronunciation Key

Phonetic Spelling	Examples
a	at, bad, plaid, laugh
ā	ape, pain, day, break
ä	father, calm
âr	care, pair, bear, their, where
e	end, pet, said, heaven, friend
ē	equal, me, feet, team, piece, key
i	it, big, give, hymn
ī	ice, fine, lie, my
îr	ear, deer, here, pierce
o	odd, hot, watch
ō	old, oat, toe, low
ô	coffee, all, taught, law, fought
ôr	order, fork, horse, story, pour
oi	oil, toy
ou	out, now, bough
u	up, mud, love, double
ū	use, mule, cue, feud, few
ü	rule, true, food, fruit
u̇	put, wood, should, look
ûr	burn, hurry, term, bird, word, courage
ə	about, taken, pencil, lemon, circus
b	bat, above, job
ch	chin, such, match

Phonetic Spelling	Examples
d	dear, soda, bad
f	five, defend, leaf, off, cough, elephant
g	game, ago, fog, egg
h	hat, ahead
hw	white, whether, which
j	joke, enjoy, gem, page, edge
k	kite, bakery, seek, tack, cat
l	lid, sailor, feel, ball, allow
m	man, family, dream
n	not, final, pan, knife, gnaw
ng	long, singer
p	pail, repair, soap, happy
r	ride, parent, wear, more, marry
s	sit, aside, pets, cent, pass
sh	shoe, washer, fish, mission, nation
t	tag, pretend, fat, dressed
th	thin, panther, both
th	these, mother, smooth
v	very, favor, wave
w	wet, weather, reward
y	yes, onion
z	zoo, lazy, jazz, rose, dogs, houses
zh	vision, treasure, seizure

Aa

a•ban•don (ə ban′dən) *verb.* To leave and not return. *The sailors jumped into the ocean when they were given the order to* **abandon** *the ship.*

ac•com•pa•ny (ə kum′pə nē) *verb.* To go together with. *My friend decided to* **accompany** *me to the store so that I would have someone to talk to.*

ad•ap•ta•tions (ad′əp tā′shənz) *noun, plural.* Changes in a plant or animal so that it is better suited to survive in its environment. *Fur and the shape of an animal's teeth are* **adaptations***.*

ad•just•ed (ə jus′tid) *verb.* Changed or arranged to fit a need or demand. *We* **adjusted** *the schedule to include two more singers in the program.*

ad•ver•tise•ment (ad′vûr tīz′mənt, ad vûr′tis mənt) *noun.* A public notice that tells people about a product, event, or something a person needs. *A successful* **advertisement** *will convince shoppers to buy a product.*

a•lert (ə lûrt′) *noun.* A heightened sense of watchfulness for possible danger. *The navy ship was put on* **alert** *after an ice storm was reported in the area.*

a•mend•ment (ə mend′mənt) *noun.* A change in a law caused by voting of government officials or changes to the Constitution. *Women were given the right to vote in all states by an* **amendment** *to the Constitution.*

a•nat•o•my (ə nat′ə mē) *noun.* The structure of an animal or plant or any of its parts. *Medical students study* **anatomy** *to learn how to treat illnesses in people.*

an•chored (ang′kərd) *verb.* Being held in place by a heavy metal device or object. *The crew is lucky they* **anchored** *the boat to a rock because the sudden storm would have blown them far from shore.*

ap•pre•ci•a•tion (ə prē′shē ā′shən) *noun.* A feeling of being thankful. *To show his* **appreciation***, Javier gave the boy who found his wallet a small reward.*

ar•chae•ol•o•gists (är′kē ol′ə jists) *noun, plural.* Students of or experts in past cultures and histories. **Archaeologists** *dig in the earth for clues to Earth's past.*

a•rous•ing (ə rouz′ing) *verb.* Stirring up or causing excitement. *The opposing team's fans were* **arousing** *a lot of attention in the bleachers with their cheering.*

ar•roy•o (ə roi′ō) *noun.* A small river or stream. *The small* **arroyo** *had plenty of fish.*

ar•ti•facts (är′tə fakts′) *noun, plural.* Things left over from an earlier time. *Some tools are* **artifacts** *from a time when they were useful to people.*

at•mos•phere (at′məs fîr′) *noun.* **1.** The layer of gases that surrounds Earth. *We watched on television as the space shuttle entered the* **atmosphere** *after its mission to the moon was over.* **2.** A surrounding mood or environment. *Our house has a merry* **atmosphere** *during the holiday season.*

at•tor•ney (ə tûr′nē) *noun.* A lawyer; one who helps with legal matters. *Before arguing your case in court, it may be a good idea to hire an* **attorney***.*

at•trac•tion (ə trak′shən) *noun.* A person or thing that draws attention. *The new baby elephant was an* **attraction** *that drew a lot of people at the zoo.*

au•to•graph (ô′tə graf′) *noun.* A person's signature written in that person's own handwriting. *My sister got her favorite singer's* **autograph.**

a•vail•a•ble (ə vāl′ə bəl) *adjective.* Possible to get. *There were seats* **available** *at the front of the theatre.*

Bb

banned (band) *verb.* Officially forbidden; prohibited. *Many school boards have* **banned** *books that contain inaccurate information.*

bed•lam (bed′ləm) *noun.* A place or condition of wild uproar and confusion. *There was* **bedlam** *in the hallways when the fire alarm sounded.*

be•hav•ior (bi hāv′yər) *noun.* A way of acting. *The campers were yelled at by the counselor for their mischievous* **behavior.**

bi•ol•o•gy (bī ol′ə jē) *adjective.* Characterized by the study of living things. *The* **biology** *teacher enjoyed the study of plants.* —*noun.* The study of living things. **Biology** *is my favorite subject in school.*

blared (blârd) *verb.* Made a loud, harsh sound. *The trumpets* **blared** *as the Olympic ceremonies began.*

blurt•ed (blûr′tid) *verb.* Said suddenly or without thinking. *I* **blurted** *out the answer before the teacher finished asking the question.*

boy•cott (boi′kot) *noun.* A planned and organized refusal to have anything to do with a person, group, or nation. *The strikers called for a* **boycott** *of the company's products.*

bri•dle (brī′dəl) *noun.* The part of a horse's or donkey's harness that fits over the head and is used to guide or control the animal. *The cowboy fitted the* **bridle** *over the horse's head before going for a ride.*

brim•ming (bri′ming) *adjective.* Full to the upper edge of a container. *The* **brimming** *mugs were filled with hot cocoa and whipped cream.*

buf•fet¹ (buf′it) *verb.* To knock about. *We felt the rough water* **buffet** *the raft.*

buf•fet² (bəf′ā, bŭf′ā) *noun.* **1.** A piece of furniture with a flat surface for serving food. *Please put the rice on the* **buffet** *after it has been passed around the table.* **2.** A meal laid out on a table so that guests can serve themselves. *The* **buffet** *at the wedding featured foods from many countries.*

bul•le•tin board (bul′i tin bôrd) *noun.* A board for posting notices, announcements, and pictures. *The teacher uses a* **bulletin board** *to report all class events.*

bun•dle (bun′dəl) *noun.* A group of things held together. *The deliveryman left a* **bundle** *of newspapers outside the grocery store.*

bur•dens (bûr′dənz) *noun, plural.* Things that are carried. *The mule carried the* **burdens** *down the trail into the canyon.*

Cc

cam•ou•flage (kam′ə fläzh′) *noun.* Any disguise, appearance, or behavior that serves to conceal or deceive, such as the protective coloring of an animal. *An octopus uses* **camouflage** *to change its skin color and blend into its surroundings.*

---

a**t**; **āp**e; f**är**; c**âr**e; **e**nd; m**ē**; **i**t; **īc**e; p**îr**ce; h**o**t; **ōl**d; s**ông**; f**ôr**k; **oi**l; **ou**t; **u**p; **ūs**e; r**ül**e; p**ůl**l; t**ûr**n; **ch**in; si**ng**; **sh**op; **th**in; **th**is; **hw** in **wh**ite; **zh** in trea**s**ure.

The symbol **ə** stands for the unstressed vowel sound in **a**bout, tak**e**n, penc**i**l, lem**o**n, and circ**u**s.

can•celed (kanʹsəld) *verb.* Did away with, stopped, or called off. *The picnic was* **canceled** *due to rain.*

ca•pa•ble (kāʹpə bəl) *adjective.* Having skill or power; able. *The new planes are* **capable** *of even greater speed.*

car•ni•vores (kärʹnə vôrzʹ) *noun, plural.* Animals or plants such as sharks, eagles, dogs, and Venus's-flytraps that feed chiefly on flesh. *Lions are* **carnivores** *who hunt and feed on smaller animals.*

cat•e•go•ries (katʹi gôrʹēz) *noun, plural.* Groups or classes of things. *The menu was divided into three* **categories**: *snacks, main courses, and desserts.*

cel•e•bra•tion (selʹə brāʹshən) *noun.* The act of honoring with festivities. *My grandma's ninetieth birthday called for a big* **celebration**.

char•ac•ter•is•tics (karʹik tə risʹtiks) *noun, plural.* Qualities or features that are typical of or serve to distinguish a person, group, or thing from others. *Courage and bravery are* **characteristics** *that my cousin possesses.*

chis•eled (chiʹzəld) *verb.* Cut or shaped with a sharp metal tool called a chisel. *The numbers were* **chiseled** *into the stone next to the front doors.*

civ•i•li•za•tion (sivʹə lə zāʹshən) *noun.* A society in which agriculture, trade, government, art, and science are highly developed. *The museum had a number of objects that showed how* **civilization** *has developed over the last 600 years.*

clenched (klencht) *verb.* Grasped or closed tightly. *The boy* **clenched** *his fist when he saw the bully walking angrily towards him.*

colo•nel (kûrʹnəl) *noun.* One of the ranks of a military officer. *Kevin Andretti was promoted to full* **colonel** *last month.*

com•bined (kəm bīndʹ) *adjective.* Characterized by being joined together or united. *Thanks to the* **combined** *efforts of the voters in our city, the mayor was reelected.* —*verb.* Joined together; united. *The baker* **combined** *eggs, butter, sugar, and flour to make cookie dough.*

com•menced (kə menstʹ) *verb.* Began or started. *When the audience was seated and quiet, the play* **commenced**.

com•mon•wealth (komʹən welthʹ) *noun.* A nation or state that is governed independently but is associated with another country. *Puerto Rico is a* **commonwealth** *of the United States.*

com•pan•ion (kəm panʹyən) *noun.* A person or animal who keeps somebody company. *A dog can be a good* **companion** *for a lonely person.*

com•pelled (kem peldʹ) *verb.* Urged, or caused with force. *The rain* **compelled** *us to postpone our picnic.*

com•pe•ti•tion (komʹpi tishʹən) *noun.* The act of trying to win or gain something from another person or other people. *We're in* **competition** *with two other teams for the swimming championship.*

com•plex (kəm pleksʹ) *adjective.* Hard to understand or do. *The math problems were very* **complex** *because they involved many steps.*

con·sent·ed (kən sen'tid) *verb.* Gave permission or agreed to. *My mom **consented** to my sleeping over at Maria's house for her slumber party.*

con·tact (kon'takt) *noun.* A touching or meeting of persons or things. *My uncle burned his arm when it came in **contact** with the hot stove.*

con·tam·i·na·tion (kən tam'ə nā'shən) *noun.* The process of spoiling or the state of being spoiled; pollution. *Food should be kept covered to prevent **contamination**.*

con·ti·nent (kon'tə nənt) *noun.* One of the seven large land areas on Earth. *I live in the United States which is on the **continent** of North America.*

co·op·er·a·tion (kō op'ə rā'shən) *noun.* Working with another or others for a common purpose. *With **cooperation**, the friends quickly decorated the room for the surprise party.*

co·or·di·na·tion (kō ôr'də nā'shən) *noun.* The ability of parts of the body to work together well. *A gymnast needs good **coordination** when performing on the balance beam.*

cor·ri·dor (kôr'i dər, kor'i dər) *noun.* A long passageway or hallway. *The students walked down the **corridor** towards the gymnasium.*

creased (krēst) *adjective.* Characterized by lines or marked by wrinkling. *My teacher would not accept my **creased** book report because it was messy looking.*

cred·it (kred'it) *noun.* **1.** Praise or honor; something owed to a person. *The students who included a visual display with their speeches earned extra **credit**.* **2.** Trust in a person to pay a debt at a later time. *The store gave me **credit** today so I could buy the shirt and pay for it on Friday.*

cross·breed·ing (krôs'brē'ding) *verb.* Breeding different kinds of plants or animals in order to produce hybrids. *The farmer was **crossbreeding** small, sweet peppers with large, tasteless peppers to get large, sweet peppers.*

Dd

dam·ag·es (dam'ij iz) *noun, plural.* Harm that makes things less valuable or useful. ***Damages** to the city totaled in the millions of dollars after the storm.*

dan·gling (dang'ling) *verb.* Hanging loosely. *The diamonds **dangling** from Erin's ears looked pretty in the light.*

de·cen·cy (dē'sən sē) *noun.* Proper behavior, as in speech, actions, and dress. *Mary had the **decency** to admit she made a mistake.*

ded·i·cat·ed (ded'i kā'tid) *verb.* Set apart for a special purpose or use. *The mayor **dedicated** a new museum to the memory of the founders of the city.*

de·fec·tive (di fek'tiv) *adjective.* Having a flaw or weakness; not perfect. *The zipper was **defective** so the coat wouldn't close all the way up.*

at; āpe; fär; câre; end; mē; it; īce; pîerce; hot; ōld; sông; fôrk; oil; out; up; ūse; rüle; pùll; tûrn; chin; sing; shop; thin; this; hw in white; zh in treasure.

The symbol ə stands for the unstressed vowel sound in about, taken, pencil, lemon, and circus.

del•i•ca•cies (del′i kə sēs) *noun, plural.* Rare or excellent food. *At the food festival there were **delicacies** from around the world.*

de•liv•er•ing (di liv′ə ring) *verb.* Taking or carrying something to a particular place or person. *My job is **delivering** groceries to people's homes.*

dense (dens) *adjective.* Packed closely together. *The smoke was very **dense**, making it difficult for the firefighters to see anything.*

de•scend•ed (di sen′did) *verb.* Moved from a higher place to a lower one. *The woman **descended** down the mountain on skis.*

de•spair (di spâr′) *noun.* A complete loss of hope. *The student was filled with **despair** when he couldn't complete his assignment for tomorrow's deadline.*

de•struc•tion (di struk′shən) *noun.* Great damage or ruin. *The tornadoes caused a lot of **destruction** in our neighborhood.*

di•ag•nose (dī′əg nōs′) *verb.* To make a ruling as to the nature of an illness. *The doctor can **diagnose** the patient's illness based on a description of the symptoms.*

dic•ta•tors (dik′tā tərz, dik tā′tərz) *noun, plural.* Rulers who have absolute power and authority, ruling a country without sharing power or consulting anyone else. ***Dictators** can pass laws that take away people's rights, such as the right to vote.*

dis•as•ters (di zas′tərz) *noun, plural.* Events that cause much suffering, distress, or loss. *Hurricanes are examples of natural **disasters**.*

dis•cus•sions (di skush′ənz) *noun, plural.* Acts of talking about something or exchanging opinions. *There were many **discussions** among the voters about what the politician promised them.*

dis•in•te•grate (dis in′ti grāt′) *verb.* To break into many small pieces or fragments. *A blow with the heavy hammer caused the stone to **disintegrate**.*

dis•man•tled (dis man′təld) *verb.* Took something apart piece by piece. *The workers dismantled the outdooor stage after the concert.*

dis•miss (dis mis′) *verb.* To take away the job of, or fire. *The manager needed to **dismiss** one of his workers for doing a poor job.*

dis•re•spect•ful (dis′ri spekt′fəl) *adjective.* Having or showing disrespect; rude; impolite. *It is **disrespectful** behavior to make fun of your guests.*

di•verse (di vûrs′, dī vûrs′) *adjective.* Not all the same; varied. *The people in my neighborhood come from **diverse** backgrounds.*

dor•mant (dôr′mənt) *adjective.* Temporarily quiet or not active. *Many tourists visited the dormant volcano because the chance of an eruption was low.*

Ee

ease (ēz) *verb.* To move slowly or carefully. *I tried to **ease** the heavy clock off the table without dropping or scratching it.*

ed•u•cate (ej′ə kāt′) *verb.* To teach or train. *It is important to **educate** the students about dangers in the science lab so that no one gets hurt.*

e•lect•ed (i lek′tid) *verb.* Chosen by voting. *The class **elected** a representative to discuss the issue of recess with the principal.*

el•e•gant (el′i gənt) *adjective.* Showing richness and good taste; showing grace and dignity. *The **elegant** dress was trimmed with gold lace.*

el•e•ment•ar•y (el′ə mən′tə rē, el′ə mən′trē) *adjective.* Dealing with the simple parts or beginnings of something. *We learned **elementary** facts about life cycles by observing how things change as they grow.*

el•e•ments (el′ə mənts) *noun, plural.* Basic parts from which something is made or formed. *A story should have these basic **elements**: a beginning, a middle, and an end.*

e•lim•i•nates (i lim′ə nāts′) *verb.* Gets rid of; removes. *The new detergent **eliminates** tough stains on clothing.*

e•merged (i mûrjd′) *verb.* Came into view. *After the giant wave knocked over Pietro, he **emerged** from the water with a piece of seaweed in his mouth.*

en•light•ened (en lī′tend) *verb.* Gave knowledge or wisdom to; freed from prejudice or ignorance. *The teacher **enlightened** her students to the customs of the foreign tribe.*

en•list•ed (en lis′tid) *verb.* Joined the military voluntarily. *Michael's brother **enlisted** in the army after he graduated from high school.*

en•thu•si•asm (en thü′zē az′əm) *noun.* Eager and lively interest. *The audience expressed great **enthusiasm** for the play by applauding loudly.*

en•vi•ron•ment (en vī′rən mənt, en vī′ərn mənt) *noun.* The air, water, soil, and all the other things that surround a person, animal, or plant. *Living things need time to get used to changes in their **environment**.*

e•qual•i•ty (i kwol′i tē) *noun.* The quality or condition of being equal. *The Constitution of the United States provides for the **equality** of all Americans under the law.*

e•rupt•ed (i rup′tid) *verb.* Forced out or burst forth. *The area was filled with lava after the volcano **erupted**.*

e•vap•o•rates (i vap′ə rāts′) *verb.* To be changed from a liquid or solid into a vapor. *Water **evaporates** when it is boiled.*

ex•ag•ger•at•ing (eg zaj′ə rā′ting) *verb.* Making something seem greater, larger, or more than it is; overstating. *I was **exaggerating** when I described the fish I had caught.*

ex•hib•its (eg zib′its) *noun, plural.* Things shown on display. *We went to see the **exhibits** of African art at the museum.*

ex•pe•di•tion (ek′spi dish′ən) *noun.* A journey with a specific purpose. *The members of the **expedition** had to go back down the mountain because the wind was too strong.*

Ff

fare (fâr) *noun.* The cost of a ride on a bus, train, airplane, ship, or taxi. *My mother paid my **fare** on the bus.*

fea•tures (fē′chərz) *noun, plural.* Important or distinctive parts or characteristics of something. *Great speed and power steering are **features** of this car.*

fire•ball (fīr′bôl′) *noun.* A bright body from space that may trail bright sparks. *The **fireball** shot across the sky and briefly lit up our backyard.*

---

at; āpe; fär; câre; end; mē; it; īce; pîerce; hot; ōld; sông; fôrk; oil; out; up; ūse; rüle; pùll; tûrn; chin; sing; shop; thin; this; hw in white; zh in treasure.

The symbol ə stands for the unstressed vowel sound in about, taken, pencil, lemon, and circus.

flick•ered (flik´ərd) *verb.* Shone or burned with an unsteady or wavering light. *The candles **flickered** in the breeze.*

flukes (flüks) *noun, plural.* Chance happenings; unexpected or accidental events, especially lucky ones. *Some discoveries were **flukes** and resulted when scientists were trying to find other things.*

fo•cused (fō´kəst) *verb.* Concentrated or directed attention on. *The basketball player was so **focused** on scoring that he didn't hear the fans roaring.*

for•bid•den (fər bid´ən, fôr bid´ən) *verb.* Ordered not to do something; not allowed. *The children were **forbidden** to play outside after dark.*

for•ma•tions (fôr mā´shənz) *noun, plural.* Things that have been formed in a certain way and place. *Geologists study rock **formations** to understand Earth's history.*

frac•tures (frak´chərz) *noun, plural.* Cracks, splits, or breaks, as in a bone. *The boy's leg had multiple **fractures** after he fell out of the tree.*

fra•grance (frā´grəns) *noun.* A sweet or pleasing smell. *Roses have a strong **fragrance**.*

frig•id (frij´id) *adjective.* Very cold. *The **frigid** water was full of ice and snow.*

frus•trat•ed (frus´trā tid) *verb.* Kept from doing something. *Lita was **frustrated** in trying to light the candle because of the wind.*

func•tion (fungk´shən) *verb.* To work or act; to serve. *Mr. Martinez will **function** as the principal while Mrs. Arnold is out of town.*

fused (fūzd) *verb.* To blend or unite. *All the crayons in the box were **fused** together because they were left in the hot sun.*

Gg

gey•sers (gī´zərz) *noun, plural.* A natural hot spring from which steam and hot water shoot into the air after being heated below the surface by surrounding masses of hot rock. *Many people visit national parks to see the **geysers** spurt water.*

gi•gan•tic (jī gan´tik) *adjective.* Like a giant; huge and powerful. *The airplane looked **gigantic** when I saw it up close.*

glimpse (glimps) *noun.* A brief look or a passing glance. *I caught a **glimpse** of the actor as he dashed into the car.*

gnarled (närld) *adjective.* Having many rough, twisted knots. *The worker's hands looked as **gnarled** as a tree trunk.*

gos•siped (gos´ipt) *verb.* Talked or spread rumors, often unfriendly, about matters related to another person. *Kayla **gossiped** to her friends about Beth because she was jealous of Beth's good grades.*

gov•er•nor (guv´ər nər) *noun.* The person elected to be the head of a state government in the United States, or of a territory. *The **governor** of my state will sign the new law.*

grav•i•ty (grav´i tē) *noun.* The force that pulls things toward the center of Earth, causing objects to have weight. *Because of **gravity**, a ball thrown in the air will fall back to the ground.*

guar•an•teed (gar´ən tēd´) *verb.* Made sure or certain. *The salesman **guaranteed** this was the lowest price for a mountain bike.*

gushed (gusht) *verb.* Poured out suddenly and in large amounts. *The quiet fountain suddenly **gushed**, surprising the children.*

Hh

hem•i•sphere (hem´i sfîr´) *noun.* One half of Earth. *The equator divides Earth into the Northern and Southern **Hemispheres.** Earth is also divided into the Western Hemisphere and the Eastern Hemisphere.*

her•it•age (her´i tij) *noun.* Something that is handed down from the past; tradition. *Celebrating festivals is part of the Native American **heritage**.*

hes•i•ta•tion (hez´i tā´shən) *noun.* A delay due to fear or doubt. *The talented dancers showed no **hesitation** on stage.*

ho•ri•zon (hə rī´zən) *noun.* The line where the sky and the earth or sea seem to meet. *We watched as the ship seemed to disappear into the **horizon**.*

hu•man•i•ty (hū man´i tē, ū man´i tē) *noun.* The quality or condition of being human; human character or nature. *Keeping our air and water clean will help all **humanity**.*

hur•ri•canes (hûr´i kānz´, hur´i kānz´) *noun, plural.* Storms with strong winds and heavy rain. ***Hurricanes** can rip trees out of the ground.*

hy•brids (hī´bridz) *noun, plural.* The offspring of two animals or plants of different varieties. *Pluots are **hybrids** that combine the qualities of plums and apricots.*

hy•dro•gen (hī´drə jən) *noun.* A gas that has no odor, color, or taste and burns easily. *Today in class we learned that **hydrogen** was used in early balloons because it was the lightest element.*

Ii

i•den•ti•ty (ī den´ti tē) *noun.* Who or what a person or place is. *The man at the bank used his driver's license as proof of his **identity**.*

im•press (im pres´) *verb.* To have a strong effect on the mind or feelings. *The display of artwork will **impress** the audience.*

in•ev•i•ta•ble (in ev´i tə bəl) *adjective.* Not able to be avoided; bound to happen. *An **inevitable** result of closing your eyes is not being able to see.*

in•flate (in flāt´) *verb.* To cause to swell by filling with air or gas. *My father used the air pump at the gas station to **inflate** the front tires.*

in•ju•ry (in´jə rē) *noun.* Damage or harm done to a person or thing. *Luckily, Roberto's football **injury** was not serious.*

in•quire (in kwīr´) *verb.* To ask questions or seek information. *I went into the restaurant to **inquire** about getting a job as a waitress.*

in•still (in stil´) *verb.* To put in or introduce little by little. *Good teachers **instill** a love of learning in their students.*

in•struct (in strukt´) *verb.* To provide with knowledge, information, or skill; to teach. *The dance teacher will **instruct** the students in tap, ballet, and jazz.*

---

at; āpe; fär; cåre; end; mē; it; īce; pîerce; hot; ōld; sông; fôrk; oil; out; up; ūse; rüle; pùll; tûrn; chin; sing; shop; thin; <u>th</u>is; hw in white; zh in treasure.

The symbol ə stands for the unstressed vowel sound in about, taken, pencil, lemon, and circus.

in•ten•tions (in ten´shənz) *noun, plural.* Plans to act in a certain way; purposes. *Franklin hated baseball so his* **intentions** *for joining the team were unclear.*

in•ter•act (in´tə rakt´) *verb.* To act upon one another. *Members of the band walked into the audience so they could* **interact** *with fans.*

in•ter•sec•tion (in´tər sek´shən, in´tər sek´shən) *noun.* A place where two or more things meet and cross each other, such as roads or streets. *Look both ways before crossing an* **intersection**.

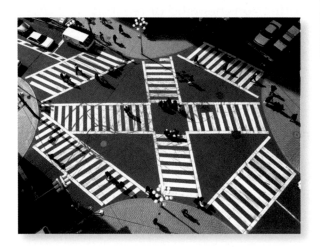

in•va•sion (in vā´zhən) *noun.* The entering of an army into a region to conquer it. *When planning an* **invasion**, *generals pay close attention to where the enemy troops are stationed.*

ir•re•sist•i•ble (ir´i zis´tə bəl) *adjective.* Not capable of being resisted or opposed. *On a hot day, a cold drink is so tempting that it is* **irresistible**.

Ll

la•bor (lā´bər) *noun.* Hard work; toil. *The construction workers were tired from the backbreaking* **labor** *they were hired to do.* —*verb.* To do hard work. *Tired runners* **labor** *up the steep hill at the end of the race.*

land•scape (land´skāp´) *noun.* The stretch of land or scenery viewed from one point or place. *The* **landscape** *was filled with tall trees and green pastures.*

Word History

The term **landscape** comes from the Dutch *landschap*, meaning "province, or painting of a land scene." The Dutch word came from the root *land* and the suffix *-schap*, which means "ship."

launched (lôncht) *verb.* Sent off or started in motion. *The science club* **launched** *a rocket into the air.*

leg•is•la•ture (lej´is lā´chər) *noun.* A government body having the power to make laws. *People depend on members of the* **legislature** *to make laws that are fair.*

lim•it•less (lim´it lis) *adjective.* Without bounds or restrictions. *There seems to be a* **limitless** *number of stars in the sky.*

lo•ca•tion (lō kā´shən) *noun.* An exact position or place. *The airplane flew by several times before spotting the* **location** *of the lost hikers.*

lu•mi•nous (lü´mə nəs) *adjective.* Bright; shining. *The* **luminous** *glow coming from the windows made the house look warm.*

lung•ing (lun´jing) *verb.* Making a sudden forward movement. *The pitcher was* **lunging** *for the ball when the runner tagged the base.*

Mm

ma•jor (mā´jər) *adjective.* Greater in size, amount, value, importance, or rank. *The Rockies are a* **major** *mountain system in America.* —*noun.* An officer in the armed forces. *My uncle is a* **major** *in the Army.*

mam•mals (mam′əlz) *noun, plural.* Creatures that are warm-blooded and have a backbone. *Female mammals produce milk to feed their young. Human beings, cattle, bats, and whales are* **mammals.**

maze (māz) *noun.* A confusing series of paths or passageways through which people may have a hard time finding their way. *There is a* **maze** *in my town where people try to find their way through tall stalks of corn.*

me•chan•i•cal (mi kan′i kəl) *adjective.* Produced or operated by a machine. *John likes to play with* **mechanical** *toys.*

me•di•a (mē′dē ə) *noun, plural.* Means or form of communication that reaches a large audience. A plural of **medium.** *Television and newspapers are* **media** *that influence our daily life.*

mer•chan•dise (mûr′chən dīz′, mûr′chən dīs′) *noun.* Things for sale. *A shipment of new* **merchandise** *was delivered to the electronics store last night.*

me•te•or (mē′tē ər) *noun.* A mass of metal or rock that enters Earth's atmosphere from space. *It is rare for a* **meteor** *to strike Earth, but it can happen.*

mim•ic•ry (mim′i krē) *noun.* The close outward resemblance of one kind of animal to another or to an object in its natural environment. *One type of fly uses* **mimicry** *to fool animals into thinking it is a wasp.*

mis•chie•vous (mis′chə vəs) *adjective.* Full of mischief, or conduct that is often playful but causes harm. *Cal likes to be* **mischievous** *by playing practical jokes.*

mis•sion (mish′ən) *noun.* A special job or task. *My mom sent me on a* **mission** *to find my sister's favorite stuffed bear.*

moist•ened (moi′sənd) *verb.* Dampened or made slightly wet. *Ellen* **moistened** *the flaps of the envelopes with a damp sponge.*

mourn•ful (môrn′fəl) *adjective.* Feeling, expressing, or filled with grief or sorrow. *The* **mournful** *song on the radio made the listeners feel sad.*

murk•y (mûr′kē) *adjective.* Dark or cloudy. *It was scary sitting in the row boat because there was* **murky** *water all around us.*

Nn

nat•u•ral•ist (nach′ər ə list) *noun.* A person who specializes in the study of things in nature, especially plants and animals. *The* **naturalist** *spent a lot of time hiking and camping in the woods.*

nav•i•ga•tion (nav′i gā′shən) *noun.* The art or science of figuring out the position and course of boats, ships, and aircraft. *For proper* **navigation,** *pilots rely on equipment to direct them.*

nes•tled (nes′əld) *verb.* Located in a snug and sheltered spot. *Her desk was* **nestled** *between piles of books in the back corner of the warehouse.*

---

at; āpe; fär; câre; end; mē; it; īce; pîerce; hot; ōld; sông; fôrk; oil; out; up; ūse; rūle; púll; tûrn; chin; sing; shop; thin; this; hw in white; zh in treasure.

The symbol ə stands for the unstressed vowel sound in about, taken, pencil, lemon, and circus.

no•mads (nō′madz) *noun, plural.* Members of groups or tribes that have no permanent home and move from place to place in search of food or land on which to graze their animals. **Nomads** *often live in desert areas.*

Word History

The word **nomad** comes from the Latin word *nomas*, meaning "wanderer." It is related to the Greek word *nomas*, which means "wandering, as in search of pasture."

Oo

ob•ser•va•tions (ob′zər vā′shənz) *noun, plural.* The act, practice, or power of seeing and noticing. *The detective's careful* **observations** *helped to solve the crime.*

ob•serv•er (əb zûr′vər) *noun.* A person who watches carefully and with attention. *The nature photographer was a keen* **observer** *of flowers and insects.*

o•ral•ly (ôr′əl ē) *adverb.* Using speech as opposed to writing. *Each contestant was given a chance to spell the word* **orally**.

or•gan•isms (ôr′gə niz′əmz) *noun, plural.* Living things. Animals, plants, mushrooms, protozoans, and bacteria are all organisms. *The scientist studied* **organisms** *that live in ponds.*

o•rig•i•nal (ə rij′ə nəl) *adjective.* Made, done, thought of, or used for the first time. *All of the wood floors in the old house are* **original**.

out•cast (out′kast′) *noun.* A person rejected by and driven out of a group. *Jason felt like an* **outcast** *when he was thrown off the debating team.*

Pp

parched (pärcht) *adjective.* Dry or thirsty. *The* **parched** *land seemed to cry out for rain.*

par•ti•cles (pär′ti kəlz) *noun, plural.* Small bits or pieces of an element. *Tiny* **particles** *connect together to make up solid objects.*

pa•tri•ots (pā′trē əts) *noun, plural.* People who love and enthusiastically support their country. *American history views George Washington and John Adams as true* **patriots**.

per•mis•sion (pər mish′ən) *noun.* Consent or agreement from someone in authority. *I had to get* **permission** *from my parents before leaving on the school trip.*

phy•si•cal (fiz′i kəl) *adjective.* Having to do with the body. *Doing* **physical** *activities that increase your heart rate will help you stay in shape.*

poll•ing (pōl′ling) *adjective.* The casting and recording of votes in an election. *Voters go to a* **polling** *station to cast their votes.*

post•pone (pōst pōn′) *verb.* To put off to a later time. *The officials decided to* **postpone** *the baseball game until tomorrow because of rain.*

pre•cip•i•ta•tion (pri sip′i tā′shən) *noun.* Any form of water that falls to Earth, such as rain, hail, or snow. *Desert regions get very little* **precipitation** *each year.*

pred•a•tors (pred′ə tərz) *noun, plural.* Animals that live by preying on, or hunting and eating, other animals. *Lions and wolves are natural* **predators** *who hunt smaller animals for food.*

pre•oc•cu•pied (prē ok′yə pīd′) *adjective.* Absorbed in thought; engrossed. *The bride was so* **preoccupied** *with wedding plans that she couldn't concentrate on her work.*

pres•ence (prez′əns) *noun.* Something felt to be present in a specific place at a given time. *I could sense my mother's **presence** even before I saw her.*

pres•i•den•tial (prez′ə den′shəl) *adjective.* Of or relating to the president. *The candidates prepared for a **presidential** debate.*

pre•vail•ing (pri vā′ling) *adjective.* Most common at a particular time. *The **prevailing** winds made the day really cold.*

prey (prā) *noun.* Any animal hunted or killed by another animal for food. *Nature films often show lions hunting down their **prey**.*

prog•ress (prog′res) *noun.* A forward movement or gradual betterment. *This century has seen a lot of **progress** in computer science.*

prop•er•ty (prop′ər tē) *noun.* A piece of land. *If you're thinking of building a house, the **property** next to my house is for sale.*

Qq

qual•i•fy (kwol′ə fī′) *verb.* To make fit, as for a certain job or task. *In order to **qualify** for the Olympics, you must be one of the best athletes in the country.*

quest (kwest) *noun.* A search or pursuit. *The explorers went on a **quest** for gold.*

Word History

The word **quest** comes from the Old French word *queste,* which means "search." It goes back to Latin *quaesīta,* meaning "thing sought."

Rr

ra•vine (rə vēn′) *noun.* A deep, narrow valley, especially one worn by running water. *As you walk along the edge of the road, be careful not to fall into the **ravine**.*

re•duce (ri dūs′, ri dūs′) *verb.* To make less or become smaller in size, number, or degree. *The store should **reduce** its prices.*

re•flect•ed (ri flek′təd) *verb.* Light, sound, images, or heat that is turned, thrown, or bent back at an angle. *The white tents **reflected** the heat from the hot sun onto the sand.*

re•lays (n., rē′lāz; v. rē′lāz, ri lāz′) *noun, plural.* Fresh sets or teams, as of workers or animals, prepared to replace or relieve another. *The Pony Express used **relays** to deliver mail across long distances.* —*verb.* Passes along. *When I'm not home, my mother **relays** your messages to me.*

re•luc•tant (ri luk′tənt) *adjective.* Unwilling or hesitant. *My friend wants to try the high dive, but I am **reluctant** to join him because I'm afraid.*

re•pet•i•tive (ri pet′i tiv) *adjective.* Full of, marked by, or containing repetition. *Some factories use robots to do **repetitive** tasks.*

at; āpe; fär; câre; end; mē; it; īce; pîerce; hot; ōld; sông; fôrk; oil; out; up; ūse; rüle; pull; tûrn; chin; sing; shop; thin; **th**is; hw in white; zh in treasure.

The symbol ə stands for the unstressed vowel sound in about, taken, pencil, lemon, and circus.

rep·re·sent·a·tive (rep´ri zen´tə tiv) *noun.* A person who is chosen to represent or stand for another or others. *A **representative** from each district was sent to City Hall to vote for the law.*

re·search (ri sûrch´, rē´sûrch´) *noun.* A careful study to find and learn facts about a subject. *Fawn had to do a lot of **research** at the library before she wrote her paper.*

res·er·va·tion (rez´ər vā´shən) *noun.* **1.** Land set aside by a government for a special purpose, such as for Native American tribes to live on. *Native Americans preserved their culture and traditions on the **reservation** where they lived.* **2.** An arrangement to have something kept for another person or persons. *We asked the travel agent to make a plane **reservation** for us.* **3.** Something that causes doubt. *Her serious **reservations** about walking home after dark made sense.*

re·trieve (ri trēv´) *verb.* To get back; recover; regain. *The golfer tried to **retrieve** the golf ball from the lake.*

re·veal (ri vēl´) *verb.* To make known. *The journalist would not **reveal** the source of her story.*

re·versed (ri vûrst´) *verb.* Moved in the opposite direction from what is usual. *We **reversed** our direction when we realized we were going the wrong way.*

rig·id (rij´id) *adjective.* Not changing; fixed. *Our **rigid** schedule did not allow us to make an unplanned stop at the new park.*

riv·er·bank (riv´ər bangk´) *noun.* The raised ground bordering a river. *The **riverbank** was a very popular place for summer picnics.*

ro·bot (rō´bot) *noun.* A machine designed to perform certain human tasks. *The **robot** did a job that was too dangerous for humans to do.*

ro·tat·ed (rō tā´tid) *verb.* Turned around on an axis. *As the wheels **rotated**, the car moved forward.*

Ss

sagged (sagd) *verb.* Drooped down in the middle from weight. *The tent **sagged** from all the rainwater that had collected on top.*

sat·is·fac·to·ry (sat´is fak´tə rē) *adjective.* Good enough to meet a need or desire. *The work done on the house was **satisfactory**, so the owners could move in.*

saun·tered (sôn´tərd) *verb.* Walked in a slow or relaxed way; strolled. *The family **sauntered** through the lush grass in the park.*

scald (skôld) *verb.* To heat to a temperature just below the boiling point. *The cook taught us how to **scald** the milk by taking it off the burner before it bubbles.*

scen·er·y (sē´nə rē) *noun.* The sights of a place or region. *We admired the beautiful **scenery** while we rode through the mountain range on the train.*

sci·en·tif·ic (sī´ən tif´ik) *adjective.* Having to do with or used in science. *The **scientific** discovery of gravity changed the way people thought about Earth.*

scorch•ing (skôr´ching) *adjective.* Causing intense heat to dry or burn the surface of something. *The scorching sun dried up all the plants.*

scoured (skourd) *verb.* Cleaned, cleared, or worn away. *We scoured the pan with cleanser until it shone.*

scraw•ny (skrô´nē) *adjective.* Thin, bony, or skinny. *The cat was scrawny because she hadn't eaten in days.*

se•clud•ed (si klü´did) *adjective.* Shut off from view. *We found a quiet, secluded area in the park for our picnic.*

seg•re•ga•tion (seg´ri gā´shən) *noun.* The practice of separating one racial group, especially African Americans, from the rest of society by making them use different schools and social facilities or making them live in certain areas. *Segregation forced African American children to attend schools with poor facilities.*

set•tings (set´ingz) *noun, plural.* The surroundings of something; background; environment. *The gallery showed paintings of cottages in forest settings.*

shield (shēld) *noun.* A person or thing that protects against danger, injury, or distress. *I used a magazine as a shield against the bright sunlight because I forgot my sunglasses.*

short•age (shôr´tij) *noun.* A small amount or lack of supply. *The storm destroyed many farms, so there was a shortage of watermelon.*

shrieks (shrēks) *verb.* Makes loud, shrill cries or sounds. *My little sister shrieks when I tickle her.*

site (sīt) *noun.* The position or location of something. *Our house is at a mountain site with a beautiful view.*

slumped (slumpt) *verb.* Fell or sunk heavily. *The tired woman slumped down in the back seat.*

slurp (slûrp) *verb.* To drink or eat noisily. *It is impolite to slurp soup, especially in public.*

sog•gy (sog´ē) *adjective.* Very wet or damp; soaked. *The juicy tomatoes on the sandwich made the bread soggy.*

spe•cies (spē´shēz) *noun.* A group of animals or plants that have many characteristics in common. *German shepherds belong to one species, and wolves belong to another.*

spec•i•mens (spes´ə mənz) *noun, plural.* Items or parts typical of a group. *The scientist collected specimens of some germs that could make people sick.*

spec•tac•u•lar (spek tak´yə lər) *adjective.* Very impressive or unusual. *We watched the spectacular fireworks display from our backyard.*

sprawled (sprôld) *verb.* Lay or sat with the body stretched out in an awkward or careless manner. *My brother was so tired from swimming that he sprawled out on the blanket and left no room for anyone else.*

spunk (spungk) *noun.* An informal word for courage, spirit, or determination. *The gymnast showed her spunk by climbing back up on the balance beam after falling.*

stag•gered (sta´gərd) *verb.* Moved unsteadily or with a swaying motion. *The tired runners staggered to the finish line.*

stam•i•na (stam´ə nə) *noun.* The physical ability to withstand fatigue, disease, or hardship; endurance. *A long-distance runner must have stamina to finish a race.*

stark (stärk) *adjective.* Bare. *All of the trees had been cut down so the landscape appeared stark.*

---

at; āpe; fär; câre; end; mē; it; īce; pîerce; hot; ōld; sông; fôrk; oil; out; up; ūse; rüle; pull; tûrn; chin; sing; shop; thin; this; hw in white; zh in treasure.

The symbol ə stands for the unstressed vowel sound in about, taken, pencil, lemon, and circus.

strands (strandz) *noun, plural.* Things similar to threads. ***Strands** of spaghetti were wrapped around the fork.*

strat•e•gy (strat´i jē) *noun.* A careful plan for achieving a goal. *Our coach used a new **strategy** that confused the best team in the league.*

stunned (stund) *verb.* Shocked or overwhelmed. *Everyone was **stunned** when I won the essay contest because I usually needed help with my writing assignments.*

sub•mit (səb mit´) *verb.* **1.** To give up; to give in to someone's power. *Soldiers may **submit** to the enemy if they are too weak to fight.* **2.** To present. *My teacher asked us to **submit** our reports on Friday.*

suc•ceed (sək sēd´) *verb.* **1.** To follow in sequence, especially immediately. *The prince was able to **succeed** to the throne after the king stepped down.* **2.** To have a good result. *The debating team will **succeed** in winning the award.*

suf•frage (suf´rij) *noun.* The right or privilege of voting. *The women who marched at the rally in Washington, D.C., were fighting for **suffrage**.*

su•per•hu•man (sü´pər hū´mən, sü´pər ū´mən) *adjective.* Beyond ordinary human ability or power. *Folk tale heroes often have **superhuman** strength.*

su•per•vise (sü´pər vīz´) *verb.* To watch over and direct. *It was a huge responsibility to **supervise** all the children swimming in the pool.*

surge (sûrj) *noun.* A large wave or series of waves during a storm. *The storm **surge** caused a lot of damage along the coast.*

sur•round•ings (sə roun´dingz) *noun, plural.* The objects, influences, or conditions of a place. *The cabin had beautiful **surroundings**: flowers, plants, and a nearby lake.*

sur•vive (sər vīv´) *verb.* To live and be active through and after an event. *One must know how to find food and shelter to **survive** in the woods.*

sus•pend•ed (sə spen´dəd) *verb.* Held in place as if attached from above. *The spider was **suspended** from the roof by a strand of web.*

swag•ger (swag´ər) *noun.* A walk or behavior that is bold, rude, or arrogant. *The star athlete walked into the room with a **swagger**.*

swerved (swûrvd) *verb.* Turned aside suddenly. *The car **swerved** to miss the dog crossing the road.*

sym•pa•thy (sim´pə thē) *noun.* The ability to share the feelings of another or others. *I felt great **sympathy** for Jim because I knew what it felt like to have my feelings hurt.*

Tt

the•o•ry (thē´ə rē) *noun.* An idea that explains a group of facts or an event; something that has not been proven true. *Do you have a **theory** that explains why leaves turn color in the fall?*

to·kens (tō′kənz) *noun, plural.* **1.** Pieces that mark movement on a board game. *Andrea moved her **tokens** six spaces ahead and won the game.* **2.** Pieces of metal, like coins, used as substitutes for money. *We put **tokens** in the machine to play video games at the mall.*

tra·di·tion·al (trə dish′ə nəl) *adjective.* The knowledge, beliefs, or customs that one generation passes to another. *Our **traditional** Thanksgiving includes eating turkey and watching television.*

traits (trāts) *noun, plural.* Aspects, qualities, or characteristics that a person or thing possesses. *Bravery and honesty are **traits** a person can display.*

trans·formed (trans fôrmd′) *verb.* Changed in shape, form, or appearance. *The builder **transformed** the backyard by adding a patio.*

treach·er·ous (trech′ər əs) *adjective.* Full of danger. *The sharp curves on the **treacherous** road caused many traffic accidents.*

treas·ur·er (trezh′ər ər) *noun.* The person in charge of the money of a business or a group. *The **treasurer** became nervous when he realized money was missing from the company bank account.*

tri·umph (trī′umf) *verb.* To be successful or win. *Everyone is confident that we will **triumph** over the problems we are having due to the weather.*

ty·rant (tī′rənt) *noun.* A person who uses power or authority in a cruel or unjust way. *The king was a **tyrant** because he punished his subjects unfairly.*

Word History

The word **tyrant** comes from Old French *tiran*, which means "despot." The Old French word came from the Latin word *tyrannus*, which means "ruler or despot." Tyrant can also be traced to the Greek word *tyrannos*, which means "absolute ruler."

Uu

un·con·sti·tu·tion·al (un′kon sti tü′shə nəl) *adjective.* Not in keeping with the constitution of a country, state, or group, especially the Constitution of the United States. *The Supreme Court in this country decides if a law is **unconstitutional**.*

un·en·thu·si·as·ti·cal·ly (un′en thü′zē as′tik ə lē) *adverb.* Not in an enthusiastic manner; not zealous. *The crowd laughed **unenthusiastically** at the comedian's bad jokes.*

un·for·tu·nate (un fôr′chə nit) *adjective.* Unlucky. *It was very **unfortunate** that it rained on the day we had tickets to the outdoor concert.*

un·heed·ed (un hē′did) *adjective.* Not paid attention to; disregarded. *The disaster occurred because warnings were **unheeded**.*

---

at; āpe; fär; câre; end; mē; it; īce; pîerce; hot; ōld; sông; fôrk; oil; out; up; ūse; rüle; pull; tûrn; chin; sing; shop; thin; <u>th</u>is; **hw** in **wh**ite; **zh** in treasure.

The symbol ə stands for the unstressed vowel sound in **a**bout, tak**e**n, penc**i**l, lem**o**n, and circ**u**s.

un·in·hab·it·ed (un´in hab´i tid) *adjective.* Not lived in. *The **uninhabited** house had broken windows and a leaky roof.*

un·pleas·ant (un plez´ənt) *adjective.* Offensive or not pleasing. *There was a very **unpleasant** smell near the restaurant's garbage container.*

un·rea·son·a·ble (un rē´zə nə bəl) *adjective.* Not showing or using good sense or judgment. *The teacher was being **unreasonable** when he punished the whole class for the bad behavior of one student.*

Vv

va·cant (vā´kənt) *adjective.* Not having anyone or anything in it; empty. *If that seat is **vacant**, you can sit in it.*

va·ri·e·ty (və rī´i tē) *noun.* A number or collection of different things; things of various kinds or parts. *I enjoy eating a wide **variety** of fruits and vegetables.*

vast·ness (vast´nis) *noun.* Greatness in size, extent, or number. *The **vastness** of the desert made it seem to stretch for miles.*

ven·tured (ven´chərd) *verb.* Went despite risk or danger. *Lucy **ventured** out into the storm to look for her dog.*

ver·sions (vûr´zhənz) *noun, plural.* Different or changed forms of an original. *I wrote many **versions** of the story before I completed the final draft.*

vet·er·i·nar·i·an (vet´ər ə när´ē ən, vet´rə när ē ən) *noun.* A person trained and licensed to give medical or surgical treatment to animals. *I took my dog to the **veterinarian** for a checkup.*

vi·brates (vī´brāts) *verb.* Moves back and forth or up and down very fast. *The cell phone **vibrates** instead of making a loud ring when someone calls.*

vol·ume (vol´ūm, vol´yəm) *noun.* The amount of space occupied. *Find the **volume** of a building block by multiplying its height by its length by its width.*

Ww

wares (wârz) *noun, plural.* Things for sale. *My mother inspects the quality of the **wares** at the market before buying anything.*

wheel·chair (hwēl´châr´, wēl´châr´) *noun.* A chair on wheels that is used by someone who cannot walk to get from one place to another. *My grandmother needed to use a **wheelchair** after she fell and broke her hip.*

wring (ring) *verb.* To squeeze or twist; to get by force. *I had to **wring** out my swimsuit before hanging it in the laundry room.*

Zz

zone (zōn) *noun.* A region or area that has some special quality, condition, or use. *There is a "No Parking" **zone** on this street.*

(Continued from Copyright page.)

"Miss Alaineus" by Debra Frasier. Copyright © 2000 by Debra Frasier. Reprinted by permission of Harcourt, Inc.

"My Great-Grandmother's Gourd" by Cristina Kessler, illustrations by Walter Lyon Krudop. Text copyright © 2000 by Cristina Kessler. Illustrations copyright © 2000 by Walter Lyon Krudop. Reprinted by permission of Orchard Books, A Grolier Company.

"The Night of San Juan" is from SALSA STORIES by Lulu Delacre. Copyright © 2000 by Lulu Delacre. Reprinted by permission of Scholastic Press, a division of Scholastic Inc.

"Paul Revere's Ride" by Henry Wadsworth Longfellow is from OUR NATION. Copyright © 2003 by Macmillan/McGraw-Hill.

"Pipiolo and the Roof Dogs" by Brian Meunier, illustrations by Perky Edgerton. Text copyright © 2003 by Brian Meunier. Illustrations copyright © 2003 by Perky Edgerton. Reprinted by permission of Dutton Children's Books, a division of Penguin Young Readers Group.

"Rattlers!" by Ellen Lambeth (sidebar by John Cancalosi) is from RANGER RICK. Copyright © 1998 by the National Wildlife Federation. Reprinted by permission of the National Wildlife Federation.

"Shiloh" is from SHILOH by Phyllis Reynolds Naylor. Copyright © 2000 by Phyllis Reynolds Naylor. Reprinted by permission of Aladdin Paperbacks, an imprint of Simon & Schuster Children's Publishing Division.

"Skunk Scout" is from SKUNK SCOUT by Laurence Yep. Copyright © 2003 by Laurence Yep. Reprinted by permission of Hyperion Books for Children.

"Sleds on Boston Common" by Louise Borden, illustrations by Robert Andrew Parker. Text copyright © 2000 by Louise Borden. Illustrations copyright © 2000 by Robert Andrew Parker. Reprinted by permission of Margaret K. McElderry Books, an imprint of Simon & Schuster Children's Publishing Division.

"Spirit of Endurance" by Jennifer Armstrong, illustrations by William Maughan. Text copyright © 2000 by Jennifer Armstrong. Illustrations copyright © 2000 by William Maughan. Reprinted by Crown Publishing, a division of Random House Inc.

"Suffrage for Women" is from OUR NATION. Copyright © 2003 by Macmillan/McGraw-Hill.

"Suspense" is from THE BIG SKY by Pat Mora. Copyright © 1998 by Pat Mora. Reprinted by permission of Scholastic Press, a division of Scholastic, Inc.

"Through My Eyes" is from THROUGH MY EYES by Ruby Bridges. Copyright © 1999 by Ruby Bridges. Reprinted by permission of Scholastic Press, a division of Scholastic, Inc.

"Ultimate Field Trip 5: Blasting Off to Space Academy" is from ULTIMATE FIELD TRIP 5: BLASTING OFF TO SPACE ACADEMY by Susan E. Goodman. Text copyright © 2001 by Susan E. Goodman. Illustrations copyright © 2001 by Michael J. Doolittle. U.S. Space Camp and U.S. Space Academy are registered trademarks of the U.S. Space Rocket Center. Reprinted by permission of Atheneum Books for Young Readers, an imprint of Simon & Schuster Children's Publishing Division.

"The Unbreakable Code" by Sara Hoagland Hunter, illustrations by Julia Miner. Text copyright © 1996 by Sara Hoagland Hunter. Illustrations copyright © 1996 by Julia Miner. Reprinted by permission of Rising Moon Books for Young Readers from Northland Publishing.

"Weslandia" by Paul Fleischman, illustrations by Kevin Hawkes. Text copyright © 1999 by Paul Fleischman. Illustrations copyright © 1999 by Kevin Hawkes. Reprinted by permission of Candlewick Press.

"When Esther Morris Headed West" by Connie Nordhielm Wooldridge, illustrations by Jacqueline Rogers. Text copyright © 2001 by Connie Nordhielm Wooldridge. Illustrations copyright © 2001 by Jacqueline Rogers. Reprinted by permission of Holiday House.

"Zathura" by Chris Van Allsburg. Copyright © 2002 by Chris Van Allsburg. Reprinted by permission of Houghton Mifflin Company.

ILLUSTRATIONS
Cover Illustration: Leland Klanderman

20-41:Debra Frasier 50-51:Jeff Crosby 52-69:Rosalyn Schanzer 72-73: Owen Smith 75: Owen Smith 95:Susan E. Goodman 108-109:David Gordon III:John Hovell 116-133:Perky Edgerton 140,142:Erika LeBarre 148-163:Joel Spector 169:Erika LeBarre 178:Richard Orr 186-187: Siede Preis/Getty Images 188-189:Mercedes McDonald 208-221:Edel Rodriguez 222:Joe LeMonnier 232-251:Jerry Pinkney 252-253:Jeff Slemons 263:John Hovell 265-283:Robert Andrew Parker 284-286: Greg Newbold 287:John Burgoyne 289:Neal Armstrong 294-307: Jacqueline Rogers 330-349:Walter Lyon Krudop 351:Argosy 358: Tyson Mangelsdorf 360-383:Chris Van Allsburg 394:Rick Powell 396-413:Jerry Pinkney 419:John Hovell 422-423:Loretta Krupinski 424-441:Jeanne Arnold 478-479:Susan Swan 484-485:Mark Weber 486-505:Wendy Born Hollander 506-507:Daniel Powers 518-519, 526,528-532: William Maughan 533:Kailey LeFaiver 534-535: William Maughan 539:Joe LeMonnier 541:Erika LeBarre 544-545: John Parra 546-561:Kevin Hawkes 562-563 Argosy 565:Erika LeBarre 571:Rick Nease for TFK 582-599:Julia Miner 603:(bg)Julia Miner (tr)Kevin Hawkes 606:Donna Perrone 608-627:Marla Baggetta 634-635:Cezanne Studios 640-641:Rebecca Walsh 642-661:Ruth Sanderson 662-665:Maryana Beletskaya 672-690:Winson Trang 693:Joe LeMonnier 695:John Hovell 702-705:Courtesy of Boundless Playgrounds 727:Sharon and Joel Harris 732-733:Tom Foty 735:Erika LeBarre 764-765:Wendy Born Hollander

PHOTOGRAPHY
All photographs are by Macmillan/McGraw-Hill except where noted below

16-17: Zelick Nagel/Getty. 17: Glenn Mitsui/Getty. 18: (tcr) Royalty-free/CORBIS; (bl) SW Productions/Photodisc/Getty. 19: Tony Freeman/PhotoEdit. 40: Courtesy Debra Frasier. 42: (tr) Steve Cole/Getty; (inset) Linda Spillers/AP. 43: Royalty-Free/CORBIS 44: (tl) Matthew Cavanaugh/Stringer/Getty; (tr), (c) Linda Spillers/Stringer/AP. 46: Thinkstock/Getty. 47: SW Productions/Getty. 48-49: Joe Sohm/Alamy. 49: Arthur Tilley/PictureQuest. 50-51: C Squared Studios/Getty. 70: Courtesy Rosalyn Schanzer. 76: Scott T. Baxter/Photodisc/Getty. 77: Tom Carter/PhotoEdit. 78-79: Photo 24/Brand X/Getty. 80: Thomas Pakenham. 81: (tl) Goodshot/Punchstock; (l) Courtesy Ohio Department of Natural Resources; (2) John Serrao/Photo Researchers; (3) Dan Tenaglia, (4), (5) Courtesy Time for Kids. 82: (bl) CORBIS/Punchstock. 82-83: (t) Stuart Franklin/Magnum. 83: David Lorenz Winston/Brand X. 84: Stuart Franklin/Magnum. 85: (tl) Rick Nease for TFK; (tr) Ryan McVay/Photodisc/Getty; (bl) CORBIS/Punchstock. 86: David McNew/Getty. 88: SW Productions/Brand X. 89: (tr) C Squared Studios/Getty; (bl) Photodisc/Getty; (br) Dian Lofton for TFK. 90-91: James McDivitt/NASA/AP. 91: StockTrek/Getty. 92: Photodisc/Getty. 92-93: (t) Ian McKinnell/Getty. 94: (cl) Michael J. Doolittle/Image Works. 94-95: StockTrek/Getty. 95: Bettmann/CORBIS. 96: Michael J. Doolittle/Image Works. 96-97: StockTrek/Getty. 97-98: Michael J. Doolittle/Image Works. 98-99: StockTrek/Getty. 99-100: Michael J. Doolittle/Image Works. 100-101: StockTrek/Getty. 102: Michael J. Doolittle/Image Works. 102: (c) CORBIS SYGMA/CORBIS; (l) Michael J. Doolittle/Image Works. 102-103: StockTrek/Getty. 103: Michael J. Doolittle/Image Works. 104: Michael J. Doolittle/Image Works 104-105: StockTrek/Getty 105: (t) Michael J. Doolittle/Image Works; (b) NASA/AP. 106: (tr) Michael J. Doolittle/Image Works; (inset) Courtesy Susan E. Goodman. 106-107: StockTrek/Getty. 110: MedioImages/Getty. 112-113: Tom Kidd/Alamy. 113: Photodisc/Getty. 114: Alley Cat Productions/Brand X/Getty. 115: American Images/Getty. 132: Courtesy Brian Meunier. 134: Carrie McLean Museum/Alaska Stock Images. 135: (tr) Bettmann/CORBIS; (l) Tracy Morgan/Getty; (2) Yann Arthus-Bertrand/CORBIS; (3) David Ward/DK Images. 136: Jack Sauer/AP. 137: Peter Skinner/Photo Researchers. 138: Royalty-free/CORBIS. 139: GK & Vikki Hart/Photodisc/Getty. 144-145: Paul Wayne Wilson/PhotoStockFile/Alamy. 145: Edmond Van Hoorick/Photodisc/Getty. 146-147: Chas & Elizabeth Schwartz Trust/Animals Animals. 147: Eric and David Hosking/CORBIS. 162: Courtesy Simon & Schuster. 164: zefa/Masterfile. 164-165: Jack Hollingsworth/Photos.com. 165: RaeAnn Meyer/Struve Labs. 166: Joe Munroe/Getty. 166-167: Jack Hollingsworth/Photos.com. 168: Tom L. Geoff/Digital Vision/Getty. 170-171: David A. Northcott/CORBIS. 171: Photodisc/Getty. 172: Joe McDonald/CORBIS. 173: OSF/Fogden, M./Animals Animals. 174-175: Tom McHugh/Photo Researchers. 176: Paul Chesley/Getty. 177: (tl) Will Crocker/Getty; (br) Lee Kline. 178: Breck P. Kent/Animals Animals. 179: (t) Joe McDonald/Animals Animals; (br) John Cancalosi/DRK. 180: John Cancalosi. 181: David Boag/Alamy. 182: (t) David A. Northcott/DRK; (br) Deborah Allen. 183: (tr) Stephen Cooper/Animals Animals; (bl) Zigmund Leszczynski/Animals Animals. 184-185: Gary McVicker/Index Stock. 185: John Cancalosi. 186: (tl) Courtesy Ellen Lambeth; (c) Breck P. Kent/